Parallel and Distributed Computing

Edited by

Alberto Ros

Parallel and Distributed Computing
Edited by Alberto Ros

Republished by InTech

Janeza Trdine 9, 51000 Rijeka, Croatia

Parallel and Distributed Computing,
Edited by Alberto Ros
p. cm.
ISBN 978-953-307-057-5

For EU product safety concerns:
IN TECH d.o.o., Prolaz Marije Krucifikse Kozulić 3, 51000 Rijeka, Croatia,
info@intechopen.com or visit our website at intechopen.com.

Preface

Parallel and distributed computing has offered the opportunity of solving a wide range of computationally intensive problems by increasing the computing power of sequential computers. Although important improvements have been achieved in this field in the last 30 years, there are still many unresolved issues. These issues arise from several broad areas, such as the design of parallel systems and scalable interconnects, the efficient distribution of processing tasks, or the development of parallel algorithms.

This book provides some very interesting and highquality articles aimed at studying the state of the art and addressing current issues in parallel processing and/or distributed computing. The 14 chapters presented in this book cover a wide variety of representative works ranging from hardware design to application development. Particularly, the topics that are addressed are programmable and reconfigurable devices and systems, dependability of GPUs (General Purpose Units), network topologies, cache coherence protocols, resource allocation, scheduling algorithms, peertopeer networks, largescale network simulation, and parallel routines and algorithms. In this way, the articles included in this book constitute an excellent reference for engineers and researchers who have particular interests in each of these topics in parallel and distributed computing.

I would like to thank all the authors for their help and their excellent contributions in the different areas of their expertise. Their wide knowledge and enthusiastic collaboration have made possible the elaboration of this book. I hope the readers will find it very interesting and valuable.

Alberto Ros

Departamento de Ingeniería y Tecnología de Computadores

Universidad de Murcia, Spain

a.ros@ditec.um.es

Contents

1

Fault tolerance of programmable devices

Minoru Watanabe
Shizuoka University
Japan

1. Introduction

Currently, we are frequently facing demands for automation of many systems. In particular, demands for cars and robots are increasing daily. For such applications, high-performance embedded systems are necessary to execute real-time operations. For example, image processing and image recognition are heavy operations that tax current microprocessor units. Parallel computation on high-capacity hardware is expected to be one means to alleviate the burdens imposed by such heavy operations.

To implement such large-scale parallel computation onto a VLSI chip, the demand for a large-die VLSI chip is increasing daily. However, considering the ratio of non-defective chips under current fabrications, die sizes cannot be increased (1),(2). If a large system must be integrated onto a large die VLSI chip or as an extreme case, a wafer-size VLSI, the use of a VLSI including defective parts must be accomplished.

In the earliest use of field programmable gate arrays (FPGAs) (3)–(5), FPGAs were anticipated as defect-tolerant devices that accommodate inclusion of defective areas on the gate array because of their programmable capability. However, that hope was partly shattered because defects of a serial configuration line caused severe impairments that prevented programming of the entire gate array. Of course, a spare row method such as that used for memories (DRAMs) reduces the ratio of discarded chips (6),(7), in which spare rows of a gate array are used instead of defective rows by swapping them with a laser beam machine. However, such methods require hardware redundancy. Moreover, they are not perfect. To use a gate array perfectly and not produce any discarded VLSI chips, a perfectly parallel programmable capability is necessary: one which uses no serial transfer.

Currently, optically reconfigurable gate arrays (ORGAs) that support parallel programming capability and which never use any serial transfer have been developed (8)–(15). An ORGA comprises a holographic memory, a laser array, and a gate-array VLSI. Although the ORGA construction is slightly more complex than that of currently available FPGAs, the parallel programmable gate array VLSI supports perfect avoidance of its faulty areas; it instead uses the remaining area. Therefore, the architecture enables the use of a large-die VLSI chip and even entire wafers, including fault areas. As a result, the architecture can realize extremely high-gate-count VLSIs and can support large-scale parallel computation.

This chapter introduces an ORGA architecture as a high defect tolerance device, describes how to use an optically reconfigurable gate array including defective areas, and clarifies its high fault tolerance. The ORGA architecture has some weak points in making a large VLSI, as

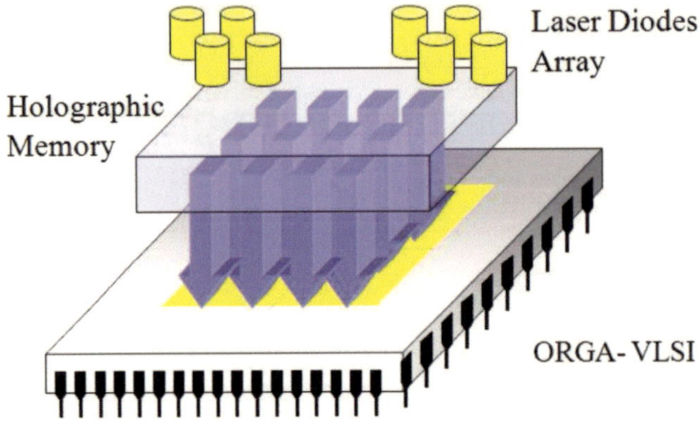

Fig. 1. Overview of an ORGA.

do FPGAs. Therefore, this chapter also presents discussion of more reliable design methods to avoid weak points.

2. Optically Reconfigurable Gate Array (ORGA)

The ORGA architecture has the following features: numerous reconfiguration contexts, rapid reconfiguration, and large die size VLSIs or wafer-scale VLSIs. A large die size VLSI can produce large physical gates that increase the performance of large parallel computation. Furthermore, numerous reconfiguration contexts achieve huge virtual gates with contexts several times more numerous than those of the physical gates. For that reason, such huge virtual gates can be reconfigured dynamically on the physical gates so that huge operations can be integrated onto a single ORGA-VLSI. The following sections describe the ORGA architecture, which presents such advantages.

2.1 Overall construction

An overview of an Optically Reconfigurable Gate Array (ORGA) is portrayed in Fig. 1. An ORGA comprises a gate-array VLSI (ORGA-VLSI), a holographic memory, and a laser diode array. The holographic memory stores reconfiguration contexts. A laser array is mounted on the top of the holographic memory for use in addressing the reconfiguration contexts in the holographic memory. One laser corresponds to a configuration context. Turning one laser on, the laser beam propagates into a certain corresponding area on the holographic memory at a certain angle so that the holographic memory generates a certain diffraction pattern. A photodiode-array of a programmable gate array on an ORGA-VLSI can receive it as a reconfiguration context. Then, the ORGA-VLSI functions as the circuit of the configuration context. The reconfiguration time of such ORGA architecture reaches nanosecond-order (14),(15). Therefore, very-high-speed context switching is possible. Since the storage capacity of a holographic memory is extremely high, numerous configuration contexts can be used with a holographic memory. Therefore, the ORGA architecture can dynamically treat huge virtual gate counts that are larger than the physical gate count on an ORGA-VLSI.

2.2 Gate array structure

This section introduces a design example of a fabricated ORGA-VLSI chip. Based on it, a generalized gate array structure of ORGA-VLSIs is discussed.

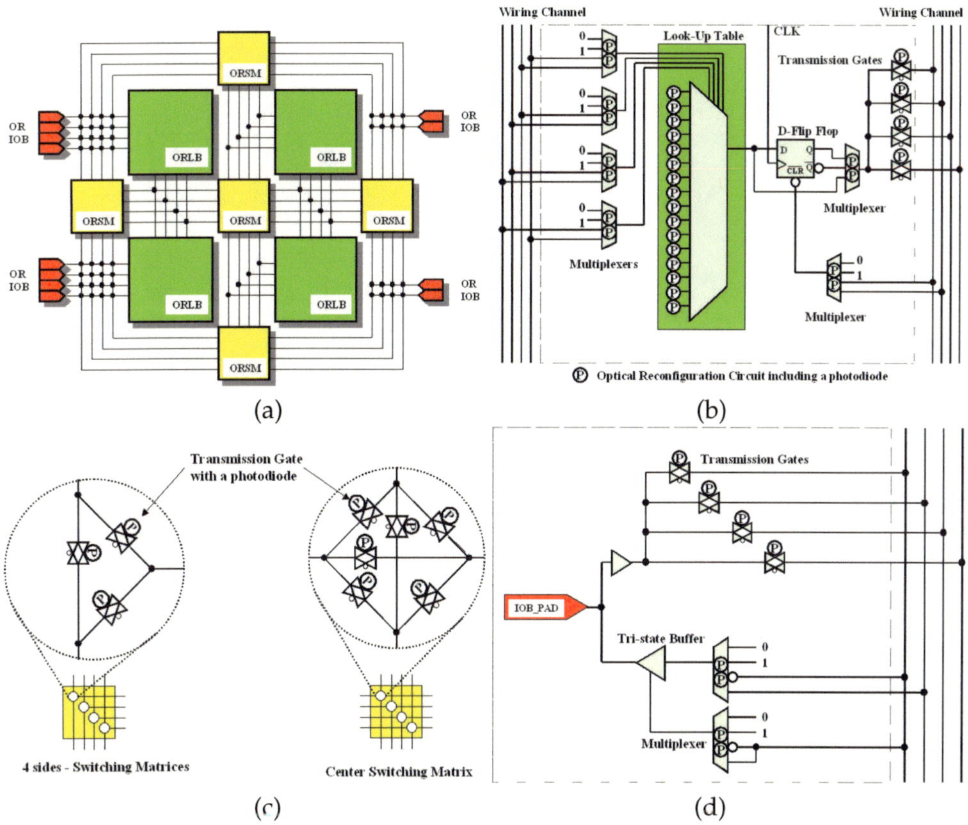

Fig. 2. Gate-array structure of a fabricated ORGA. Panels (a), (b), (c), and (d) respectively depict block diagrams of a gate array, an optically reconfigurable logic block, an optically reconfigurable switching matrix, and an optically reconfigurable I/O bit.

2.2.1 Prototype ORGA-VLSI chip

The basic functionality of an ORGA-VLSI is fundamentally identical to that of currently available field programmable gate arrays (FPGAs). Therefore, ORGA-VLSI takes an island-style gate array or a fine-grain gate array. Figure 2 depicts the gate array structure of a first prototype ORGA-VLSI chip. The ORGA-VLSI chip was fabricated using a 0.35 μm triple-metal CMOS process (8). The photograph of a board is portrayed in Fig. 3. Table 1 presents the specifications. The ORGA-VLSI chip consists of 4 optically reconfigurable logic blocks (ORLB), 5 optically reconfigurable switching matrices (ORSM), and 12 optically reconfigurable I/O bits (ORIOB) portrayed in Fig. 2(a). Each optically reconfigurable logic block is surrounded by wiring channels. In this chip, one wiring channel has four connections. Switching matrices are located on the corners of optically reconfigurable logic blocks. Each connection of the switching matrices is connected to a wiring channel. The ORGA-VLSI has 340 photodiodes to program its gate array. The ORGA-VLSI can be reconfigured perfectly in parallel. In this fabrication, the distance between each photodiode was designed as 90 μm. The photodiode size was set as 25.5×25.5 μm^2 to ease the optical alignment. The photodiode was constructed between the N-well layer and P-substrate. The gate array's gate count is 68. It was confirmed experimentally that the ORGA-VLSI itself is reconfigurable within a nanosecond-order period

Fig. 3. Photograph of an ORGA-VLSI board with a fabricated ORGA-VLSI chip. The ORGA-VLSI was fabricated using a 0.35 μm three-metal 4.9 $\times$ 4.9 mm^2 CMOS process chip. The gate count of a gate array on the chip is 68. In all, 340 photodiodes are used for optical configurations.

(14),(15). Although the gate count of the chip is too small, the gate count of future ORGAs was already estimated (12). Future ORGAs will achieve gate counts of over a million, which is similar to gate counts of FPGAs.

2.2.2 Optically reconfigurable logic block

The block diagram of an optically reconfigurable logic block of the prototype ORGA-VLSI chip is presented in Fig. 2(b). Each optically reconfigurable logic block consists of a four-input one-output look-up table (LUT), six multiplexers, four transmission gates, and a delay type flip-flop with a reset function. The input signals from the wiring channel, which are applied through some switching matrices and wiring channels from optically reconfigurable I/O blocks, are transferred to a look-up table through four multiplexers. The look-up table is used for implementing Boolean functions. The outputs of the look-up table and of a delay type flip-flop connected to the look-up table are connected to a multiplexer. A combinational circuit and sequential circuit can be chosen by changing the multiplexer, as in FPGAs. Finally, an output of the multiplexer is connected to the wiring channel again through transmission gates. The last multiplexer controls the reset function of the delay-type flip-flop. Such a four-input one-output look-up table, each multiplexer, and each transmission gate respectively have 16 photodiodes, 2 photodiodes, and 1 photodiode. In all, 32 photodiodes are used for programming an optically reconfigurable logic block. Therefore, the optically reconfigurable logic block can be reconfigured perfectly in parallel. In this prototype chip, since the gate array is too small, a CLK for each flip-flop is provided through a single CLK buffer tree. However, for a large gate array, CLKs of flip-flops are applied through multiple CLK buffer trees as programmable CLKs, as well as that of FPGAs.

Technology	0.35μm double-poly triple-metal CMOS process
Chip size	4.9 mm $\times$ 4.9 mm
Photodiode size	25.5 μm $\times$ 25.5 μm
Distance between photodiodes	90 μm
Number of photodiodes	340
Gate count	68

Table 1. ORGA-VLSI Specifications.

2.2.3 Optically reconfigurable switching matrix

Similarly, optically reconfigurable switching matrices are optically reconfigurable. The block diagram of the optically reconfigurable switching matrix is portrayed in Fig. 2(c). The basic construction is the same as that used by Xilinx Inc. One four-directional with 24 transmission gates and 4 three-directional switching matrices with 12 transmission gates were implemented in the gate array. Each transmission gate can be considered as a bi-directional switch. A photodiode is connected to each transmission gate; it controls whether the transmission gate is closed or not. Based on that capability, four-direction and three-direction switching matrices can be programmed, respectively, as 24 and 12 optical connections.

2.2.4 Optically reconfigurable I/O block

Optically reconfigurable gate arrays are assumed to be reconfigured frequently. For that reason, an optical reconfiguration capability must be implemented for optically reconfigurable logic blocks and optically reconfigurable switching matrices. However, the I/O block might not always be reconfigured under such dynamic reconfiguration applications because such a dynamic reconfiguration arises inside the device and each mode of Input, Output, or Input/Output, and each pin location of the I/O block must always be fixed due to limitations of the external environment. However, the ORGA-VLSI supports optical reconfiguration for I/O blocks because reconfiguration information is provided optically from a holographic memory in ORGA. Consequently, electrically configurable I/O blocks are unsuitable for ORGAs. Here, each I/O block is also controlled using nine optical connections. Always, the optically reconfigurable I/O block configuration is executed only initially.

3. Defect tolerance design of the ORGA architecture

3.1 Holographic memory part

Holographic memories are well known to have a high defect tolerance. Since each bit of a reconfiguration context can be generated from the entire holographic memory, the damage of some fraction rarely affects its diffraction pattern or a reconfiguration context. Even though a holographic memory device includes small defect areas, holographic memories can correctly record configuration contexts and can correctly generate configuration contexts. Such mechanisms can be considered as those for which majority voting is executed from an infinite number of diffraction beams for each configuration bit. For a semiconductor memory, single-bit information is stored in a single-bit memory circuit. In contrast, in holographic memory, a single bit of a reconfiguration context is stored in the entire holographic memory. Therefore, the holographic memory's information is robust while, in the semiconductor memory, the defect of a transistor always erases information of a single bit or multiple bits. Earlier studies have shown experimentally that a holographic memory is robust (13). In the experiments, 1000 impulse noises and 10% Gaussian noise were applied to a holographic memory. Then the holographic memory was assembled to an ORGA architecture. All configuration experiments were successful. Therefore, defects of a holographic memory device on the ORGA are beyond consideration.

3.2 Laser array part

In an ORGA, a laser array is a basic component for addressing a configuration memory or a holographic memory. Although configuration context information stored on a holographic memory is robust, if the laser array becomes defective, then the execution of each configuration becomes impossible. Therefore, the defect modes arising on a laser array must be analyzed. In an ORGA, many discrete semiconductor lasers are used for switching configuration contexts. Each laser corresponds to one holographic area including one configuration context. One laser addresses one configuration context. The defect modes of a certain laser are categorizable as a turn-ON defect mode and a full-time turn-ON defect mode or a turn-OFF defect mode. The turn-ON defect mode means that a certain laser cannot be turned on. The full-time turn-ON defect mode means the state in which a certain laser is constantly turned ON and cannot be turned OFF.

3.2.1 Turn-ON defect mode

A laser might have a Turn-ON defect. However, laser source defects can be avoided easily by not using the defective lasers, and not using holographic memory areas corresponding to the lasers. An ORGA has numerous reconfiguration contexts. A slight reduction of reconfiguration contexts is therefore negligible. Programmers need only to avoid the defective parts when programming reconfiguration contexts for a holographic memory. Therefore, the ORGA architecture allows Turn-ON defect mode for lasers.

3.2.2 Turn-OFF defect mode

Furthermore, a laser might have a Turn-OFF defect mode. This trouble level is slightly higher than that of the Turn-ON defect mode. The corresponding holographic memory information is constantly superimposed to the other configuration context under normal reconfiguration procedure if one laser has Turn-OFF defect mode and turns on constantly. Therefore, the Turn-OFF defect mode of lasers presents the possibility that all normal configuration procedures are impossible. Therefore, if such Turn-OFF defect mode arises on an ORGA, a physical action to cut the corresponding wires or driver units is required. The action is easy and can perfectly remove the defect mode.

3.2.3 Defect mode for matrix addressing

Such laser arrays are always arranged in the form of a two-dimensional matrix and addressed as the matrix. In such matrix implementation, the defect of one driver causes all lasers on the addressing line to be defective. To avoid simultaneous defects of many lasers, a spare row method like that used for memories (DRAMs) is useful (6)(7). By introducing the spare row method, the defect mode can be removed perfectly.

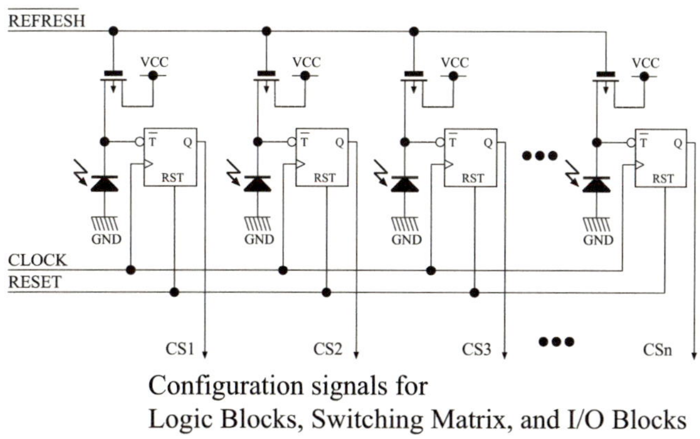

Fig. 4. Circuit diagram of reconfiguration circuit.

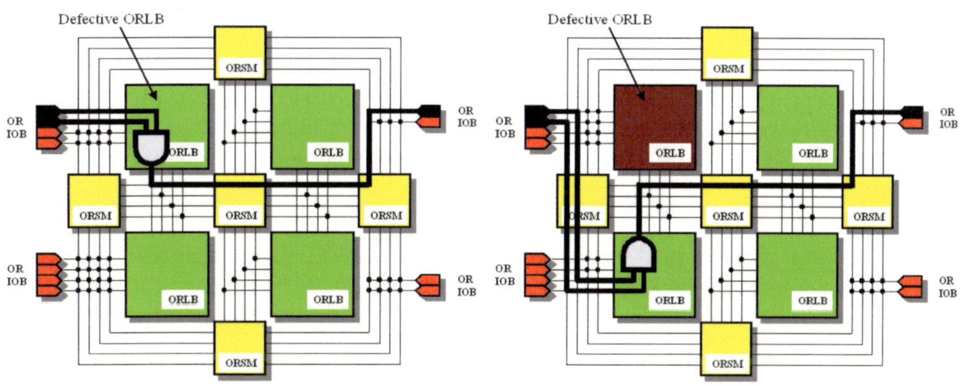

Fig. 5. Defective area avoidance method on a gate array. Here, it is assumed that a defective optically reconfigurable logic block (ORLB) exists, as portrayed in the upper area of the figure. In this case, the defective area is avoided perfectly using parallel programming with the other components, as presented in the lower area of the figure.

3.3 ORGA-VLSI part

In the ORGA-VLSIs, serial transfers were perfectly removed and optical reconfiguration circuits including static memory functions and photodiodes were placed near and directly connected to programming elements of a programmable gate array VLSI. Figure 4 shows that the toggle flip-flops are used for temporarily storing one context and realizing a bit-by-bit configuration. Using this architecture, the optical configuration procedure for a gate array can be executed perfectly in parallel. Thereby, the VLSI part can achieve a perfectly parallel bit-by-bit configuration.

3.3.1 Simple method to avoid defective areas

Using configuration, a damaged gate array can be restored as shown in Fig. 5. The structure and function of an optically reconfigurable logic block and optically reconfigurable switching matrices on a gate array are mutually similar. If a part is defective or fails, the same function can be implemented onto the other part. Here, the upper part of Fig. 5 shows that it is assumed that a defective optically reconfigurable logic block (ORLB) exists in a gate array. In that case, the lower part of Fig. 5 shows that another implementation is available. By reconfiguring the gate array VLSI, the defective area can be avoided perfectly and its functions can be realized using other blocks. For this example, we assumed a defective area of only one optically reconfigurable logic block. For the other cells, for optically reconfigurable switching matrices, and for optically reconfigurable I/O blocks, a similar avoidance method can be adopted. Such a replacement method can be adopted onto FPGAs; however, such a replacement method is based on the condition that the configuration is possible. Regarding FPGAs, the defect or failure probability of configuration circuits is very high because of the serial configuration. On the other hand, the ORGA architecture configuration is very robust because of the parallel configuration. For that reason, the ORGA architecture has high defect and fault tolerance.

3.3.2 Weak point

However, a weak point exists on the ORGA-VLSI design. It is a common clock signal line. When using a single common clock signal line to distribute a clock for all delay-type flip-flops, damage to one clock tree renders all delay-type flip-flops useless. Therefore, the clock line must be programmable with many buffer trees when a large gate count VLSI or a wafer scale VLSI is made. In currently available FPGAs, each clock line of delay-type flip-flops has already been programmable with several clock trees. To reduce the probability of the clock death trouble, sufficient programmable clock trees should be prepared. If so, along with FPGA, defects for clock trees in ORGA architecture can be beyond consideration.

3.3.3 Critical weak points

Figure 4 shows that more critical weak points in the ORGA-VLSIs are a refresh signal, a reset signal, and a configuration CLK signal of configuration circuits to support optical configuration procedures. These signals are common signals on VLSI chip and cannot be programmable since the signals are necessary for programming itself. Therefore, along with the laser array, a physical action or a spare method is required in addition to enforcing the wire and buffer trees for defects so that critical weak points can be removed.

3.4 Possibility of greater than tera-gate capacity

In ORGA architecture, a holographic memory is a very robust device. For that reason, defect analysis is done only for an ORGA-VLSI and a laser array. In ORGA-VLSI part, even if defect parts are included on the ORGA-VLSI chip, almost all defect parts can be avoided using parallel programming capability. The only remaining concern is the common signals used for controlling configuration circuits. For those common signals, spare hardware or redundant hardware must be used. On the other hand, in a laser array part, only a spare row method must be applied to matrix driver circuits. The other defects are negligible.

Therefore, exploiting the defect tolerance and using methods of ORGA architecture described above, a very large die size VLSI is possible. At that time, according to an earlier paper (12), if it is assumed that an ORGA-VLSI is built on a 0.18 μm process 8 inch wafer and that 1 million configuration contexts are stored on a corresponding holographic memory, then greater than 10-tera-gate VLSIs will be realized. Currently, although this remains only a distant objective, optoelectronic devices might present a new VLSI paradigm.

4. Conclusion

Optically reconfigurable gate arrays have perfectly parallel programmable capability. Even if a gate array VLSI and a laser array include defective parts, their perfectly parallel programmable capability enables perfect avoidance of defective areas. Instead, it uses the remaining area of a gate array VLSI, remaining laser resources, and remaining holographic memory resources. Therefore, the architecture enables fabrication of large-die VLSI chips and wafer-scale integrations using the latest processes, even those chips with a high defect fraction. Finally, we conclude that the architecture has a high defect tolerance. In the future, optically reconfigurable gate arrays will be a type of next-generation three-dimensional (3D) VLSI chip with an extremely high gate count and with a high manufacturing-defect tolerance.

5. References

[1] C. Hess, L. H. Weiland, "Wafer level defect density distribution using checkerboard test structures," International Conference on Microelectronic Test Structures, pp. 101–106, 1998.

[2] C. Hess, L. H. Weiland, "Extraction of wafer-level defect density distributions to improve yield prediction," IEEE Transactions on Semiconductor Manufacturing, Vol. 12, Issue 2, pp. 175-183, 1999.

[3] Altera Corporation, "Altera Devices," http://www. altera.com.

[4] Xilinx Inc., "Xilinx Product Data Sheets," http://www. xilinx.com.

[5] Lattice Semiconductor Corporation, "LatticeECP and EC Family Data Sheet," http://www. latticesemi.co.jp/products, 2005.

[6] A. J. Yu, G. G. Lemieux, "FPGA Defect Tolerance: Impact of Granularity," IEEE International Conference on Field-Programmable Technology,pp. 189–196, 2005.

[7] A. Doumar, H. Ito, "Detecting, diagnosing, and tolerating faults in SRAM-based field programmable gate arrays: a survey," IEEE Transactions on Very Large Scale Integration (VLSI) Systems, Vol. 11, Issue 3, pp. 386 – 405, 2003.

[8] M. Watanabe, F. Kobayashi, "Dynamic Optically Reconfigurable Gate Array," Japanese Journal of Applied Physics, Vol. 45, No. 4B, pp. 3510-3515, 2006.

[9] N. Yamaguchi, M. Watanabe, "Liquid crystal holographic configurations for ORGAs," Applied Optics, Vol. 47, No. 28, pp. 4692-4700, 2008.

[10] D. Seto, M. Watanabe, "A dynamic optically reconfigurable gate array - perfect emulation," IEEE Journal of Quantum Electronics, Vol. 44, Issue 5, pp. 493-500, 2008.

[11] M. Watanabe, M. Nakajima, S. Kato, "An inversion/non-inversion dynamic optically reconfigurable gate array VLSI," World Scientific and Engineering Academy and Society Transactions on Circuits and Systems, Issue 1, Vol. 8, pp. 11- 20, 2009.

[12] M. Watanabe, T. Shiki, F. Kobayashi, "Scaling prospect of optically differential reconfigurable gate array VLSIs," Analog Integrated Circuits and Signal Processing, Vol. 60, pp. 137 - 143, 2009.

[13] M. Watanabe, F. Kobayashi, "Manufacturing-defect tolerance analysis of optically reconfigurable gate arrays," World Scientific and Engineering Academy and Society Transactions on Signal Processing, Issue 11, Vol. 2, pp. 1457- 1464, 2006.

[14] M. Miyano, M. Watanabe, F. Kobayashi, "Optically Differential Reconfigurable Gate Array," Electronics and Computers in Japan, Part II, Issue 11, vol. 90, pp. 132-139, 2007.

[15] M. Nakajima, M. Watanabe, "A four-context optically differential reconfigurable gate array," IEEE/OSA Journal of Lightwave Technology, Vol. 27, No. 24, 2009.

2

Fragmentation management for HW multitasking in 2D Reconfigurable Devices: Metrics and Defragmentation Heuristics

Julio Septién, Hortensia Mecha, Daniel Mozos and Jesus Tabero
University Complutense de Madrid
Spain

1. Introduction

Hardware multitasking has become a real possibility as a consequence of FPGA advances along the last decade, such as partial run-time reconfiguration capability and increased FPGA size. Partial reconfiguration times are small enough, and FPGA sizes large enough, to consider reconfigurable environments where a single FPGA managed by an extended operating system can store and run simultaneously several whole tasks, even belonging to different users. The problem of HW multitasking management involves decisions such as the structure used to keep track of the free FPGA resources, the allocation of FPGA resources for each incoming task, the scheduling of the task execution at a certain time instant, where its time constraints are satisfied, and others that have been studied in detail in (Wigley & Kearney, 2002a).

The tasks enter and leave the FPGA dynamically, and thus FPGA reuse due to hardware multitasking leads to fragmentation. When a task finishes execution and has to leave the FPGA, it leaves a hole that has to be incorporated to the FPGA free area. It becomes unavoidable that such process, repeated once and again, generates an external fragmentation that can lead to difficult situations where new tasks are unable to find room in the FPGA though there are free resources enough. The FPGA free area has become fragmented and it can not be used to accommodate future incoming tasks due to the way the free resources are spread along the FPGA.

For 1D-reconfiguration architectures such as that of commercial Xilinx Virtex or Virtex II (only column-programmable, though they consist of 2D block arrays), simple management techniques based, for example, on several fixed-sized partitions or even arbitrary-sized partitions, are used, and fragmentation can be easily detected and managed (Steiger et al., 2004) (Ahmadinia et al., 2003). It is a linear problem alike to that of memory fragmentation in SW multitasking environments. The main problem for such architectures is not the management of the fragmented free area, but how defragmentation is accomplished by performing task relocation (Brebner & Diessel, 2001). Some systems even propose a 2D management of the 1D-reconfigurable, Virtex-type, architecture (Hübner et al., 2006) (van der Veen et al., 2005).

For 2D-reconfigurable architectures such as Virtex 4 (Xilinx, Inc "Virtex-4 Configuration Guide) and 5 (Xilinx, Inc "Virtex-5 Configuration User Guide), more sophisticated techniques must be used to keep track of the available free area, in order to get an efficient FPGA resource management (Bazargan et al., 2000) (Walder et al., 2003) (Diessel et al., 2000) (Ahmadinia et al., 2004) (Handa & Vemuri, 2004a) (Tabero et al., 2004). For such architectures the estimation of the FPGA fragmentation status through an accurate metric is an important issue, and some researchers have proposed estimation metrics as in (Handa & Vemuri, 2004b), (Ejnioui & DeMara, 2005) and (Septien et al., 2008). What the 2D metric must estimate is how idoneous is the geometry of the free FPGA area to accommodate a new task.

A reliable fragmentation metric can be used in different ways: first, as a cost function when the allocation decisions are being taken (Tabero et al., 2004). The use of a fragmentation metric as cost function would guarantee future FPGA status with lower fragmentation (for the same FPGA occupation level), that would give a better probability of finding a location for the next task.

It can be used, also, as an alarm in order to trigger defragmentation measures as preventive actions or in extreme situations, that lead to relocation of one o more of the currently running tasks (van der Veen et al., 2005), (Diessel et al., 2000), (Septien et al., 2006) and (Fekete et al., 2008).

In this work, we are going to review the fragmentation metrics proposed in the literature to estimate the fragmentation of the FPGA resources, and we'll present two fragmentation metrics of our own, one of them based on the number and shape of the FPGA free holes, and another based on the relative quadrature of the free area perimeter. Then we´ll show examples of how these metrics behave in different situations, with one or several free holes and also with islands (isolated tasks). We'll also show how they can be used as cost functions in a location selection heuristic, each time a task is loaded into the FPGA. Experimental results show that though they maintain a low complexity, these metrics, specially the quadrature-based one, behave better than most of the previous ones, discarding a lower amount of computing volume when the FPGA supports a heavy task load.

We will review also the different approaches to FPGA defragmentation considered in the literature, and we'll propose a set of FPGA defragmentation techniques. Two basic techniques will be presented: preventive and on-demand defragmentation. Preventive measures will try to anticipate to possible allocation problems due to fragmentation. These measures will be triggered by a high fragmentation metric value. When fired, the system performs an immediate global or partial defragmentation, or a delayed global one depending on the time constraints of the involved tasks. On-demand measures try an urgent move of a single candidate task, the one with the highest relative adjacency with the hole border. Such battery of defragmentation measures can help avoiding most problems produced by fragmentation in HW multitasking on 2D reconfigurable devices.

2. Previous work

The problems of fragmentation estimation and defragmentation are very different when FPGAs managed in one or two dimensions are considered. For 1D, a few simple solutions have been used, but for 2D a nice amount of interesting research has been done, and in this section we'll focus on such work.

2.1 Fragmentation estimation

Fragmentation has been considered in the existing literature as an aspect of the area management problem in HW multitasking, and thus most fragmentation metrics have been proposed as part of different management techniques, most of them rectangle-based.

Bazargan presented in (Bazargan et al., 2000) a free area management and task allocation heuristic that is broadly referenced. Such heuristic is based on MERs, maximum empty rectangles. Bazargan´s allocator keeps track, with a high complexity algorithm, of all the MERs (which can overlap) available in the free FPGA area. Such approach is optimal, in the sense that if there is free room enough for an incoming task, it is contained in one of the available MERs. To select one of the MERs, Bazargan uses several techniques: First-Fit, Worst-Fit, Best-fit… Though Bazargan does not estimate fragmentation directly, the availability of large MERs at a given time is an indirect measure of the fragmentation status of a given FPGA situation.

The MER approach, though, is so expensive in terms of update and search time that Bazargan finally opted for a non-optimal approach to area management, by dividing the free area into a set of non-overlapping rectangles.

Wigley proposes in (Wigley & Kearney, 2002b) a metric that must keep track of all the available MERs. Thus what we have just stated about the MER approach applies also to this metric. It considers fragmentation then as the average size of the maximal squares fitting into the more relevant set of MERs. Moreover, this metric does not discriminate enough, giving the same values for very different fragmentation situations.

Walder makes in (Walder & Platzner, 2002) an estimation of the free area fragmentation, using non-overlapping rectangles similar to those of Bazargan. It considers the number of rectangles with a given size. It uses a normalized, device-independent formula, to compute the free area. Its main problem comes from the complexity of the technique needed to keep track of such rectangles.

Handa in (Handa & Vemuri, 2004b) computes fragmentation referred to the average task size. Holes with a size two times such value or more are not considered for the metric. Fragmentation then has not an absolute value for a given FPGA situation, but depends on the incoming task. It gives in general very low fragmentation values, even for situations with very disperse tasks and holes not too large compared to the total free area.

Ejnoui in (Ejnioui & DeMara, 2005) proposes a fragmentation metric that depends only on the free area and the number of holes, and not on the shape of the holes. It can be considered then a measure of the FPGA occupation, more than of FPGA fragmentation. There is a fragmentation value of 0 only for an empty chip. When the FPGA is heavily loaded the metric approaches to 1 quickly, independently from the hole shape.

Cui in (Cui et al., 2007) computes fragmentation for all the MERs of the free area. For each MER this fragmentation is based on the probable size of the arriving task, and involves computations for each basic cell inside the MER. Thus the technique presents a heavy complexity order that, as for other MER-based techniques, makes it difficult to use in a real environment.

All that has been explained above allows to make some assertions. The main feature of a good fragmentation metric should be its ability to detect when the free FPGA area is more or less apt to accommodate future incoming taks, that is, it must detect if it is efficiently or inefficiently organized, and give a value to such organization. It must separate the fragmentation estimation from the occupation degree, or the amount of available free area. For example, an FPGA status with a high occupation but with all the free area concentred in a single, almost-square, rectangle, cannot be considered as fragmented as some of the metrics previously presented do. Also, the metric must be computationally simple, and that suggests the inconvenience of the MER-based approach of some of the metrics reviewed.

2.2 Defragmentation techniques

As it was previously stated, the problem of defragmentation is different for 1D or 2D FPGAs. For FPGAs allowing reconfiguration in a single dimension, Compton (Compton et al., 2002), Brebner (Brebner & Diessel, 2001) or Koch (Koch et al., 2004) have proposed architectural features to perform defragmentation through relocation of complete columns or rows.

For 2D-reconfigurable FPGAs, though many researchers estimate fragmentation, and even use metrics to help their allocation algorithms to choose locations for the arriving tasks, as section 2.1 has shown, only a few perform explicit defragmentation processes.

Gericota proposes in (Gericota et al., 2003) architectural changes to a classical 2D FPGA to permit task relocation by replication of CLBs, in order to solve fragmentation problems. But they do not solve the problems of how to choose a new location or how to decide when this relocation must be performed.

Ejnioui (Ejnioui & DeMara, 2005) has proposed a fragmentation metric adapted from the one shown in (Tabero et al., 2003). They propose to use this estimation to schedule a defragmentation process if a given threshold is reached. They comment several possible ways of defining such threshold, though they do not seem to choose any of them. Though they suggest several methodologies, they do not give experimental results that validate their approach.

Finally, Van der Veen in (van der Veen et al., 2005) and (Fekete et al., 2008) uses a branch-and bound approach with constraints, in order to accomplish a global defragmentation process that searches for an optimal module layout. It is aimed to 2D FPGAs, though column-reconfigurable as current Virtex FPGAs. This process seems to be quite time-consuming, of an order of magnitude of seconds. The authors do not give any information about how to insert such defragmentation process in a HW management system.

3. HW management environment

Our approach to reconfigurable HW management is summarized in Figure 1. Our environment is an extension of the operating system that consists of several modules. The Task Scheduler controls the tasks currently running in the FPGA and accepts new incoming tasks. Tasks can arrive anytime and must be processed on-line. The Vertex-List Updater keeps track of the available FPGA free area with a Vertex-List (VL) structure that has been described in detail in (Tabero et al., 2003), updating it whenever a new event happens. Such structure can be travelled with different heuristics ((Tabero et al., 2003), (Tabero et al., 2006), and (Walder & Platzner, 2002)) by the Vertex Selector in order to choose the vertex where each arriving task will be placed. Finally, a permanent checking of the FPGA status is made by the Free Area Analyzer. Such module estimates the FPGA fragmentation and checks for

isolated islands appearing inside the hole defined by the VL, every time a new event happens.
As Figure 1 shows, we suppose a 2D-managed FPGA, with rectangular relocatable tasks made of a number of basic reconfigurable basic blocks, each block includes processing elements and is able to access to a global interconnection network through a standard interface, not depicted in the figure.

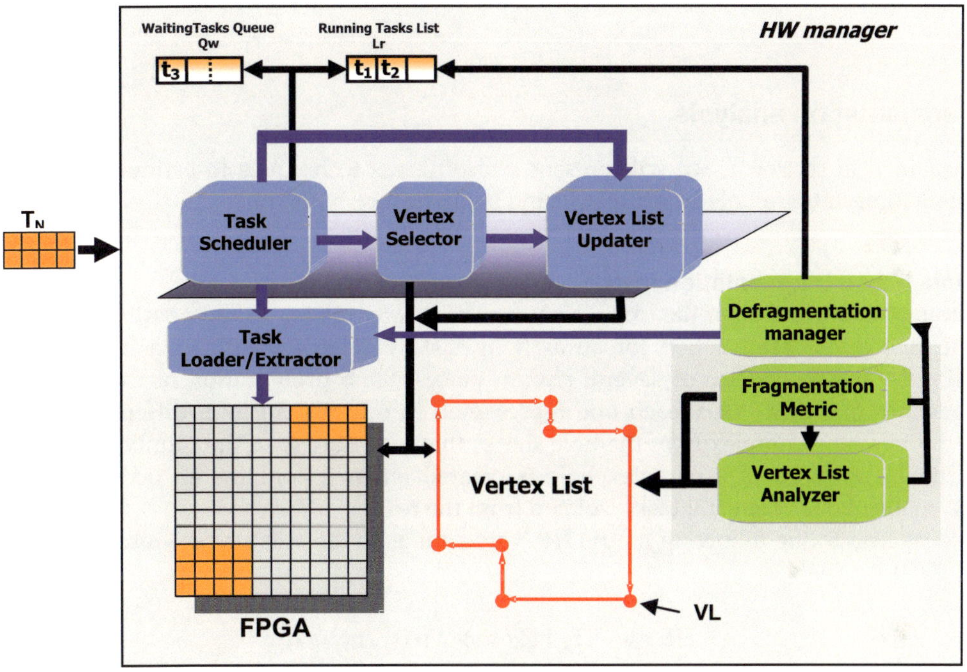

Fig. 1. HW management environment.

Each incoming task T_i is originally defined by the tuple of parameters:

$$T_i = \{w_i, h_i, t\_ex_i, t\_arr_i, t\_max_i\}$$

where w_i times h_i indicates the task size in terms of basic reconfigurable blocks, t_ex_i is the task execution time, t_arr_i the task arrival time and t_max_i the maximum time allowed for the task to finish execution. These parameters are characteristic for each incoming task.
If a suitable location is found, task T_i is finally allocated and scheduled for execution at an instant t_start_i. If not, the task goes to the queue Qw, and it is reconsidered again at each task-end event or after defragmentation. We call the current time t_curr. All the times but t_ex_i are absolute (referred to the same time origin). We estimate t_conf_i, the time needed to load the configuration of the task, proportional to its size: $t\_conf_i = k * w_i * h_i$.

We also define t_marg_i, as the time margin each task is allowed to delay its completion, the time interval between the task scheduled finishing instant and its time-out (defined by t_max_i). If the task has been scheduled at time t_start_i it must be computed as:

$$t\_marg_i = t\_max_i - (t\_start_i + t\_conf_i + t\_ex_i) \quad (1)$$

But if the task has not been allocated yet, and is waiting at Qw, *t_curr* should be used instead of t_start_i. In this case, t_marg_i value decreases at each time cycle as *t_curr* advances. When t_marg_i reaches a value of 0 the task must be definitively rejected and deleted from Qw.

4. Fragmentation analysis

As explained in section 1, we will present two different techniques to estimate the FPGA fragmentation status: a hole-based metric and a quadrature-based one.

4.1 Hole-based fragmentation metric

The fragmentation status of the free FPGA area is directly related to the possibility of being able to find a suitable location for an arriving task. We have identified a fragmentation situation by the occurrence of several circumstances. First, proliferation of the number of independent free area holes, each one represented in our system by a different VL. And second, increasing complexity of the hole shape, that we relate with the number of vertices. A particular instance of a complex hole is created when it contains an occupied island inside, made of one of several tasks isolated from the rest.

This ideas lead to the following metric ***HF***, very similar to the one we presented in (Tabero et al., 2004):

$$\boldsymbol{HF} = 1 - \Pi_h \left[(4/V_H)^n * (A_H/A_{F\_FPGA}) \right] \quad (2)$$

Where the term between brackets represents a kind of "suitability" for a given hole H, with area A_H and V_H vertices:

- $(4/V_H)^n$ represents the suitability of the shape of hole H to accommodate rectangular tasks. Notice that any hole with four vertices has the best suitability. For most of our experiments we employ n=1, but we can use higher or lower values if we want to penalize more or less the occurrence of holes with complex shapes and thus difficult to use.
- (A_H/A_{F_FPGA}) represents the relative normalized hole area. A_{F_FPGA} stands for the whole free area in the FPGA. That is $A_{F\_FPGA} = \sum A_H$.

This ***HF*** metric penalizes the proliferation of independent holes in the FPGA, as well as the occurrence of holes with complex shapes and small sizes. Figure 2 shows several fragmentation situations in an example FPGA of 20x20 basic blocks, and the fragmentation values estimated by the formula in (2).

A new estimation is done every time a new event occurs, that is, when a new task is placed in the FPGA, when a finishing task leaves the FPGA, or when relocation decisions are taken during a defragmentation process. The *HF* estimation can be used to help in the vertex selection process, as it is done in (Tabero et al., 2004), (Tabero et al., 2006) and (Tabero et al., 2008), or to check the FPGA status in order to fire a defragmentation process when needed (Septién et al. 2006). In the next sections we will focus in how we accomplish defragmentation.

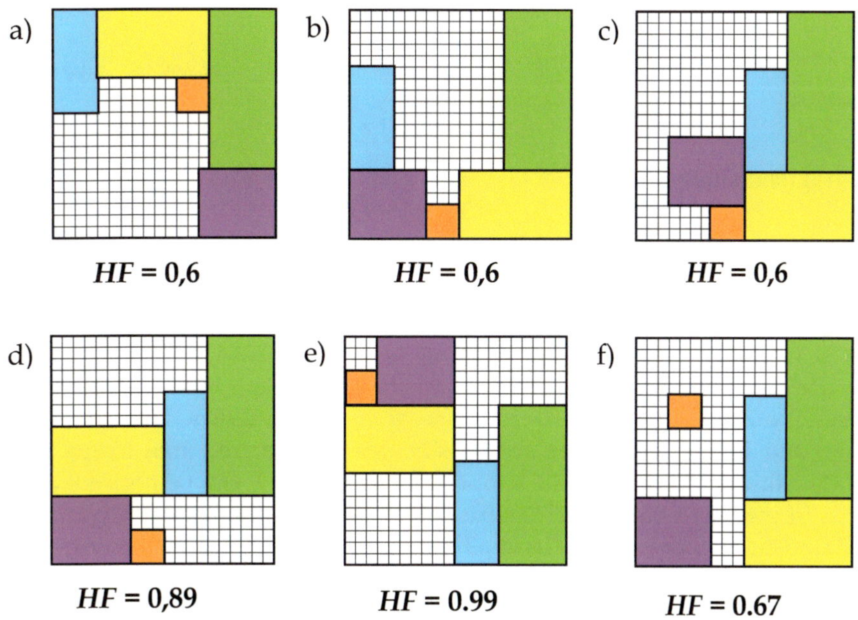

Fig. 2. Different FPGA situations and fragmentation values given by the *HF* metric.

4.2 Perimeter quadrature-based metric

The *HF* metric presented in section 4.1 gives adequate fragmentation values for many situations, but does not handle well a few, particular ones. The main problem for such vertex-based metric is that sometimes a hole with a complex boundary with many vertices can contain a significantly usable portion of free area. Also, the metric does not discriminate among holes with different shapes but the same number of vertices, as in Figures 2.a, 2.b and 2.c. Moreover, as Figure 2.f shows the metric is not too sensible to islands. Finally, another drawback is that the occurrence of several holes as in Figures 2.d and 2.e is severely penalized with very high (close to 1) fragmentation values.

We will try to solve this problem with a new metric, derived form a different approach.

A) Quadrature fragmentation metric basics

The new metric starts from a simple idea: we do consider the ideal free hole H as such one able to accommodate most of the incoming tasks with a variety of shapes and a total task area similar or smaller than the size of the hole H. The assumption we make is that such ideal free hole should have a perfect square shape. Such hole would be able to accommodate most incoming tasks. One of the advantages of a square shape task would be that the longest interconnections inside the task would be shorter than for irregular shape tasks with the same area, or even rectangular ones.

For any hole H with an area A_H a perimeter P_H and a non-square shape, we define its **relative quadrature** Q as "how its shape is near from being a perfect square". We estimate such magnitude dividing its actual area A_H by the area A_Q of a perfect square with the same perimeter P_H. A_Q that is computed as:

$$A_Q = (P_H \ / \ 4)^2 \tag{3}$$

where $P_H \ / \ 4$ would be the length of each one of the square sides. Then the relative quadrature is:

$$Q = A_H \,/ A_Q \tag{4}$$

and thus fragmentation is:

$$\boldsymbol{QF} = 1 - Q \tag{5}$$

It can be seen that our quadrature-based metric ***QF*** will consider that fragmentation for a given hole H is minimal (0) when it has a square shape. On the contrary, the longest perimeter gives a higher fragmentation value.

In Figure 3 we can see a set of five running tasks in a 20x20 FPGA, placed at different locations. The free area is of 169 basic area units for all of them. But the perimeter P an thus the A_Q and Q values are different for each one, as the figure shows. Thus the fragmentation ***QF*** differs, and is smaller for the FPGA situation with a free area shape more apt to accommodate future incoming tasks, supposedly Figure 3.f. It can be noticed, also, how the ***QF*** metric, in contrast with the ***HF*** metric, gives different fragmentation values for holes with the same number of vertices (10 in all the cases) but different shapes, as in Figures 3.a, 3.e or 3.f.

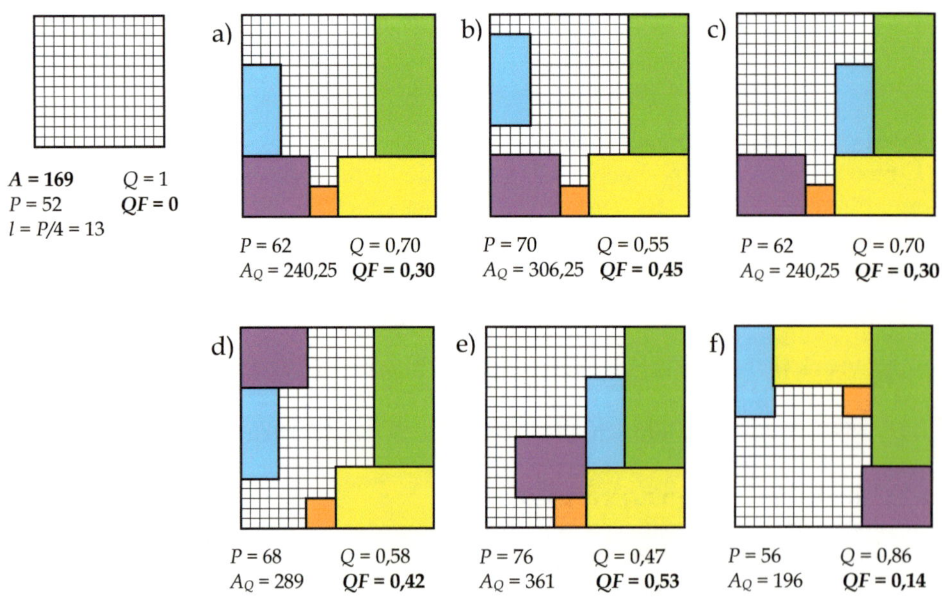

Fig. 3. ***QF*** metric values for different task locations and a single hole.

B) *QF* metric for multiple holes

The *QF* metric can be easily extended to a more complex free area made of several holes, by considering the whole boundary between the free and the occupied area as a single perimeter. Then *P* and *A* values would be used computed as:

$$P = \sum_i P_i \quad \text{and} \tag{6}$$

$$A = \sum_i A_i \tag{7}$$

And the global fragmentation is computed as:

$$\boldsymbol{QF} = 1 - A/(P\,/\,4)^2 \tag{8}$$

The global fragmentation value given by ***QF*** would be, then, a measure of how far from being an ideal single hole is the whole available free area delimited by *P*.

Figure 4 shows several situations for the same 20x20 FPGA and five running tasks than Figure 3. Now the tasks are located at different positions, and the free area *A* is divided into two (Figures 4.a and 4.b) or even three (Figure 4.c) independent holes. The figure shows how our metric does not need to take into account the number of holes to estimate the quality of the different FPGA situations.

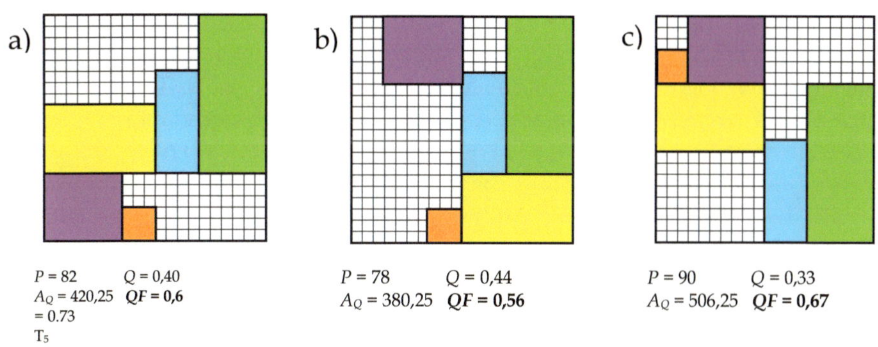

Fig. 4. ***QF*** metric values for different tasks locations and multiple holes

C) *QF* metric for islands

A situation that our metric deals with automatically is the occurrence of islands. Islands are high fragmentation, undesirable situations that can happen as some tasks finish and leave the FPGA, while others remain. It is important that a fragmentation metric is able to deal with such situations.

Our metric deals with it automatically, because in our representation of the free area perimeter (a vertex list), the island is connected to the rest of the perimeter with virtual edges, as depicted in Figure 5. These virtual edges are considered as part of the perimeter when *P* is computed. Thus, an island close to the perimeter will have short virtual edges and the *P* value will be lower than when the island is more distant. As an island, even a small one, can be quite annoying when it is located in the middle of a large hole, virtual edges can

have an associated weight factor that multiplies its length as desired, in order to penalize such event.
The figure shows how our metric takes into account how far from the hole perimeter is the island, giving a higher fragmentation value for Figures 5.a than for Figures 5.b or 5.c. In this example we have weighted the virtual edges with a penalty factor of 2.
As we said, this metric is very simple to compute, at least for an allocation algorithm that takes control of the free area boundary.

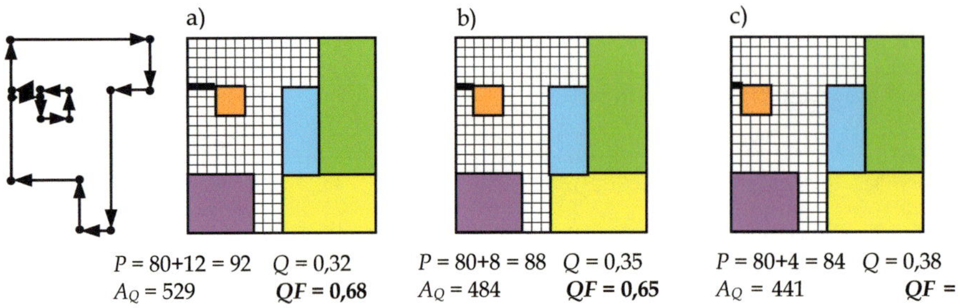

Fig. 5. ***QF*** metric values for a hole with an island at different locations

4.3 Comparison of different fragmentation metrics

A) Experiment #1

In order to compare our metrics ***HF*** and ***QF*** with others proposed in the literature, we have computed fragmentation values given by some of these metrics for some of the simple FPGA examples in Figures 3, 4 and 5. These results are shown in Table 1. The table also shows the size of largest MER available (L-MER), that though not viable as a real technique due to its high complexity, it can be used as a reference.
The purpose of this table is to show that the fragmentation value computed by our ***QF*** metric (with the quadrature *Q* value also given between parentheses) is a reliable estimation of the fragmentation status of a FPGA.
If compared with the L-MER, the lowest and highest fragmentation cases match, as most of the others. Only for cases 3.d and 3.e there is a noticeable difference, that comes from the fact that in case 3.e there exist several medium-sized rectangles, all of them good for accommodating incoming tasks, though the largest MER is smaller that in other cases. For the other metrics, it can be seen that F1 and F2 match with L-MER and ***QF*** for the less fragmented case, but do behave not so well with islands: F1 does not discriminate among 5.a and 5.c and F2 chooses as more fragmented the case where the island is closer to the perimeter. F3 chooses as less fragmented 3.a instead of 3.f. Finally, F4 and ***HF*** do not discriminate among many of the cases proposed, and assign excessive fragmentation values to cases with several independent holes.

	Single hole (Fig. 3)				Several holes (Fig. 4)			Island (Fig. 5)	
	3.a	3.d	3.e	3.f	4.a	4.b	4.c	5.a	5.c
F1 (Wigley)	10	7	10	**11**	7	10	7	**6**	6
F2 (Walder)	0.16	0.36	0.32	**0.14**	0.39	0.32	0.39	**0.43**	0.45
F3 (Handa)	0.07	0.18	0.21	**0.08**	0.28	0.22	0.33	**0.21**	0.20
F4 (Ejnoui)	0.58	0.58	0.58	**0.58**	0.96	0.98	1	**0.58**	0.58
HF	0.60	0.67	0.60	**0.60**	0.89	0.98	0.99	**0.67**	0.67
QF (*Q*)	**0,30 (0,70)**	**0,42 (0,58)**	**0,53 (0,47)**	**0,14 (0,86)**	**0,60 (0,40)**	**0,56 (0,44)**	**0,67 (0,33)**	**0,68 (0,32)**	**0,62 (0,38)**
L-MER	140	98	100	**154**	80	110	80	**70**	84

Table 1. Comparison of ***HF*** and ***QF*** with different metrics

B) Experiment #2

The previous section showed how our ***QF*** metric was able to assign appropriate fragmentation values to each FPGA situation.

We have made also experiments using ***HF*** and ***QF*** as a cost functions to select the most appropriate location to place each new arriving task. We have used our Vertex-list based manager, that allows choosing among several different vertex selection heuristics. Among such, heuristic based on 2D (space) adjacency or 3D (space-time) adjacency can be found in (Tabero et al., 2006). These heuristics are used to select one of the candidate vertices each time a new task is considered for allocation. For adjacency-based heuristics, the vertex with a higher adjacency is selected. For fragmentation-based heuristics, the one with lower fragmentation value, as given by the metric, is chosen.

As a reference we have also used two MER-based heuristics, implementing Best-Fit (choosing the smaller MER able to contain the task) and Worst-Fit (choosing the largest MER) as in (Bazargan et al., 2000).

We have not used other metrics as in the previous section, due to the difficulties in programming all them and incorporating them to the allocation environment (that for some of them is not possible).

The experimental results are summarized in Table 2 and Figures 6, 7, 8 and 9. We have used a 20x20 FPGA with 400 area units, and as benchmarks several task sets with 100 tasks and different features each one.

We have used four different task size ranges. Set S1 is made of small tasks, with each randomly generated dimension *X* or *Y* ranging from 1 to 10 units. Set S2 is made of medium tasks, with side sizes ranging from 2 to 14 basic block units. Set S3 is made of large tasks with side size ranging from 4 to 18 units. S4 is a more heterogeneous set, with small, medium and large tasks combined. The average number of running tasks comes from the average task size and is approximately of 12 for S1, 8 for S2, and 6 for S3. For S4 it is more unpredictable.

All the task sets have an excess of workload that forces the allocator to store some tasks temporally in a queue, and even discard them when their latest starting time constraint is reached.

For each one of the sets, we have used three different time constraint types: hard (H), soft (S) or nonexistent (N). Thus the 12 experiment sets are labelled S1-H, S1-S, S1-N, S2-H… up to S4-N.
As mentioned earlier, results are shown for the MER approach, with Best-Fit (labelled as MER-BF) and Worst-Fit (MER-WF), the 2D adjacency heuristic (A-2D), the 3D adjacency heuristic (A-3D), the hole-based metric ***HF*** and the quadrature -based metric ***QF***.
The parameters we have used to characterize each experiment are the number of cycles used to complete the executed computing volume, the average area occupation, and the computing volume rejected. The number of cycles is only significant if related with the computing volume executed, and only when no task has been rejected it allows direct comparison between the heuristics. The average FPGA occupation ranges between 66 and 75 %, this means that a significant amount of the FPGA area (34 to 25%) cannot be used, due to fragmentation. The computing volume rejected is the sum, for all the rejected tasks, of the area of each task multiplied by its execution time.

	Parameter	S1-H	S1-S	S1-N	S2-H	S2-S	S2-N	S3-H	S3-S	S3-N	S4-H	S4-S	S4-N
MER-WF	# cycles	144	158	158	146	186	199	154	256	302	152	212	200
	% area	67	68	68	66	68	66	72	72	73	66	62	68
	Vol. rej.	12	0	0	27	4	0	50	17	0	25	5	0
MER-BF	# cycles	147	156	156	141	192	203	154	264	321	152	197	207
	% area	69	69	69	65	67	65	72	71	68	63	68	66
	Vol. rej.	7	0	0	31	3	0	50	16	0	29	3	0
A-2D	# cycles	142	158	158	144	185	200	149	268	308	155	199	202
	% area	70	68	68	64	67	66	71	73	71	63	67	67
	Vol. rej.	8	0	0	30	7	0	52	12	0	28	3	0
A-3D	# cycles	140	158	158	148	181	192	150	266	299	151	211	208
	% area	70	68	68	64	68	69	70	73	73	63	63	65
	Vol. rej.	10	0	0	21	7	0	53	12	0	30	3	0
HF	# cycles	145	154	154	141	181	188	153	265	294	156	207	196
	% area	68	70	70	68	71	70	72	72	75	65	64	70
	Vol. rej.	9	0	0	28	3	0	50	14	0	28	3	0
QF	# cycles	143	150	150	144	180	190	150	265	300	148	194	194
	% area	71	72	72	72	71	70	75	73	73	66	70	70
	Vol. rej.	7	0	0	22	3	0	49	12	0	27	0	0

Table 2. Experimental results

The results of Table 2 are summarized in some figures. Figures 6 and 7 show how much computing volume (in percentage with respect to the whole computing volume of the task set) is discarded for each set and for each one of the selection heuristics, for hard and soft time constraints, respectively. We suppose all the other tasks have been successfully loaded and executed before their respective time constraints have been reached.
As the figures show, the ***QF*** based heuristic discards a smaller percentage of the set computing volume for most of the task sets that the other heuristics. Only for a single case it behaves slightly worst, and for a few it does alike to some of the other ones. We must state that some of the heuristics mentioned have a quite good performance on their own, as it has been shown in (Tabero et al., 2006).

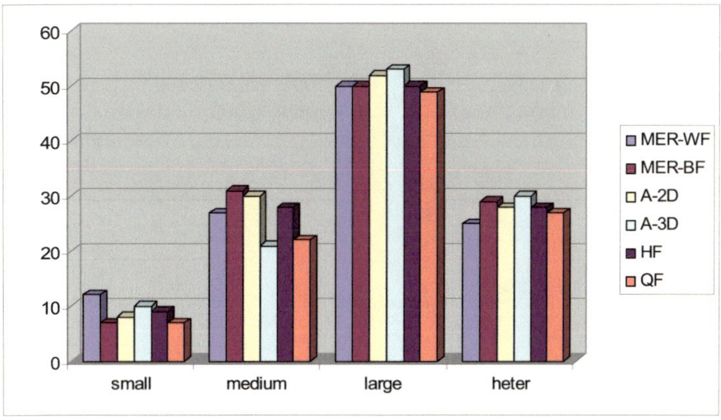

Fig. 6. Percentage of computing volume discarded for task sets with hard time constraints

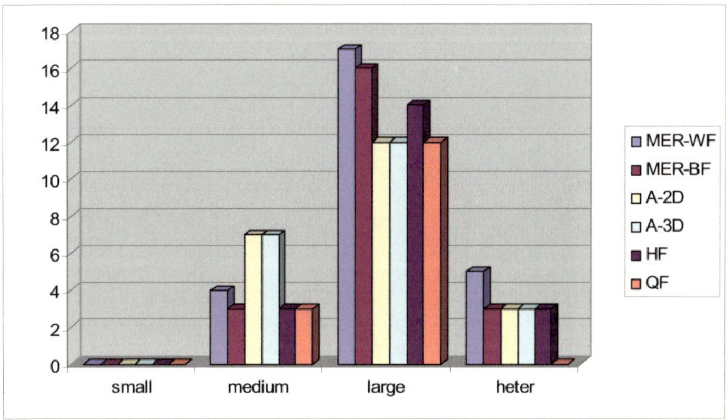

Fig. 7. Percentage of computing volume discarded for task sets with soft time constraints

When time constraints are non-existent, or for soft time constraints in some of the sets, no tasks are discarded by any heuristic, and the comparison must be established in terms of how many cicles have been used to complete the whole task set by each one of the heuristics. Figure 8 shows that the QF heuristic is able to execute the complete set workload in less cycles than most of the others and for most of the task sets. As Figure 9 shows, the average FPGA area occupation behaves similarly. We want to outline also that though the MER approaches are given only as a reference, because their complexity makes them unusable in a real on-line allocation environment, they can give a hint of how other rectangle-based heuristic will behave. As our heuristic compares favourably with the MER-based approaches, we can also expect it will stand against non-optimal techniques based on non-overlapping rectangles.

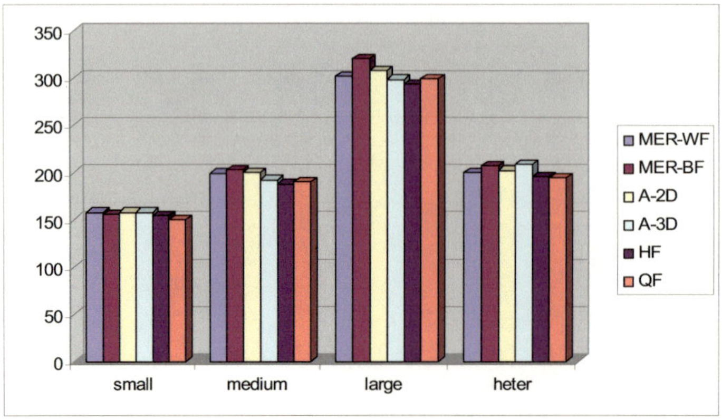

Fig. 8. Number of cycles for task sets without time constraints

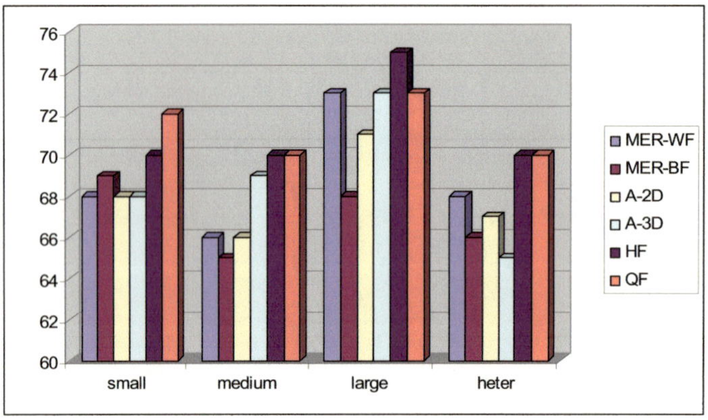

Fig. 9. Average area occupation for task sets without time constraints

Though the difference of the results for both fragmentation metrics, ***QF*** and ***HF***, are not always significant, it must be mentioned that ***QF*** is much simpler to compute than ***HF***, because there is no need to consider each independent hole in the FPGA free area. If a Vertex list-based allocator is used, then the free area perimeter is exactly the Vertex list length.

5. Defragmentation techniques

Even if we use intelligent (fragmentation-aware) heuristics to select the location for each incoming task, it is unavoidable that situations where fragmentation becomes a real problem will eventually arise.
In order to be able to defragment the free area available in an FPGA with several running tasks, we are making some considerations: we will suppose a pre-emptive system, that is, that we have the resources needed to interrupt anytime a currently running task, to relocate or reload the task configuration at a different location without modifying its status, and then to continue its execution.

We will consider two different defragmentation techniques, each one for a different situation:

- First, a routine, **preventive defragmentation** will be initiated if an alarm is fired by the Free Area Analyzer module. This alarm has two possible causes: the appearing of an occupied island inside a free hole, as in Figure 5, or a high fragmentation FPGA status detected by the metric above, as in Figures 2.d or 2.e. This preventive defragmentation is desired but not urgent, and will be performed only if time constraints for currently running tasks are not too severe.
- Second, an urgent **on-demand defragmentation** will be initiated, if an arriving task cannot find a suitable location in the FPGA, though there is enough free area to accommodate it. This emergency defragmentation will try to get room by moving a single currently running task.

5.1 Defragmentation time-cost estimation

It becomes clear that defragmentation is a time-consuming process, and therefore an estimation of the defragmentation time t_D will be needed in order to decide when, how or even if defragmentation will be performed. We must state also that we will not consider the time spent by the defragmentation algorithms themselves, which run in software in parallel with the tasks in the FPGA.

We have supposed that the defragmentation time cost due to each task will be proportional to the number of basic blocks of the task. And thus the total defragmentation time cost could be estimated as:

$$t_D = 2 * \sum_i t\_conf_i = 2\boldsymbol{k} * \sum_i (w_i * h_i) \quad \text{for all tasks } \boldsymbol{T_i} \text{ in the FPGA to be relocated} \qquad (9)$$

The proportionality factor $\boldsymbol{k}$ will depend on the technique we use to relocate the task configuration and on the configuration interface features (for example, the 8-bit SelectMap interface for Virtex FPGAs described in (www.xilinx.com). The factor of 2 appears because we have supposed that configuration reloading is done for each task through a readback of the task configuration and status from the original task location, that are later copied to the new one.

We would get a lower $2\boldsymbol{k}$ value if relocation could be done inside the FPGA, with the help of architectural changes such as the buffer proposed by Compton in (Compton et al., 2002). Such buffer, though, poses problems because relocation of each task must take into account the locations of other tasks in the FPGA. But we suppose it is not done by a task shifting technique such as the one explained in (Diessel et al., 2000), because in such case relocation time would depend for each task on the initial and final task locations.

The solution that would get the most significant reduction of $2\boldsymbol{k}$ would be using an FPGA architecture with two different contexts, a simplified version of the classical multicontext architecture proposed by Trimberger in (Trimberger et al., 1997). A second context would allow to schedule and accomplish a global defragmentation with a minimal time cost. The configuration load in the second context could be done while tasks go on running, and we would have to add only the time needed to transfer the status of each currently running task from the active context to the other one.

5.2 Preventive defragmentation

This defragmentation is fired by the Free Area Analyzer module, and it will be performed only if the free area is large enough, and it will try first to relocate islands inside the free hole, if they exist, or to relocate most of the currently running tasks if possible. There are two possible alarm causes: an **island alarm**, or a **fragmentation metrics alarm**.

The first alarm checked is the island alarm. An island is made of one or more tasks that have become isolated when all the tasks surrounding them have already finished. An island can appear only when a task-end event happens. It is obvious that to remove an island by relocating its tasks can lead to a significant reduction of the fragmentation value, and thus we treat it separately.

The second alarm cause is that the fragmentation value rises above a certain threshold. This can happen as a consequence of several different events, and the system will try to perform, if possible, a global or quasi-global relocation of the currently running tasks.

This routine defragmentation is not urgent, or at least it is not fired by the immediate need to allocate an incoming task, and its goal is to get a significantly lower fragmentation FPGA status by taking one of the mentioned actions.

A) Island alarm management

Though islands are not going to appear frequently, when they appear inside a hole they must be dealt with before any other consideration is done. An island inside a hole is represented in our system as part of the hole frontier, its vertices belonging to the VL defining the hole as all the other vertices do. We connect the island vertices with the external ones by using two virtual edges, which do not represent, as normal vertices do, a real frontier, and thus they are not considered when intersections are checked. Figure 10.a shows an example with a simple island made of two tasks and its VL is shown in Figure 10.b. The island alarm is then only a bit that is set whenever the Free Area Analyzer module detects the presence of a pair of virtual edges in VL, that in the example appear as discontinued arrows.

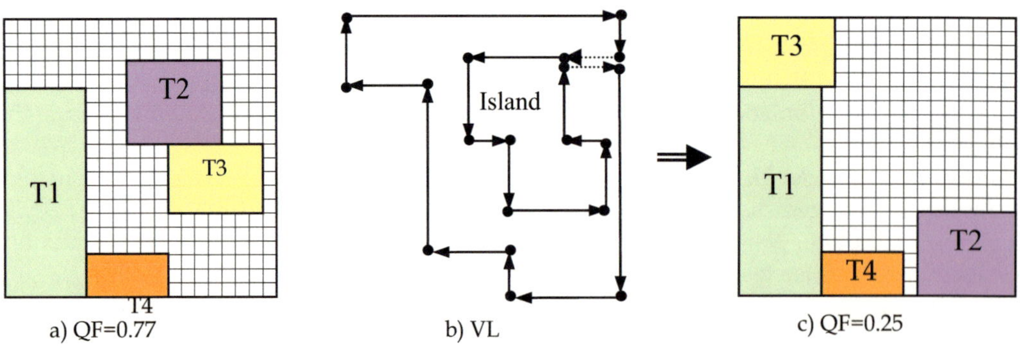

Fig. 10. FPGA status with an island (a) and its vertex list (b), and FPGA status after defragmentation (c).

If the island alarm has been fired, we check first if we can relocate it or not, by demanding that for every task T_i in the island the following condition is satisfied:

$$\textbf{C1:}\quad t\_marg_i \geq t_{D\_island} \tag{10}$$

where t_marg_i is computed as in (1) and t_{D_island} is the time needed to relocate the complete island, proportional to the island block size and computed as in (9). If condition C1 is satisfied, then new locations for the island tasks are selected by the 3D-adjacency allocation heuristic explained in (Tabero et al., 2004) o (Tabero et al., 2006). The tasks are allocated by decreasing values of t_rem_i, the time the will still remain in the FPGA, that is given by:

$$t\_rem_i = t\_start_i + t\_conf_i + t\_ex_i - t\_curr. \quad (11)$$

Figure 10.c shows the FPGA status once the island has been removed. Usually, the fragmentation estimation after island removal will lower substantially, below the alarm firing value, and thus we can consider the defragmentation accomplished.

If the island cannot be moved because the C1 condition is not met, then the defragmentation process will not be done.

B) Fragmentation alarm firing

The Free Area Analyzer module checks continuously the fragmentation status of the FPGA, estimating its value with the fragmentation metric used. The fragmentation alarm fires whenever the estimated value surpasses a given threshold. The exact threshold value would depend on the metric used.

For the examples shown in this paper, with an average running task number between four and five tasks, we have chosen as threshold a value of 0.75.

Finally, even when the fragmentation estimation reaches a high value, we have set another condition in order to decide if defragmentation is started: we only perform it if the hole has a significant size. We have set a minimum size value of two times the average task size:

$$A_{F\_FPGA} \geq 2 * average(A_i) \quad (12)$$

Only when this happens the theoretical fragmentation value can be taken as truly significant, and the alarm is actually fired. When such is the case, three different approaches can be considered, depending on the time constraints of the running tasks: immediate global defragmentation, delayed global defragmentation, or immediate partial defragmentation.

C) Immediate global defragmentation

If a high fragmentation alarm has fired, the system can try an **immediate global defragmentation** of the FPGA resources. In order to decide if such a defragmentation is possible, it must check if all the currently running tasks can be relocated or not, by demanding that for every task $\mathbf{T_i}$ in the FPGA the following condition is satisfied:

$$\textbf{C2:} \quad t\_marg_i \geq t_D \quad (13)$$

where t_D is the time needed to relocate all the running tasks computed as in (9). If all the tasks satisfy condition C2, then a defragmentation is performed where all the tasks are relocated, starting from an empty FPGA. The task configurations are readback first, and then relocated at their new locations. In order to reduce the probability of a new fragmentation situation too soon, tasks are relocated in order of decreasing values of t_rem_i, and the allocation heuristic used is based on the 3D-adjacency concept. Figure 11.a shows a FPGA situation with six running tasks and a high fragmentation status (QF=0.76). For each task T_i, example t_rem_i and t_marg_i values are shown. A global defragmentation will lead to the situation of Figure 11.b. We have supposed all tasks meet condition C2, and a t_D value of 20 cycles.

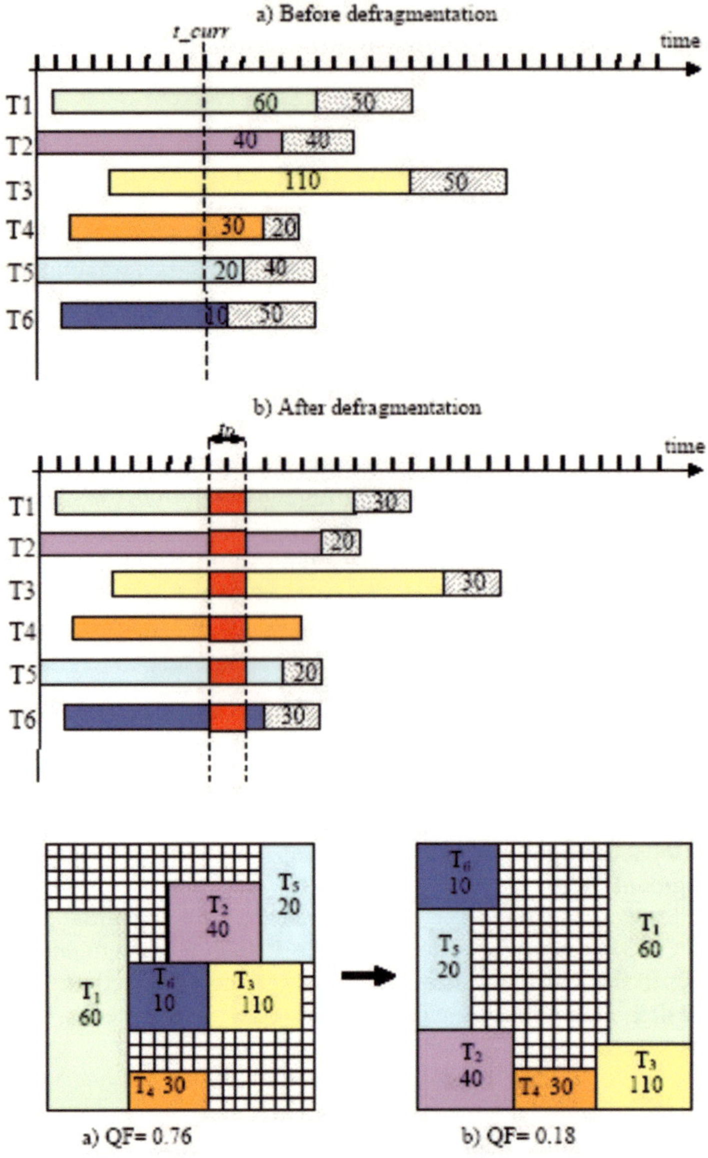

Fig. 11. Immediate global defragmentation process.

On the contrary, if there are one or more tasks T_j not meeting the condition above, we say these tasks have **severe time constraints**. In such case, a global immediate defragmentation cannot be made and we have to try a different approach. Then we set as a reference the time interval defined by the average time-lapse between consecutive task arrivals, *t_av*. Two situations can happen, depending on the instant the problematic tasks are going to finish, related to *t_av*. If the condition:

$$\textbf{C3:}\quad t\_rem_j < t\_av \tag{14}$$

is met by all tasks T_j not satisfying C2, that is, if these problematic tasks are expected to finish before a new task can arrive, then a **delayed global fragmentation** will be tried. If this is not the case, an **immediate partial defragmentation** will be performed, affecting only the non-problematic tasks.

D) Delayed global defragmentation

This heuristic is used when condition C3 is met by all tasks T_j not satisfying C2, that is, the task or tasks T_j with severe time constraint will end "soon". If all the problematic tasks finish before this reference threshold is reached, then we can wait the largest t_rem_j value and accomplish a delayed global defragmentation. During this defragmentation we do not perform new incoming task allocations. If any task arrives during this time-lapse it will be directly copied to the waiting tasks queue Qw, if the task has not severe time constraints. When a task with a severe time constraint arrives the defragmentation process is instantly aborted. Figure 12.a shows a situation derived from Figure 11.a, where condition C2 is not met now by task T6 due to a t_marg_6 value of only 10 cycles, though it satisfies C3. The situation depicted in Figure 12.b corresponds to a time instant after 10 cycles when task T6 has already finished. We also suppose no tasks arrive before task T6 is completed. Figure 12.c shows how it is possible to get a much better fragmentation status, though not immediately.

E) Immediate partial defragmentation

This approach is chosen if the tasks with severe time constraints will finish "late", that is, the condition C3 is not met. In such case, a partial defragmentation is performed immediately, by relocating all the tasks except the problematic ones. Such defragmentation is not optimal, but it can reduce the fragmentation value very soon. The configurations of the tasks to be relocated are readback, and then they are relocated as in a global defragmentation, but with a Vertex-List including the problematic tasks, instead of with an empty FPGA.

Figure 13.a shows a situation derived from Figure 12.a, where task T6, with a t_marg_6 value of 10 cycles and a t_rem_6 value of 60, does not satisfy conditions C2 and C3. Thus immediate relocation is performed for all tasks except T6. The resulting FPGA fragmentation status shown in Figure 13.b is not as good as the delayed one of Figure 12.c, but it is immediate.

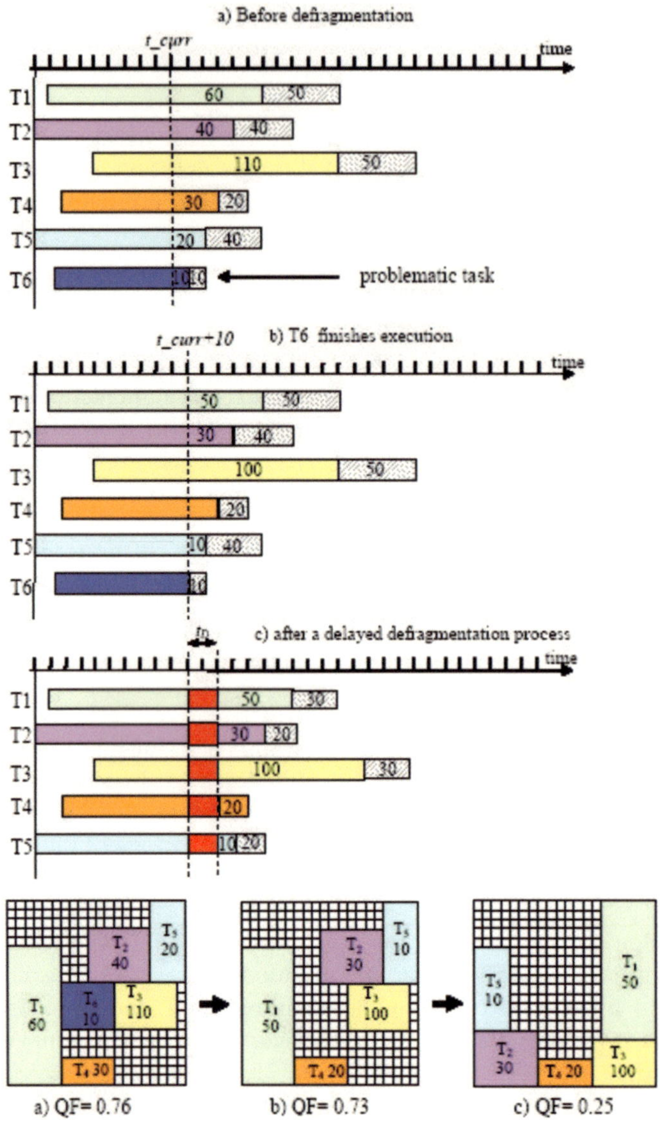

Fig. 12. Delayed global defragmentation process

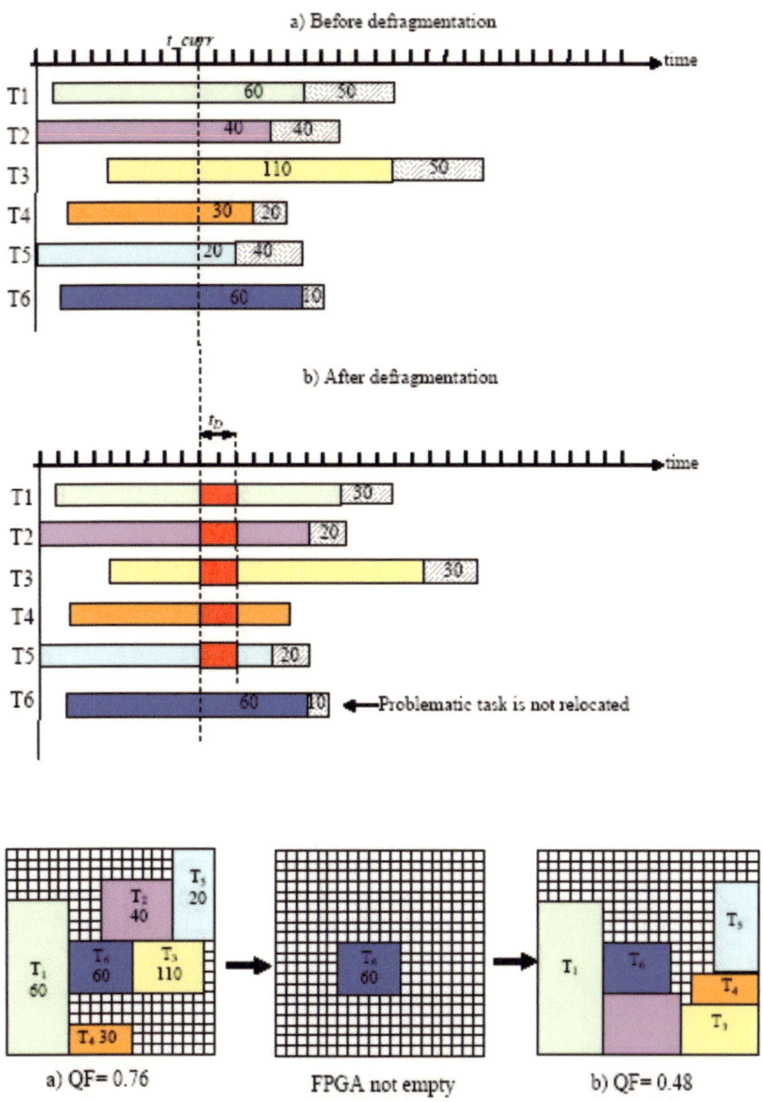

Fig. 13. Immediate partial defragmentation process

5.3 On-demand defragmentation

The on-demand defragmentation is only accomplished on an urgent basis, when a new task T_N cannot fit inside the FPGA due to fragmentation in spite of all the preventive measures already explained. Reasons for such failure can be the presence of many tasks with severe time constraints in the FPGA, or a fragmentation level below the alarm threshold. Then, as a final action, we try to move a single task in order to get room for the new one.

First, it must be guaranteed that the real problem is fragmentation and not the lack of space. Thus, we will take defragmenting actions only if the free FPGA area is two times the area of the incoming task:

$$A_{F\_FPGA} \geq 2 * (w_N * h_N). \tag{15}$$

If this condition is met, we choose as **best candidate task for relocation, T_R**, the task T_i with the highest percentage of its perimeter P_i belonging to the hole borders, what we have called its **relative adjacency** $radj_i$, that can be actually moved. The $radj_i$ value is computed by the allocation algorithm for every task in the hole border as:

$$radj_i = [(P_i \cap \mathrm{VL}) \,/\, 2(w_i + h_i)] \tag{16}$$

T_R will be thus the task T_i with the maximal value of *radj*. The allocation algorithm keeps continuous track of such relocation candidate, anytime the VL is modified, considering only values of $radj_i$ greater than 0.5. Any task forming an island would give the highest possible value of $radj_i$, that is 1. Good candidates would be tasks "joined" with a single side to the rest of the hole perimeter. Figure 14.a shows a candidate T_R intermediate between such two situations, with a *radj* value of 0.9286. On the contrary in Figure 14.c, with all tasks having a *radj* value of 0.5 or lower, no candidate T_R is available any longer because an advantageous quick task move is not obvious.

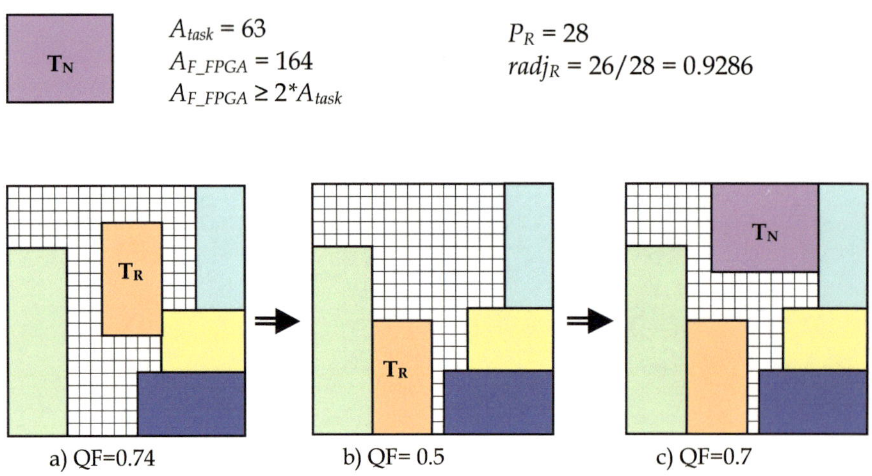

Fig. 14. FPGA status before (a) and after (b, then c) an on-demand defragmentation.

Moreover, T_R must satisfy: $t\_marg_R \geq t_{DR}$, t_{DR} being the relocation time of the candidate task T_R. A similar condition must be satisfied by the incoming task T_N as well: $t\_marg_N \geq t_{DR}$. If these two conditions are met, T_R is relocated with a 3D-adjacency heuristic, and then the new task T_N is considered again, and a suitable location perhaps can be found as in Figure 14.c.

If there is not a valid T_R candidate, though, then the on-demand defragmentation will not take place and the task T_N will go directly to Qw, in hope of a future chance before its *t_marg*$_N$ is spent. It happens the same if the defragmentation does not give the desired results.

5.4 Defragmentation experiments

In order to show that the defragmentation techniques proposed do work, we have made an experiment with a 100x100 FPGA. For this experiments, five new task sets have been generated with the same criteria than in Section 4. These sets generate situations where the preventive and on-demand defragmentation techniques can be applied.
We have compared how the Vertex List manager behaves, using as vertex selection heuristic the ***QF***-based cost function, with and whitout defragmentation. Figures 15 and 16 show, respectively, the rejected computing volume and the FPGA occupation level.

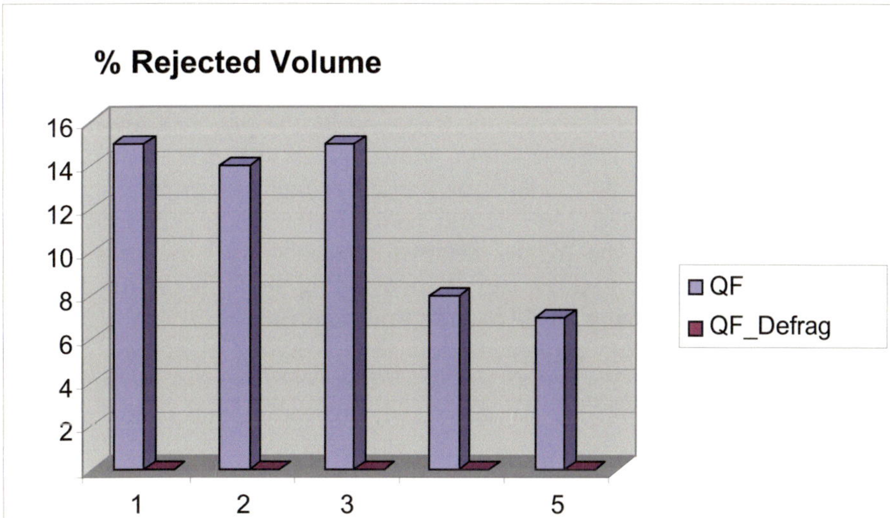

Fig. 14. Rejected computing volume.

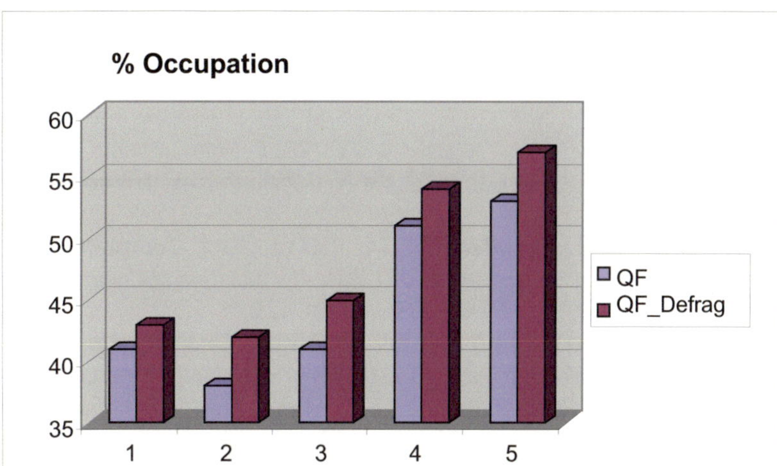

Fig. 15. FPGA occupation level.

Both figures confirm that when defragmentation techniques are used, the rejected computing volume reduces considerably, and the occupation level rises.

6. Conclusions and Future Work

We have presented an approach to 2D hardware multitasking upon a reconfigurable, FPGA-type, device. Our approach manages the FPGA resources with a Vertex list structure, allocates tasks to vertices of the list, estimates the fragmentation status of the FPGA and takes defragmentation decisions when needed.

Two fragmentation metrics have been proposed based on different concepts, one of them on the shape and area of each hole, and the other one on the relative quadrature of the whole free area. One of them, the quadrature-based one, has revealed very simple to compute and reliable enough to be used as cost function for the vertex selection process.

Two basic approaches have been shown to the defragmentation problem: preventive and on-demand defragmentation. Preventive techniques try to anticipate to possible allocation problems due to fragmentation. They can be triggered by the presence of an island in the vertex list, or by a high fragmentation value given by the metric. Preventive defragmentation can be immediate, global or partial, or delayed, depending on the time constraints of the involved tasks. On-demand heuristics try an urgent move of a single candidate task, the one with the highest relative adjacency with the hole border. Such battery of defragmentation measures can help avoiding most problems produced by fragmentation in HW multitasking on 2D reconfigurable hardware.

Future work-plans include the implementation of a working prototype based on the techniques described, upon a 2D-reconfigurable, Virtex 5 FPGA, and the development of preemption-supporting mechanisms, that allow task suspending and restoring trough task status storing and recovering.

7. References

Ahmadinia, A., Bobda, C., Bednara, M. & Teich, J. (2004). A new approach for on-line placement on reconfigurable devices. *Proceedings of the Parallel and Distributed Processing Symposium (IPDPS 2004),* pp. 134-, ISBN: 0-7695-2132-0, New Mexico USA, April 2004.

Ahmadinia, A.; Bobda, C. & Teich, J. (2003). Temporal task clustering for online placement on reconfigurable hardware, *Proceedings of the IEEE International Conference on Field-Programmable Technology,* pp. 359-362, ISBN: 0-7803-8320-6, Tokyo Japan, December 2003, IEEE.

Bazargan, K.; Kastner, R. & Sarrafzadeh, M. (2000). Fast Template Placement for Reconfigurable Computing Systems, *IEEE Design and Test of Computers,* Vol. 17, No. 1, (January-March 2000) pp. 68–83, ISSN: 0740-7475.

Brebner, G. & Diessel, O. (2001). Chip-Based Reconfigurable Task Management, *Proceedings of the 11th International Conference on Field-Programmable Logic and Applications,* pp. 182–191, ISBN: 3-540-42499-7, Belfast, U.K., August 2001, Springer.

Compton, K.; Cooley, J.; Knol, S. & Hauck S. (2002). Configuration Relocation and Defragmentation for Reconfigurable Computing. *IEEE Transactions on VLSI Systems,* Vol. 10, No. 3, (June 2002) pp. 209-220, ISSN 1063-8210.

Cui, J., Gu, Z., Liu, W. & Deng, Q. (2007). An Efficient Algorithm for Online Soft Real-Time Task Placement on Reconfigurable Hardware Devices. *Proceedings of the 10th IEEE International Symposium On Object and Component-Oriented Real-Time Distributed Computing (ISORC'07)*, pp. 222-227, ISBN:0-7695-2765-5, Santorini Greece, May 2007.

Diessel, O.; ElGindy, H.; Middendorf, M.; Schmeck, H. & Schmidt, B. (2000). Dynamic scheduling of tasks on partially reconfigurable FPGAs. *IEE Proc.-Computer Digital Technology*, Vol. 147, No. 3, (May 2000), pp. 181-188, ISSN : 1751-8601.

Ejnioui, A. & DeMara, R.F. (2005). Area Reclamation Metrics for SRAM-based Reconfigurable Device. *Proceedings of the International Conference on Engineering of Reconfigurable Systems and Algorithms (ERSA'05)*, pp. 196-202, ISBN 1-932415-74-2, Las Vegas, USA, June 2005. CSRAE Press.

Fekete, S.; van der Veen, J.; Ahmadinia, A.; Gohringer, D.; Majer, M. & Teich, J. (2008). Offline and Online aspects of Defragmenting the Module Layout of a Partially Reconfigurable Device, *IEEE Transactions on VLSI*, Vol. 16, No. 9, (September 2008), pp 1210-1219, ISSN: 1063-8210.

Gericota, M.; Alves, G.; Silva, M. & Ferreira, J. (2003). Run-Time Management of Logic Resources on Reconfigurable Systems, *Proceedings of the conference on Design, Automation and Test in Europe (DATE'03)*, pp. 974-979, ISBN:0-7695-1870-2, Munich Germany, March 2003, IEEE.

Handa, M. & Vemuri, R. (2004a). An Efficient Algorithm for Finding Empty Space for Online FPGA Placement. *Proceedings of the 41st Design Automation Conference (DAC'04)*, pp. 960-965, ISBN: 1-51183-828-8, San Diego USA, June 2004, IEEE.

Handa, M. & Vemuri, R. (2004b). Area Fragmentation in Reconfigurable Operating Systems, *Proceedings of the International Conference on Engineering of Reconfigurable Systems and Algorithms (ERSA'04)*, pp.77-83, ISBN 1-932415-42-4, Las Vegas USA, June 2004, CSREA Press.

Hübner, M., Schuck, C. & Becker, J. (2006). Elementary Block Based 2-Dimensional Dynamic and Partial Reconfiguration for Virtex-II FPGAs, *Proceedings of the Parallel and Distributed Processing Symposium (IPDPS 2006)*, ISBN: 1-4244-0054-6, Rodas Greece, April 2006.

Koch, D.; Ahmadinia, A.; Bobda, C. & Kalte, H. (2004). FPGA Architecture Extensions for Preemptive Multitasking and Hardware Defragmentation. *Proceedings of the IEEE International Conference on Field-Programmable Technology*, pp. 433-436. ISBN: 0-7803-7574-2, Brisbane, Australia, December 2004, IEEE.

Septién, J.; Mecha, H.; Mozos, D. & Tabero, J., (2006). 2D Defragmentation Heuristics for Hardware Multitasking on Reconfigurable Devices. *Proceedings of the Parallel and Distributed Processing Symposium (IPDPS 2006)*, ISBN: 1-4244-0054-6, Rodas Greece, April 2006.

Septién, J.; Mozos, D.; Mecha, H.; Tabero, J. & García, M.A. (2008). Perimeter Quadrature-based metric for estimating FPGA fragmentation in 2D HW multitasking, *Proceedings of the Parallel and Distributed Processing Symposium (IPDPS 2008)*, ISBN: 978-1-4244-1693-6, Miami, Florida USA , April 2008.

http://csdl.computer.org/comp/trans/tc/2004/11/t1393abs.htmSteiger, C.; Walder, H. & Platzner, M. (2004). Operating Systems for Reconfigurable Embedded Platforms: Online Scheduling of Real-Time Tasks. *IEEE Transactions on Computers* vol. 53, No. 11, (November 2004) pp.1393-1407, ISSN 0018-9340.

Tabero, J.; Septien, J.; Mecha, H. & Mozos, D. (2004). A Low Fragmentation Heuristic for Task Placement in 2D RTR HW Management, *Proceedings of the 14th International Conference on Field-Programmable Logic and Applications*. pp. 241-250, ISBN: 978-3-540-22989-6, Antwerp Belgium, August 2004, Springer-Verlag, Berlin.

Tabero, J.; Septién, J.; Mecha, H. & Mozos, D. (2006). Task Placement Heuristic Based on 3-D Adjacency and Look-Ahead in Reconfigurable Systems, *Proceedings of the 11th Asia and South Pacific Design Automation Conference (ASP-DAC 2006)*, pp. 396-401, ISBN:0-7803-9451-8, Yokohama Japan, January 2006.

Tabero, J.; Septién, J.; Mecha, H. & Mozos, D. (2008). Allocation heuristics and defragmentation measures for reconfigurable systems management. *Integration, the VLSI Journal*, Vol. 41, No. 2, (February 2008), pp. 281-296, ISSN:0167-9260.

Tabero, J.; Septien, J.; Mecha, H.; Mozos, D. & Roman, S. (2003). Efficient Hardware Multitasking through Space Multiplexing in 2D RTR FPGAs. *Euromicro Symposium on Digital System Design*, ISBN 0-7695-2003-0, Belek Turkey, September 2003, Elsevier.

Trimberger, S.; Carberry, D.; Johnson, A. & Wong, J. (1997). A time-multiplexed FPGA, *Proceedings of the 5th IEEE Symposium on FPGA-Based Custom Computing Machines (FCCM 97)*, pp. 22-28, ISBN: 0-8186-8159-4, Napa Valley, USA, April 1997, IEEE.

http://citebase.eprints.org/cgi-bin/search?author=Bobda%3BMajer%3BAhmadinia%3BKoch%3BTeich%3BField%3BComputer%3BScience&yearfrom=2003&yearuntil=2004&title=title%3A%28A+dynamic+NoC+approach+for+communication%29&submit=1van der Veen, J.; Fekete, S.; Majer, M.; Ahmadinia, A.; Bobda, C.; Hannig, F. & Teich, J. (2005). Defragmenting the Module Layout of a Partially Reconfigurable Device. *Proceedings of the Proc. of the International Conference on Engineering of Reconfigurable Systems and Algorithms (ERSA´05)*, pp. 92-104, ISBN 1-932415-74-2, Las Vegas, USA. June 2005. CSREA Press.

Walder, H. & Platzner, M. (2002). Non-preemptive Multitasking on FPGAs: Task Placement and Footprint Transform, *Proceedings of the International Conference on Engineering of Reconfigurable Systems and Algorithms (ERSA'02)*, pp. 24-30, ISBN: 1-892512-96-3, Las Vegas, USA. June 2002. Editors: T. P. Plaks & P. M. Athanas, Las Vegas.

Walder, H.; Steiger, C. & Platzner , M. (2003). Fast online task placement on FPGAs: free space partitioning and 2D-Hashing. *Proceedings of the Parallel and Distributed Processing Symposium (IPDPS 2003)*, ISBN: 0-7695-1926-1, France, April 2003.

Walder, H.; Steiger, C. & Platzner, M. (2003). Fast online task placement on FPGAs: free space partitioning and 2D-Hashing. *Proceedings of the Parallel and Distributed Processing Symposium (IPDPS 2003)*, ISBN: 0-7695-1926-1, Nice, France, April 2003.

Wigley, G. & Kearney, D. (2002a). Research Issues in Operating Systems for Reconfigurable Computing, *Proceedings of the International Conference on Engineering of Reconfigurable Systems and Algorithms (ERSA'02)*, pp. 569-572 ISBN: 1-892512-96-3, Las Vegas, USA. June 2002. Editors: T. P. Plaks & P. M. Athanas, Las Vegas.

Wigley, G. & Kearney, D. (2002b). The Management of Applications for Reconfigurable Computing Using an Operating System. *Australian Computer Science Communications*, Vol. 6, No. 3, (January-February 2002), pp. 73-81.

Xilinx, Inc. "Virtex-4 Configuration Guide", UG071, http://www.xilinx.com.

Xilinx, Inc. "Virtex-5 Configuration User Guide", UG191, http://www.xilinx.com.

TOTAL ECLIPSE—An Efficient Architectural Realization of the Parallel Random Access Machine

Martti Forsell
Platform Architectures
VTT
Finland

1. Introduction

In the beginning of this millennium power density and related heating problems practically stopped the exponential frequency increase of single core processors and limited availability of *instruction-level parallelism* (ILP) in general purpose applications started to limit the speedup achievable by increasing the number of simultaneously executed instructions in superscalar processors that along with architectural improvements in exploitation of memory hierarchies used to roughly duplicate the performance of processors in every second year for decades. In order to be able to continue the increasing trend of computational performance, all major processor manufacturers have switched to *chip multiprocessors* (CMP) integrating multiple processor cores on a single chip and switching the focus of parallelism from ILP to *thread-level parallelism* (TLP), because the number of transistors per chip still tends to increase exponentially with every new generation of silicon technology (ITRS, 2007) and high amounts of TLP is easier to extract than ILP. Manufacturers have ambitious plans to continue this development by roughly duplicating the number of cores per chip every second year, resulting to constellations with over 100 cores in ten years (Intel, 2006). This will, however, not happen without problems, because current CMP architectures and related programming models do not support simple migration to parallel computing, so called automatic parallelization of existing sequential code has been turned out to be extremely difficult for general purpose programs, writing explicitly parallel versions of programs has turned out to be tedious, error-prone and expensive, and achieving linear speed-ups with respect to the number of cores appears to be limited to only small classes of well-behaving algorithms. These problems are caused by inability of current architectures to hide the latency of shared memory accesses (or intercommunication), lack of synchronicity in execution of computational threads as well as too weak models and low-level primitives of parallel computing forcing a programmer to explicitly take care of data partitioning to maximize locality, functionality mapping supporting data partitioning, synchronization of subtasks, and communication. Without solving these problems, it is hard to imagine that parallel computing would be able to supersede sequential computing from being the main paradigm of general purpose computing. Furthermore, if nothing is done, the performance of future processors will remain the same while the utilization of processor cores for single computational problems will decrease as the number of cores per chip increases.

The importance of providing easy-to-use programming models has been discovered in parallel computing research long before the era of CMPs (Schwarz, 1966; Karp and Miller, 1969). The culmination of this early active research period was achieved with the invention of the *parallel random access machine* (PRAM) in the late 70's being able to abstract the essence of parallel computing into a conceptually simple and beautiful model being a logical extension the widely used model of sequential computation (Fortune and Wyllie, 1978). A PRAM consists of a set of processors working under the same clock and a uniform single step accessible shared memory connected to them (see Figure 1). Programming with the PRAM model is much easier than with the weaker asynchronous models since with PRAM a programmer knows all the time the exact state of the threads due to synchrony of instruction execution, partitioning and mapping problems are eliminated—a programmer can just put all the data requiring interaction to the shared memory so that all processors can uniformly access it—and communication happens simply via accessing synchronously shared variables in the shared memory. One clear evidence for this is that there exists a rich theory of algorithms for the PRAM model (Jaja, 1992; Keller et al., 2001), which can not be said for the other models that are typically asynchronous and highly architecture dependent. Unfortunately, realization of a computer supporting the PRAM model has turned out to be very challenging. Namely, in our early research (Forsell, 1994) we have shown that the direct implementation of the multiport memory being the key to PRAM implementation is not physically feasible with the known silicon technology if the number of ports is higher than, say 4, due to quadratic wiring area increase with respect to the number of ports. An indirect implementation, based on executing multiple threads per processor core to hide the latency of the memory system, high-bandwidth intercommunication network with randomization to avoid congestion, and wave-based synchronization mechanism, is known from the early 90's (Ranade, 1991), but so far the proposed architectures (Schwarz, 1980; Ranade et al., 1987; Alverson et al., 1990; Abolhassan et al., 1993; Imai, et al., 2000; Vishkin et al., 2008) have been unable to provide feasibility, scalability, instruction-level parallelism (ILP) support, low thread-level parallelism (TLP) support, and cost-efficiency to lure processor manufacturers to employ them in their products.

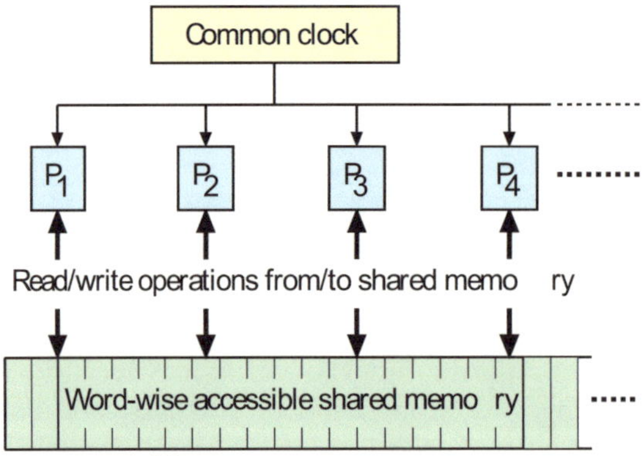

Fig. 1. Parallel random access machine.

In this chapter, we introduce a configurable chip multiprocessor architecture, TOTAL ECLIPSE, for realizing one of the most powerful PRAM variants, the *arbitrary multioperation concurrent read concurrent write* (MCRCW) PRAM model. In addition to standard *arbitrary concurrent read concurrent write* (CRCW) PRAM capable of concurrent reads and writes so that in the case of a write arbitrary of the participating threads succeeds, MCRCW provides multioperations that can e.g. sum the values sent by all participating threads into a memory location concurrently. The architecture is optimized for efficient execution of programs containing enough TLP to hide the latency of the intercommunication network and co-exploitation of virtual ILP with TLP but it is also able to execute programs with low TLP efficiently by providing seamless configurability of PRAM threads to *non-uniform memory access* (NUMA) (Swan et.al., 1977) bunches combining the computational power of two or more threads within a processor core. We will describe the principles of PRAM realization, integration of NUMA bunching to TOTAL ECLIPSE operation, as well as overall architectural structure and operation of the TOTAL ECLIPSE architecture. Performance evaluation by executing simple programs with a clock-accurate simulator is provided and silicon area and power consumption estimations of selected TOTAL ECLIPSE CMP configurations are given. This chapter acts also as a case-driven introduction to novel techniques for parallel architectures, unknown from the theory of sequential architectures.
The rest of the chapter is organized so that in Section 2 we describe the principles of realizing PRAM on a physically feasible silicon platform. In Section 3 we describe the TOTAL ECLIPSE architecture making use of these principles and additional architectural techniques, in Section 4 we evaluate the performance, silicon area and power consumption of selected TOTAL ECLIPSE CMPs, and finally in Section 5 we give conclusions.

2. Realizing the Parallel Random Access Machine

Realizing PRAM on silicon has turned out to be very challenging problem. In addition to the theoretical complexity of direct implementation mentioned in Section 1 (Forsell, 1994), a stronger claim arguing that required bandwidth rules any realization unfeasible was published already in the previous year with the introduction of the LogP model (Culler, 1993). While the complexity of direct implementation can be overcome by using an indirect implementation technique reported a few years earlier (Valiant, 1990; Ranade, 1991), the latter claim has been controversial from the very beginning. The tremendous progress in VLSI technology currently allowing for more than billion transistors and ten on-chip wiring layers with wiring pitch of only 45 nm has raised the capacity and practically achievable bisection bandwidth of a single microchip to a level where these old capacity/bandwidth precautions do not hold any more. In addition, these numbers are predicted to grow for still more than ten years making even more complex integrated systems feasible (ITRS, 2007). Finally, recent estimations on the area and power, and even FPGA and silicon prototypes of PRAM or PRAM-like CMPs (Vishkin, 2007; Forsell and Roivainen, 2008) prove that PRAM realizations are indeed physically feasible. In this section we describe the principles of realizing the PRAM model as formulated by (Ranade, 1991; Leppänen 1996).
The current approach for advanced CMPs is to use a *cache coherent distributed shared memory* (CC-SM) machine consisting of a number of processor cores with local caches connected to memory modules via an asynchronous communication network (see Figure 2). In order to try to hide the latency of the distributed memory system, caches are being kept coherent

during execution by using a high-speed cache coherence mechanism, usually based on distributed directories (Lenoski, 1992). The problems of CC-SMs are that for general purpose parallel algorithms the cache coherence maintenance traffic consumes already the most of the intercommunication network bandwidth, for demanding memory access patterns caches would need to be multiported, thus non-scalable (Forsell, 1994) or severe performance degrading sequentialization will occur, and for fine-grained parallel functionality the asynchrony of the machine makes programming very difficult. It is hard to solve all these problems together without taking a radically different approach like shared memory emulation connecting a set of processor cores without caches to memory modules via a high-bandwidth synchronous intercommunication network (Ranade, 1991; Leppänen, 1996). In it, the latency is hidden with low-overhead multithreading exploiting slackness of parallel computation, i.e. executing other threads while one is referring the memory in a pipelined way. We call the obtained solution *emulated shared memory* (ESM) machine (see Figure 2). A bit similar cacheless solution is used with some synchronous SIMD and vector machines, but they can not execute code including control parallelism efficiently.

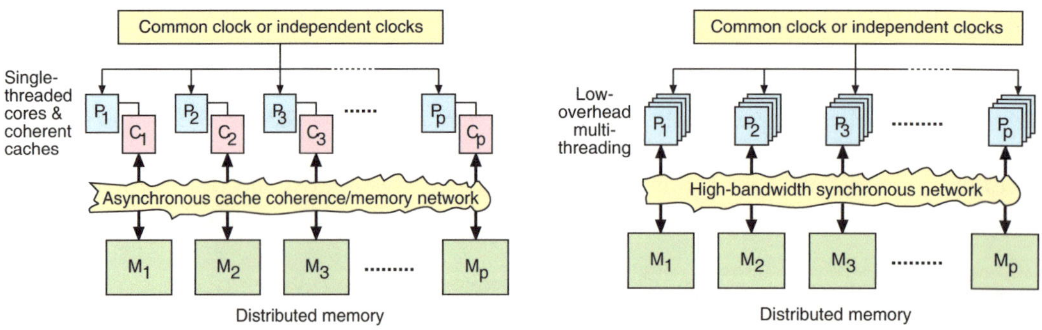

Fig. 2. Cache coherent shared memory (left) versus emulated shared memory approach (right) (P=processor core, C=local cache, M=memory module).

There exists a number of theoretical studies summarized in (Leppänen, 1996) that formally prove that this kind of on ESM can work-optimally simulate the PRAM with a high probability if the following preconditions related to the network topology, and congestion avoidance are guaranteed:

(i) The bandwidth requirements of certain extreme cases causing all the references to be headed to a low number of (or even single) memory module(s) are reduced to an ability to route random traffic by using a hashing of memory locations that is randomly selected from a family of hashings (Dietzfelbinger et.al., 1994).

(ii) To handle random communication the bisection bandwidth of the network must be at least *O(number of cores)*.

(iii)Synchronization of memory references can be handled by the synchronization wave technique that works with acyclic networks in which special synchronization packets are sent by the processors to the memory modules and vice versa (Ranade, 1991). The idea is that when a processor has sent all its packets on their way, it sends a synchronization packet. Synchronization packets from various sources push on the actual packets, and spread to all possible paths, where the actual packets could go. When a node receives a synchronization packet from one of its inputs, it waits, until it has received a synchronization packet from all of its inputs, then it forwards the synchronization wave to all of its outputs. The synchronization wave may not bypass any actual packets and vice versa. When a synchronization wave sweeps over a network, all nodes and processors receive exactly one synchronization packet via each input link and send exactly one via each output link.

Another necessary condition for practical PRAM implementations is that the used CMP architecture needs to be ultimately implementable with current silicon technology. Due to relatively decreasing signal propagation speed on shrinking silicon technologies, variable link length intercommunication network topologies, including all logarithmic diameter constellations (trees, fat trees, butterflies, hypercubes, etc.) fail to provide performance scalability with respect to the number of processor cores, while fixed link length topologies like coated meshes, sparse meshes and multimeshes have no such scalability problems (Leppänen, 1996; Forsell, 2002; Forsell and Leppänen, 2005).

3. TOTAL ECLIPSE

Embedded Chip-Level Integrated Parallel SupErcomputer (ECLIPSE) is an architectural framework for general purpose chip multiprocessors and multiprocessor systems on chip (MP-SOC), but is extendable also to multichip constellations (Forsell, 2002). It lends many ideas from our early work on the *Instruction-Level Parallel Shared Memory* (IPSM) machine originally reported in (Forsell, 1997) as well as earlier PRAM realization research (Ranade, 1991; Leppänen, 1996) and *network on chip* (NOC) research (Jantsch, 2003). Unfortunately, the original ECLIPSE architecture is only able to support the *exclusive read exclusive write* (EREW) PRAM model which is not able to match the performance of MCRCW PRAM, but requires logarithmically longer execution times for a large number of parallel computational problems even though optimal parallel algorithms are used. In addition, it fails to support efficient execution of low-TLP functionalities because for organizational reasons it features a relatively high minimum number of threads per processor, dropping the utilization of a core to as low as the reciprocal of that value in the case of a functionality having only one thread.

Our renewed proposal for a universal general purpose CMP is the TOTAL ECLIPSE architecture that realizes the arbitrary MCRCW PRAM model and supports NUMA execution for processor-wise thread bunches making execution of low-TLP functionalities as efficient as with standard sequential processors using the NUMA convention. A TOTAL ECLIPSE consists of P T_P-threaded (constituting total $T = PT_P$ threads) F-functional unit MBTAC processor cores with dedicated instruction memory and local data memory modules, P T_P-line step caches and scratchpads attached to processors, P fast data memory modules, and a high-bandwidth multimesh interconnection network (see Figure 3).

In the following subsections we describe the processor, memory system, and communication network of the TOTAL ECLIPSE architecture as well as the key architectural techniques used in them to realize the properties of it. Due to simplicity reasons and lack of space, we limit ourselves to describing an integer-only version of the architecture. Inclusion of floating point support to this class of architectures should be, however, as straightforward as for any other architecture. Supporting application-specific acceleration of functionalities, like graphics, multimedia, and communications, is also left out because they can be implemented efficiently with already relatively well-known architectural solutions that may be used along with TOTAL ECLIPSE, making the overall system architecture slightly heterogeneous (Forsell, 2009). In such a heterogeneous TOTAL ECLIPSE system, however, the performance of TOTAL ECLIPSE unit in general purpose parallel execution would make useless techniques used in some current heterogeneous systems that map even some general purpose functionality to general purpose GPUs rather than standard multicore CPUs to gain modest speedups (although this happens often with the cost of reduced utilization, increased power consumption, and more difficult programmability).

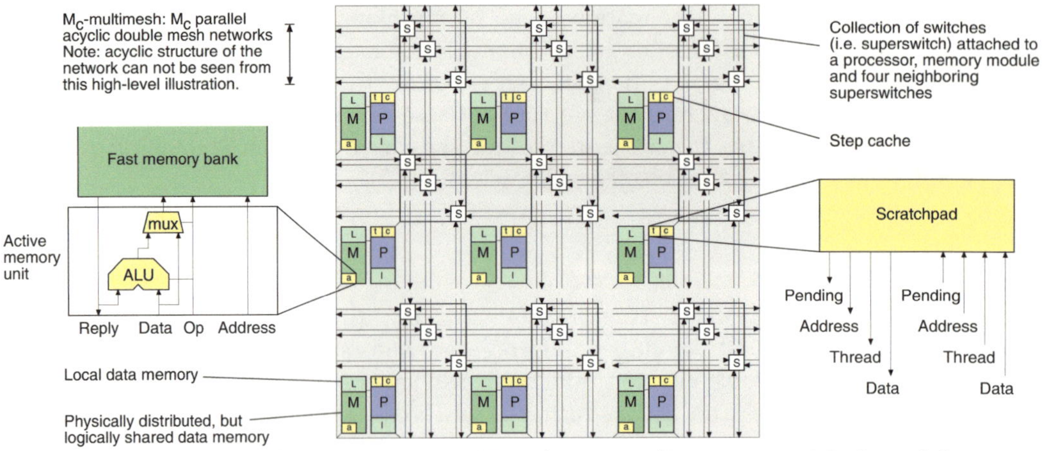

Fig. 3. Block diagram of the TOTAL ECLIPSE architecture (P=processor, M=shared data memory module, L=local data memory module, I=instruction memory module, a= active memory unit, c=step cache, t=scratchpad, and s=switch).

3.1 Processor

Multibunched/threaded Architecture with Chaining (MBTAC) is a dual-mode VLIW processor architecture designed for realizing both a strong PRAM model on a physically distributed memory architecture (so called PRAM mode) and an efficient NUMA model for low TLP locality-optimized code (so called NUMA mode) (Forsell, 2009). An MBTAC processor has A ALUs, M memory units, M hash address calculation units, a compare unit, a sequencer, and a register file of R registers per thread on a deep, cyclic, hazard-free interthread pipeline for the PRAM mode execution and a local ALU, a local memory unit, a local sequencer, and a register file of R registers per thread bunch on a four stage pipeline for the NUMA mode execution (see Figure 4). The NUMA mode pipeline is overlapped/merged with the first four stages of the PRAM mode pipeline so that most of the hardware, including one ALU and all registers, can be shared between the modes. Other parts of the processor include a step cache and scratchpad that are used to implement concurrent memory access and multioperations. MBTAC has a VLIW-style instruction set with a chain-like fixed execution ordering of subinstructions with a mechanism for using the result of a subinstruction as an operand of the following subinstructions in the chain for the PRAM mode and standard parallel organization of functional units for the NUMA mode (see Appendix A for the list of subinstructions). There is a hardware assisted synchronization mechanism for a limited number of concurrent fast barriers, while a bit slower software based solution utilizing multioperations can be used to provide an arbitrary number of simultaneous barriers (Forsell, 2006).

MBTAC supports overlapped execution of a variable number of threads and thread bunches and seamless dynamic switching between them with special instructions. Multithreading is implemented as a T_p-stage, cyclic interthread pipeline for hiding the latency of the memory system and maximizing the overlapping of execution in the PRAM mode. Switching between threads and bunch slots happens in zero time, because threads proceed in the pipeline only during the forward time. If a thread tries to refer memory when the intercommunication network is busy, the whole pipeline is suspended until the network becomes available again. After issuing a memory read, the thread can wait the reply for at most $M_w<T_p$ clock cycles before the pipeline freezes until the reply arrives. For the NUMA mode, forwading is used to reduce the number of pipeline hazards to two delay slots per each executed control transfer instruction.

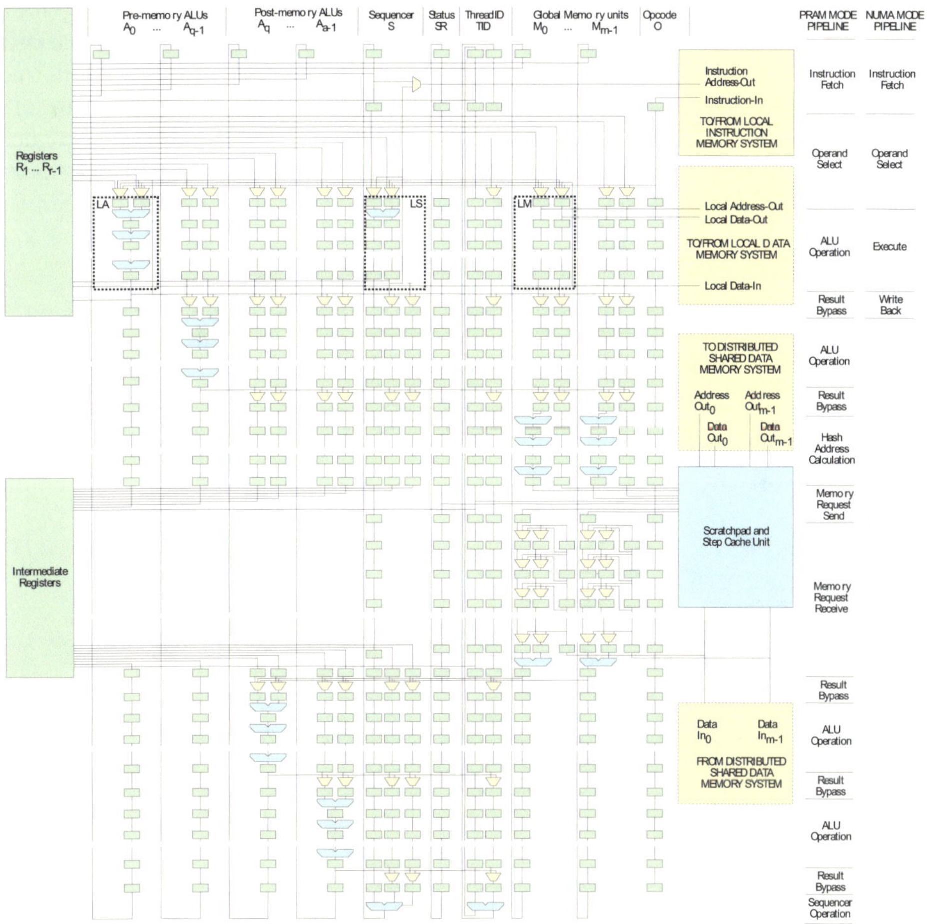

Fig. 4. Block diagram of the MBTAC processor

The PRAM and NUMA models are linked to the architecture so that a full cycle in the pipeline corresponds typically to a single PRAM step and a full cycle of execution for a bunch with B thread slots corresponds typically to executing B consecutive instructions. During a step, each thread of each processor of the CMP executes an instruction, including

at most M shared memory reference subinstructions, and sends a synchronization wave. Therefore a step lasts for multiple, at least T_p+1, clock cycles.
In the following subsections we take a detailed look at special architectural techniques, chaining, step caches, and scratchpads, used in TOTAL ECLIPSE.

3.1.1 Low and low-level parallelism exploitation via chaining and bunching

The organization of the PRAM mode functional units in MBTAC is targeted for exploiting ILP during steps of parallel execution. Therefore functional units in MBTAC are connected as a chain, so that a unit is able to use the results of its predecessors in the chain (Forsell, 1997; Forsell, 2003). Since multiple threads are executed in an overlapped way, it possible to execute dependent subinstructions during a step unlike with parallel functional unit organization of sequential processors (see Figure 5). We call this new class of parallelism *virtual instruction level parallelism*. In order to maximize the obtained speedup, the ordering of functional units in the chain is selected according to the average ordering of instructions in a basic block: Two thirds of the ALUs form the beginning of the chain. They are followed by the memory units and the rest of the ALUs. The compare unit and the sequencer are located in the end of the chain, because comparing and branching happen always in the end of basic blocks. In the NUMA mode, the local functional units are organized in parallel like in a standard single threaded VLIW processor because chaining would cause a lot of pipeline hazards for bunches and actually degrade the performance.

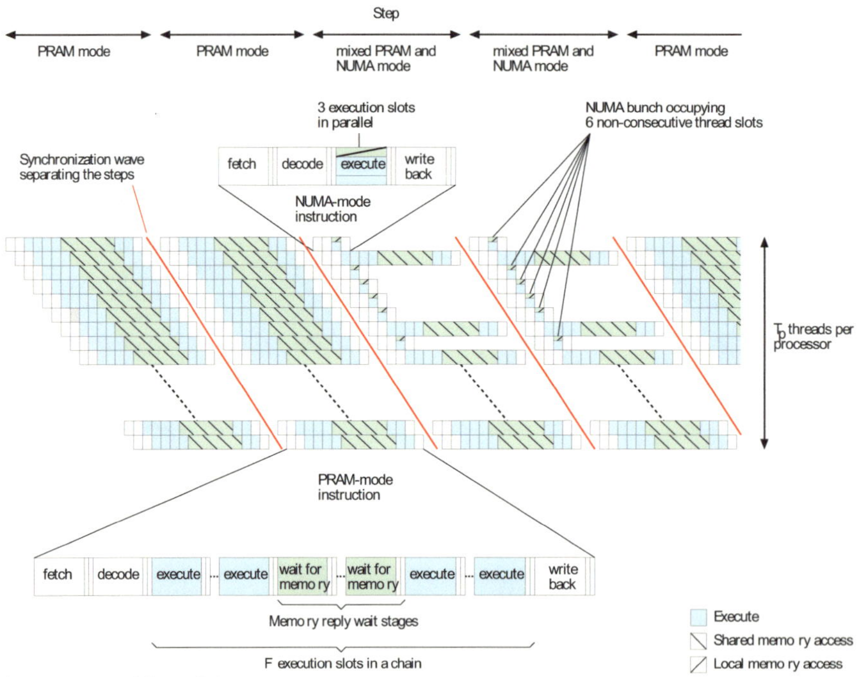

Fig. 5. Chaining and bunching.

Efficient execution of low TLP code is implemented by making the thread storage configurable/indirect and pipeline suitable for sequential execution so that multiple thread execution slots can be assigned to efficiently execute a single NUMA mode thread bunch by just using the same thread storage address for all of them (Forsell, 2009). This way a bunch can use thread slots to execute multiple instructions during a step removing the low TLP performance bottleneck of the original Eclipse (see Figure 5). The number of concurrent bunches per processor can be everything from zero (PRAM mode) to $T_P/2$ and they can occur in parallel with PRAM mode threads. Bunches can only access local memories since there is no efficient and easy-to-use mechanism to hide the latency of memory references in low TLP situations. Required indirect thread storaging is implemented by storing threads into a multiported and multithreaded register block (like in the SUN Sparc Tx-series) rather than in the pipeline registers, and by adding a thread address storage pointer for each thread (see leftmost registers of the TID dual chain in Figure 4). In order to set a group of threads to use just one thread storage, i.e. to execute a single thread for all the thread slots, a programmer needs just to set the thread storage pointers to a single value selected out of the values of the thread storage pointers with the JOIN instruction. Similarly, splitting the bunch back to separate threads happens by restoring the old numbering of the thread slots with the SPLIT instruction.

3.1.2 Concurrent access and step caches

The PRAM support machinery of TOTAL ECLIPSE allows for arbitrary concurrent reads and writes to memory locations. For a concurrent read, all threads participating the access give the same results. In the case of a concurrent write, the data of an arbitrary thread participating the write will be written to the target location. This is implemented by using step caches, which are associative memory buffers in which data stays valid only to the end of ongoing step of multithreaded execution (Forsell, 2005). The main contribution of step caches to concurrent accesses is that they step-wisely filter out everything but the first reference for each referenced memory location. This reduces the number of requests per location to P allowing them to be processed sequentially on a single ported memory module assuming $T_P \geq P$ (see Figure 6).

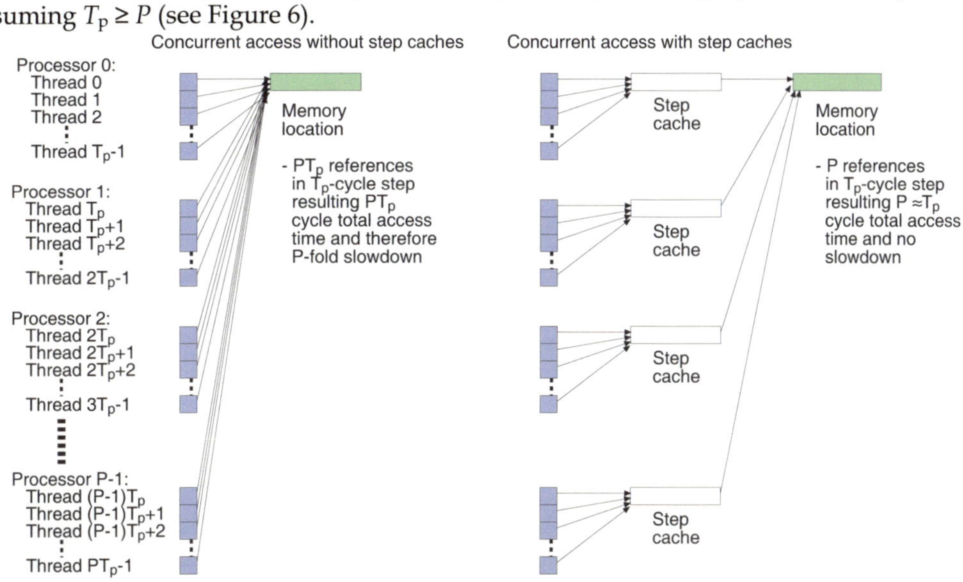

Fig. 6. Step caches for implementing concurrent memory access.

Step caches operate similarly as ordinary caches with a few notable exceptions: Each time a multithreaded processor refers to the shared data memory a step cache search is performed. A hit is detected on a cache line if the line is in use, the address tag matches the tag of the line, and the least significant bits of step of the reference matches the step of the line. In the case of a hit, a write is just ignored while a read is just completed by accessing the data from the cache. In the case of a miss, the reference is stored into the cache using the replacement policy at hands and marked as pending (for reads). At the same time with storing the reference information to the cache line, the reference itself is sent to the lower-level memory system. When a reply of a read arrives from the memory, the data is put to the data field of the line storing the reference information and the pending field is cleared. The structure of a step cache is similar to ordinary caches, but it has two extra fields—pending and step—and a block for decaying (Kaxiras, 2001) the data belonging to previous steps before their step field matches again to the least significant bits of current step (see Figure 7). Cache coherency problems are avoided due to a short life-time of references in the cache, since operations made during a step are independent by the definition parallel execution. The TOTAL ECLIPSE CMPs involved in our evaluations in Section 4 use A_s -way set associative step caches with *the least recently used* (LRU) replacement policy of size T_p lines attached to each processor and scratchpads.

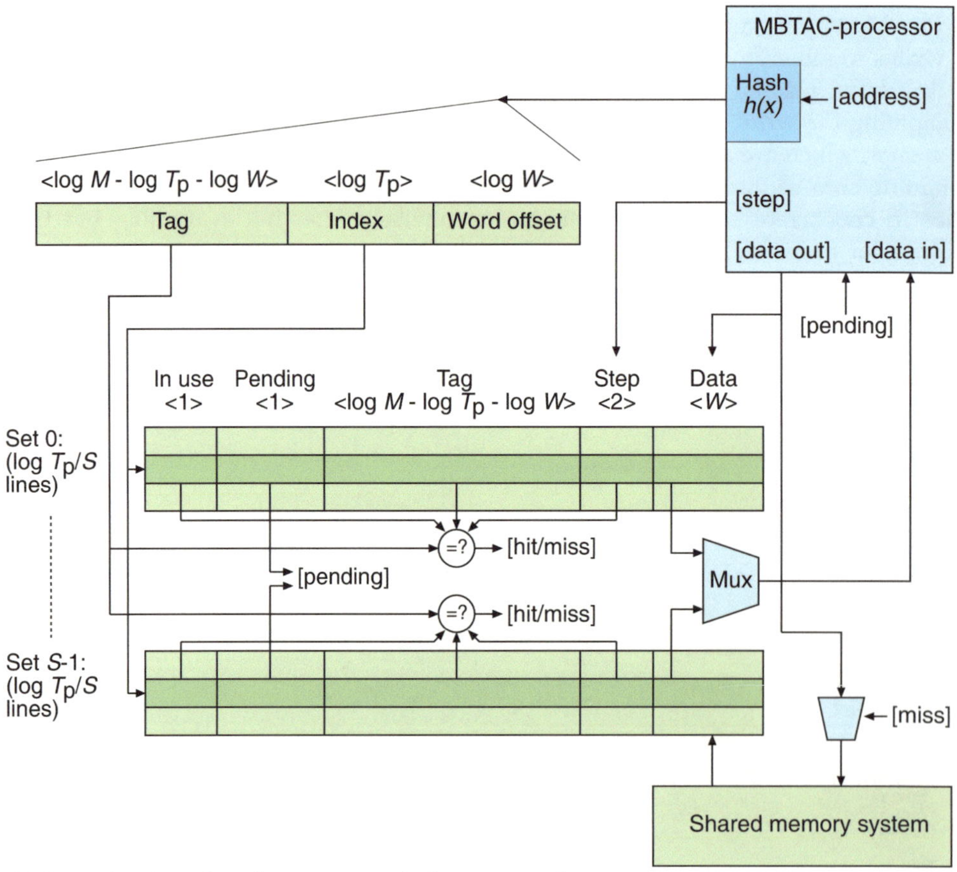

Fig. 7. Organization of an A_s -way associative step cache.

3.1.3 Multioperations and scratchpads

Scratchpads are addressable memory buffers that are used to store memory access data to keep the associativity of step caches limited in implementing multioperations and thread bunches with a help of step caches, and minimal on-core and off-core ALUs that take care of actual intra-processor and inter-processor computation for multioperations (Forsell, 2006) (see Figures 3 and 4). Scratchpads are organized with step caches to so called scratchpad - step cache units. A scratchpad - step cache unit for MBTAC processor consists of a T_P-line scratchpad, a T_P-line step cache, and a simple multioperation ALU for executing incoming concurrent references, multioperations and arbitrary ordered multiprefixes sequentially (see Figure 8).

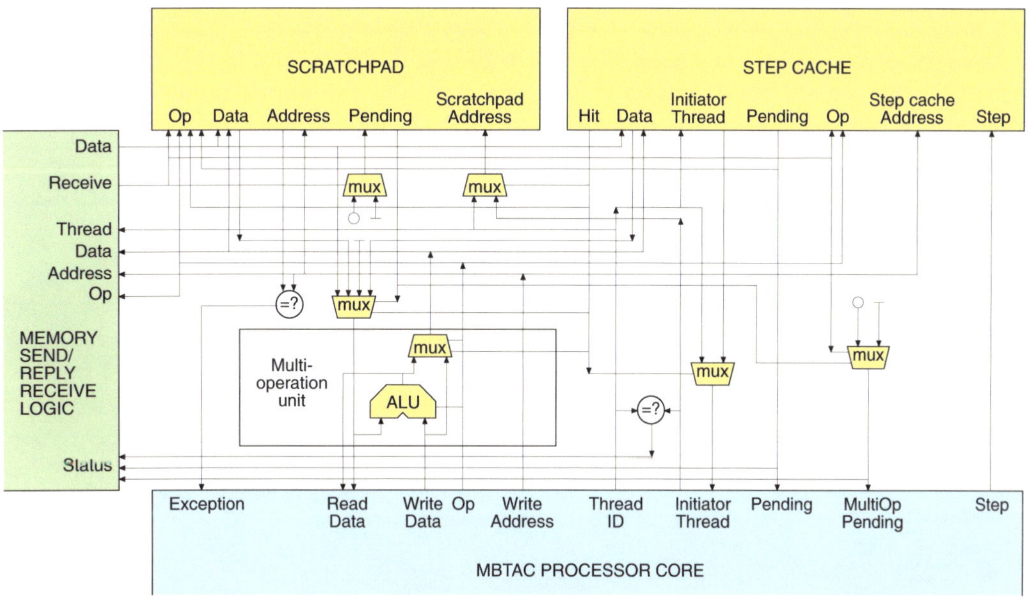

Fig. 8. Implementation of multioperations with scratchpads and step caches. Detailed description of this logic can be found in (Forsell, 2006).

Ordinary multioperations are implemented as two consecutive single step operations (see Appendix A for a list of available multioperations). During the first step, a starting operation (BMxx for multioperations or BMPxx for arbitrary ordered multiprefix operations) executes a processor-wise multioperation against a step cache location without making any reference to the external memory system (see Figure 9). During the second step, an ending operation (EMxx for multioperations or EMPxx for arbitrary ordered multiprefix operations) performs the rest of the multioperation so that the first reference to a previously initialized memory location triggers an external memory reference using the processor-wise multioperation result as an operand. The external memory references that are targeted to the same location are processed in the active memory unit of the corresponding memory module according to the type of the multioperation. In the case of arbitrary ordered multiprefixes the reply data is sent back to scratchpads of participating processors. The consecutive references are completed against the step cached reply data. It can happen that a consecutive reference is made to a location while the external reference is being processed.

In that case, the operation is marked as pending and completed as the result is available. This does not slow down the processing any way since one additional simple ALU is located to the end of memory access pipeline segment in MBTAC (see Figure 4). Since MBTAC uses limited associativity step caches, scratchpads are used to store the id of the initiator thread of each multioperation sequence to the step cache and internal initiator thread id (IT) register as well as reference information to a storage that saves the information regardless of possible conflicts that may wipe away information on references from the step cache. A scratchpad has a field for data, address and pending for each thread of the processor. With a help of scratchpads, multioperations are implemented by using sequences of two instructions: Data to be written in the step cache is also written to the scratchpad, id of the first thread referencing a certain location is stored to the step cache and IT register (for the rest of references), the pending bit for multioperations is kept in the scratchpad rather than in the step cache, reply data is stored to the scratchpad rather than to the step cache, and reply data for the ending operation is retrieved from the scratchpad rather than from the step cache (Forsell, 2006).

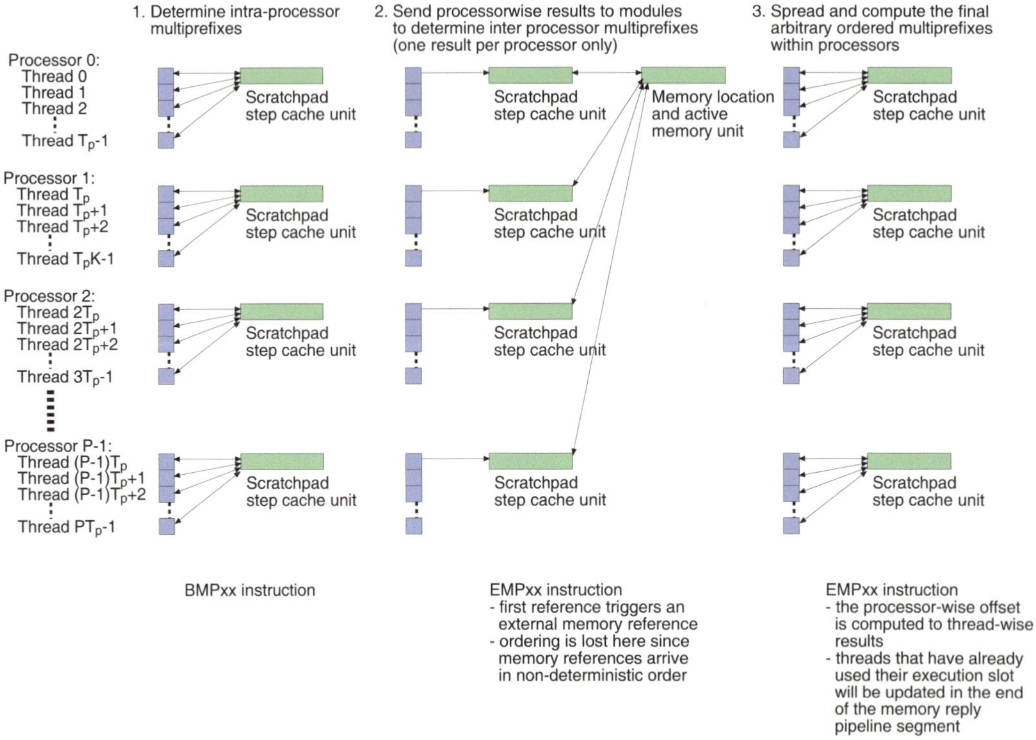

Fig. 9. Implementation of multioperations with scratchpads and step caches.

Since many efficient parallel algorithms make use of limited concurrent access, constituting of, say, at most square root T references per step, we have implemented faster single instruction limited multioperations that execute in single step. These instructions do not use multioperation units of processors but just active memory ALUs to perform their operations.

3.2 Memory modules

Total ECLIPSE has three types of memory modules—local data memory modules, shared data memory modules, and instruction memory modules. For performance reasons, they are accessed via dedicated local data, shared data, and instruction memory ports of processors, respectively (see Figure 10). The local memory modules are aimed for storing data local to threads of a processor and NUMA mode data while all the shared data is located to distributed shared data memory modules emulating the ideal PRAM memory. Instruction memory modules are aimed to keep the program code for each processor. The modules are connected together so that all memory locations can be accessed via the shared data memory port but giving high priority to accesses from local data memory and instruction memory ports (see Figure 10).

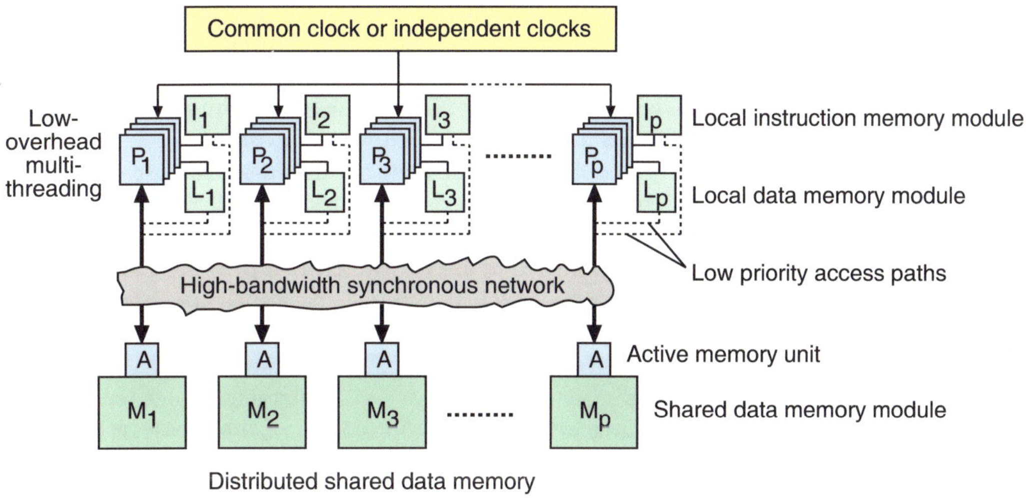

Fig. 10. Organization of the memory system

During normal operation, the on-chip shared data, local data, and instruction memory modules are isolated from each other to guarantee high-bandwidth local data, shared data, and instruction streams to processors. The access (and cycle) times of local data and instruction modules equal to one system clock cycle. The access time of shared data modules need to be half of the system clock cycle or alternatively T_p must be at least $2P$ or a small and fast module-level cache (allowing for multioperation related data to be read and written during a single clock cycle) is needed for each memory module. A local data memory module is just a standard memory module. A shared data memory module consists of an active memory unit and data memory itself (see Figure 3). An active memory unit consists of a simple ALU and fetcher (Forsell, 2006). Active memory units allow one to perform arbitrary ordered multiprefix operations and multioperations that e.g. sum all the references that are targeted to a memory location during a step helping to drop the lower bound of the execution time of some parallel algorithms by a logarithmic factor and perform flexible synchronizations (including arbitrary number of simultaneous barriers) between threads. Instruction memory modules are similar to data memory modules except they do not have active memory units, the length of instruction words is different to that of data words depending on the architectural parameters, and there are no write lines from the instructions fetcher to instruction memory modules. If the data or program code of the application does not fit into the on-chip memory, expensive external memory access prefetches with interleaving, banking and module-level caching are needed. In this chapter, however, we consider on-chip memory configurations only.

3.3 Interconnection network

The TOTAL ECLIPSE network is a M_c-way double acyclic two-dimensional multi mesh (Forsell and Leppänen, 2005) (see Figure 11). It has separate lines for references going from processors to memories and for replies from memories to processors to maximize the throughput for read-intensive portions of code. Memory locations are distributed across the data modules by a randomly chosen polynomial hashing function for avoiding congestion of messages and hot spots (Ranade, 1991; Dietzfelbinger et.al., 1994). References are routed by using a simple greedy algorithm on a randomly selected submesh. Deadlocks are not possible during communication because the network is acyclic. Separation of steps and their synchronization is guaranteed with the synchronization wave technique allowing for independent clocking or asynchronous links between the processor cores.

To exploit locality, the switches related to processor-memory module pairs are grouped as superswitches (see Figure 11). This kind of a two-level structure allows for sending a message from a resource to any of the switches belonging to a superswitch in a single clock cycle. A superswitch consists of M_c switches that are connected to a processor and memory module via dedicated output decoders and switch elements. Each switch consists of 8 switch elements that have two to three input and output links. A switch element consists of logic blocks for determining the right output link (select direction), arbitration logic, and output queues storing the outgoing messages (see Figure 11). A switch element routes an incoming message to an output buffer according to the target information of the message if there is room for it in the buffer. If multiple incoming messages need to be routed to a single output buffer simultaneously it is waited until there is room in the buffer for all of them before transferring them simultaneously to the output buffer. If an incoming message is not allowed to proceed to the output buffer, the busy signal is activated in the corresponding input.

The processors send memory requests (reads and writes) and synchronization messages to the memory modules and modules send replies and synchronization messages back to processors. A message is built of a single parallel flit consisting of dedicated fields for message type, data access width, target address, return address and data (Forsell, 2005). Messages are routed at the rate of at most one hop per clock cycle by using a simple greedy algorithm with two intermediate targets (see Figure 11): A message is first sent to a first intermediate target, which is a randomly chosen switch in a superswitch related to the sending resource (this determines the submesh to be used for routing). Then the message is routed greedily (go to the right row and then go to the right column) to the second intermediate target, which is the switch of the selected submesh in the superswitch related to the target resource. Finally the message is routed from the second intermediate target to the target resource. Routing memory replies back to the processors is made in the same way, but using the memory reply network. Synchronization messages follow the same paths from processors to memories and back to processors.

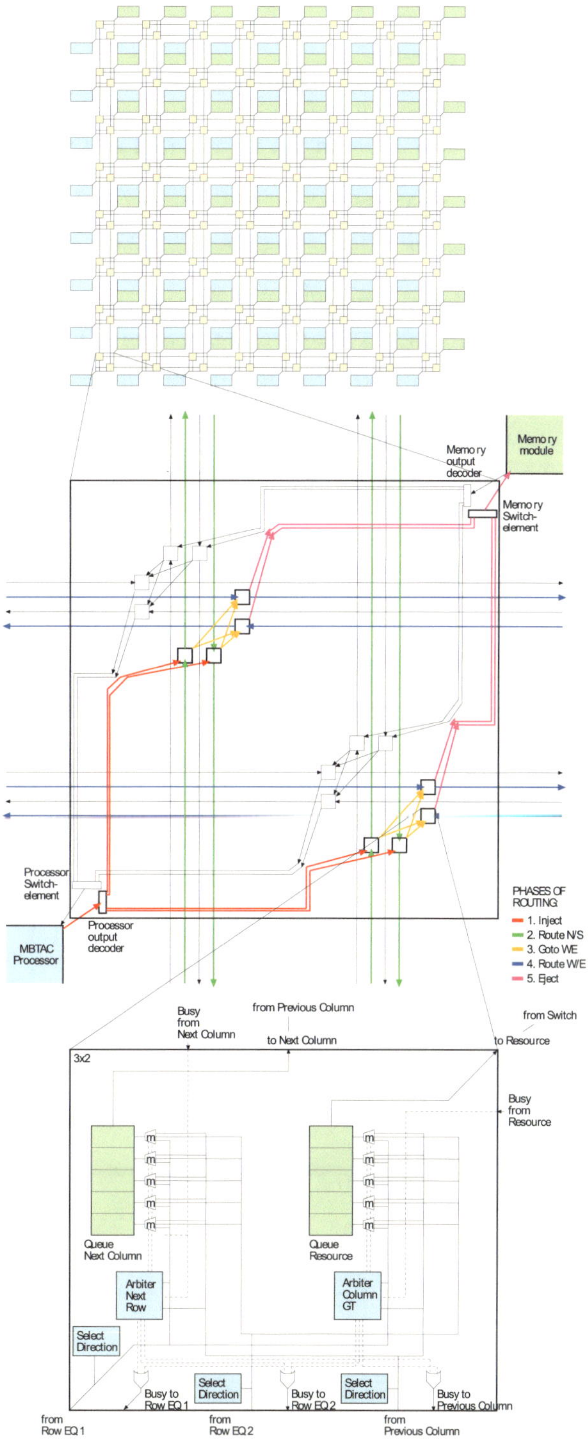

Fig. 11. Block diagrams of a M_c-way double acyclic multimesh network (top), superswitch (middle), and switch element (bottom) for a 64-processor TOTAL ECLIPSE CMP.

4. Evaluation

In order to evaluate the performance and scalability achievable with the TOTAL ECLIPSE architecture on realistic and physically feasible CMPs we made a number of simulations on different CMP configurations and estimated the silicon area and power consumption of the used configurations with analytical modeling.

For performance tests, we mapped parallel and sequential e-language versions of seven parallel computational problems of which three are fixed size and others depend on the number of threads in a processor core (see Table 1) to PRAM thread groups and NUMA bunches, compiled, optimized (e-compiler options -O2 -ilp -fast) and loaded them to three CMP configurations having 4, 16 and 64 ten-FU 512-threaded MBTAC processors (see Table 2), and executed them with our clock accurate CMP simulator modified for the TOTAL ECLIPSE architecture.

In order to evaluate the PRAM mode execution performance, we executed the parallel versions of the programs in the TOTAL ECLIPSE CMPs in the PRAM mode and in ideal PRAMs having similar configurations. The results as relative execution time are shown in Figure 12. We can observe that the PRAM mode execution speed of TOTAL ECLIPSE is very close to that of ideal PRAM, mean overheads being 0.8%, 1.7%, and 1.4% for E4, E16, and E64, respectively.

	SEQUENTIAL				**PARALLEL**		
Name	*N*	*E*	*P*	*W*	*E*	*P*=*W*	**Explanation**
aprefix	*T*	*N*	1	*N*	1	*N*	Determine an arbitrary ordered multiprefix of an array of *N* integers
fft	64	*N* log *N*	1	*N* log *N*	1	N^2	Perform a 64-point complex Fourier transform using fixed point arithmetic on integer ALUs
max	*T*	*N*	1	*N*	1	*N*	Find the maximum of a table of *N* words
mmul	16	N^3	1	N^3	1	N^3	Compute the product of two 16-element matrixes
sort	64	*N* log *N*	1	*N* log *N*	1	N^2	Sort a table of 64 integers
spread	*T*	*N*	1	*N*	1	*N*	Spread an integer to all *N* threads
sum	*T*	*N*	1	*N*	1	*N*	Compute the sum of an array of *N* integers

Table 1. Evaluated computational problems and features of their sequential and parallel implementations (*E*=execution time, *M*=size of the key string, *N*=size of the problem, *P*=number of processors, *T*=number of threads, *W*=work). Note that fft, mmul, and sort are fixed size problems, while others depend on *T*.

	Symbol	E4	E16	E64	DLX
Model of computing	M_{tlp}	PRAM / NUMA	PRAM / NUMA	PRAM / NUMA	RAM
ILP model in the PRAM mode	M_{ilpp}	chained VLIW	chained VLIW	chained VLIW	
ILP model in the NUMA mode	M_{ilpn}	VLIW	VLIW	VLIW	5-stage pipelin e
Processors	P	4	16	64	1
Threads per processors	T_p	512	512	512	1
Total number of threads	T	2048	8192	32768	1
FUs in the PRAM mode	F_p	10	10	10	-
FUs in the NUMA mode	F_n	3	3	3	4
On-chip shared data memory	M_{sd}	2 MB	8 MB	32 MB	-
On-chip local data memory	M_{ld}	2 MB	8 MB	32 MB	-
On-chip banks access time	A_b	1 c	1 c	1 c	1 c
On-chip bank cycle time	C_b	1 c	1 c	1 c	1 c
Length of FIFOs	Q	16	16	16	
Step cache associativity	A_c	4	4	4	-

Table 2. Evaluated configurations (c=processor clock cycles). DLX is a single threaded RISC processor described in (Hennessy and Patterson, 2003). The Random Access Machine (RAM) model is a computing model used in sequential computers.

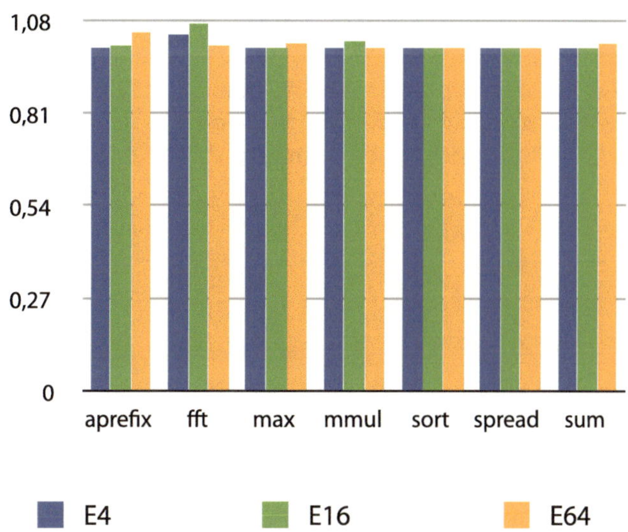

Fig. 12. The relative execution time of TOTAL ECLIPSE CMPs compared to ideal PRAMs with similar configuration (PRAM=1.0, shorter is better).

The NUMA mode performance was measured by executing the sequential versions of the programs in a single thread of a CMP in both PRAM and NUMA modes. In NUMA mode execution all the threads of a single processor were joined to a single NUMA bunch. The results of these simulations as execution time are illustrated in Figure 13. We see that the NUMA mode indeed provides better performance for sequential programs than the PRAM mode, but is not able to exploit virtual ILP up to degree possible in the PRAM mode. The mean speedups of using the NUMA mode are 13200%, 13196%, and 13995% for E4, E16, and E64, respectively. This does not, however, mean that these NUMA bunches can solve these computational problems faster than the PRAM mode if parallel solutions are used. Namely, the parallel solutions are 1421%, 3111%, and 6889% faster than the best sequential ones for E4, E16, and E64, respectively. Note that the speedup is not linear with respect to the number of processors, since 3 out of 7 benchmarks are fixed size computational problems.

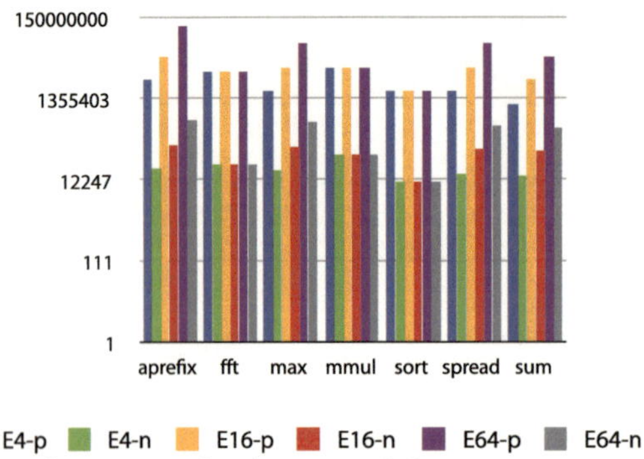

Fig. 13. The execution time of sequential solutions of the computational problems on a single thread of a singe MBTAC processor core in the PRAM mode and on a 512-thread NUMA bunch in a single MBTAC processor core.

To show seamless configurability between NUMA and PRAM modes in the TOTAL ECLIPSE architecture, we measured the NUMA mode execution time for sort algorithm for a bunch with different number of threads ranging from 1 to 512 threads per bunch in the E4 configuration. The results are shown in Figure 14. We can see linear performance increase as the number of threads per the bunch increases (note that the thread scale is exponential).

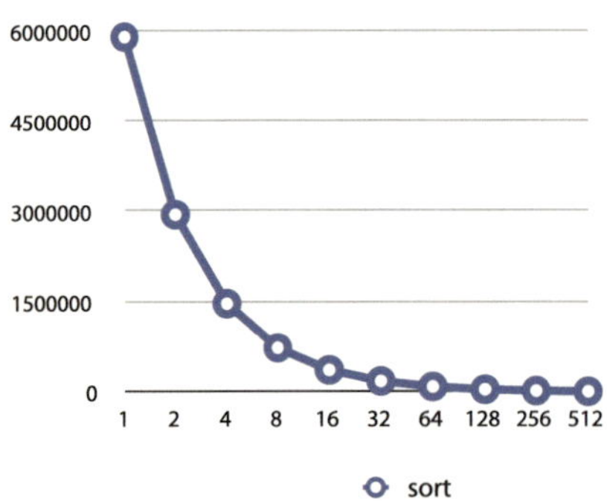

Fig. 14. Execution time of as a function of number of threads in the bunch for E4 CESM configuration.

We compared also the NUMA mode performance of TOTAL ECLIPSE CMPs to that of a single threaded five-stage basic pipelined RISC processor DLX (Hennessy and Patterson,

2003) by executing all the sequential programs in a single DLX processor with a single step accessible on-chip memory (like the local memories of TOTAL ECLIPSE cores) and in a single NUMA bunch composed of the threads of a single processor of TOTAL ECLIPSE. In order to commit fair comparison, we took the variable size of the problems aprefix, max, spread, and sum into account in our measurements so that the amount of actual computation (and the computational problem itself) is the same for the both architectures. In addition, the same compiler and even compilation were used to eliminate the effect of the compiler. TOTAL ECLIPSE code was obtained from DLX code just by doing binary translation (Forsell, 2003). The results are shown in Figure 15. Although the code is not optimized with a VLIW compiler for TOTAL ECLIPSE's NUMA bunching, it provides a bit better performance than DLX, the average speedup being 8.8%. This is due to more efficient ILP architecture of TOTAL ECLIPSE cores.

Finally, we estimated silicon area, power consumption, and maximum clock frequency figures for E4, E16, and E64 with configurable memory modules implemented on a high-performance 65 nm silicon process. The estimations are based on models presented (Pamunuwa et. al., 2003), ITRS 2007, and careful counting of architectural elements broken down to gate counts. The wire delay model gives maximum clock frequency 1.29 GHz for E4, E16 and E64 assuming 135 nm global interconnect wiring with repeaters. The area and power results are shown in Figure 16. These figures except the clock frequency are somewhat comparable to those of a X86 class multi-core high-frequency superscalar processor.

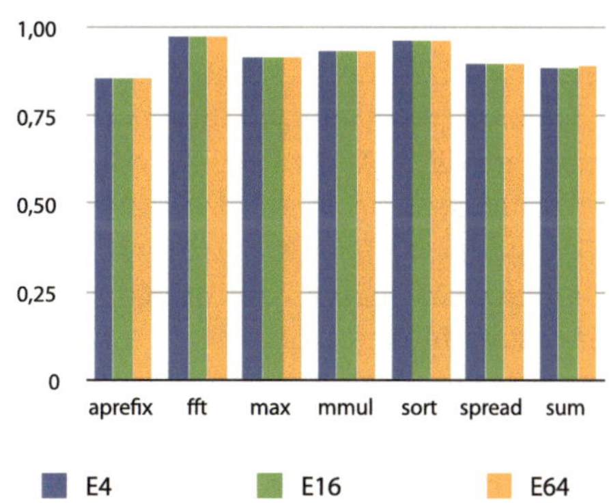

Fig. 15. Relative execution time of 512-thread NUMA bunches compared to 5-stage pipelined DLX processor with the same memory setup (DLX=1.0, shorter is better).

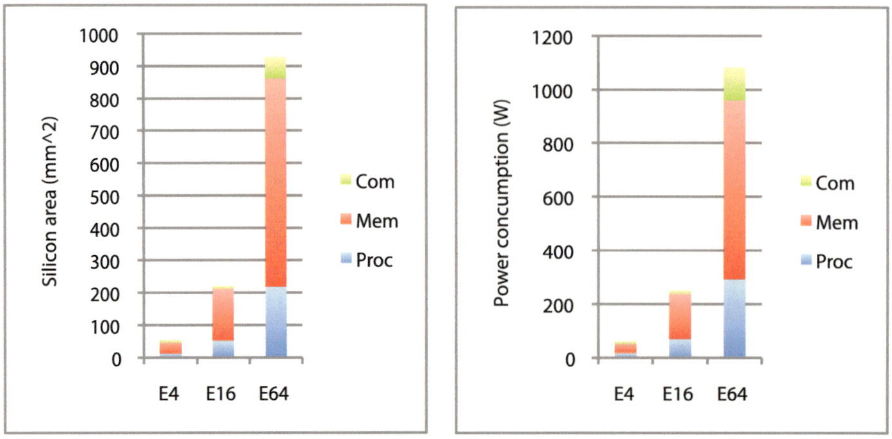

Fig. 16. Silicon area and power consumption estimates for E4, E16, and E64 with configurable memory module at 1.29 MHz on a high-performance 65 nm technology (Com=communication network, Mem=memory modules, and Proc=processors).

5. Conclusion

We have introduced the TOTAL ECLIPSE CMP architecture providing an efficient realization of PRAM. In addition to providing synchronous access to the shared memory, it allows for concurrent references to memory location, special multioperations performing computations between the participating threads, modes for efficient parallel execution and fast sequential operation combining the computational power of threads and seamless configurability between these modes. According to our evaluation TOTAL ECLIPSE provides in many cases performance close to similarly configured ideal PRAM, while the silicon area and power consumption are somewhat comparable to the current commercial CMPs. This chapter acts also as a case-driven introduction to novel parallel architecture techniques, including synchronization wave, cacheless memory organization, chaining, step caching, bunching, and scratchpads, that are unknown from the theory of sequential architectures. Our future research interests related to this topic include building FPGA and silicon prototypes of TOTAL ECLIPSE, addressing the off-chip memory efficiency problem, as well as investigating the limits of practical scalability of this kind of architectures.

6. Acknowledgements

This work was supported by the grants 122462 and 128733 of the Academy of Finland.

7. References

Abolhassan, F., Drefenstedt, R., Keller, J., Paul, W. Scheerer, D. (1993) On the Physical Design of PRAMs, *Computer Journal* 36, 8 (1993), 756-762.

Alverson, R., Callahan, D., Cummings, D., Kolblenz, B., Porterfield, A., Smith, B. (1990). The Tera Computer System, *Proceedings of the International Conference on Supercomputing*, Association for Computing Machinery, New York, 1990, 1-6.

Culler, D., Karp, R., Patterson, D., Sahay, A., Schauser, K., Santos, E., Subramonian, R., von Eicken, T. (1993). LogP: Towards a Realistic Model of Parallel Computation, *Proceedings of the 4th ACM Conference on Principles & Practicies of Parallel Programming*, 1-12.

Dietzfelbinger, M., Karlin, A., Mehlhorn, K., Mayer auf der Heide, F., Rohnert, H., Tarjan, R. (1994). Dynamic Perfect Hashing: Upper and Lower Bounds, *SIAM Journal on Computing* 23, (August 1994), 738-761.

Forsell, M. (1994). Are Multiport Memories Physically Feasible?, *Computer Architecture News* 22, 4 (September 1994), 47-54.

Forsell, M. (1997). Implementation of Instruction-Level and Thread-Level Parallelism in Computers, *Dissertations* 2, Department of Computer Science, University of Joensuu, Joensuu, 1997.

Forsell, M. (2002). A Scalable High-Performance Computing Solution for Network on Chips, *IEEE Micro* 22, 5 (September-October 2002), 46-55.

Forsell, M. (2003). Using Parallel Slackness for Extracting ILP from Sequential Threads, *Proceedings of the SSGRR-2003s, International Conference on Advances in Infrastructure for Electronic Business, Education, Science, Medicine, and Mobile Technologies on the Internet*, July 28 - August 3, 2003, L'Aquila, Italy.

Forsell, M., Leppänen, V. (2005). High-Bandwidth on-chip Communication Architecture for General Purpose Computing, *Proceedings of the 9th World Multiconference on Systemics, Cybernetics and Informatics (WMSCI 2005)* Volume IV, July 10-13, 2005, Orlando, USA, 1-6.

Forsell, M. (2005). Step Caches—a Novel Approach to Concurrent Memory Access on Shared Memory MP-SOCs, *Proceedings of the 23th IEEE NORCHIP Conference*, November 21-22, 2005, Oulu, Finland, 74-77.

Forsell, M. (2006). Realizing Multioperations for Step Cached MP-SOCs, *Proceedings of the International Symposium on System-on-Chip 2006 (SOC'06)*, November 14-16, 2006, Tampere, Finland, 77-82.

Forsell, M., Roivainen, J. (2008). Performance, Area and Power Trade-Offs in Mesh-Based Emulated Shared Memory CMP Architectures, *Proceedings of the 2008 International Conference on Parallel and Distributed Processing Techniques and Applications (PDPTA'08)*, July 14-17, 2008, Las Vegas, USA, 471-477.

Forsell, M. (2009). Configurable Emulated Shared Memory Architecture for general purpose MP-SOCs and NOC regions, *Proceedings of the 3rd ACM/IEEE International Symposium on Networks-on-Chip*, May 10-13, 2009, San Diego, USA, 163-172.

Fortune, S., Wyllie, J. (1978). Parallelism in Random Access Machines, *Proceedings of 10th ACM STOC*, Association for Computing Machinery, New York, 1978, 114-118.

Hennessy, J., Patterson, D. (2003). *Computer Architecture: A Quantitative Approach*, third edition, Morgan Kaufmann Publishers Inc., Palo Alto, 2003.

Imai, M., Hayakawa, Y., Kawanaka, H., Chen, W., Wada, K., Castanho, C., Okajima, Y., Okamoto, H. (2000). A Hardware Implementation of PRAM and Its Performance Evaluation, *Proceedings of the 15 IPDPS 2000 Workshops on Parallel and Distributed Processing*, May 1-5, 2000, Cancun, Mexico, LNCS 1800, 143 - 148.

Intel. (2006). Research at Intel From a Few Cores to Many: A Tera-scale Computing Research Overview, *White Paper*, Intel, 2006.

ITRS (2007). International Technology Roadmap for Semiconductors, Semiconductor Industry Assoc., 2007; http://public.itrs.net/.

Jaja, J. (1992). *Introduction to Parallel Algorithms*, Addison-Wesley, Reading, 1992.
Jantch, A. (2003). *Networks on Chip* (edited by A. Jantsch and H. Tenhunen), Kluver Academic Publishers, Boston, 2003, 173-192.
Kaxiras, S., Hu, Z. (2001). Cache Decay: Exploiting Generational Behavior to Reduce Cache Leakage Power, *Proceedings of the International Symposium on Computer Architecture*, June 30-July 4, 2001, Göteborg, Sweden, 240-251.
Karp, R., Miller, R. (1969). Parallel Program Schemata, *Journal of Computer and System Sciences* 3, 2 (1969), 147-195.
Keller, J., Keßler, C., Träff, J. (2001). *Practical PRAM Programming*, Wiley, New York, 2001.
Lenoski, D., Laudon, J., Gharachorloo, K., Weber, W., Gupta, A., Hennessy, J., Horowitz, M., Lam, M. (1992). The Stanford Dash Multiprocessor, *IEEE Computer* 25, (March 1992), 63-79.
Leppänen, V. (1996). Studies on the realization of PRAM, *Dissertation* 3, Turku Centre for Computer Science, University of Turku, Turku, 1996.
Pamunuwa, D., Zheng, L-R., Tenhunen, H. (2003). Maximizing Throughput Over Parallel Wire Structures in the Deep Submicrometer Regime, *IEEE Transactions on Very Large Scale Integration (VLSI) Systems* 11, 2 (April 2003), 224-243.
Ranade, A., Bhatt, S., Johnson, S. (1987). The Fluent Abstract Machine, *Technical Report Series* BA87-3, Thinking Machines Corporation, Bedford, 1987.
Ranade, A. (1991). How to Emulate Shared Memory, *Journal of Computer and System Sciences* 42, (1991), 307--326.
Schwarz, J. (1966). Large Parallel Computers, Journal of the ACM 13, 1 (1966), 25-32.
Schwarz J. (1980). Ultracomputers, *ACM Transactions on Programming Languages and Systems* 2, 4 (1980), 484-521.
Swan, R., Fuller, S., Siewiorek, D. (1977). Cm*—A Modular Multiprocessor, *Proceedings of NCC*, 645-655, 1977.
Valiant L. (1990). A Bridging Model for Parallel Computation, *Communications of the ACM* 33, 8 (1990), 103-111.
Vishkin, U. (2007). Towards Realizing a PRAM-On-Chip Vision, *Workshop on Highly Parallel Processing on a Chip (HPPC)*, August 28, 2007, Rennes, France (see http://www.hppc-workshop.org/HPPC07/talks.html).
Vishkin, U., Caragea, G., Lee, B. (2008). Models for Advancing PRAM and Other Algorithms into Parallel Programs for a PRAM-On-Chip Platform, *Handbook of Parallel Computing – Models, Algorithms and Applications* (editors S. Rajasekaran and J. Reif), Chapman & Hall/CRC, Boca Raton, 2008, 5-1—5-60.

Appendix A. Core instruction set of TOTAL ECLIPSE

The core instruction set of the integer-only version of the proposed MBTAC processor of TOTAL ECLIPSE consists of an instruction that can be further divided to the A ALU subinstructions, M memory subinstructions, a single compare unit subinstruction, a single sequencer subinstruction, O immediate operand subinstructions, and W_b write back subinstructions in the PRAM mode and to an ALU subinstruction, a memory subinstruction, a sequencer subinstruction, and two write back subinstructions in the NUMA mode. The following list shows the available subinstructions for each class of units:

Memory Unit subinstructions

LDBn	Xx	Load byte from memory n address Xx in MU n
LDBUn	Xx	Load byte from memory n address Xx unsigned in MU n
LDHn	Xx	Load halfword from memory n address Xx in MU n
LDHUn	Xx	Load halfword from memory n address Xx unsigned in MU n
LDn	Xx	Load word from memory n address Xx in MU n
STBn	Xx,Xy	Store byte Xx to memory n address Xy in MU n
STHn	Xx,Xy	Store halfword Xx to memory n address Xy in MU n
STn	Xx,Xy	Store word Xx to memory n address Xy in MU n
MADDn	Xx,Xy	Add multiple Xx to active memory Xy in MU n
MSUBn	Xx,Xy	Subtract multiple Xx to active memory Xy in MU n
MANDn	Xx,Xy	And multiple Xx to active memory Xy in MU n
MORn	Xx,Xy	Or multiple Xx to active memory Xy in MU n
MMAXn	Xx,Xy	Max multiple Xx to active memory Xy in MU n
MMAXUn	Xx,Xy	Max unsigned multiple Xx to active memory Xy in MU n
MMINn	Xx,Xy	Min multiple Xx to active memory Xy in MU n
MMINUn	Xx,Xy	Min unsigned multiple Xx to active memory Xy in MU n
MPADDn	Xx,Xy	Arbitrary multiprefix add Xx to active memory Xy in MU n
MPSUBn	Xx,Xy	Arbitrary multiprefix subtract Xx to active memory Xy in MU n
MPANDn	Xx,Xy	Arbitrary multiprefix and Xx to active memory Xy in MU n
MPORn	Xx,Xy	Arbitrary multiprefix or Xx to active memory Xy in MU n
MPMAXn	Xx,Xy	Arbitrary multiprefix max Xx to active memory Xy in MU n
MPMAXUn	Xx,Xy	Arbitrary multiprefix max unsigned Xx to active memory Xy in MU n
MPMINn	Xx,Xy	Arbitrary multiprefix min Xx to active memory Xy in MU n
MPMINUn	Xx,Xy	Arbitrary multiprefix min unsigned Xx to active memory Xy in MU n
BMADDn	Xx,Xy	Begin add multiple Xx to active memory Xy in MU n
BMSUBn	Xx,Xy	Begin subtract multiple Xx to active memory Xy in MU n
BMANDn	Xx,Xy	Begin and multiple Xx to active memory Xy in MU n
BMORn	Xx,Xy	Begin or multiple Xx to active memory Xy in MU n
BMMAXn	Xx,Xy	Begin max multiple Xx to active memory Xy in MU n
BMMAXUn	Xx,Xy	Begin max unsigned multiple Xx to active memory Xy in MU n
BMMINn	Xx,Xy	Begin min multiple Xx to active memory Xy in MU n
BMMINUn	Xx,Xy	Begin min unsigned multiple Xx to active memory Xy in MU n
EMADDn	Xx,Xy	End add multiple Xx to active memory Xy in MU n
EMSUBn	Xx,Xy	End subtract multiple Xx to active memory Xy in MU n
EMANDn	Xx,Xy	End and multiple Xx to active memory Xy in MU n
EMORn	Xx,Xy	End or multiple Xx to active memory Xy in MU n
EMMAXn	Xx,Xy	End max multiple Xx to active memory Xy in MU n
EMMAXUn	Xx,Xy	End max unsigned multiple Xx to active memory Xy in MU n
EMMINn	Xx,Xy	End min multiple Xx to active memory Xy in MU n
EMMINUn	Xx,Xy	End min unsigned multiple Xx to active memory Xy in MU n
BMPADDn	Xx,Xy	Begin arbitrary multiprefix add Xx to active memory Xy in MU n
BMPSUBn	Xx,Xy	Begin arbitrary multiprefix subtract Xx to active memory Xy in MU n
BMPANDn	Xx,Xy	Begin arbitrary multiprefix and Xx to active memory Xy in MU n
BMPORn	Xx,Xy	Begin arbitrary multiprefix or Xx to active memory Xy in MU n

BMPMAXn	Xx,Xy	Begin arbitrary multiprefix max Xx to active memory Xy in MU n
BMPMAXUn	Xx,Xy	Begin arbitrary multiprefix max unsigned Xx to active memory Xy in MU n
BMPMINn	Xx,Xy	Begin arbitrary multiprefix min Xx to active memory Xy in MU n
BMPMINUn	Xx,Xy	Begin arbitrary multiprefix min unsigned Xx to active memory Xy in MU n
EMPADDn	Xx,Xy	End arbitrary multiprefix add Xx to active memory Xy in MU n
EMPSUBn	Xx,Xy	End arbitrary multiprefix subtract Xx to active memory Xy in MU n
EMPANDn	Xx,Xy	End arbitrary multiprefix and Xx to active memory Xy in MU n
EMPORn	Xx,Xy	End arbitrary multiprefix or Xx to active memory Xy in MU n
EMPMAXn	Xx,Xy	End arbitrary multiprefix max Xx to active memory Xy in MU n
EMPMAXUn	Xx,Xy	End arbitrary multiprefix max unsigned Xx to active memory Xy in MU n
EMPMINn	Xx,Xy	End arbitrary multiprefix min Xx to active memory Xy in MU n
EMPMINUn	Xx,Xy	End arbitrary multiprefix min unsigned Xx to active memory Xy in MU n

Write Back subinstructions

WBn	Xx	Write Xx to register Rn.

Arithmetic and Logical Unit subinstructions

ADDn	Xx,Xy	Add Xx and Xy in ALU n
SUBn	Xx,Xy	Subtract Xy from Xx in ALU n
MULn	Xx,Xy	Multiply Xx by Xy in ALU n
MULUn	Xx,Xy	Multiply Xx by Xy in ALU n unsigned
DIVn	Xx,Xy	Divide Xx by Xy in ALU n
DIVUn	Xx,Xy	Divide Xx by Xy in ALU n unsigned
MODn	Xx,Xy	Determine Xx modulo Xy in ALU n
MODUn	Xx,Xy	Determine Xx modulo Xy in ALU n unsigned
LOGDn	Xx	Determine ROUNDDOWN(Log2 Xx) in ALU n
LOGUn	Xx	Determine ROUNDUP(Log2 Xx) in ALU n
SELn	Xx,Xy	Select Xx or Xy according to the result of previous compare operation in functional unit chain (Xx if res=1, Xy if res=0)
MAXU	Xx,Xy	Determine maximum of Xx,Xy in ALU n unsigned
MAX	Xx,Xy	Determine maximum of Xx,Xy in ALU n
MINU	Xx,Xy	Determine minimum of Xx,Xy in ALU n unsigned
MIN	Xx,Xy	Determine minimum of Xx,Xy in ALU n
SHRn	Xx,Xy	Shift right Xx by Xy in ALU n
SHLn	Xx,Xy	Shift left Xx by Xy in ALU n
SHRAn	Xx,Xy	Shift right Xx by Xy in ALU n arithmetic
RORn	Xx,Xy	Rotate right Xx by Xy in ALU n
ROLn	Xx,Xy	Rotate left Xx by Xy in ALU n
ANDn	Xx,Xy	And of Xx and Xy in ALU n
ORn	Xx,Xy	Or of Xx and Xy in ALU n
XORn	Xx,Xy	Exclusive or of Xx and Xy in ALU n
ANDNn	Xx,Xy	And not of Xx and Xy in ALU n

ORNn	Xx,Xy	Or not of Xx and Xy in ALU n
XNORn	Xx,Xy	Exclusive nor of Xx and Xy in ALU n
CSYNCn	Xx	Set up barrier synchronization group Xx in ALU n
SEQn	Xx,Xy	Set result=-1 if Xx = Xy else result=0 in ALU n
SNEn	Xx,Xy	Set result=-1 if Xx ≠ Xy else result=0 in ALU n
SLTn	Xx,Xy	Set result=-1 if Xx < Xy else result=0 in ALU n
SLEn	Xx,Xy	Set result=-1 if Xx ≤ Xy else result=0 in ALU n
SGTn	Xx,Xy	Set result=-1 if Xx > Xy else result=0 in ALU n
SGEn	Xx,Xy	Set result=-1 if Xx ≥ Xy else result=0 in ALU n
SLTUn	Xx,Xy	Set result=-1 if Xx < Xy unsigned else result=0 in ALU n
SLEUn	Xx,Xy	Set result=-1 if Xx ≤ Xy unsigned else result=0 in ALU n
SGTUn	Xx,Xy	Set result=-1 if Xx > Xy unsigned else result=0 in ALU n
SGEUn	Xx,Xy	Set result=-1 if Xx ≥ Xy unsigned else result=0 in ALU n

Immediate Operand Input subinstructions

OPn	d	Input value d into operand n

Compare Unit subinstructions

SEQ	Xx,Xy	Set IC if Xx equals Xy
SNE	Xx,Xy	Set IC if Xx not equals Xy
SLT	Xx,Xy	Set IC if Xx is less than Xy
SLE	Xx,Xy	Set IC if Xx is less than or equals Xy
SGT	Xx,Xy	Set IC if Xx is greater than Xy
SGE	Xx,Xy	Set IC if Xx is greater than or equals Xy
SLTU	Xx,Xy	Set IC if Xx is less than Xy unsigned
SLEU	Xx,Xy	Set IC if Xx is less than or equals Xy unsigned
SGTU	Xx,Xy	Set IC if Xx is greater than Xy unsigned
SGEU	Xx,Xy	Set IC if Xx is greater than or equals Xy unsigned

Sequencer subinstructions

BEQZ	Ox	Branch to Ox if IC equals zero
BNEZ	Ox	Branch to Ox if IC not equals zero
JMP	Xx	Jump to Xx
JMPL	Xx	Jump and link PC+1 to register RA
TRAP	Xx	Trap
JOIN	Xx	Join all the threads to a NUMA bunch Xx
SPLIT	Xx	Split all the current NUMA bunches back to PRAM mode threads

4

Facts, Issues and Questions - GPUs for Dependability

Bernhard Fechner
FernUniversität in Hagen
Parallel Computing and VLSI Group

1. Introduction

Graphics Processing Units (GPUs) offer massive parallelism, comprising many actual paradigms like manycore, multithreading and SIMD. Today, nearly every computer is equipped with at least one graphics card, containing one or more GPUs bringing massive parallelism to the desktop. GPUs are usually used in their main function, that is, to compute visibility, lightning, perspective, etc. in games. As this technology is widely used, it is low-cost. In the majority of the cases, graphic cards do not spend their entire lives by executing game code. Thus, such a massive parallel system is underchallenged most of the time. Shortly after the availability of comfortable programming environments, based on CUDA (Compute Unified Device Architecture) or HLSL (high-level shader language), researchers have become interested in using this power for general-purpose computing (GPGPU, General-Purpose computing on the GPU). Thus, different applications originated, e.g. physics, cryptography 0, DNA sequencing 0 and medical imaging. For further examples and overview, see 0 and 0.
The trend to compute such workloads with GPUs will go on as the DirectX 11 (compute) or the OpenCL 0 standards show. The fault-tolerant execution of (sensible) workloads on GPUs was - to the knowledge of the author - never proposed. Sensible computations should be carried out in a reliable way. What is the sense of a computation to find a private key if the program is correct but the hardware is subjected to faults and the program never finds the key? E.g. transient faults can be caused from fluctuations in the main current, radiation or RAMs not running within their specification etc. What if an encryption is faulty due to temporal faults or how can we detect a faulty medical diagnosis? The need to do computations precisely has led to the development of more sophisticated and sometimes expensive graphics processing units 0, needed by CAD applications. Larrabee 0 is a many-core visual computing architecture. It uses multiple in-order x86 CPU cores that are augmented by a wide vector processor unit, as well as some fixed function logic blocks. This provides much higher performance per watt and per unit of area than out-of-order CPUs on highly parallel workloads. Vision4ce 0 launched a new line of General-purpose Rugged Image Processing (GRIP) products at the recent SPIE Defense and Security Symposium. The GRIP-Beta showed GPGPU-based image processing demonstrations, analog and Gigabit

Ethernet video streams and the functionality in the Gripworkx image processing framework. Vision4ce addresses rugged embedded computing challenges that might normally be served by more expensive FPGA approaches.

This work presents fundamental research, answering the question of how a system, equipped with multiple graphics cards can be harnessed to detect, predict, prevent and tolerate faults. Naturally, we do not restrict ourselves to computations running on the GPUs alone and also consider the outsourcing of application parts from the CPU to the GPU. We are aware of the fact that this evaluation can only be exemplary - but it can serve as a starting point and a priming of future work. All mechanisms are fully implementable in software and do not require special or modified hardware.

This work is structured as follows: we first present examples of current GPU implementations in Section 2. Section 0 shows how the massive parallelism of modern GPUs can be exploited for dependability. Section 0 summarizes and concludes the chapter.

2. Case Study and Programming Model

2.1 Case Study: The NVidia GeForce 8800 GTX

In this Section, we describe the basic architecture of the G80 GPU family from NVidia as this will help to understand the possibilities for dependability. The GeForce 8800 GTX is divided into 16 *streaming multiprocessors* (SMs), each containing eight *streaming processors* (SPs), making a total of 128 SPs. Each SM has 8,192 registers that are shared among all threads assigned to the SM. The threads on a SM core execute in SIMD (single-instruction, multiple-data) fashion, with the instruction unit (IU) broadcasting the current instruction to the eight SPs. Each SP has one arithmetic unit that performs single-precision floating point arithmetic and 32-bit integer operations. Fig. 1 shows an overview of the GeForce 8800 GTX.

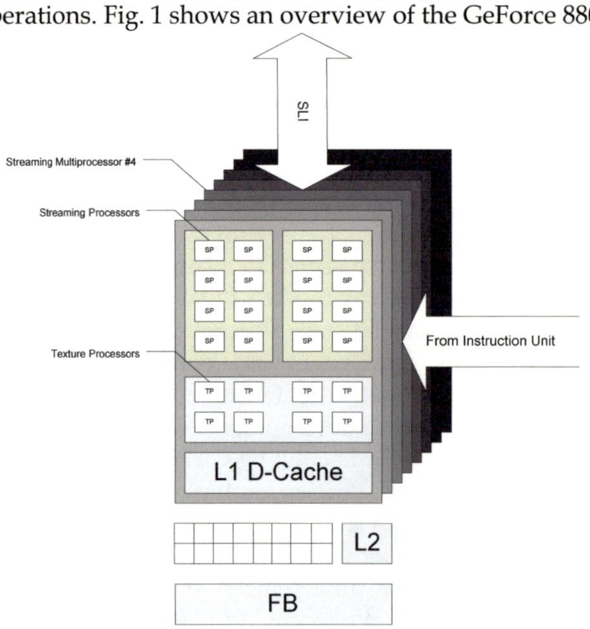

Fig. 1. The NVidia GeForce 8800 GTX

Each SM has two *special functional units* (SFUs), which perform more complex FP operations such as transcendental functions. The arithmetic units and the SFUs are fully pipelined. Each FP instruction is operating on up to 8 bytes of data. An important factor that affects both performance and quality is the precision for operations and registers. The GeForce Series support 32 bit and 16 bit floating point formats (called float and half, respectively) 0. The float data type resembles IEEE754 (s23e8), half has an s10e5 format. Some models, e.g. the G200 also support double precision in IEEE754R-format (one double-precision unit per SM). The processors support gathering and scattering. Thus, they are capable of reading and writing anywhere in local memory on the graphics card or in other parts of the system. The G80 has several on-chip memories that can exploit data locality and data sharing, e.g. a 64 KB off-chip *constant memory* and an 8 KB single-ported constant memory cache in each SM. If multiple threads access the same address during the same cycle, the cache broadcasts the address to those threads with the same latency as a register access. In addition to the constant memory cache, each SM has a 16 KB *shared (data) memory* that is either written and reused or shared among threads. Finally, for read-only data that is shared by threads but not necessarily to be accessed simultaneously, the off-chip texture memory and the on-chip texture caches exploit 2D data locality.

2.2 The CUDA Programming Model

The CUDA programming model consists of ANSI C supported by several keywords and constructs. CUDA treats the GPU as a coprocessor that executes data-parallel kernel functions. The developer supplies a single source program encompassing both host (CPU, c) and kernel (GPU, cu) code. The host code transfers data and code to and from the GPU's global memory via API calls and initiates the kernel. At the highest level, each kernel creates a single *grid*, which consists of many *thread blocks*. Each thread block is assigned to a single SM for the duration of its execution. A thread block consists of a limited number of threads which can cooperate. The maximum number of threads per block is 512. Threads from different blocks cannot cooperate. Each thread can read/write from/to thread registers, thread-local memory, shared memory in a block, the global memory and read from *constant memory* or the texture memory in a grid. The host has read/write access on the constant, global and texture memory. Threads in the same block can share data through the shared memory and can perform barrier synchronization. Threads are otherwise independent, and synchronization across thread blocks is safely accomplished only by terminating the kernel.
The IU manages things in groups of parallel threads, called *warps*. SMs can perform zero-overhead scheduling to interleave warps on an instruction-by-instruction basis to hide the latency of global memory accesses and long-latency arithmetic operations. When one warp stalls, the SM can switch to a ready warp in the same or different thread block assigned to the SM. Each warp executes in SIMD fashion, with the IU broadcasting the same instruction to the eight cores on a SM on four consecutive clock cycles. Since one pixel equals one thread, and since the SPs are scalar, the compiler schedules pixel elements for execution sequentially: red, then green, then blue, and then alpha.
Fig. 2 shows a Thread Processing Cluster (TPC) used on the G200 series with 10 TPCs in total. As depicted, a TPC comprises multiple IUs, SPs and local memory.

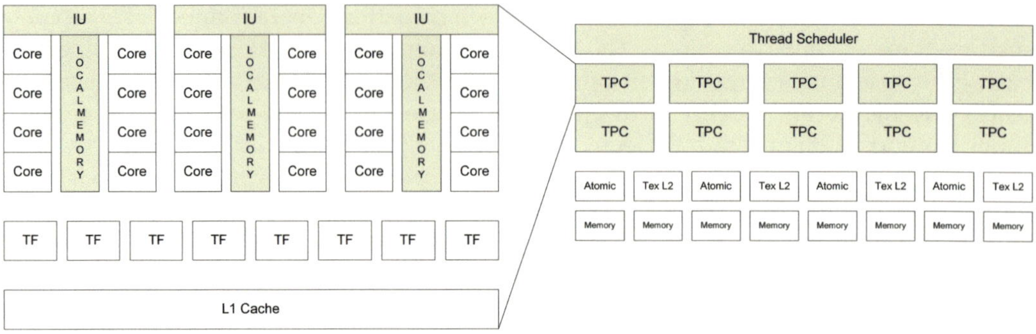

Fig. 2. A Thread Processing Cluster (TPC)

2.3 Experimental Setup and Clock Variation

In this Section we present the results from a first experimental evaluation by clock variation, since we wanted to artificially increase the fault rate, observe the system behavior concerning reliability and depict basic performance figures.

Our experimental setup consists of a 6 GB main memory Core i7 system, configured with two NVidia GTX260 cards (PCIe 2.0 x16). The two hard disks (500 GB) are in RAID 0 mode. In the first experiment with SLI, we adjusted the engine, shader and memory clock frequency. A SLI-system is constructed on hardware level and must be configured on software level. Either the GPUs work independently in non-SLI mode to support multi-view displays or all GPUs in a SLI configuration appear as a single unit, mainly used to speed up 3D applications and computations. For the CUDA programming environment, a non-SLI system appears as a set of graphics cards, a SLI system as one graphics card. Multiple GPUs appear as multiple host threads. The clock rate adjustment in SLI mode is done for both cards simultaneously, in non-SLI mode, both cards have to be configured separately. The maximum clock rate of (engine=800, shader=1650, memory=2700) MHz sometimes resulted in execution faults of a kernel in non-SLI mode and *complete system failures* in SLI mode. Therefore, we applied less aggressive settings and varied the clock frequency between (engine=500, shader=1150, memory=1900) and (700, 1400, 2500) MHz. The workload consisted of a computation of the blackscholes formula for 512 iterations. The same workload was also computed on the CPU. Besides precision issues (see Section 0) no deviation except for the highest clock settings occurred. Fig. 3 shows the influence of the variation of the clock frequencies of the engine, shader and memory on performance (SLI). Note that the bandwidth is the internal card bandwidth and not the bandwidth of the external interface (PCIe). From the experiments two simple but important conclusions can be derived:

1) a system in SLI mode is less reliable than one in non-SLI mode. Reliable calculations should be carried out on a non-SLI system. A SLI system has more advantage in computing-intensive applications. For bandwidth-intensive applications a non-SLI system should be preferred.
2) Within the overclocking experiments, the GPU rather tended to completely reject the execution of a kernel instead of doing faulty computations (overclocking applied at the beginning of the execution).

We are aware of the fact that these figures are only exemplary, but the results can serve as an orientation.

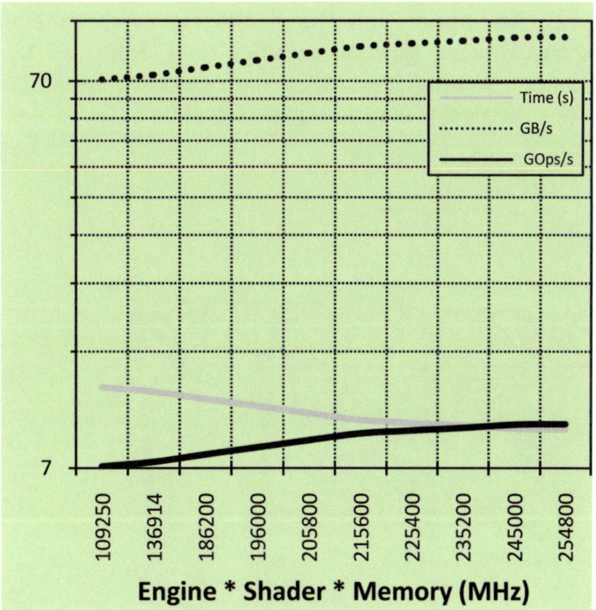

Fig. 3. System performance while varying clock frequencies

2.4 Bandwidth Experiments

The question in this Section is to determine the bandwidth in Mbytes per second for different transfer sizes and different configurations of a SLI and non-SLI system. The bandwidth is important e.g. when the results of a redundant computation must be transferred back to the CPU for a comparison. The basic bandwidths of PCIe 2.0 interfaces are depicted in Table 1.

PCIe-Slot	Lanes/ Direction	Bandwidth	Clock
x1	1	0.5 GByte/s	2.5 GHz
x4	4	2 GByte/s	2.5 GHz
x8	8	4 GByte/s	2.5 GHz
x16	16	8 GByte/s	2.5 GHz
x32	32	16 GByte/s	2.5 GHz

Table 1. Basic bandwidths of PCIe 2.0

Blocks with a certain size were either transferred from the host to the device, from the device to the host and from device to device. The maximum bandwidth for each device within the experiments is 8 GBytes/s. Fig. 4 shows the bandwidths for pageable and pinned memory. Pinned memory allows the compute kernels to access and share the host's memory. We applied the lowest clock settings (engine=500, shader=1150, memory=1900) to determine a lower bandwith bound. From the results, we see that the host to device transfer (pinned memory) is the slowest form to transfer data, followed by the device to host (pageable) communication. Starting from block sizes greater than 65536 bytes, the device to device communication is the fastest way to transfer data.

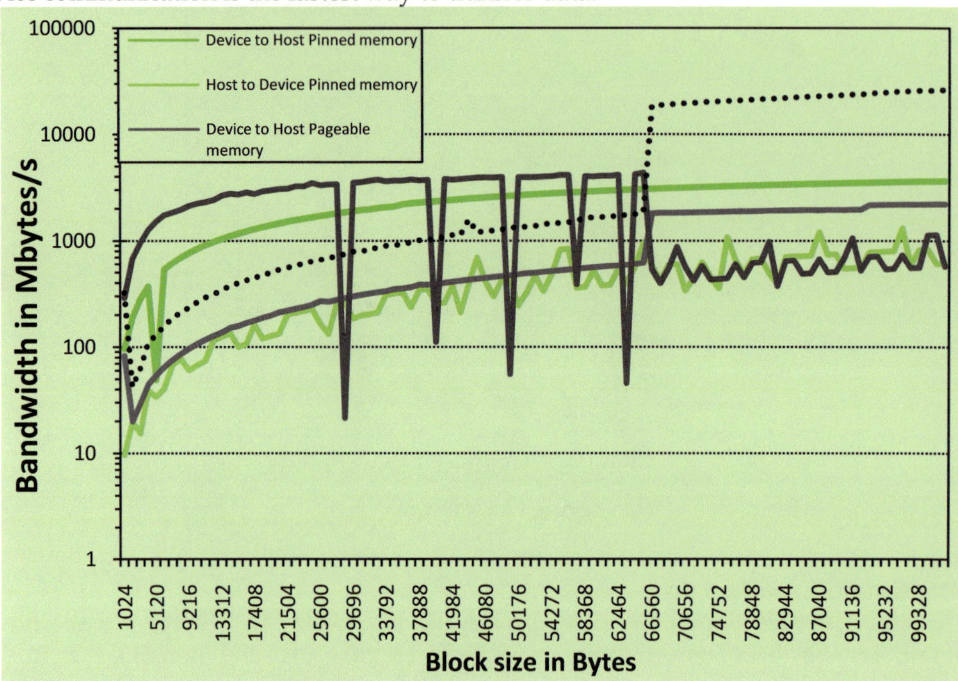

Fig. 4. Bandwidth for different block transfer sizes

We note that the experimental bandwidth for the device to device communication is well above the limit of the PCIe 2.0 x16 specification. The reason for this is that transfers are done on the graphics card and do not pass the external PCIe bus.

2.5Precision Experiments

The realm of (COTS) GPUs is not precision, it is speed. Thus, applications running on GPUs must be questioned in general. Most GPUs use IEEE754R as floating-point format. In comparison to IEEE754 rounding occurs, leading to imprecision. But there are several work-arounds, including mixed-precision 0.

In this Section, we do not focus on rounding errors. We prefer an empirical analysis, since we do not know the implementation of the floating-point algorithms within the GPU. Especially the implementation of transcendental functions implies approximation algorithms, which we cannot know if we do not have a disclosure of the GPU implementation, which is not available to the public due to commercial reasons. To the knowledge of the author, this approach to examine the precision of GPUs is a novelty.

We present benchmarks to compute the deviation of GPU operations in comparison to a CPU implementation and regard three different data types: integer, float and double. Half-floats are supported by shaders and thus are not directly accessible by CUDA. As the half-float is inspired by IEEE754, infinity exists if all bits of the exponent are one and the

mantissa is zero. A half-float is a NaN if all exponent bits are one and the mantissa is not zero. The set of precision benchmarks can be downloaded from 0.
The benchmarks implement vector operations in dim(2^{24}) with different data types and operations, listed in Table 2. The vector data is randomized in each run. Each cell in Table 2 contains the maximum unsigned deviation from the CPU implementation. For computations which could cause overflows, such as the exponential function, the size of the numbers within the randomized vectors was limited.

Type	Single	Double	INT32
Add	0	0	0
Sub	0	0	0
Mul	0	0	0
Div	0.125	0	0
Sqrt	0.0000152588	0	0
Sin	0.000000119209	$1*10^{-16}$	0
Cos	0.000000119209	$1*10^{-16}$	0
Log	0.000000953674	$9*10^{-16}$	0
Exp	0.00195313	$4*10^{-16}$	0

Table 2. Maximum absolute deviation from CPU implementation

Astonishingly, basic arithmetic operations such as add and sub or mul and all integer operations do not lead to imprecision. From this, we can conclude that a scaling of small floats to integers can improve the precision in such a way that the CPU and the GPU results will not differ.

2.6Timing and mid-term Experiments

In this Section, we present the results of mid-term experiments to determine the timing variance and reliability/ stability of results. By a mid-term evaluation, we mean an observation interval of one week. A longer observation interval, e.g. over more than one month would be appreciated, but was not feasible due to the timely restrictions of this work. The precision benchmarks from subsection 0 were calculated 18^5 times. Additionally, we calculated the workload on the CPU with one core and a parallelized version on the 8 available cores. We measured the time for each calculation, GPU and CPU and calculated the average arithmetic mean. The graphics cards were configured in non-SLI mode. The results are depicted in Fig. 5. For some cases (INT operations), the OpenMP implementation was even faster than the GPU.

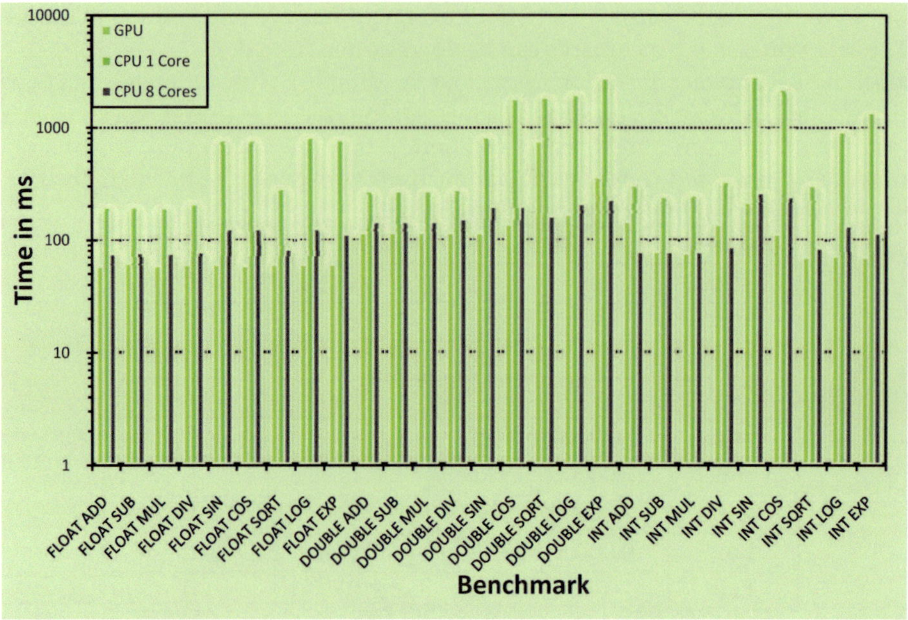

Fig. 5. Timing Results

From the results, we first see that complex operations and transcendental functions need more time - which is not surprising, since there are only two SFUs on one SM. Integers approximately need twice the same time than floats, doubles approximately twice the time than integers (in average). We noticed that the timings varied for both implementations, GPU and CPU. Thus, we calculated the maximum, minimum and average timing values for both implementations, GPU and multicore (even columns), depicted in Fig. 6. (floats).

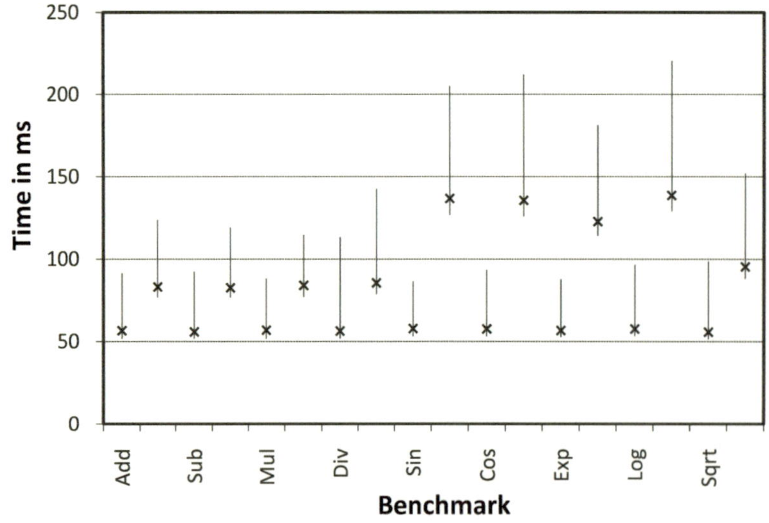

Fig. 6. Benchmark timing, variation, lowest, highest, average

The variations are e.g. caused by normal user interactions. We conclude that results cannot be expected at a certain time. Thus, computations on graphics cards may not be currently suitable for realtime applications. Interesting is that the timings from CPU and GPU have a connection, i.e. if the timing for the GPU was large, the timing of the corresponding CPU implementation was also higher. The deviation resulted in each run and the results seem to correlate. This is surprising, since we implemented an asynchronous version for the GPU which ran independently from the CPU. During the experiments, no unusual deviation (except precision) between CPU and GPU occurred. The results were stable during the whole observation period.

3. Opportunities for Dependability

In this Section, we will discuss the opportunities for dependability offered by graphics cards. Note, that our terminology is based on 0. We will first have a look at the section *means* from the dependability tree (from 0) in Fig. 7. Then we will discuss the means fault prevention, fault-tolerance, fault removal and fault forecasting in the following subsections. We do not specify the exact nature (e.g. bit-flip faults, transmission faults, permanent) of faults within a model, since we do not want to restrict our horizon by regarding at a special set of fault types but we are aware of the fact, that a fault model has to be developed later on.

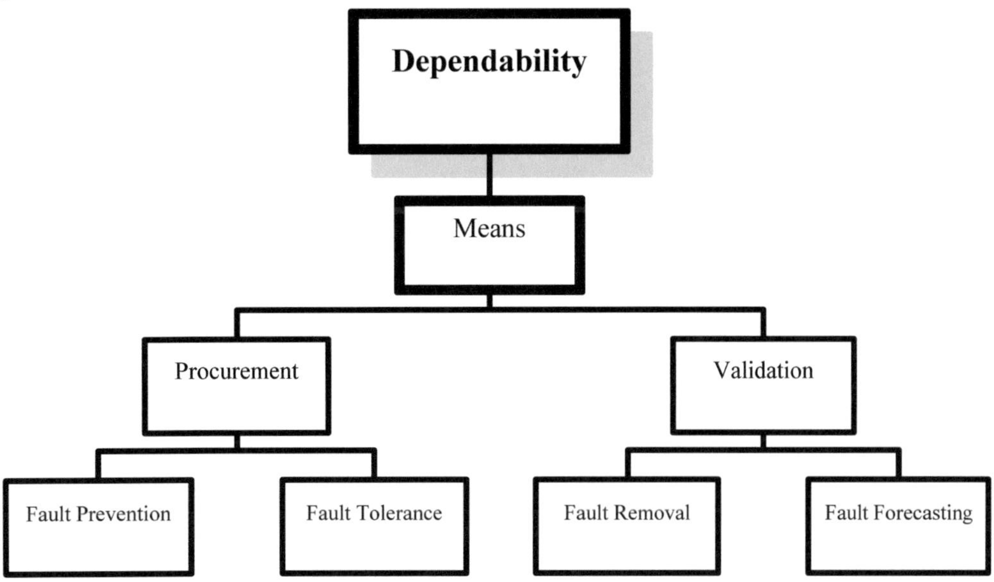

Fig. 7: A section from the dependability tree

We distinguish different levels on which different dependability means can be applied. Therefore, we depict the notational conventions in Table 3 and note the level, where zero (0) means the top level.

Level	Name	Meaning
0	Host	The host or the system; a computing system containing one or more CPUs and graphics hardware
		Integrated Computing Hardware
1	CPU	The central processing unit
2	Processing core	A core within a CPU
3	Thread	A hardware thread, consisting of registers etc.
		Graphics Hardware
1	Device	A single graphics card
2	GPU	A graphics processing unit
3	GP core	A core within a GPU
4	Grid	A set of thread blocks
5	Thread Block (TB)	A thread block consists of multiple threads

Table 3. Notational Conventions

3.1 Fault Prevention

We note that the development of an additional GPU kernel, doing the same task as the CPU at the same time, automatically involves diversity in hardware, software and design, since through different implementations and by using different compilers, we have diversity, considering the fact that we have only one system, but multiple versions of a program and multiple hardware realizations. Note, that the forecast of faults can also be seen as essential part of fault prevention (see Section 0 for details).

3.2 Fault-Tolerance

Basic means of fault-tolerance are structural, temporal, informational and functional redundancy. Naturally, all codes involving informational redundancy can be computed by graphics cards. An interesting idea is to speed up the calculation of Reed-Solomon-Codes by GPUs 0. Functional redundancy can be easily achieved by either computing a calculation on the CPU and the GPU, involving diversity in software or by programming a set of functions again for the GPU. When voting between the results, we can use the inherent voting capability supported by CUDA.

3.2.1 Structural Redundancy

Structural redundancy can be achieved by integrating multiple graphics cards into a single computing system. The result is massive redundancy, e.g. via dual, triple, quadruple configurations. Naturally, we are not able to tolerate permanent CPU faults, but permanent GPU faults. Note, that it is also possible to combine mainboard GPUs and external graphics cards. One should be aware of the fact that multiple (PCIe) graphics cards can be installed simultaneously, deriving diversity in hardware. The multiprocessing-paradigm has also arrived for GPUs. NVidia's GeForce 9800 GX2 contains a pair of 65 nm G92 graphics processors running at 600 MHz. The ATI Radeon™ HD 4870 X2 has two 55 nm GPUs, a 512-bit GDDR3 memory interface and the option to construct a dual-mode CrossfireX configuration, resulting in a total of four GPUs. To lower physical dependencies, one should carry out redundant computations on different cards, then on different GPUs, then on different grids. The program/ operating system can additionally implement a scheduler, issuing different redundant computations to different parts of the graphics subsystem. The redundant computations can be called from the main program and run in parallel to the CPU calculation. A comparison can be done by the CPU or the GPU. However, the production of results must be synchronized. Fig. 8 shows the integration. Disadvantages besides synchronization are that the user must decide which code should be verified by the GPU and the source code of the application must be modified. Additionally, only system relevant routines could be modified.

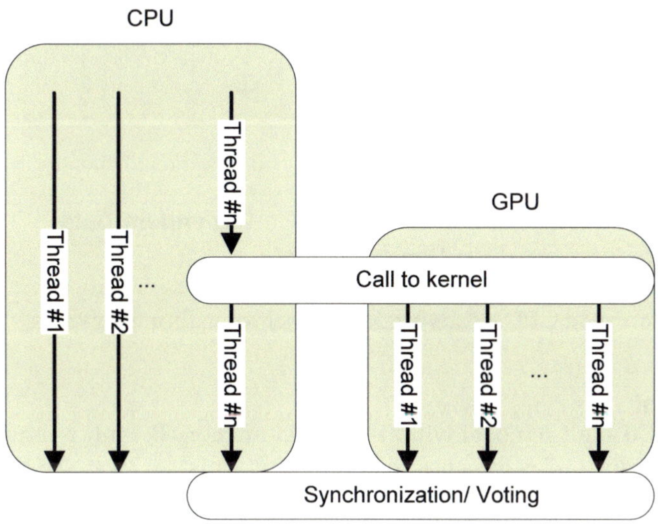

Fig. 8. CPU/ GPU redundant computations

From Fig. 8 we see that the combination of multiple host thread callers and GPU threads is possible. To do a synchronization without waiting times for the CPU and/ or the GPU, the results could be written into a buffer, where each calculation receives its very own identification. Thus, we do not have to wait for the results to arrive. A disadvantage is that in case of a rollback, already calculated results must be discarded. The synchronization of host and GPU threads offers a new perspective for research.

3.2.2 Temporal Redundancy

Temporal redundancy is an essential property of a multithreaded system, thus also for graphics cards comprising hundreds or thousands of threads. A temporal redundant computation can be done on every accessible element of the graphics card by redoing the calculation on the same or (better) on a different component. The only point where structural or temporal redundant threads are dependent is at the checking of results. The implementation in software is difficult, since CUDA does not differ between physical and virtual threads. Here, data dependencies have to be regarded. Fig. 9 illustrates two possible forms of temporal redundancy.

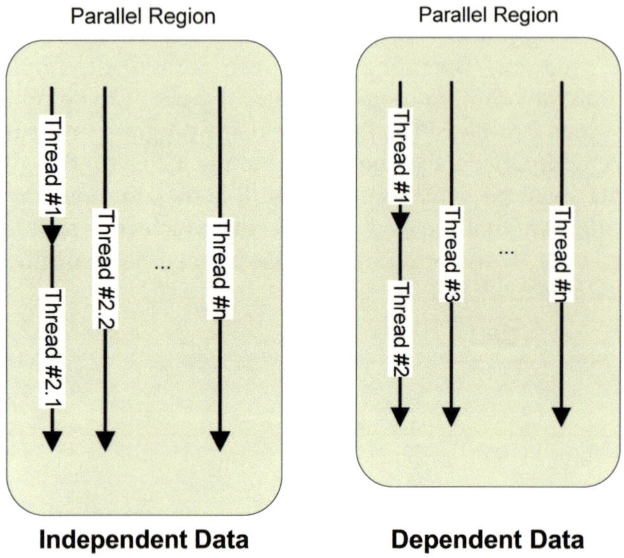

Fig. 9. Temporal Redundancy, Data Dependencies

Temporal redundancy on GPUs leads again to synchronization problems.

3.3 Fault Removal

Apart from the ECC fault removal within the GPU memory 0, fault removal is a hard thing to implement by using GPUs, because the faulty unit must be located and a prior and sane state must be restored. On a fault-free computation we must store a checkpoint. Here, we can fallback to classical schemes storing the checkpoint on hard disks or to store the checkpoint on the cards. The first thing is to use a triple card configuration to detect, locate and remove the fault within the graphics configuration. Here, the graphics cards ought to execute the same code, not strictly synchronously, but in a way that faults cannot propagate between cards. We do not discuss the removal of faults initiated from the CPU to the GPU ($CPU \Rightarrow GPU$) here, since our aim is to assist CPU calculations.

3.3.1 Watchdogs

A GPU can be periodically triggered by an external timer to monitor activities. The timer routine must be able to directly access the memory of the graphics card. The external timer is needed, because GPUs do not possess such a capability at the moment. The activities are e.g. CPU or fixed disk functionalities. Any activity and the current time are e.g. written to the texture memory. On a write of the current time, the last time will be copied to a different location within memory. If the new timer value does not differ from the last one, a fault is signaled. Furthermore, the GPU checks the activities. If no activities are recorded in the timer interval (no value has been written to memory) a wakeup signal can be issued. Fig. 10 shows the algorithm.

```
Startup:              E={}      // Empty event list E in mem
On timer:             // Compare new timestamp N with previous P in mem
        If N>P:       write P to previous timestamp in mem (P=>PP)
       Else Signal "Timer Fault"
            If E={}:Signal "Event List Empty - Wakeup"

On event:      Write event to E // Note that timer is also an event
```

Fig. 10. Watchdog Algorithm

The wakeup signal can be issued by writing to a dedicated memory location within the host's memory. If no OS restrictions apply, the GPU could write the recovery entry address to the CPU program counter.

3.3.2 Fault Removal GPU ⇒ GPU

We can imagine something like a RAIGx configuration (Redundant Array of Independent Graphics cards, according to a RAIDx - Redundant Array of Independent Disks). As we have not hardware controller to support RAIG, we only support Software-RAIG. As RAIG, we can consider the usual modes, listed in Table 4.

Mode	Meaning, Configuration
0	Two or more graphics cards doing independent calculations
1	Two of more graphics cards doing the same calculations in parallel
5	Two graphics cards doing the same calculations in parallel, securing the operands and the results in memory by a checksum, e.g. parity

Table 4. RAIG Modes

On the detection of a fault, we can vote among the results. If we include the CPU in the calculations, we have a TMR configuration and therefore can locate the faulty unit, if two results are equal. If the kernels are data independent, we can simply continue. If we have dependencies among the calculations, we have the option to either copy all memory contents and processing states of an assumed fault-free card to other all cards or copy the modified parts (see subsection 0).

3.3.3 Removal GPU ⇒ CPU

Fault removal within a CPU from a GPU is possible but far more difficult. CPU states must be written into the memory of the graphics card, also updated memory locations. We suggest checkpoint intervals between 10^6 (~4 MBytes written) and 10^7 (~40 MBytes written) memory writes. The checkpoint interval is restricted by the main memory of the graphics card, expected reliability and system performance. The CPU state is also stored in the main memory of the card. On a fault, the memory and CPU state must be transferred back. In Fig. 4 it is shown what bandwidth can be achieved. Since we cannot usually map the whole main memory of the host to the device memory, since it is smaller than that of the host's memory, we must either do every memory write of the CPU simultaneously on the card, significantly decreasing performance or do a fault removal for a single (system relevant) application running on the CPU such as a daemon. For CPU states, there is no problem, because the amount of data to transfer is very small. Difficult is the injection of a previous state in the CPU. Here we can imagine a state memory for each CPU which can be written from the GPU and read by the CPU. Within a multicore system another (healthy) CPU can inject the state into the faulty CPU.

3.4 Fault Forecasting (with GPUs)

For the prediction of faults, a history of faults must be stored in the graphics card memory, because without knowledge of the past, we cannot predict future faults. The prediction can be done with various methods, e.g. causal Bayesian networks, Hidden Markov Models (HMMs) and the forward algorithm, etc. We propose to use the MCE (machine check exception) of modern processors to enter a special routine to compute the prediction. We assume the history to be organized as simple ring buffer of length N. The algorithm in Fig. 11 briefly sketches the method without going into details.

```
Startup:  History (h2) location h=0;

CPU:
          On_MCE:   Write MCE-Flag, time to GPU memory, location h2
            h=h+1 % N
            Call prediction on GPU
GPU:
  On_Call: Do prediction using h2
```

Fig. 11. Basic (abstract) prediction of faults

Note, that the forecast with HMMs implies very small numbers and hence precision problems. A small deviation can lead to faulty results. The scaling to big integers can limit these effects.

4. Summary and Outlook

This work presents a first step and innovative approach to use GPUs for dependability. We are aware of the fact that this work is rudimentary – but it can serve as a starting point and a priming of future work. It has been shown how the existing parallelism of GPUs can be exploited for dependability. Although we did not specify the exact nature of faults, since we did not want to restrict our horizon by regarding at a special set of fault types, the results and the physical context of the experimental setup strongly suggest to model transient faults. To lower physical dependencies, one should carry out redundant computations on different cards, then on different GPUs, then on different grids. From the experimental results some conclusions can be derived: a system in SLI mode is less reliable than one in non-SLI mode. Reliable calculations should be carried out on a non-SLI system. A system configured in SLI has more (proven) advantage in computing-intensive applications. For bandwidth-intensive applications a non-SLI system should be preferred. During the mid-term experiments, no unusual deviation (except precision) between CPU and GPU results occurred. The results were stable during the whole observation period.

Not everything is golden in this new world of opportunities. There are a few critical points which must be regarded by future research:

- The precision of results: fortunately all basic arithmetic operations such as add, sub and mul and all integer operations do not lead to imprecise results. A scaling of small floats to integers can improve the precision in such a way that the CPU and the GPU results will not differ.
- The synchronization of host and GPU threads offers a whole new perspective for research. The varying timings from CPU and GPU have a connection per computation, i.e. if the timing for the GPU was large, the timing of the corresponding CPU implementation was also higher. This is surprising, since we implemented an asynchronous version for the GPU which ought to run independently on the CPU. In their current implementation, graphics cards are not suitable for realtime applications.

Future work will include the implementation and analysis of the discussed dependability means and a long-term reliability evaluation.

5. References

[1]ACM Queue, GPUs Not Just for Graphics, Vol. 6, No. 2, March/ April 2008, ISSN: 1542-7730.

[2]J.-S. Huang et al. (NVidia corporation), United States Patent 7053901, System and method for accelerating a special purpose processor

[3]GPGPU. *General-Purpose Computation Using Graphics Hardware*, http://gpgpu.org, checked 05/15/2008.

[4]NVidia. *Technical Brief. NVidia GeForce 8800 GPU Architecture Overview*, Nov. 2006. http://www.NVidia.com/object/IO_37100.html, checked 05/15/2008.

[5]Larrabee: A Many-Core x86 Architecture for Visual Computing. Seiler, L., Carmean, D., Sprangle, D., Forsyth, T., Abrash, M., Dubey, P., Junkins, S., Lake, A., Sugerman, J., Cavin, R., Espasa, R., Grochowski, E., Juan, T., Hanrahan, P. Proceedings of SIGGRAPH 2008.

[6]www.vision4ce.com, checked 06/16/2009.

[7]Schatz, M.C., Trapnell, C., Delcher, A.L., Varshney, A. (2007). "*High-throughput sequence alignment using Graphics Processing Units*". BMC Bioinformatics ***8:474***: *474*. doi:10.1186/1471-2105-8-474

[8]J.C. Laprie, *Dependability: Basic Concepts and Terminology* Springer-Verlag, 1992. ISBN 0387822968

[9]I. Pharr, Matt. II. Fernando, Randima. *GPU gems 2: programming techniques for high-performance graphics and general-purpose computation,* edited by Matt Pharr; Randima Fernando, series editor. ISBN 0-321-33559-7.

[10]John D. Owens et al. *A Survey of General-Purpose Computation on Graphics Hardware, Computer Graphics Forum*", 2007, http://www.blackwell-synergy.com/doi/pdf/10.1111/j.1467-8659.2007.01012.x , pp. 80-113, vol. 26 , no. 1

[11]Khronos OpenCL Working Group. *The OpenCL Specification. Version: 1.0, Revision: 33,* Aaftab Munshi (ed.), http://www.khronos.org/registry/cl/specs/opencl-1.0.33.pdf

[12]http://pv.fernuni-hagen.de/~fechner/GPU.html, checked 06/03/2009

[13]http://www.NVidia.de/page/tesla_computing_solutions.html, checked, 06/03/2009.

[14]Curry, M.L.; Skjellum, A.; Ward, H.L.; Brightwell, R. *Accelerating Reed-Solomon coding in RAID systems with GPUs.* In Proc. Of the IEEE International Symposium on Parallel and Distributed Processing, pp. 1 - 6, 2008.
[15]R. Strzodka, D. Göddeke. *Mixed precision methods for convergent iterative schemes.* In Proc. of the 2006 Workshop on Edge Computing Using New Commodity Architectures, pp. D-59–60, 2006.
[16]A. Moss, D. Page, N. Smart, *Toward Acceleration of RSA Using 3D Graphics Hardware.* Cryptography and Coding, pp. 369–388. December 2007.
[17]N. Maruyama, A. Nukada, S. Matsuoka, Software-Based ECC for GPUs, Symp. on Application Accelerators in High Performance Computing, 2009.

5

Shuffle-Exchange Mesh Topology for Networks-on-Chip

Reza Sabbaghi-Nadooshan[1], Mehdi Modarressi[2,3]
and Hamid Sarbazi-Azad[2,3]
[1]*Islamic Azad University Central Tehran Branch, Tehran, Iran*
[2]*IPM School of computer science, Tehran, Iran*
[3]*Sharif University of Technology, Tehran, Iran*

1. Introduction

Network-on-Chip (NoC) is a promising communication paradigm for multiprocessor system-on-chips. This communication paradigm has been inspired from the packet-based communication networks and aims at overcoming the performance and scalability problems of the shared buses in multi-core SoCs (System on Chips)(Benini & Mecheli, 2002).
Although the concept of NoCs is inspired from the traditional interconnection networks, they have some special properties which are different from the traditional networks. Compared to traditional networks, power consumption is the first order constraint in NoC design (Ogras et al., 2005). As a result, not only should the designer optimize the NoC for delay (for traditional networks), but also for power consumption.
The choice of network topology is an important issue in designing a NoC. Different NoC topologies can dramatically affect the network characteristics, such as average inter-IP distance, total wire length, and communication flow distributions. These characteristics, in turn, determine the power consumption and average packet latency of NoC architectures.
In general, the topologies proposed for NoCs can be classified into two major classes, namely regular tile-based and application-specific. Compared to regular tile-based topologies, application-specific topologies are customized to give a higher performance for a specific application. Moreover, if the sizes of the IP cores of a NoC vary significantly, regular tile-based topologies may impose a high area overhead. This area overhead can be compensated by some advantages of regular tile-based architectures. Regular NoC architectures provide standard structured interconnects which ensures well-controlled electrical parameters. Moreover, usual physical design problems like crosstalk, timing closure, and wire routing and architectural problems such as routing, switching strategies and network protocols can be designed and optimized for a regular NoC and be reused in several SoCs.
The mesh topology is the simplest and most popular topology for today's regular tile-based NoCs. On the other hand, the shuffle-exchange topology is a well-known network structure which was initially proposed by stone (Stone, 1971) as an efficient topology for multicomputer interconnection networks. Several researchers have studied the topological

properties, routing algorithms, efficient VLSI layout and other aspects of shuffle-exchange networks (Steinberg & Rodeh, 1981; Sparso et al., 1991).
The fact that shuffle-exchange networks have smaller diameter than equal sized meshes motivates us to investigate them as the underlying topology for on-chip networks. In this chapter, we propose a 2D shuffle-exchange mesh (SEM) topology for NoC implementation. We compare the two most important NoC factors (latency and power) of the same sized mesh and SEM NoC architectures. To this end, we have implemented the networks in question in a NoC simulator. Using this simulator, a routing scheme for the SEM has been developed and the performance and power consumption of the two networks have been evaluated under similar working conditions. The simulation results show that the SEM, while having equal implementation cost, consumes lesser energy and exhibits higher performance compared to the traditional mesh network.
In this chapter, we will introduce the two-dimensional SEM topology, and develop a deadlock-free routing algorithm for it. We also compare the power consumption and network performance of equal sized SEM and mesh NoCs.

2. The 2D SEM topology

2.1 The structure

The traditional shuffle–exchange network (Figure 1 shows an 8-node shuffle exchange network) is first proposed in (Stone, 1971). This topology is one of the most popular interconnection architectures for multiprocessors and multicomputers due to its scalability and distributed self routing capability (Kim & Veidenbaum, 1995). Several researchers have studied the topological properties (Park & Agrawal, 1995; Pifarre et al., 1994) and efficient VLSI layout (Steinberg & Rodeh, 1981; Sparso et al., 1991) of the shuffle-exchange networks.
In a shuffle-exchange network, each node is identified by a unique n-bit binary address, hence the network size (number of nodes), N, equals 2^n. Two nodes are connected to each other if either their addresses differ in the last bit or one is a one-bit cyclic shift of the other. To establish these connections, two operations namely, shuffle and exchange, are used. With shuffle and exchange operations, message is circulated among network nodes until it reaches the destination node.
These operators that are defined on an n-bit address pattern $(A_{n-1}A_{n-2}\ldots A_1A_0)$ as follows:

Shuffle: $(A_{n-1}A_{n-2}\ldots A_1A_0) = A_{n-2}A_{n-3}\ldots A_1A_0\,A_{n-1}$
Exchange: $(A_{n-1}A_{n-2}\ldots A_1A_0) = A_{n-1}A_{n-2}\ldots A_1\overline{A_0}$

Each node generates two connections to other nodes via shuffle and exchange operations and accepts two connections from other nodes. Since these connections are unidirectional, the degree of the network is the same as the one-dimensional mesh (linear array). The diameter of a shuffle-exchange network with size N is $2\times log(N)$-1 which is the minimum distance between nodes 0 and 2^n-1.
Some researchers, e.g. in (Padmanabhan, 1991), have proposed different flavors of shuffle-exchange network structures and corresponding routing algorithms to allow more flexible network sizes instead of a complete size of 2^n.
In this chapter we propose a two-dimensional shuffle-exchange network architecture for network-on-chips. The architecture of this network is depicted in Figure 2. In this network, the nodes in each row and column form a shuffle-exchange network.

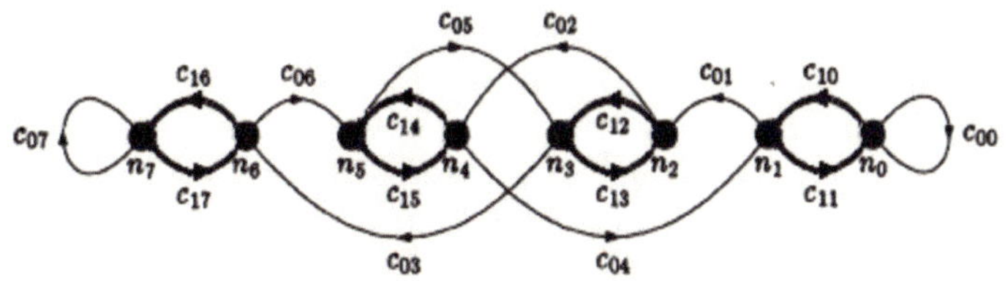

Fig. 1. An 8-node shuffle-exchange network; the bold lines are generated by exchange operation and other lines are generated by shuffle operation (Dally & seitz, 1987).

In each direction, each node has two outgoing edges along which it can send data packets to other nodes and two incoming links in each dimension and thus, has 8 unidirectional links in two dimensions. Thus, the number of links per node in the 2D SEM is equal to that in a traditional mesh network (i.e., 4 bidirectional links). Since the node degree of a topology has an important contribution in (and usually acts as the dominant factor of) the network cost, the 2D SEM and mesh NoCs have almost the same cost.
However, the network diameter of the 2D SEM is smaller than the diameter of the equivalent mesh. More precisely, the diameters of a 2D SEM and a mesh are $4\times log(2N^{0.5})-2$ and $2(N^{0.5}-1)$, respectively where N is the network size.

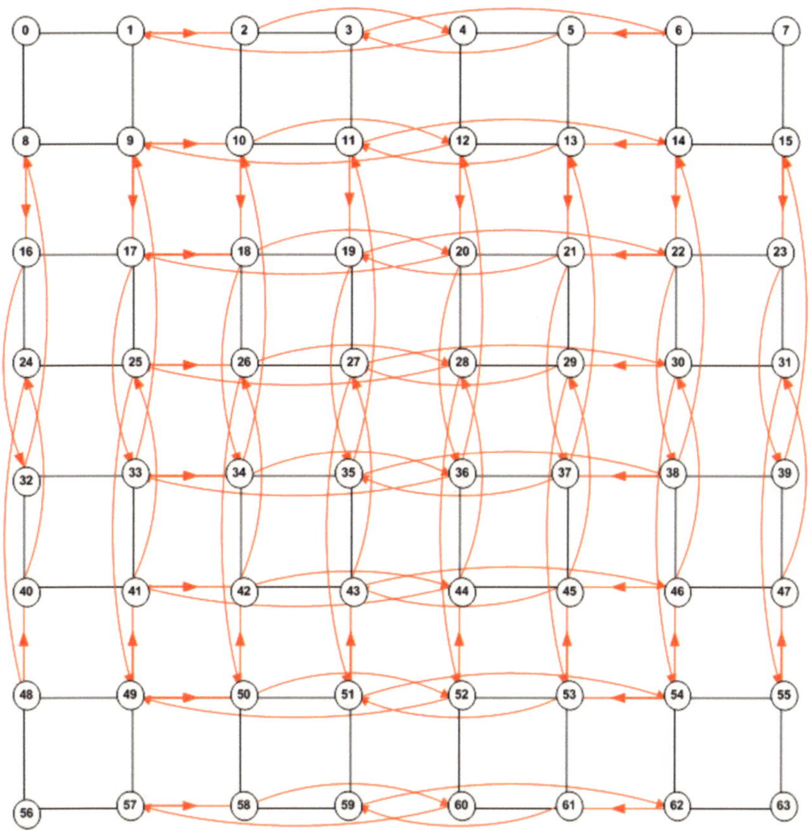

Fig. 2. A 2D SEM with 64 nodes

In shuffle-exchange networks, every link generated by an exchange operation has one corresponding link in the mesh network. However, the links generated by shuffle operations connect some non-adjacent nodes (in equivalent mesh) and reduce the distance between two end points of the network. Compared to a mesh, although establishing the shuffle links remove the link between some adjacent nodes (for example 2 to 1, 6 to 5 and 3 to 4 connections in Figure 1) and increases their distance by one hop, the distance between a larger number of nodes is decreased by one or multiple hops and this leads to a considerable reduction in average distance of the network.

Although the dominant factor of the network cost, the node degree, in 2D SEM and mesh networks are exactly the same, unlike the mesh topology the 2D SEM links do not always connect the adjacent nodes and hence, their lengths are not the same. This can lead to some variations in the delay and power of the network links and may also have link placement difficulty. The latter can be solved by a number of efficient VLSI layouts proposed for shuffle-exchange networks (Steinberg & Rodeh, 1981; Sparso et al., 1991). Moreover, since the operating frequency of a NoC is often determined by the router critical path, the long wires may not degrade the NoC speed. However, in the case of frequency degradation, the pipelined packet switching technique (Duato et al., 2002) which involves inserting some one-flit buffers for the links can solve the problem. The effect of longer links on power consumption has been considered in our simulation results (presented in the next section).

2.2 Routing algorithm

During past years, a number of routing algorithms have been developed for traditional shuffle-exchange networks. Dally (Dally & Seitz, 1987) presented a routing algorithm which routes the packets from the source node toward the destination by changing the address one bit at a time, starting from the most significant bit of the n-bit source address in a 2^n–node network. At the i-th step of the algorithm, the (n-i)-th bit of the destination address is compared to the LSB of the current address. If these two bits are equal, the message is routed over the shuffle channel to keep the bit unchanged and rotate the address. Otherwise, the message is routed over the exchange channel to make the two bits identical and then over to exchange channel to rotate the address. This algorithm involves a maximum of $2n$ communication steps between adjacent nodes along the path from the source to the destination node. However, this algorithm can not always find the shortest path for some source and destination pairs (Dally & Seitz, 1987). In order to be deadlock-free, this algorithm requires n virtual channels per physical channel and the message uses the i-th virtual channel at the (n-i)-th step. Since in this virtual channel selection scenario routing is performed in order of decreasing order of virtual channel number, the dependency graph of virtual channels is acyclic and the routing is deadlock-free (Dally & Seitz, 1987).

Park (Park & Agrawal, 1995) improved Dally's routing (Dally & Seitz, 1987) using lower number of virtual channels per physical channel. They logically partition the network into several acyclic sub-networks and assign a rank to the sub-networks. Applying Dally's routing, the virtual channel number is increased only if the message enters a new partition with higher rank. As a result, the number of required virtual channels is reduced to $n-\lfloor (n-1)/2 \rfloor$.

Pifarre (Pifarre et al., 1994) introduced another deadlock-free routing algorithm for shuffle-exchange networks using only 4 virtual channels per physical channel regardless of the network size. However, in this algorithm, the maximum number of hops taken by a message increases from $2n$ (in Dally's algorithm (Dally & Seitz, 1987)) to $3n$. It first decomposes the network into some so called shuffle cycles by considering the network without exchange links. Note that every node in a shuffle cycle has the same number of 1s in its binary address which is defined as the level of a shuffle cycle. The routing algorithm involves two phases. In phase 1, at any step, a message stays in a shuffle cycle (if it is routed along a shuffle arc) or it is routed to a shuffle cycle of a higher level (if it is routed along a shuffle-exchange arc). In phase 2, the message is successively routed in shuffle cycles of decreasing levels. Consequently, every path has at most $3n$ steps: at most $2n$ shuffle steps and n exchange steps. The shuffle cycles can be made deadlock-free, in phase 1, by allocating two virtual channels. By allocating two more virtual channels for each shuffle arc, routing in shuffle cycles can be made deadlock-free, in phase 2.

For shuffle-exchange, we use a routing algorithm based on the algorithm proposed in (Pifarre et al., 1994). The algorithm decomposes the entire graph into several shuffle-cycles and constructs two increasing (in which the nodes are traversed in increasing number) and decreasing (in which the nodes are traversed in decreasing number) graphs as shown Figure 3. The algorithm involves two phases. The first phase, the increasing phase, visits the shuffle cycles in increasing order and the bit positions which are '0' in the source address and '1' in the destination address are changed to '1'. The other phase (the decreasing phase) visits the nodes in decreasing order in respect to their levels and bit positions which are '1' in the source address and '0' in the destination address are changed to '0'. We used the modified algorithm which removes the self loops and makes the path shorter.

As can be seen in Figure 3, the shuffle cycles in the increasing graph can be made deadlock-free by allocating two virtual channels which break the cycle. By allocating two more virtual channels for each shuffle cycle, routing in shuffle cycles can be made deadlock-free along the decreasing graph in phase 2, as well. Therefore, the network should have 4 virtual channels per physical channel to make our algorithm deadlock-free.

Now, after designing a routing scheme for the shuffle-exchange, we develop a deterministic and an adaptive routing mechanism for the 2D SEM. Like XY routing algorithm in mesh networks, the deterministic routing applies the above-mentioned routing mechanism in rows first in order to deliver the packet to the column at which the destination is located. Afterwards, the message is routed to the destination by applying the same routing algorithm in that column. Obviously, adding the second dimension in this routing scheme does not generate a cycle and is deadlock-free provided that the routing in each dimension is deadlock-free (Duato et al., 2002).

In the adaptive routing mechanism, on the other hand, all possible minimal paths between a source and a destination node are of potential use along the path depending on the traffic congestion and network conditions. Since each node is connected to the nodes in its row and column via a shuffle-exchange network, in each node, the routing algorithm routes the packets along one of the two networks based on the traffic congestion and resource availability. We avoid deadlocks using a deadlock-free routing methodology presented in (Duato, 1995) which divides the virtual channels into two adaptive and deterministic parts and uses the deterministic part upon message blockage in adaptive part.

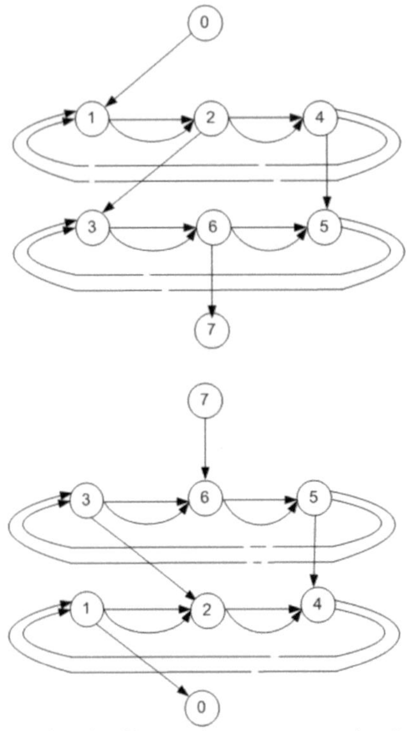

Fig. 3. The logical partitioning of a shuffle-exchange network of size 8

3. Comparison results

In order to compare the energy dissipation and performance of the 2D SEM with the mesh, we have used a modified version of the Popnet NoC simulator (Popnet, 2007). The simulator can simulate and calculate the performance measures of NoCs under different traffic patterns and supports virtual channel-based wormhole switching. It also includes the Orion power library (Wang et al., 2002) that can calculate the energy dissipated in the NoC under simulation. For our experiments, we set the network link width to 32 bits (flit size = phit size =32 bits). The power is calculated based on a NoC with 180 nm technology whose routers operate at 250 MHz.

The simulation results is obtained for an 8×8 mesh interconnection network with XY routing algorithm and an 8×8 2D SEM using the routing algorithms described in the previous section. The message length is assumed to be 32 and 64 flits and 4 and 6 virtual channels per physical channel are used. Messages are generated according to a Poisson distribution with rate λ, and the destinations of the messages are uniformly selected from the network nodes.

In Figure 4, the average message latency is plotted as a function of message generation rate at each node for the mesh and 2D SEM networks using deterministic routing (which involves 4 virtual channels) for two different message sizes. As can be seen in the figure, the 2D SEM has smaller average message latency with respect to the equivalent mesh network. The reason is that the average inter-node distance of the 2D SEM network is lower than the equivalent mesh network.

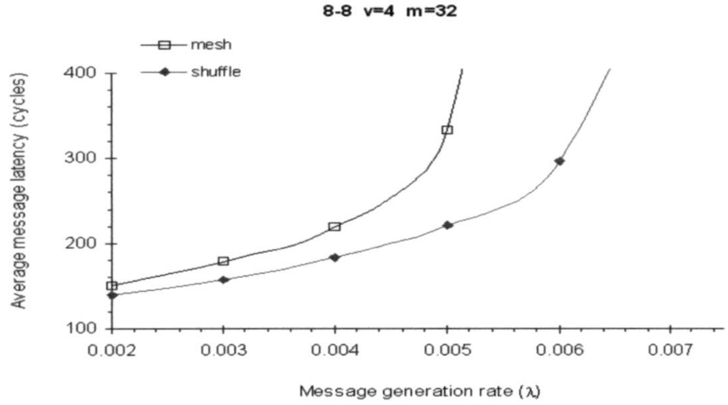

a)

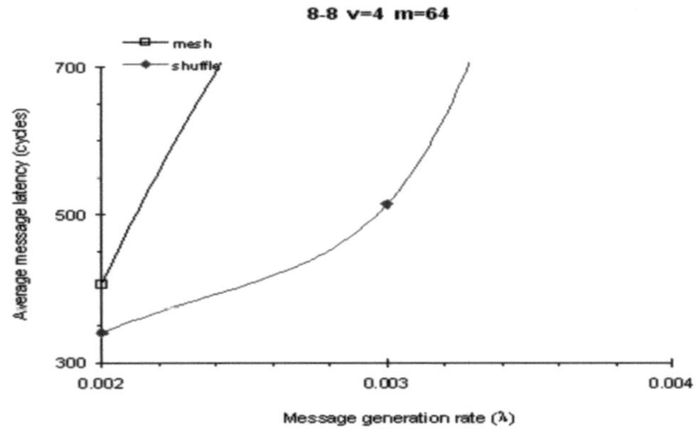

b)

Fig 4. The average message latency of deterministic routing in the 64-node 2D SEM and mesh networks using 4 virtual channels per physical channel with message length a) 32 flits and b) 64 flits.

Figure 5 compares the latency results of adaptive and deterministic routing schemes in a 2D SEM. In order to conduct a fair comparison, both routing algorithms use 6 virtual channels per physical channel (deterministic routing algorithm employs 6 virtual channels per physical channel while adaptive routing algorithm divides the virtual channels into 2-virtual channel adaptive and 4-virtual channel deterministic parts). It can be seen that the adaptive routing algorithm has improved the average message latency compared to the deterministic routing. The improvement is more significant in high-traffic regions where adaptivity resolves contentions more effectively.

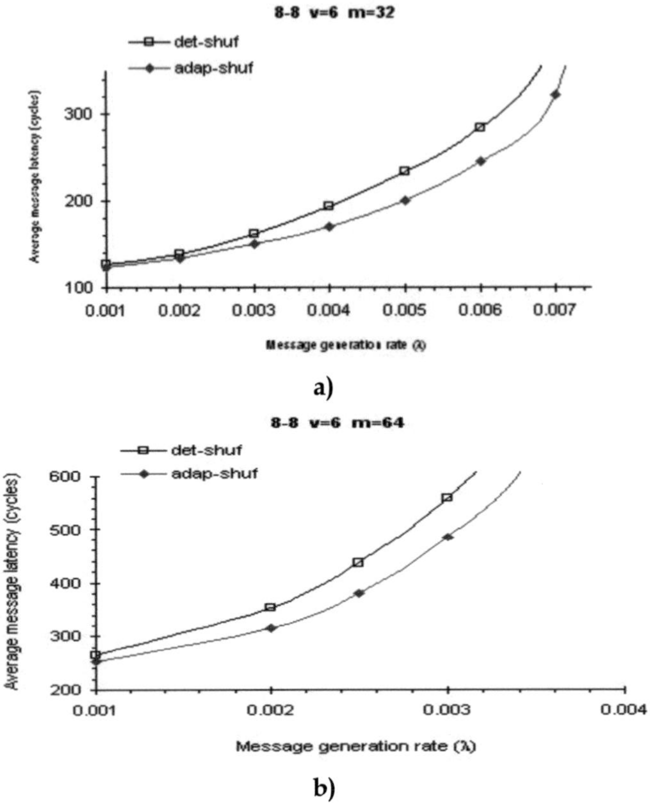

Fig. 5. The average message latency of the deterministic and adaptive routing algorithms in a 64-node 2D SEM using 6 virtual channels per physical channel with a) 32-flit messages and b) 64-flit messages.

As mentioned before, the effect of wire lengths in power consumption is considered in the calculation of consumed power by Orion. Based on the core size information presented in (Mullins et al., 2006), we set the side size of the cores of our simulated 8×8 NoCs to 2 mm. The length of the shuffle wires in the 2D SEM is set based on the number of cores they pass. Figure 6 displays the power consumption of the mesh and 2D SEM networks using deterministic routing scheme in the scenario used in figure 4. As can be seen in the figure, the proposed 2D SEM topology can effectively reduce the power consumption of the NoC. The main source of this reduction is the long wires which bypass some nodes and hence save the power which is consumed in intermediate routers in an equivalent mesh topology. Note that when the mesh network reaches to its saturation region, the 2D SEM network still can handle the traffic and thus the saturation rate for the 2D SEM is higher than that in the mesh. The extra messages communicated in the network have increased the total power consumption in the 2D SEM after the saturation rate of the mesh network. This is of course natural to have more energy consumed for higher traffic crates.

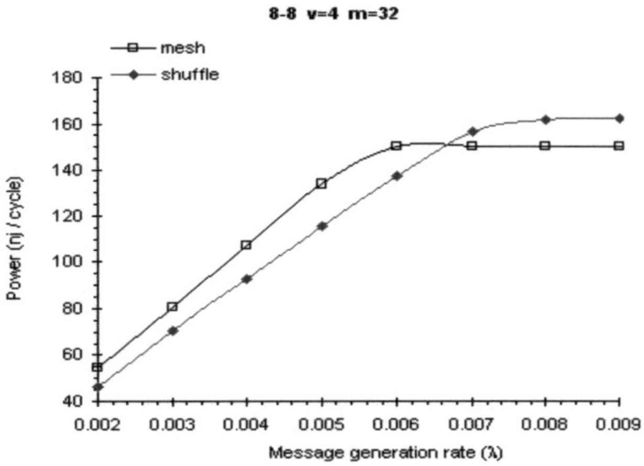

a)

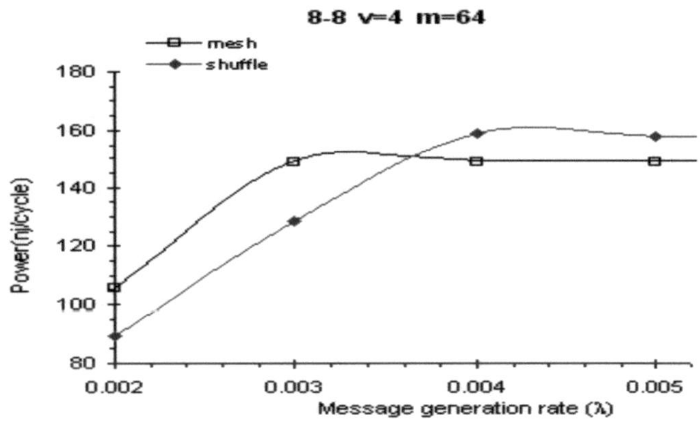

b)

Fig. 6. The power consumption of 64-node mesh and 2D SEM NoCs using deterministic routing and 4 virtual channels per physical channel with a) 32-flit and b) 64-flit messages.

The area estimation is done based on the hybrid synthesis-analytical area models presented in (Mullins et al. , 2006; Kim et al., 2006; Kim et al. 2008). In these papers, the area of the router building blocks is calculated in 90nm standard cell ASIC technology and then analytically combined to estimate the router total area. Table 1 outlines the parameters. The analytical area models for NoC and its components are displayed in Table 2. The area of a router is estimated based on the area of the input buffers, network interface queues, and crossbar switch, since the router area is dominated by these components.

The area overhead due to the additional inter-router wires is analyzed by calculating the number channels in a mesh-based NoC. A $n \times n$ mesh has $2 \times n \times (n-1)$ channels. The 2D SEM has the same channels as mesh with longer wires. In the analysis, the lengths of packetization and depacketization queues are considered as large as 64 flits.

In Table 3, the area overhead of 2D SEM NoC is calculated for 8×8 network size in a 32-bit wide system. The results show that, in an 8×8 mesh, the total area of the 2mm links and the routers are 0.0633 mm^2 and 0.1089 mm^2, respectively. Based on these area estimations, the area of the network part of the 2D SEM network shows a 27% increase compared to a simple 2D mesh with equal size. Considering 2mm×2mm processing elements, the increase in the entire chip area is less than 2%. Obviously, by increasing the buffer sizes, the network node/configuration switch area increases, leading to much reduction in the area overhead of the proposed architecture.

Parameter	**Symbol**
Flit Size	F
Buffer Depth	B
No. of Virtual channels	V
Buffer area (0.00002 *mm²/bit* (Kim et al., 2008))	B_{area}
Wire pitch (0.00024 *mm* (ITRS, 2007)	W_{pitch}
No. of Ports	P
Network Size	N (= n×n)
Packetization queue capacity	PQ
Depacketization queue capacity	DQ
Channel Area (0.00099 mm²/bit/mm (Mullinset al. , 2006)	W_{area}
Channel Length (2mm)	L
No. of Channels	$N_{channel}$

Table 1. Parameters

	Symbol	**Model**
Crossbar	RCX_{area}	$W^2_{pitch}\times P\times P\times F^2$
Buffer (per port)	RBF_{area}	$B_{area}\times F\times V\times B$
Router	R_{area}	$RCX_{area}+P\times RBF_{area}$
Network Adaptor	NA_{area}	$PQ\times B_{area}+DQ\times B_{area}$
Channel	CH_{area}	$F\times W_{area}\times L\times N_{channel}$
NoC Area	NoC_{area}	$n^2\times (R_{area}+NA_{area})+CH_{area}$

Table 2. Area analytical model

Network	Link Area	Router Area	Increase percent to mesh	increase percent in the entire chip
mesh	.06338	.1089	0	0
2D SEM	.0905	.1089	27.69	1.91

Table 3. 2D SEM area overhead

4. Conclusion

The mesh topology has been used in a variety of interconnection network applications especially for NoC designs due to its desirable properties in VLSI implementation. In this chapter, we proposed a new topology based on the shuffle-exchange topology, the 2D shuffle-exchange mesh (2D SEM), and conducted latency and power consumption comparative simulation experiments for the proposed topology and mesh network. Simulation results showed that the 2D SEM can improve the latency of the network especially for high traffic loads. The power consumption in the 2D SEM is also shown to be less than that of the equivalent mesh network.

We also analyzed the effects of the various wire lengths in the implementation of the 2D SEM. Finding an optimal mapping scheme for the 2D SEM NoCs and also a VLSI layout based on the design considerations in deep sub-micron era is the future work in this line.

5. References

http://www.princeton.edu/~lshang/popnet.html, August 2007.

Benini, L. & Micheli GD. (2002). Networks on Chip: A New Paradigm for Systems on Chip Design, *Design Automation and Test in Europe (DATE)*, pp. 418–419.

Dally, WJ. & Seitz, C. (1987). Deadlock-free Message Routing in Multiprocessor Interconnection Networks, *IEEE Trans. on Computers*, Vol. 36, No. 5, pp. 547-553.

Duato, J. (1995). A Necessary and Sufficient Condition for Deadlock-free Adaptive Routing in Wormhole Networks, *IEEE Transactions on Parallel and Distributed Systems*, Vol. 6, No. 10, pp. 1055–1067.

Duato, J.; Yalamanchili, S. & Ni, L. (2002). *Interconnection Networks: An Engineering Approach*, Morgan Kaufmann Publishers.

ITRS. (2006). International technology roadmap for semiconductors. *Tech. rep.*, International Technology Roadmap for Semiconductors.

Kim, M.; Kim, D. & Sobelman, E. (2006). NoC link analysis under power and performance constraints, *IEEE International Symposium on Circuits and Systems (ISCAS)*, Greece.

Kim, MM.; Davis, JD.; Oskin, M & Austin, T. (2008). Polymorphic on-Chip Networks, *International Symposium on Computer Architecture(ISCA)*, pp. 101 -112.

Kim, S. & Veidenbaum, AV. (1995). On Shortest Path Routing in Single Stage Shuffle-Exchange Networks, *In Proc. 7th Annual ACM Symposium on Parallel Algorithms and Architectures*, pp. 298-307.

Mullins, R.; West, A. & Moore, S. (2006). The Design and Implementation of a Low-Latency On-Chip Network, *Asia and South Pacific Design Automation Conference(ASP-DAC)*, pp. 164-169.

Ogras, UY.; HU, J. & Marculescu, R. (2005). Key Research Problems in NoC Design: A Holistic Perspective, *CODES+ISSS*, Jersey City, NJ, pp. 69-74.

Padmanabhan, K. (1991). Design and Analysis of Even-Sized Binary Shuffle-Exchange Networks for Multiprocessors, *IEEE Transactions on Parallel and Distributed Systems*, Vol. 2, No. 4, pp. 385-397.

Park, H.; Agrawal, DP. (1995). Efficient Deadlock-free Wormhole Routing in Shuffle-based Networks, *7th IEEE Symposium on Parallel and Distributed Processing*, pp. 92-99.

Pifarre, GD. et al. (1994). Fully Adaptive Minimal Deadlock-Free Packet Routing in Hypercubes, Meshes, and other Networks: Algorithms and Simulations, *IEEE transaction on Parallel and Distributed Systems*, Vol. 4, pp. 247-263.

Sparso, J. et al. (1991). An Area-efficient Topology for VLSI Implementation of Viterbi decoders and Other Shuffle-Exchange type Structures, *IEEE journal of solid-state circuits*, Vol. 24, No. 2, pp.90-97.

Steinberg, D. & Rodeh, M. (1981). A Layout for the Shuffle-Exchange Network with $O(N^2/\log^{3/2}N)$ Area, *IEEE Trans. On Computers,* Vol. C-30, No. 12, pp. 971-982.
Stone, H. (1971). Parallel Processing With Perfect Shuffle, *IEEE Trans. on Computers,* Vol. 20, pp. 153–161.
Wang, H.; Zhu, X.; Peh, L. & Malik, S. (2002). Orion: A Power-Performance Simulator for Interconnection Networks, *35th International Symposium on Microarchitecture (MICRO)* , Turkey, pp. 294-305.

6

Cache Coherence Protocols for Many-Core CMPs

Alberto Ros, Manuel E. Acacio and José M. García
Universidad de Murcia
Spain

1. Introduction

Multi-core architectures have emerged as the best alternative to take advantage of the increasing number of transistors currently offered in a single die. For example, the dual-core IBM Power6 (Le et al., 2007) and the eight-core Sun UltraSPARC T2 (Shah et al., 2007) have a relatively small number of cores, which are typically connected through a shared medium, i.e., a bus or a crossbar. However, CMP architectures that integrate tens of processor cores (usually known as many-core CMPs) are expected for the near future, after Intel recently unveiled the 80-core Polaris prototype (Azimi et al., 2007). Since the area required by a shared interconnect becomes impractical as the number of cores grows (Kumar et al., 2005), it seems that the processing cores of future CMPs will be connected by means of unordered point-to-point networks. Hence, tiled CMP architectures (Taylor et al., 2002; Zhang & Asanovic, 2005), which are designed as arrays of replicated tiles connected over a point-to-point network, have arisen as a scalable alternative to current small-scale CMP designs and they will help in keeping complexity manageable.

On the other hand, most CMP systems provide programmers with the intuitive shared-memory model, which requires efficient support for cache coherence. Although a great deal of attention was devoted to scalable cache coherence protocols in the last decades in the context of shared-memory multiprocessors, the technological parameters and constraints entailed by many-core CMPs demand new solutions to the cache coherence problem (Bosschere et al., 2007; Azimi et al., 2007).

In this chapter, we focus on three main design goals for cache coherence protocols aimed at being employed in many-core CMPs: performance, on-chip network traffic, and area requirements. For example, area constraints prevent from using an ordered interconnection network and, consequently, the popular snooping-based cache coherence protocol. Additionally, on-chip network traffic has been previously reported to constitute a significant fraction (approaching 50% in some cases) of the overall chip power (Wang et al., 2003; Magen et al., 2004).

We will firstly describe two cache coherence protocols which are used in current commodity chip multiprocessors, discussing their scalability constraints and bottlenecks: *Hammer*, implemented in the AMD Opteron^{TM}(Ahmed et al., 2002), and *Directory* used in Piranha (Barroso et al., 2000). *Hammer* avoids keeping coherence information at the cost of broadcasting requests to all cores. Although it is very efficient in terms of area requirements, it generates a prohibitive amount of network traffic, which translates into excessive power consumption. On the other hand, *Directory* reduces network traffic compared to *Hammer* by storing in a directory structure precise information about the private caches holding memory blocks. Unfortunately, the storage overhead that directories entail could become prohibitive for many-core CMPs (Azimi et al., 2007). Since neither the network traffic generated by *Hammer* nor the extra area required by *Directory* scale with the number of cores, a great deal of attention was paid in the past to address this traffic-area trade-off (Agarwal et al., 1988; Gupta et al., 1990; Chaiken et al., 1991; Mukherjee & Hill, 1994; Acacio et al., 2001).

On the other hand, these traditional cache coherence protocols introduce indirection in the critical path of cache misses. In both protocols, the ordering point for the requests to the same memory block is the *home* node or tile. Therefore, all cache misses must reach this ordering point before any coherence actions can be performed, a fact that adds extra latency to cache misses. Recently, Token-CMP (Martin et al., 2003) and DiCo-CMP (Ros et al., 2008a) protocols have been proposed to deal with the indirection problem. These indirection-aware protocols avoid the access to the home node through alternative serialization mechanisms. In this way, they reduce the latency of cache misses compared to *Hammer* and *Directory*, which translates into performance improvements. Although Token-CMP entails low memory overhead, it is based on broadcasting requests to all nodes, which is clearly non-scalable. Otherwise, DiCo-CMP sends requests to just one node, but it adds a full-map sharing code that keeps track of sharers to each cache entry, which does not scale with the number of cores.

In this chapter, we discuss both protocols that are used nowadays, such as *Hammer* and *Directory*, and these two novel indirection-aware protocols (Token-CMP and DiCo-CMP). We also study how they can scale up to a greater number of cores. In particular, we perform this study by considering direct coherence (DiCo) protocols and, therefore we first describe this kind of protocols in detail. Finally, we compare all the described protocols in terms of performance, network traffic and area requirements, thus performing a detailed evaluation of a wide range of cache coherence protocols for many-core CMPs in a common framework.

The rest of the chapter is organized as follows. Section 2 introduces tiled CMP architectures. Section 3 discusses and presents a classification of some cache coherence protocols that could be used in tiled CMPs. Section 4 offers a detailed description of direct coherence protocols, and Section 5 discusses several implementations that differ in the amount of coherence information that they keep. Section 6 focuses on the evaluation methodology. Section 7 shows and analyses performance results. In Section 8, we present a review of the related work and, finally, Section 9 concludes the chapter.

2. Tiled CMPs

Tiled CMP architectures are designed as arrays of identical or close-to-identical building blocks known as *tiles*. In these architectures, each tile is comprised of a processing core, one or several levels of caches, and a network interface or router that connects all tiles through a tightly integrated and lightweight point-to-point interconnection network (e.g., a two-dimensional mesh). Differently from shared networks, point-to-point interconnects are suitable for many-core CMPs because their peak bandwidth and area overhead scale with the number of cores. Tiled CMPs can easily support families of products with varying number of tiles, including the option of connecting multiple separately tested and speed-binned dies within a single package. Therefore, it seems that they will be the choice for future many-core CMPs.

In this chapter, we assume a tiled CMP with two levels of on-chip caches, as shown in Figure 1. The first one (L1 cache) is private to its local processing core. In contrast, the second one (L2 cache) is logically shared (but physically distributed) among the processing cores. Therefore, each cache block maps to a particular L2 cache bank, which is called the *home* tile for that block.

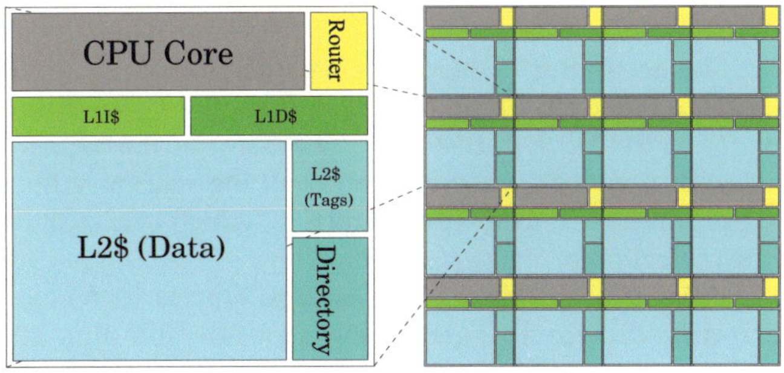

Fig. 1. Organization of a tile (left) and a 4×4 tiled CMP (right).

The home bank of each block is commonly obtained from its address bits. Particularly, the bits usually chosen for the mapping to a particular bank are the less significant ones without considering the block offset (Huh et al., 2005; Zhang & Asanovic, 2005; Shah et al., 2007).

Since, wire delay of future CMPs will cause cross-chip communications to reach tens of cycles (Agarwal et al., 2000; Ho et al., 2001), the access latency to a multibanked shared cache will be dominated by the delay to reach each particular cache bank rather than the time spent accessing the bank itself. In this way, the access latency to the shared cache can be drastically different depending on the cache bank where the requested block maps. The resulting cache design is what is known as non-uniform cache architecture (NUCA) (Kim et al., 2002).

The main downside of a NUCA organization is the long cache access latency (on average), since it depends on the bank wherein the block is allocated, especially when home banks are assigned by taking some fixed bits from the block address. Since, in this case, the distribution of the blocks is performed in a round-robin fashion without considering the distance from the requesting cores to the home banks, it is more important to avoid the indirection to the home tile, because for most misses the requested block could map to a remote cache bank.

3. Cache coherence protocols for tiled CMPs

As introduced at the beginning of this chapter, traditional snooping-based protocols require an ordered interconnect to keep cache coherence, but such interconnects do not scale in terms of area requirements. This section describes and classifies the four cache coherence protocols considered in this chapter as potential candidates to be employed in tiled CMPs (i.e., with unordered networks): *Hammer*, *Directory*, *Token*, and *DiCo*. In particular, we classify these cache coherence protocols into *traditional* protocols, in which cache misses suffer from indirection, and *indirection-aware* protocols, which try to avoid the indirection problem. For each type, we also differentiate between area-demanding and traffic-intensive protocols.

We discuss the implementation of these cache coherence protocols for a tiled CMP in which each tile includes a private L1 cache and a slice of the shared L2 cache, as described in the previous section. In this way, cache coherence is maintained among data stored in the L1 caches. We also assume that private caches use MOESI states, and that L1 and L2 caches are non-inclusive.

3.1 Traditional protocols

In traditional protocols, the requests issued by several cores to the same block are serialized through the home tile, which enforces cache coherence. Therefore, all requests must be sent to the home tile before any coherence action can be performed. Then, requests are forwarded to the corresponding tiles according to the coherence information (if needed). All processors that receive a forwarded request answer to the requesting core by sending either an acknowledgment (and invalidating the block in case of write misses) or the requested data block. The requesting core can access the block when it receives all the acknowledgment and data messages. The access to the home tile introduces indirection, which causes that most cache misses take three hops in the critical path.

Examples of these traditional protocols are *Hammer* and *Directory*. As commented in the introduction, *Hammer* has the drawback of generating a considerable amount of network traffic. On the other hand, directory protocols that use a precise sharing code to keep track of cached blocks introduce an area overhead that does not scale with the number of cores.

3.1.1 Hammer-CMP

Hammer (Owner et al., 2006) is the cache coherence protocol used by AMD in their Opteron systems (Ahmed et al., 2002). Like snooping-based protocols, *Hammer* does not store any coherence information about the blocks held in the private caches and, therefore, it relies on broadcasting requests to all tiles to solve cache misses. Its key advantage with respect to snooping-based protocols is that it targets systems that use unordered point-to-point interconnection networks. In contrast, the ordering point in this protocol is the home tile, a fact that introduces indirection on every cache miss.

We have implemented a version of the AMD's Hammer protocol for tiled CMPs that we call *Hammer-CMP*. As an optimization, our implementation adds a small structure to each home tile. This structure stores a copy of the tags for the blocks that are held in the private L1 caches. In this way, cache miss latencies are reduced by avoiding off-chip accesses when the block can be obtained on-chip. Moreover, the additional structure has small size and it does not increase with the number of cores.

On every cache miss, *Hammer-CMP* sends a request to the home tile. If the memory block is present on chip (this information is given by the structure that we add to each home tile), the request is forwarded to the rest of tiles to obtain the requested block, and to eliminate potential copies of the block in case of a write miss. Otherwise, the block is requested to the memory controller.

All tiles answer to the forwarded request by sending either an acknowledgment or the data message to the requesting core. The requesting core needs to wait until it receives the response from each other tile. When the requester receives all the responses, it sends an unblock message to the home tile. This message notifies the home tile about the fact that the miss has been satisfied. In this way, if there is another request for the same block waiting at the home tile, it can be processed. This unblock message prevents the occurrence of race conditions.

Figure 2(a)shows an example of how *Hammer-CMP* solves a cache-to-cache transfer miss. The requesting core (*R*) sends a write request (*1 GetX*) to the home tile (*H*). Then, invalidation messages (*2 Inv*) are sent to all other tiles. The tile with the ownership of the block (*M*) responds with the data block (*3 Data*). The other tiles that do not hold a copy of the block (*I*) respond with acknowledgment messages (*3 Ack*). When the requester receives all the responses, it sends the unblock message (*4 Unbl*) to the home tile. First, we can see that this protocol requires three hops in the critical path before the requested data block is obtained. Second, broadcasting invalidation messages increases considerably the traffic injected into the interconnection network and, therefore, its power consumption.

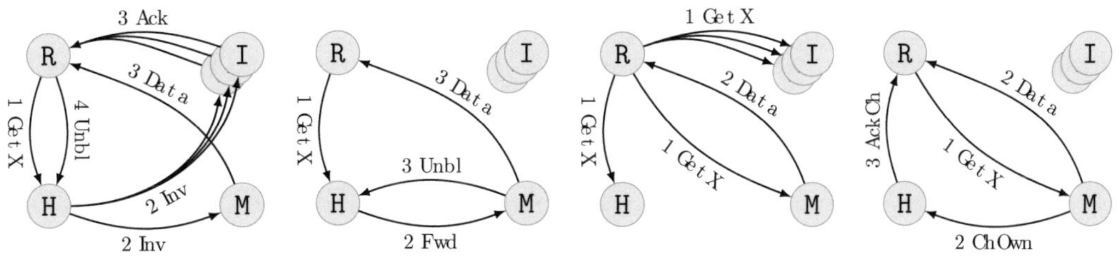

(a) Hammer-CMP. (b) Directory-CMP. (c) Token-CMP. (d) DiCo-CMP.

Fig. 2. A cache-to-cache transfer miss in each one of the described protocols.

3.1.2 Directory-CMP

The directory-based protocol that we have implemented for CMPs (*Directory-CMP*) is similar to the intra-chip coherence protocol used in Piranha (Barroso et al., 2000). In particular, the directory information consists in a full-map (or bit-vector) sharing code, that is employed for keeping track of the sharers. This sharing code allows the protocol to send invalidation messages just to the caches currently sharing the block, thus removing unnecessary coherence messages. In addition, directory-based protocols that implement MOESI states add an *owner* field that identifies the owner tile to the directory information of each block. The owner field allows the protocols to detect the tile that must provide the block in case of several sharers. In this way, requests are only forwarded to that tile. The use of directory information allows the protocol to reduce considerably network traffic when compared to *Hammer-CMP*.

In the implemented directory protocol, on every cache miss, the core that causes the miss sends the request only to the home tile, which is the serialization point for all requests issued for the same block. Each home tile includes an on-chip directory cache that stores the sharing and owner information for the blocks that it manages. This cache is used for the blocks that do not hold a copy in the shared cache. In addition, the tags' part of the shared cache also include a field for storing the sharing information for those blocks that have a valid entry in that cache. Once the home tile decides to process the request, it accesses the directory and it performs the appropriate coherence actions. These coherence actions include forwarding the request to the owner tile, and invalidating all copies of the block in case of write misses.

When a tile receives a forwarding request it provides the data to the requester if it is already available or, in other case, the request must wait until the data is available. Like in *Hammer-CMP*, all tiles must respond to the invalidation messages with an acknowledgment message to the requester. Since acknowledgment messages are collected by the requester, it is necessary to inform the requester about the number of acknowledgments that it has to receive before accessing the requested data block. In our particular implementation, this information is sent from the home tile, which knows the number of invalidation messages issued, to the requester along with the forwarding and data messages. When the requester receives all acknowledgments and the data block, data can be accessed.

Figure 2(b)shows an example of how *Directory-CMP* solves a cache-to-cache transfer miss. The request is sent to the home tile, where the directory information is stored (*1 GetX*). Then, the home tile forwards the request to the provider of the block, which is obtained from the directory information (*2 Fwd*). The provider sends the unblock message to the home tile to allow subsequent requests to be processed (*3 Unbl*) and it also sends the data to the requester (*3 Data*). When the data block arrives to the requester, the miss is considered solved. As we can see, although this protocol introduces indirection to solve cache misses (three hops in the critical path of the miss), few coherence messages are required to solve them, which finally translates into savings in network traffic and less power consumption. This characteristic allows the directory protocol to scale up to a greater number of cores than *Hammer-CMP*.

3.2 Indirection-aware protocols

Recently, new cache coherence protocols have been proposed to avoid the indirection problem of traditional protocols. *Token-CMP* avoids indirection by broadcasting requests to all tiles and maintains coherence through a token counting mechanism. Token-CMP only cares about requests ordering in case of race conditions. In those cases, a persistent requests mechanism is responsible for ordering the different requests. Although the area required to store the tokens of each block is reasonable, network requirements are prohibitive for may-core CMPs.

On the other hand, in *DiCo-CMP* the ordering point is the tile that provides the block in a cache miss and indirection is avoided by directly sending the requests to that tile. *DiCo-CMP* keeps traffic low by sending requests to only one tile. However, coherence information used in its original implementation (Ros et al., 2008a) include bit-vector sharing codes, which are not scalable in terms of area requirements.

3.2.1 Token-CMP

Token coherence (Martin et al., 2003) is a framework for designing coherence protocols whose main asset is that it decouples the correctness substrate from several different performance policies. Token coherence protocols can avoid both the need of a totally ordered network and the introduction of additional indirection caused by the access to the home tile in the common case of cache-to-cache transfers. Token coherence protocols keep cache coherence by assigning T tokens to every memory block, where one of them is the owner token. Then, a processing core can read a block only if it holds at least one token for that block and has valid data. On the other hand, a processing core can write a block only if it holds all T tokens for that block and has valid data. Token coherence avoids starvation by issuing a persistent request when a core detects potential starvation.

In this chapter, we use *Token-CMP* (Marty et al., 2005) in our simulations. *Token-CMP* is a performance policy aimed at achieving low-latency cache-to-cache transfer misses. It targets CMP systems, and uses a distributed arbitration scheme for persistent requests, which are issued after a single retry to optimize the access to contended blocks.

Particularly, on every cache miss, the requesting core broadcasts requests to all other tiles. In case of a write miss, they have to answer with all tokens that they have. The data block is sent along with the owner token. When the requester receives all tokens the block can be accessed. On the other hand, just one token is required upon a read miss. The request is broadcast to all other tiles, and only those that have more than one token (commonly the one that has the owner token) answer with a token and a copy of the requested block.

Figure 2(c)shows an example of how *Token-CMP* solves a cache-to-cache transfer miss. Requests are broadcast to all tiles (*1 GetX*). The only tile with tokens for that block is *M*, which responds by sending the data and all the tokens (*2 Data*). We can see that this protocol avoids indirection since only two hops are introduced in the critical path of cache misses. However, as happens in *Hammer-CMP*, this protocol also has the drawback of broadcasting requests to all tiles on every cache miss, which results in high network traffic and, consequently, power consumption in the interconnect.

	Traditional	Indirection-aware
Traffic-intensive	Hammer-CMP	Token-CMP
Area-demanding	Directory-CMP	DiCo-CMP

Table 1. Summary of cache coherence protocols.

3.2.2 DiCo-CMP

Direct coherence protocols where proposed both to avoid the indirection problem of traditional directory-based protocols and to reduce the traffic requirements of token coherence protocols. In direct coherence, the ordering point for the requests to a particular memory block is the current owner tile of the requested block. In this way, the tile that must provide the block in case of a cache miss is the one that keeps coherence for that block. Indirection is avoided by directly sending requests to the corresponding owner tile instead of to the home tile. In this work we evaluate *DiCo-CMP* (Ros et al., 2008a), an implementation of direct coherence for CMPs. Particularly, we implement the *Base* policy presented in that paper because it is the policy that incurs in less area and traffic requirements.
Figure 2(d)shows an example of how *DiCo-CMP* solves a cache-to-cache transfer miss. The request is directly sent to the tile that has the ownership of the requested block (*1 GetX*). This tile responds by sending the data to the requesting core (*2 Data*), thus requiring just two hops in the critical path of cache misses. Out of the critical path of the miss, the owner tile informs the home tile about the change of ownership (*2 ChOwn*). Then, the home tile acknowledges the change of ownership (*3 AckCh*) allowing to move again the ownership of the block (if requested). Direct coherence protocols are explained in detail in next section. The main drawback of this protocol is that it adds a sharing code to every cache entry, which could result in high area requirements.

3.3 Summary

Table 1 summarizes the protocols described before. This table focuses on the three main metrics evaluated throughout this chapter. The first one is the applications' execution time, which can be affected by the indirection to the home tile. The second one is the network traffic, which impacts power consumption. The third one is the area requirements, which can severely limit the scalability of the CMP. *Hammer-CMP* and *Token-CMP* are based on broadcasting requests on every cache miss. Although the storage required to keep coherence in these protocols is small, they generate a prohibitive amount of network traffic. On the other hand, *Directory-CMP* and *DiCo-CMP* achieve more efficient utilization of the interconnection network at the cost of increasing storage requirements compared to *Hammer-CMP* and *Token-CMP*. Finally, the key advantage of *Token-CMP* and *DiCo-CMP* is that they avoid the indirection problem for most cache misses, thus reducing the execution time compared to traditional protocols.

4. Direct coherence protocols

In this section, we describe the main characteristics of a direct coherence protocol and its implementation for tiled CMPs. First, we explain how direct coherence avoids indirection for most cache misses by means of changing the distribution of the roles involved in cache coherence maintenance. We also study the changes in the structure of the tiles necessary to implement *DiCo-CMP*. Then, we describe the cache coherence protocol for tiled CMPs and, finally, we study how to avoid the starvation issues that could arise in direct coherence protocols.

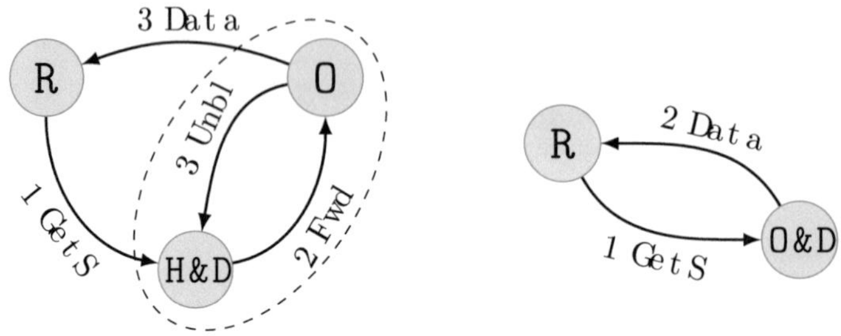

(a) Directory protocols. (b) Direct coherence protocols.

Fig. 3. How cache-to-cache transfer misses are solved in directory and direct coherence protocols. R=Requester; H=Home; D=Directory; O=Owner.

4.1 Direct coherence basis

As already discussed, directory protocols introduce indirection in the critical path of cache misses. Figure 3(a)shows a cache miss suffering indirection in a directory protocol, a cache-to-cache transfer for a read miss. When a cache miss takes place it is necessary to access the home tile to obtain the directory information and serialize the requests before performing any coherence action (*1 GetS*). In case of a cache-to-cache transfer miss, the request is subsequently forwarded to the owner tile (*2 Fwd*), where the block is provided (*3 Data*). As it can be observed, the miss is solved in three hops. Moreover, requests for the same block cannot be processed by the directory until it receives the unblock message (*3 Unbl*).

To avoid this indirection problem, direct coherence sends the request to the provider of the block, i.e., the owner tile, instead of to the home tile. This is the main motivation behind direct coherence. To allow the owner tile to process the request, direct coherence stores the sharing information along with the owner block, and it also assigns the task of keeping cache coherence and ensuring ordered accesses for every memory block to the tile that stores that block. As shown in Figure 3(b)*DiCo-CMP* sends the request directly to the owner tile (*1 GetS*), instead of to the home tile. In this way, data can be provided by the owner tile (*2 Data*), requiring just two hops to solve the cache miss.

Therefore, direct coherence requires a re-distribution of the roles involved in solving a cache miss. Next, we describe the tasks performed in cache coherence protocols and the component responsible for each task in both directory and direct coherence protocols, which are illustrated in Figure 4:

- *Order requests*: Cache coherence maintenance requires to serialize the requests issued by different cores to the same block. In snooping-based cache coherence protocols, the requests are ordered by the shared interconnection network. However, since tiled CMP architectures implement an unordered network, this serialization of the requests must be carried out by another component. Directory protocols assign this task to the home tile of each memory block. On the other hand, this task is performed by the owner tile in direct coherence protocols.

- *Keep coherence information*: Coherence information is used to track blocks stored in private caches. In protocols that include the *O* state, like MOESI protocols, coherence information also identifies the owner tile. In particular, *sharing information* is used to invalidate all cached blocks on write misses, while *owner information* is used to know

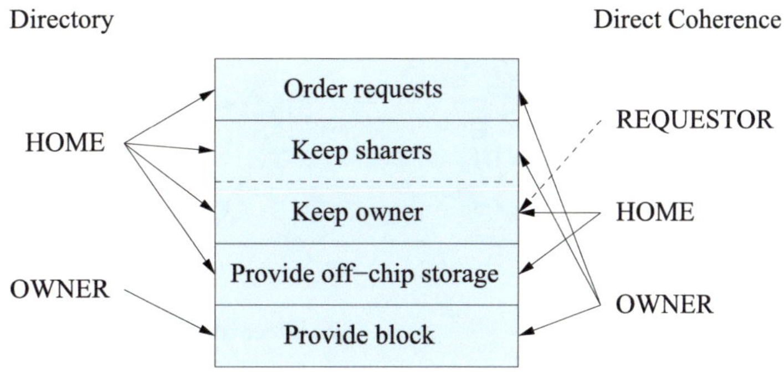

Fig. 4. Tasks performed in cache coherence protocols.

the identity of the provider of the block on every miss. Directory protocols store coherence information at the home tile, where cache coherence is maintained. Instead, direct coherence requires that sharing information be stored in the owner tile for keeping coherence there, while owner information is stored in two different components. First, the requesting cores need to know the owner tile to send the requests to it. Processors can easily keep the identity of the owner tile, e.g., by recording the last core that invalidated their copy. However, this information can become stale and, therefore, it is only used for avoiding indirection (dashed arrow in Figure 4). Then, the responsible for tracking the up-to-date identity of the owner tile is the home tile which must be notified on every ownership change.

- *Provide the data block*: If the valid copy of the block resides on chip, data is always provided by the owner tile, since it always holds a valid copy. The owner of a block is either a tile holding the block in the exclusive or the modified state, the last core that wrote the block when there are multiple sharers, or the the L2 cache bank within the home tile in case of an eviction of the owner block from some L1 cache.
- *Provide off-chip storage*: When the valid copy of a requested block is not stored on chip, an off-chip access is required to obtain the block. Both in directory and direct coherence protocols the home tile is responsible for detecting that the owner copy of the block is not stored on chip. It is also responsible for sending the off-chip request and receiving the data block.

Another example of the advantages of direct coherence is shown in Figure 5. This diagram represents an upgrade that takes place in a tile whose L1 cache holds the block in the owned state, which happens frequently in common applications (e.g., for the producer-consumer pattern). In a directory protocol, upgrades are solved by sending the request to the home tile (*1 Upgr*), which replies with the number of acknowledgements that must be received before the block can be modified (*2 Ack*), and sends invalidation messages to all sharers (*2 Inv*). Sharers confirm their invalidation to the requester (*3 Ack*). Once all the acknowledgements have been received by the requester, the block can be modified and the directory is unblocked (*4 Unbl*). In contrast, in *DiCo-CMP* only invalidation messages (*1 Inv*) and acknowledgements (*2 Ack*) are required because the directory information is stored along with the data block, thereby solving the miss with just two hops in the critical path.
Additionally, by keeping together the owner block and the directory information, control messages between them are not necessary, thus saving some network traffic (two messages in Fig-

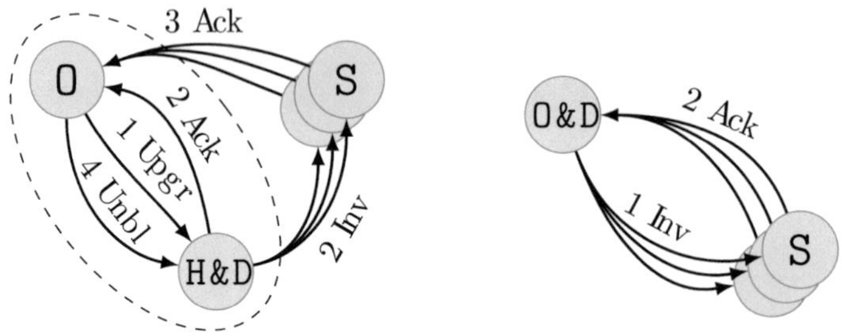

(a) Directory protocols. (b) Direct coherence protocols.

Fig. 5. How upgrades are solved in directory and direct coherence protocols. O=Owner; H=Home; D=Directory; S=Sharers.

ure 3 and three in Figure 5). Moreover, this allows the O&D node to solve cache misses without using transient states, thus reducing the number of states and making the implementation simpler than a directory protocol. Finally, the elimination of transient states at the directory reduces waiting time for the subsequent requests and, therefore, average miss latency.

4.2 Changes to the structure of the tiles of a CMP

The new distribution of roles that characterizes direct coherence protocols requires some modifications in the structure of the tiles that build the CMP. Firstly, the identity of the sharers for every block is stored in the corresponding owner tile instead of the home one to allow caches to keep coherence for the memory blocks that they hold in the owned state. Therefore, *DiCo-CMP* extends the tags' part of the L1 caches with a sharing code field, e.g., a full-map (L2 caches already include this field in directory protocols). In contrast, *DiCo-CMP* does not need to store a directory structure at the home tile, as happens in directory protocols.
Additionally, *DiCo-CMP* adds two extra hardware structures that are used to record the identity of the owner tile of the memory blocks stored on chip:

- *L1 coherence cache* (L1C$): The pointers stored in this structure are used by the requesting core to avoid indirection by directly sending local requests to the corresponding owner tile. Therefore, this structure is located close to each processor's core. Although *DiCo-CMP* can update this information in several ways, we consider in this chapter the *Base* policy presented in Ros et al. (2008a), in which this information is updated by using the coherence messages sent by the protocol, i.e., invalidation and data messages.
- *L2 coherence cache* (L2C$): Since the owner tile can change on write misses, this structure must track the owner tile for each block allocated in any L1 cache. This structure replaces the directory structure required by directory protocols and it is accessed each time a request fails to locate the owner tile. This information must be updated whenever the owner tile changes through control messages. These messages must be processed by the L2C$ in the very same order in which they were generated in order to avoid any incoherence when storing the identity of the owner tile, as described later in Section 4.3.3.

Figure 6 shows a tile design for directory protocols and for direct coherence protocols. A comparison among the extra storage and structures required by all the protocols evaluated in this chapter can be found in Section 7.4.

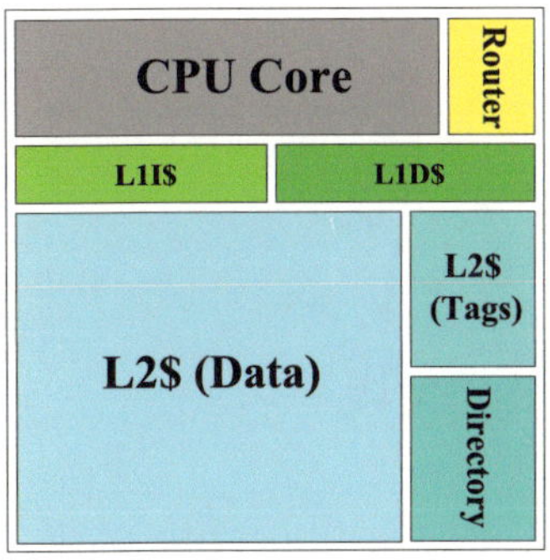

(a) Organization of a tile for directory protocols.

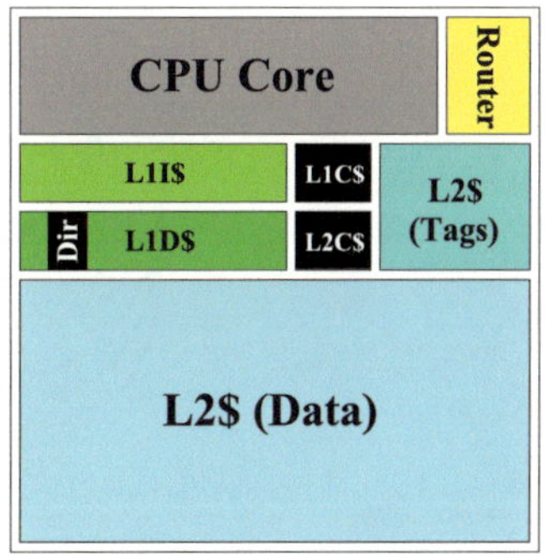

(b) Organization of a tile for direct coherence protocols.

Fig. 6. Modifications to the structure of a tile required by direct coherence protocols.

4.3 Description of the cache coherence protocol

4.3.1 Requesting processor

When a processor issues a request that misses in its private L1 cache, it sends the request directly to the owner tile in order to avoid indirection. The identity of the potential owner tile is obtained from the L1C$, which is accessed at the time that the cache miss in detected. If there is a hit in the L1C$, the request is sent to the obtained owner tile. Otherwise, the request is sent to the home tile, where the L2C$ will be accessed to get the identity of the current owner tile.

4.3.2 Request received by a tile that is not the owner

When a request is received by a tile that is not the current owner of the block, it simply re-sends the request. If the tile is not the home one, the request is re-sent to it. Otherwise, if the request is received by the home tile and there is a hit in the L2C$, the request is sent to the current owner tile. In absence of race conditions the request will reach the owner tile. Finally, if there is a miss in the L2C$ and the home tile is not the owner of the block, the request is solved by providing the block from main memory, where, in this case, a fresh copy of the block resides. This is because the L2C$ always keeps an entry for the blocks stored in the private L1 caches. If the owner copy of the block is not present in either any L1 cache or in the L2 cache, it resides off-chip. After the off-chip access, the block is allocated in the requesting L1 cache, which gets the ownership of the block, but not in the L2 cache (as occurs in the other protocols evaluated), since we assume that the L1 and the L2 cache are non-inclusive. In addition, it is necessary to allocate a new entry in the L2C$ pointing to the current L1 owner tile.

4.3.3 Request received by the owner tile

Every time a request reaches the owner tile, it is necessary to check whether this tile is currently processing a request from a different processor for the same block (a previous write waiting for acknowledgements). In this case, the block is in a busy or transient state, and the request must wait until all the acknowledgements are received.

If the block is not in a transient state, the miss can be immediately solved. If the owner is the L2 cache at the home tile all requests (reads and writes) are solved by deallocating the block from the L2 cache and allocating it in the private L1 cache of the requester. Again, the identity of the new owner tile must be stored in the L2C$.

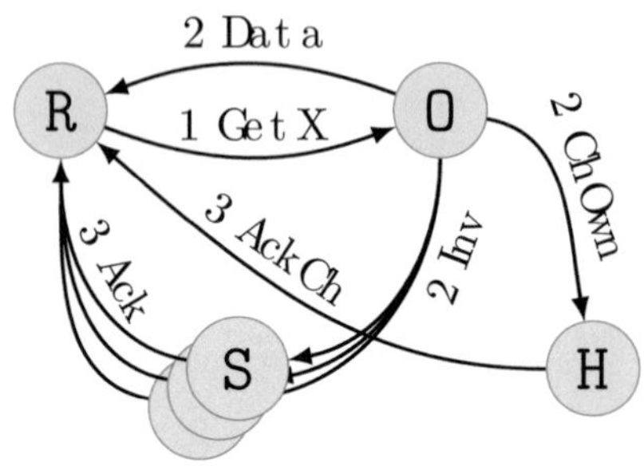

Fig. 7. Example of ownership change upon write misses. R=Requester; O=Owner; S=Sharers; H=Home.

When the owner is an L1 cache, read misses are completed by sending a copy of the block to the requester and adding it to the sharing code field kept along with the block. For write misses, the owner tile sends invalidation messages to all the tiles that hold a copy of the block in their L1 caches and, then, it sends the data block to the requester. Acknowledgement messages are collected at the requesting core. As previously shown in Figure 5, write misses (upgrade) that take place in the owner tile just need to send invalidations and receive acknowledgements (two hops in the critical path).

Finally, since the L2C$ must store up-to-date information regarding the owner tile, every time that this tile changes, the old owner tile also sends a control message to the L2C$ indicating the identity of the new owner tile. These messages must be processed by the L2C$ in the very same order in which they were generated. Otherwise, the L2C$ could fail to store the identity of the current owner tile. Fortunately, there are several approaches to ensure this order. In the implementation evaluated in this chapter, once the L2C$ processes the message reporting an ownership change from the old owner tile, it sends a confirmation response to the new one. Until this confirmation message is received by the new owner tile, it could access the data block (if already received), but cannot give the ownership to another tile. Since these two control messages are not in the critical path of the cache miss, they do not introduce extra latency.

As an example, Figure 7 illustrates a write miss for a shared block. It assumes that the requester has valid and correct information about the identity of current owner tile in the L1C$ and, therefore, it directly sends the request to the owner tile (*1 GetX*). Then the owner tile must perform the following tasks. First, it sends the data block to the requester (*2 Data*). Second, it sends invalidation messages to all the sharers (*2 Inv*), and it also invalidates its own copy. The information about the sharers is obtained from the sharing code stored along with every owner block. Third, it sends the message informing about the ownership change to the home tile (*2 ChOwn*). All tiles that receive an invalidation message respond with an acknowledgement message to the requester once they have invalidated their local copies (*3 Ack*). When the data and all the acknowledgements arrive to the requesting processor the write operation can be performed. However, if another write request arrives to the tile that previously suffered the miss, it cannot be solved until the acknowledgement to the ownership change issued by the home tile (*3 AckCh*) is received.

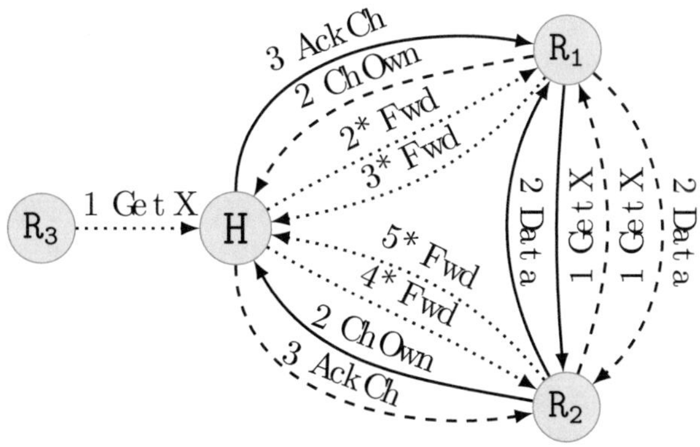

Fig. 8. Example of a starvation scenario in direct coherence protocols. R_x=Requester; H=Home. Continuous arrows represent cache misses that take place in R_1, dashed arrows represent misses in R_2 and dotted arrows represent misses in R_3.

4.3.4 Replacements

In our particular implementation, when a block with the ownership property is evicted from an L1 cache, it must be allocated at the L2 cache along with the up-to-date directory information. Differently from *Directory-CMP* and *Hammer-CMP* protocols and similarly to *Token-CMP*, replacements are performed by sending the writeback message directly to the home tile (instead of requiring three-phase replacements). This operation can be easily performed in direct coherence protocols because the tile where these blocks are stored is the responsible for keeping cache coherence and, as consequence, no complex race conditions can appear. When the writeback message reaches the home tile, the L2C$ deallocates its entry for this block because the owner tile is now the home one. On the other hand, replacements for blocks in shared state are performed transparently, i.e., no coherence actions are needed.

Finally, no coherence actions must be performed in case of an L1C$ replacement. However, when an L2C$ entry is evicted, the protocol should ask the owner tile to invalidate all the copies from the private L1 caches. Luckily, as happens to the directory cache in directory protocols, an L2C$ with the same number of entries and associativity than the L1 cache is enough to completely remove this kind of replacements (Ros et al., 2008b).

4.4 Preventing starvation

Directory protocols avoid starvation by enqueuing requests in FIFO order at the directory buffers. Differently in *DiCo-CMP*, write misses can change the tile that keeps coherence for a particular block and, therefore, some requests can take some extra time until this tile is finally found. If a memory block is repeatedly written by several processors, a request could take some time to find the owner tile ready to process it, even when it is sent by the home tile. Hence, some processors could be solving their requests while other requests are starved. Figure 8 shows an example of a scenario in which starvation appears. R_1 and R_2 tiles are issuing write requests repeatedly and, therefore, the owner tile is continuously moving from R_1 to R_2 and vice versa. On every change of owner the home tile is notified, and the requesting core is acknowledged. However, at the same time, the home tile is trying to re-send the request issued by R_3 tile to the owner one, but the request is always returned to the home tile because the write request issued by R_1 or R_2 arrives before to the owner tile.

DiCo-CMP detects and avoids starvation by using a simple mechanism. In particular, each time that a request must be re-sent to the L2C$ in the home tile, a counter into the request message is increased. The request is considered starved when this counter reaches a certain value (e.g, three accesses to the L2C$ for the evaluation carried out in this chapter). When the L2C$ detects a starved request, it re-sends the request to the owner tile, but it records the address of the block. If the starved request reaches the current owner tile, the miss is solved, and the home tile is notified, ending the starvation situation. If the starved request does not reach the owner tile is because the ownership property is moving from a tile to another one. In this case, when the message informing about the change of the ownership arrives to the home tile, it detects that the block is suffering from starvation, and the acknowledgement message required on every ownership change is not sent. This ensures that the owner tile does not change until the starved request can complete.

5. Reducing area requirements in DiCo-CMP

DiCo-CMP needs two structures that keep the identity of the tile where the owner copy of the block resides, the L1C$ and the L2C$. These two structures do not compromise scalability because they have a small number of entries and each one stores a tag and a pointer to the owner tile ($log_2 n$ bits, where n is the number of cores). The L2C$ is needed to solve cache misses in *DiCo-CMP*, since it ensures that the tile that keeps coherence for each block can always be found. On the other hand, the L1C$ is required to avoid indirection in cache misses and, therefore, it is essential to obtain good performance. Moreover, the L2C$ allows read misses to be solved by sending only one forwarding request to the owner tile, since it stores the identity of the owner tile, which significantly reduces network traffic when compared to broadcast-based protocols.

Apart from these structures, *DiCo-CMP* also adds a full-map sharing code to each data cache entry. The memory overhead introduced by this sharing code could become prohibitive in many-core CMPs. In this section, we describe some alternatives that differ in the sharing code scheme added to each entry of the data caches. Since these alternatives always include the L1C$ and the L2C$, they have area requirements of at least $O(log_2 n)$. The particular compressed sharing code employed impacts on the number of invalidations sent in write misses. Next, we comment on the different implementations of direct coherence protocols that we have evaluated.

DiCo-FM is the *DiCo-CMP* protocol described in Ros et al. (2008a) and, therefore, it adds a full-map sharing code to each data cache. Particularly, we evaluate the *Base* policy presented in that work, which obtains good performance with low traffic overhead.

DiCo-CV-K reduces the size of the sharing code field by using a *coarse vector* (Gupta et al., 1990) instead of a full-map sharing code. In a coarse vector, each bit represents a group of K tiles, instead of just one. A bit is set when at least one of the tiles in the group holds the block in its private cache. Therefore, even when just one of the tiles in the group requested a particular block, all tiles belonging to that group will receive an invalidation message before the block can be written. Particularly, we study a configuration that uses a coarse vector sharing code with $K = 2$. In this case, 8 bits are needed for a 16-core configuration. Although this sharing code reduces the memory required by the protocol, its size still increases linearly with the number of cores.

DiCo-LP-P employs a *limited pointers* sharing code (Chaiken et al., 1991). In this scheme, each entry has a limited number of pointers for the first P sharers of the block. Actually, since *DiCo-CMP* always stores the information about the owner tile in the L2C$, the first pointer

Protocol	Sharing Code	Bits L1 and L2	Bits L1C$ and L2C$	Order
DiCo-FM	Full-map	n	$log_2 n$	$O(n)$
DiCo-CV-K	Coarse vector	$\frac{n}{K}$	$log_2 n$	$O(n)$
DiCo-LP-P	Limited pointers	$1 + P \times (1 + log_2 n)$	$log_2 n$	$O(log_2 n)$
DiCo-BT	Binary Tree	$\lceil log_2(1 + log_2 n) \rceil$	$log_2 n$	$O(log_2 n)$
DiCo-NoSC	None	0	$log_2 n$	$O(log_2 n)$

Table 2. Bits required for storing coherence information.

is employed to store the identity of the second sharer of the block. When the sharing degree of a block is greater than $P + 1$, write misses are solved by broadcasting invalidations to all tiles. Therefore, apart from the pointers, it is necessary an extra bit indicating the overflow situation. However, this situation is not very frequent since the sharing degree of the applications is usually low (Culler et al., 1999). In particular, we evaluate this protocol with a P value of 1. Under this assumption, the number of bits needed to store the sharing information considering 16 cores is 5.

DiCo-BT uses a sharing code based on a *binary tree* (Acacio et al., 2001). In this approach, tiles are recursively grouped into clusters of two elements, thus leading to a binary tree with the tiles located at the leaves. The information stored in the sharing code is the smallest cluster that covers all the sharers. Since this scheme assumes that for each block the binary tree is computed from a particular leave (the one representing the home tile), it is only necessary to store the number of the level in the tree, i.e., 3 bits for a 16-core configuration.

Finally, *DiCo-NoSC* (no sharing code) does not maintain any coherence information along with the owner block. In this way, this protocol does not need to modify the structure of data caches to add any field. This lack of information implies broadcasting invalidation messages to all tiles upon write misses, although this is only necessary for blocks in shared state because the owner tile is always known in *DiCo-CMP*. This scheme incurs in more network traffic compared to the previous ones. However, it falls into less traffic than *Hammer-CMP* and *Token-CMP*. This is because *Hammer-CMP* requires broadcasting requests on every cache miss, and what is more expensive in a network with multicast support, every tile that receives the request answers with a control message. On the other hand, although *Token-CMP* avoids these response messages, it also relies on broadcasting requests for all cache misses.

Table 2 shows the number of bits required for storing coherence information in each implementation, both for the coherence caches (L1C$ and L2C$) and for the data caches (L1 and L2). Other compressed sharing codes, like *tristate* (Agarwal et al., 1988), *gray-tristate* (Mukherjee & Hill, 1994) or *binary tree with subtrees* (Acacio et al., 2001) could also be implemented instead of those shown in this table. However, for a 16-core tiled CMP, they incur in similar overhead than *DiCo-CV-2* (8, 8 and 7 bits respectively), which does not significantly increases network traffic, as we will see in Section 7.3. For a greater number of cores, these compressed sharing codes could be more appropriate.

6. Simulation environment

We perform the evaluation using the full-system simulator Virtutech Simics (Magnusson et al., 2002) extended with Multifacet GEMS 1.3 (Martin et al., 2005), that provides a detailed memory system timing model. Since the network modeled by GEMS 1.3 is not very precise, we have extended it with SICOSYS (Puente et al., 2002), a detailed interconnection network sim-

GEMS Parameters		SICOSYS Parameters	
Processor frequency	3 GHz	Network frequency	1.5 GHz
Cache hierarchy	Non-inclusive	Topology	4x4 Mesh
Cache block size	64 bytes	Switching technique	Wormhole, Multicast
Split L1 I & D caches	128KB, 4 ways, 3 hit cycles	Routing technique	Deterministic X-Y
Shared unified L2 cache	1MB/tile, 8 ways, 6 hit cycles	Data message size	4 flits
		Control message size	1 flit
L1C$ & L2C$	512 sets, 4 ways, 2 hit cycles	Routing time	2 cycles
Directory cache	512 sets, 4 ways, 2 hit cycles	Link latency (one hop)	2 cycles
Memory access time	300 cycles	Link bandwidth	1 flit/cycle

Table 3. System parameters.

ulator. We simulate CMP systems with 16 tiles. Table 3 shows the values of the main parameters used for the evaluation, where cache latencies have been calculated using the CACTI 5.3 tool (Thoziyoor et al., 2008) for 45nm technology. We also have used CACTI to measure the area of the different structures needed in each one of the evaluated protocols. In this study, we assume that the length of the physical address is 40 bits, like in the SUN UltraSPARC-III architecture (Horel & Lauterbach, 1999).

The ten applications used in our simulations cover a variety of computation and communication patterns. *Barnes* (8192 bodies, 4 time steps), *FFT* (64K points), *Ocean* (130x130 ocean), *Radix* (512K keys, 1024 radix), *Raytrace* (teapot), *Volrend* (head) and *Water-Nsq* (512 molecules, 4 time steps) are scientific applications from the SPLASH-2 benchmark suite (Woo et al., 1995). *Unstructured* (Mesh.2K, 5 time steps) is a computational fluid dynamics application. *MPGdec* (525_tens_040.m2v) and *MPGenc* (output of *MPGdec*), are multimedia applications from the APLBench suite (Li et al., 2005). We account for the variability in multithreaded workloads by doing multiple simulation runs for each benchmark in each configuration and injecting random perturbations in memory systems timing for each run.

7. Evaluation results

In this section, we compare the different alternatives described in Section 5 with all the base protocols described in this chapter. First, we show to what extent direct coherence protocols avoid indirection, and its impact on execution time. Then, we analyze the network traffic generated by each protocol, and the area required by them to store the coherence information. Finally, we summarize these results by showing the trade-off in terms of execution time, network traffic and area requirements of the protocols evaluated.

7.1 Impact on indirection

In general, *DiCo-CMP* reduces the average number of hops needed to solve a cache miss by avoiding the indirection introduced by the access to the home tile, when compared to traditional protocols. However, in *DiCo-CMP*, some misses can increase the number of hops compared to a directory protocol due to owner mis-predictions. In order to study how *DiCo-CMP* impacts on the number of hops needed to solve cache misses, we classify each miss in one of the following categories:

- *2-hop misses*: Misses belonging to this category does not suffer from indirection since the number of hops in the critical path of the miss is two. In *Hammer-CMP*, misses fall into this category when the home tile of the requested block can provide the copy of

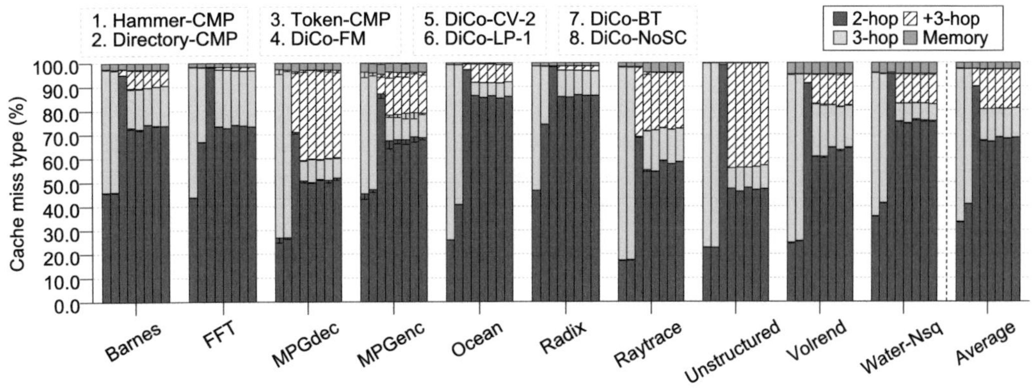

Fig. 9. How each miss type is solved for the applications evaluated in this chapter.

the block and it is not necessary to invalidate blocks from other tiles. In directory protocols, misses fall into this category in the same cases as *Hammer-CMP*, but also when the miss takes place in the home tile. *Token-CMP* solves all misses that do not require persistent requests in two hops. Finally, *DiCo-CMP* solves cache misses using two hops either when the request is directly sent to the current owner tile and invalidations are not required or when the miss takes place either in the home tile or in the owner tile (upgrades).

In all protocols, when the miss takes place in the home tile and this tile holds the owner block in the L2 cache, the miss is solved without generating network traffic (0-hop miss). These misses are also included in this category because they do not introduce indirection.

- *3-hop misses*: A miss belongs to this category when three hops in the critical path are necessary to solve it. This category represents the misses suffering from indirection in traditional protocols. In contrast, 3-hop misses never take place in *Token-CMP*.
- *+3-hop misses*: We include in this category misses that need more than three hops in the critical path to be solved. This type of misses only happens in *DiCo-CMP*, when the identity of the owner tile is mis-predicted, or in *Token-CMP*, when persistent requests are required to solve the miss. The traditional protocols evaluated in this chapter never require more than three hops to solve cache misses since the acknowledgements to invalidation messages are collected by the requesting core.
- *Memory misses*: Misses that require off-chip accesses since the owner block is not stored on chip fall into this category.

Figure 9 shows the percentage of cache misses that fall into each category. As commented in Section 2, in tiled CMP architectures it is not very frequent that the requester tile be the home one for the requested block because the distribution of blocks among tiles is performed in a round-robin fashion. Therefore, traditional protocols have a lot of cache misses with indirection. However, the fact that sometimes a coherent copy of the block is found in the L2 cache bank of the home tile, decreases the number of misses with indirection. In this way, the first and second bars in Figure 9 shows that most applications have an important fraction of misses suffering from indirection when traditional protocols are considered, like *Barnes*, *MPGdec*,

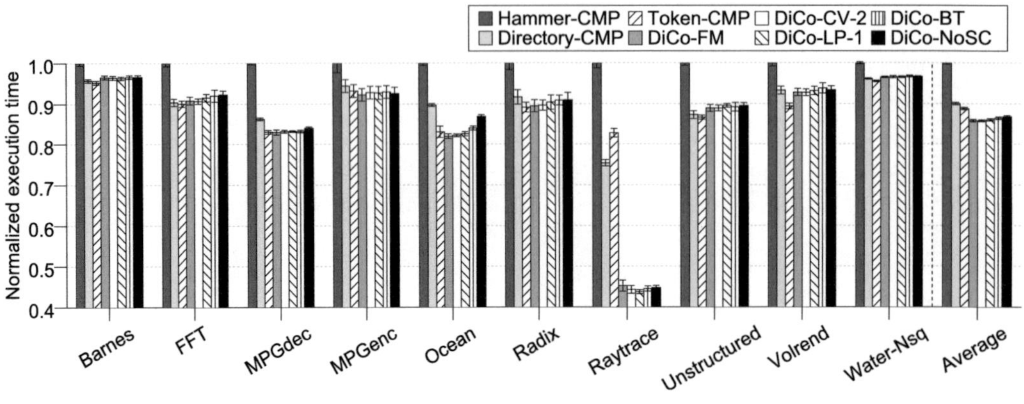

Fig. 10. Normalized execution times.

MPGenc, *Ocean*, *Raytrace*, *Unstructured*, *Volrend* and *Water-Nsq*, while other applications, like *FFT* and *Radix*, have most of the misses solved in two hops when a directory protocol is considered. *Hammer-CMP* has more cache misses suffering from indirection because sometimes it has to broadcast forwarding messages due to the lack of information about the identity of the owner tile. Obviously, *DiCo-CMP* will have more impact for the applications that suffer more indirection, although this impact will also depend on the cache miss rate of each application. We also can observe that *Token-CMP* solves most of the misses (90%) needing just two hops (see third bar).

As shown in the fourth bar of Figure 9, *DiCo-FM* increases the percentage of cache misses without indirection compared to both *Hammer-CMP* and *Directory-CMP* (from 34% and 41%, respectively, to 67% on average). On the other hand, *DiCo-FM* solves 17% of cache misses needing more than three hops. This fact is due to owner mis-predictions that can arise for two reasons: (1) staled owner information was found in the L1C$ or (2) the owner tile is changing or busy due to race conditions and the request is sent back to the home tile. Although, the first case can be removed with a precise hints mechanism, as discussed in (Ros et al., 2008a), in this chapter we do not use this mechanism in order to save network traffic.

The remaining bars show the different implementations of direct coherence aimed at reducing the area requirements entailed by this protocol. We can see that, the indirection avoidance is similar. However, the more compressed is the sharing code, the more invalidations are sent, which slightly increases the number of misses without indirection due to a better prediction of owner tiles.

7.2 Impact on execution time

Figure 10 plots the average execution times for the applications evaluated in this chapter normalized with respect to *Hammer-CMP*. Compared to *Hammer-CMP*, *Directory-CMP* improves performance for all applications as a consequence of an important reduction in terms of both misses suffering from indirection and network traffic (as we will see in next section). As discussed in the previous section, the longer latency cache misses are suffered in *Hammer-CMP*. This is because on each cache miss the requesting core must wait for all the acknowledgement messages before the miss can be solved. On the contrary, in *Directory-CMP* only write misses must wait for acknowledgements.

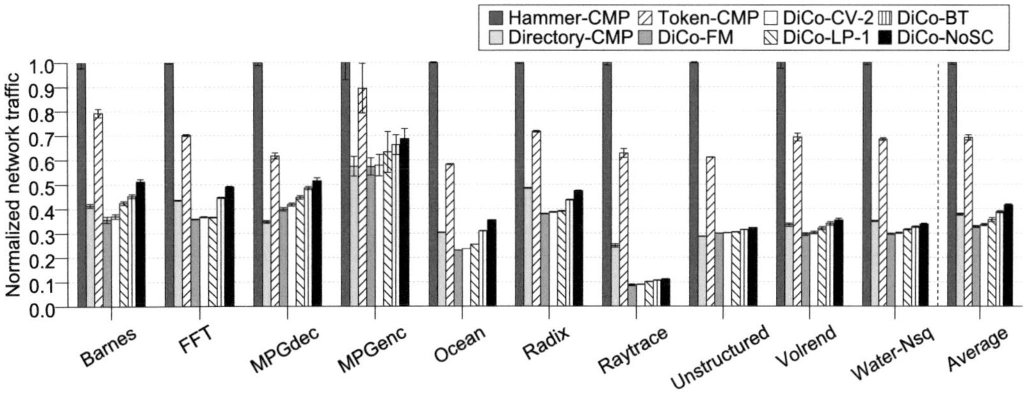

Fig. 11. Normalized network traffic.

On the other hand, indirection-aware protocols reduce average execution time when compared to traditional protocols. Particularly, *Token-CMP* obtains average improvements of 11% compared to *Hammer-CMP* and 1% compared to *Directory-CMP*. *DiCo-FM* improves the execution time by 14%, 5% and 4% compared to *Hammer-CMP*, *Directory-CMP* and *Token-CMP*, respectively. On the other hand, when *DiCo-CMP* employs compressed sharing codes, the execution time slightly increases. Although the protocol incurs in more network traffic, it also increases the accuracy of owner predictions. Therefore, it remains close to *DiCo-FM*. For *DiCo-CV-2* and *DiCo-LP-1* the increase in execution time is negligible, while *DiCo-BT* and *DiCo-NoSC* increase execution time by 1%.

7.3 Impact on network traffic

Figure 11 compares the network traffic generated by the protocols discussed previously. Each bar plots the number of bytes transmitted through the interconnection network normalized with respect to *Hammer-CMP*.

As expected, *Hammer-CMP* introduces much more network traffic than the other protocols due to the lack of coherence information, which implies broadcasting requests to all cores and receiving the corresponding acknowledgements. *Directory-CMP* reduces considerably traffic by adding a full-map sharing code that filters unnecessary invalidations. *Token-CMP* generates more network traffic than *Directory-CMP*, because it relies on broadcasting requests, and less than *Hammer-CMP*, because it does not need to receive acknowledgements from tiles without tokens (i.e., the tiles that do not share the block). Finally, *DiCo-FM* decreases traffic requirements compared to *Directory-CMP* (by 13%) due to the elimination of control messages between the owner and the home tile, as discussed in Section 4.

In general, we can see that compressed sharing codes increase network traffic compared to a full-map sharing code. However, the increase in traffic is admissible. Particularly, the most scalable alternatives, *DiCo-LP-1*, *DiCo-BT* and *DiCo-NoSC*, increase network traffic by 8%, 16% and 21% compared to *DiCo-FM*, respectively. *DiCo-BT* has similar traffic requirements than *Directory-CMP*, and *DiCo-NoSC*, which does not have any sharing code, generates an acceptable amount of network traffic (40% less traffic than *Token-CMP* and 58% less traffic than *Hammer-CMP*).

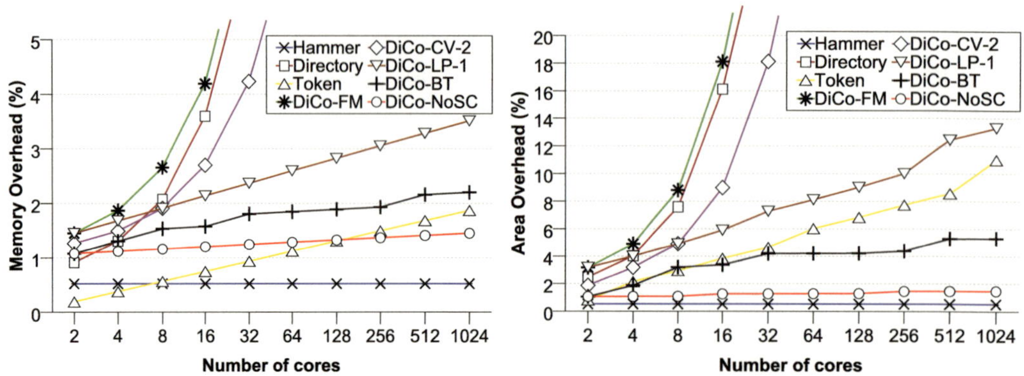

(a) Overhead in terms of bits. (b) Overhead in terms of area (mm^2).

Fig. 12. Overhead introduced by the cache coherence protocols.

7.4 Impact on area overhead

Finally, we compare the memory overhead introduced by the coherence information for the cache coherence protocols evaluated in this chapter. Although some protocols can entail extra overhead as a consequence of the additional mechanisms that they demand (e.g., timeouts for reissuing requests or large tables for keeping active persistent requests in *Token-CMP*), we only consider the amount of memory needed to keep coherence information. Obviously, the extra tags required to store this information (e.g., for the L1C$ and L2C$) are also considered in this study. Figure 12 shows the storage overhead introduced by these protocols in terms of both number of bits and estimated area (calculated with the CACTI tool). The overhead is plotted for varying number of cores from 2 to 1024.

Although the original *Hammer* protocol does not require any coherence information, our optimized version for CMPs adds a new structure to the home tile. This structure is a 512-set 4-way cache that contains a copy of the tags for blocks stored in the L1 caches but not in the L2 cache. However, this structure introduces a slight overhead which keeps constant with the number of cores.

Directory-CMP stores the directory information either in the L2 tags, when the L2 cache holds a copy of the block, or in a distributed directory cache, when the block is stored in any of the L1 caches but not in the L2 cache. Since the information is stored using a full-map sharing code, the number of required bits is n, and consequently the width of each directory entry grows linearly with the number of cores.

Token-CMP keeps the token count for any block stored both in the L1 and L2 caches. This information only requires $\lceil log_2(n+1) \rceil$ bits for both the owner-token bit and the non-owner token count. These additional bits are stored in the tags' part of both cache levels. In this way, *Token-CMP* has acceptable scalability in terms of area.

DiCo-FM stores directory information along with each owner block held in the L1 and L2 caches. Therefore, a full-map sharing code is added to the tags' part of each cache entry. Moreover, it uses two structures that store the identity of the owner tile, the L1C$ and the L2C$. Each entry in these structures contains a tag and an owner field, which requires $log_2 n$ bits. Therefore, this is the protocol that more area overhead entails.

We propose to reduce this overhead by introducing compressed sharing codes in *DiCo-CMP*. *DiCo-CV-2* saves storage compared to *DiCo-FM* but it is still non-scalable. In contrast, *DiCo-*

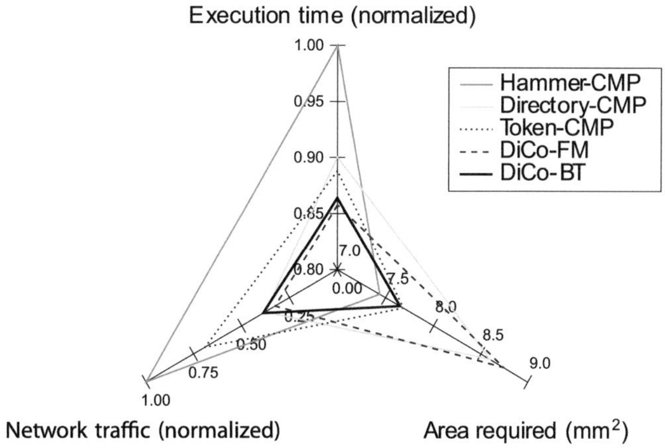

Fig. 13. Trade-off of the three main design goals.

LP-1, which only adds a pointer for the second sharer of the block (the first one is given by the L2C$) has better scalability –$O(log_2 n)$–. *DiCo-BT* reduces even more the area requirements compared to *DiCo-LP-1*, and it scales better than *Token-CMP*. Finally, *DiCo-NoSC*, which does not require to modify data caches to add coherence information, is the implementation of DiCo with less overhead (although it still has order $O(log_2 n)$ due to the need of the coherence caches), at the cost of increasing network traffic. Finally, we can see that a small overhead in the number of required bits results in a significant overhead when the area of the structures is considered.

7.5 Trade-off analysis

Figure 13 shows the trade-off among execution time, network traffic, and area requirements for the base protocols evaluated in this chapter, *DiCo-FM*, and *DiCo-BT*, which constitutes a good alternative when the three metrics evaluated in this chapter are considered. In this way, this graph summarizes the evaluation carried out in this chapter. Results in terms of execution time and network traffic represent the average of all applications, normalized with respect to *Hammer-CMP*. Results in terms of area requirements correspond to the area in mm^2 of each protocol considering both the data caches and the extra structures required to keep the coherence information.

We can see that, in general, the base protocols aimed to be used with tiled CMPs do not have a good trade-off. *Hammer-CMP* has the highest traffic levels and execution times, but also the lowest area requirements ($7.4mm^2$). In contrast, *Directory-CMP*, which reduces both execution time and network traffic compared to *Hammer-CMP* (by 10% and 61%, respectively), at the cost of increasing area requirements ($8.59mm^2$ for a 16-tiled CMP, and $O(n)$). Although *Token-CMP* has acceptable area requirements ($7.68mm^2$ for a 16-tiled CMP) it is limited by traffic, requiring twice the traffic required by *Directory-CMP*. Finally, *DiCo-FM*, that reduces both execution time and traffic requirements when compared to *Token-CMP* (by 4% and 47%, respectively), is the one with the highest area requirements ($8.74mm^2$ for a 16-tiled CMP, and $O(n)$).

However, the use of different compressed sharing codes for *DiCo-CMP* can lead to a good compromise between network traffic and area requirements, and still guaranteeing low average execution time. In general, *DiCo-LP-1*, *DiCo-BT* and *DiCo-NoSC* are very close to an ideal protocol with the best characteristics of the base protocols, for the sake of clarity, we only show the trade-off for *DiCo-BT*. *DiCo-BT* requires less area (7.65mm^2 for a 16-tiled CMP) than all evaluated protocols except *Hammer-CMP*, it also generates similar network traffic than *Directory-CMP* and, finally, it has a low average execution time (increasing just by 1% the best approach, *DiCo-FM*).

8. Related work

In the shared-memory multiprocessors domain, Acacio et al. propose to avoid the indirection for cache-to-cache transfer misses (Acacio et al., 2002a) and upgrade misses (Acacio et al., 2002b) separately by predicting the current holders of every cache block. Predictions must be verified by the corresponding directory controller, thus increasing the complexity of the protocol on mis-predictions. Hossain et al. (2008) propose different optimizations for each sharing pattern considering a chip multiprocessor architecture. Particularly, they accelerate the producer-consumer pattern by converting 3-hop read misses into 2-hop read misses. Again, communication between the cache providing the data block and the directory is necessary, thus introducing more complexity in the protocol. In contrast, direct coherence is applicable to all types of misses (reads, writes and upgrades) and just the identity of the owner tile is predicted. Moreover, the fact that the directory information is stored along with the owner of the block simplifies the protocol. Finally, differently from the techniques proposed by Acacio et al., direct coherence avoids predicting the current holders of a block by storing the up-to-date directory information in the owner tile.

Also in the context of shared-memory multiprocessors, Cheng et al. (2007) have proposed converting 3-hop read misses into 2-hop read misses for memory blocks that exhibit the producer-consumer sharing pattern by using extra hardware to detect when a block is being accessed according to this pattern. In contrast, direct coherence obtains 2-hop misses for read, write and upgrade misses without taking into account sharing patterns.

Jerger et al. (2008) propose Virtual Tree Coherence (VTC). This mechanism uses coarse-grain coherence tracking (Cantin et al., 2006) and the sharers of a memory region are connected by means of a virtual tree. Since the root of the virtual tree serves as the ordering point in place of the home tile, and the root tile is one of the sharers of the region, the indirection can be avoided for some misses. Contrarily, direct coherence protocols keep the coherence information at block granularity and the ordering point always has the valid copy of the block, which leads to less network traffic and lower levels of indirection.

Huh et al. (2005) propose to allow replication in a NUCA cache to reduce the access time to a shared multibanked cache. More recently, Beckmann et al. (2006) present ASR that replicates cache blocks only when it is estimated that the benefits of replication (lower L2 hit latency) exceeds its costs (more L2 misses). In contrast, direct coherence reduces miss latencies by avoiding the access to the L2 cache when it is not necessary, and no replication is performed. It could be also used in conjunction with techniques that try to make the best use of the limited on-chip cache storage.

Martin et al. (2000) present a technique that allows snooping-based protocols to utilize unordered networks by adding logical timing to coherence requests and reordering them on destiny to establish a total order. Likewise, Agarwal et al. (2009) propose In-Network Snoop Ordering (INSO) to allow snooping over unordered networks. Since direct coherence protocols do not rely on broadcasting requests, they generate less traffic and, therefore, less power consumption when compared to snooping-based protocols.

Martin et al. (2003) propose to use destination-set prediction to reduce the bandwidth required by a snoopy protocol. Differently from DiCo-CMP, this proposal is based on a totally-ordered interconnect (a crossbar switch), which does not scale with the number of nodes. Destination-set prediction is also used by Token-M in shared-memory multiprocessors with unordered networks (Martin, 2003). However, on mis-predictions, requests are solved by resorting on broadcasting after a time-out period. Differently, in direct coherence protocols mis-predictions are re-sent immediately to the owner cache, thus reducing both latency and network traffic.

9. Conclusions

Tiled CMP architectures have recently emerged as a scalable alternative to current small-scale CMP designs, and will be probably the architecture of choice for future many-core CMPs. On the other hand, although a great deal of attention was devoted to scalable cache coherence protocols in the last decades in the context of shared-memory multiprocessors, the technological parameters and constraints entailed by CMPs demand new solutions to the cache coherence problem. New cache coherence protocols, like *Token-CMP* and *DiCo-CMP*, have been recently proposed to cope with the indirection problem of traditional protocols. However, neither *Token-CMP* nor *DiCo-CMP* scale efficiently with the number of cores, and future cache coherence protocols need to be efficient in terms of execution time, network traffic generated and area requirements.

In this chapter, we take into consideration these three constraints, and we discuss and evaluate both protocols that are used nowadays, such as *Hammer* and *Directory*, and novel indirection-aware protocols, such as *Token-CMP* and *DiCo-CMP*. In this way, we perform a detailed evaluation of a wide range of cache coherence protocols for many-core CMPs in a common framework. We also study several implementations of *DiCo-CMP* that differ in the amount of coherence information that they store in order to achieve the best trade-off among the three constraints considered.

Particularly, we show that *DiCo-LP-1*, which only stores the identity of one sharer along with the data block, *DiCo-BT*, which codifies the directory information just using three bits, and *DiCo-NoSC*, which does not store any coherence information in the data caches (and it does not need to modify the structure of the caches), are the alternatives that achieve a better trade-off. For example, *DiCo-BT* requires less area than all evaluated protocols, except *Hammer-CMP*, it also generates similar network traffic than *Directory-CMP* and, finally, it has a low average execution time (increasing just by 1% the best approach, *DiCo-FM*).

10. Acknowledgements

This work has been jointly supported by Spanish MEC under grant "TIN2006-15516-C04-03" and European Comission FEDER funds under grant "Consolider Ingenio-2010 CSD2006-00046". Alberto Ros is supported by a research grant from Spanish MEC under the FPU national plan (AP2004-3735).

11. References

Acacio, M. E., González, J., García, J. M. & Duato, J. (2001). A new scalable directory architecture for large-scale multiprocessors, *7th Int'l Symp. on High-Performance Computer Architecture (HPCA)*, pp. 97–106.

Acacio, M. E., González, J., García, J. M. & Duato, J. (2002a). Owner prediction for accelerating cache-to-cache transfer misses in cc-NUMA multiprocessors, *SC2002 High Performance Networking and Computing*.

Acacio, M. E., González, J., García, J. M. & Duato, J. (2002b). The use of prediction for accelerating upgrade misses in cc-NUMA multiprocessors, *11th Int'l Conference on Parallel Architectures and Compilation Techniques (PACT)*, pp. 155–164.

Agarwal, A., Simoni, R., Hennessy, J. L. & Horowitz, M. A. (1988). An evaluation of directory schemes for cache coherence, *15th Int'l Symp. on Computer Architecture (ISCA)*, pp. 280–289.

Agarwal, N., Peh, L.-S. & Jha, N. K. (2009). In-Network Snoop Ordering (INSO): Snoopy coherence on unordered interconnects, *15th Int'l Symp. on High-Performance Computer Architecture (HPCA)*, pp. 67–78.

Agarwal, V., Hrishikesh, M. S., Keckler, S. W. & Burger, D. (2000). Clock rate versus IPC: the end of the road for conventional microarchitectures, *27th Int'l Symp. on Computer Architecture (ISCA)*, pp. 248–259.

Ahmed, A., Conway, P., Hughes, B. & Weber, F. (2002). AMD Opteron^{TM} shared-memory MP systems, *14th HotChips Symp.*

Azimi, M., Cherukuri, N., Jayasimha, D. N., Kumar, A., Kundu, P., Park, S., Schoinas, I. & Vaidya, A. S. (2007). Integration challenges and tradeoffs for tera-scale architectures, *Intel Technology Journal* **11**(3): 173–184.

Barroso, L. A., Gharachorloo, K., McNamara, R., Nowatzyk, A., Qadeer, S., Sano, B., Smith, S., Stets, R. & Verghese, B. (2000). Piranha: A scalable architecture based on single-chip multiprocessing, *27th Int'l Symp. on Computer Architecture (ISCA)*, pp. 12–14.

Beckmann, B. M., Marty, M. R. & Wood, D. A. (2006). ASR: Adaptive selective replication for CMP caches, *39th IEEE/ACM Int'l Symp. on Microarchitecture (MICRO)*, pp. 443–454.

Bosschere, K. D., Luk, W., Martorell, X., Navarro, N., O'Boyle, M., Pnevmatikatos, D., Ramirez, A., Sainrat, P., Seznec, A., Stenstrom, P. & Temam, O. (2007). High-performance embedded architecture and compilation roadmap, *Transactions on HiPEAC I* pp. 5–29.

Cantin, J. F., Smith, J. E., Lipasti, M. H., Moshovos, A. & Falsafi, B. (2006). Coarse-grain coherence tracking: RegionScout and region coherence arrays, *IEEE Micro* **26**(1): 70–79.

Chaiken, D., Kubiatowicz, J. & Agarwal, A. (1991). LimitLESS directories: A scalable cache coherence scheme, *4th Int. Conf. on Architectural Support for Programming Language and Operating Systems (ASPLOS)*, pp. 224–234.

Cheng, L., Carter, J. B. & Dai, D. (2007). An adaptive cache coherence protocol optimized for producer-consumer sharing, *13th Int'l Symp. on High-Performance Computer Architecture (HPCA)*, pp. 328–339.

Culler, D. E., Singh, J. P. & Gupta, A. (1999). *Parallel Computer Architecture: A Hardware/Software Approach*, Morgan Kaufmann Publishers, Inc.

Gupta, A., Weber, W.-D. & Mowry, T. C. (1990). Reducing memory traffic requirements for scalable directory-based cache coherence schemes, *Int'l Conference on Parallel Processing (ICPP)*, pp. 312–321.

Ho, R., Mai, K. W. & Horowitz, M. A. (2001). The future of wires, *Proceedings of the IEEE* **89**(4): 490–504.

Horel, T. & Lauterbach, G. (1999). UltraSPARC-III: Designing third-generation 64-bit performance, *IEEE Micro* **19**(3): 73–85.

Hossain, H., Dwarkadas, S. & Huang, M. C. (2008). Improving support for locality and fine-grain sharing in chip multiprocessors, *17th Int'l Conference on Parallel Architectures and Compilation Techniques (PACT)*, pp. 155–165.

Huh, J., Kim, C., Shafi, H., Zhang, L., Burger, D. & Keckler, S. W. (2005). A NUCA substrate for flexible CMP cache sharing, *19th Int'l Conference on Supercomputing (ICS)*, pp. 31–40.

Jerger, N. D. E., Peh, L.-S. & Lipasti, M. H. (2008). Virtual tree coherence: Leveraging regions and in-network multicast tree for scalable cache coherence, *41th IEEE/ACM Int'l Symp. on Microarchitecture (MICRO)*, pp. 35–46.

Kim, C., Burger, D. & Keckler, S. W. (2002). An adaptive, non-uniform cache structure for wire-delay dominated on-chip caches, *10th Int. Conf. on Architectural Support for Programming Language and Operating Systems (ASPLOS)*, pp. 211–222.

Kumar, R., Zyuban, V. & Tullsen, D. M. (2005). Interconnections in multi-core architectures: Understanding mechanisms, overheads and scaling, *32nd Int'l Symp. on Computer Architecture (ISCA)*, pp. 408–419.

Le, H. Q., Starke, W. J., Fields, J. S., O'Connell, F. P., Nguyen, D. Q., Ronchetti, B. J., Sauer, W. M., Schwarz, E. M. & Vaden, M. T. (2007). IBM POWER6 microarchitecture, *IBM Journal of Research and Development* **51**(6): 639–662.

Li, M.-L., Sasanka, R., Adve, S. V., Chen, Y.-K. & Debes, E. (2005). The ALPBench benchmark suite for complex multimedia applications, *Int'l Symp. on Workload Characterization*, pp. 34–45.

Magen, N., Kolodny, A., Weiser, U. & Shamir, N. (2004). Interconnect-power dissipation in a microprocessor, *Int'l workshop on System Level Interconnect Prediction (SLIP'04)*, pp. 7–13.

Magnusson, P. S., Christensson, M., Eskilson, J., Forsgren, D., Hallberg, G., Hogberg, J., Larsson, F., Moestedt, A. & Werner, B. (2002). Simics: A full system simulation platform, *IEEE Computer* **35**(2): 50–58.

Martin, M. M. (2003). *Token Coherence*, PhD thesis, University of Wisconsin-Madison.

Martin, M. M., Harper, P. J., Sorin, D. J., Hill, M. D. & Wood, D. A. (2003). Using destination-set prediction to improve the latency/bandwidth tradeoff in shared-memory multiprocessors, *30th Int'l Symp. on Computer Architecture (ISCA)*, pp. 206–217.

Martin, M. M., Hill, M. D. & Wood, D. A. (2003). Token coherence: Decoupling performance and correctness, *30th Int'l Symp. on Computer Architecture (ISCA)*, pp. 182–193.

Martin, M. M., Sorin, D. J., Ailamaki, A., Alameldeen, A. R., Dickson, R. M., Mauer, C. J., Moore, K. E., Plakal, M., Hill, M. D. & Wood, D. A. (2000). Timestamp snooping: An approach for extending SMPs, *9th Int. Conf. on Architectural Support for Programming Language and Operating Systems (ASPLOS)*, pp. 25–36.

Martin, M. M., Sorin, D. J., Beckmann, B. M., Marty, M. R., Xu, M., Alameldeen, A. R., Moore, K. E., Hill, M. D. & Wood, D. A. (2005). Multifacet's general execution-driven multiprocessor simulator (GEMS) toolset, *Computer Architecture News* **33**(4): 92–99.

Marty, M. R., Bingham, J., Hill, M. D., Hu, A., Martin, M. M. & Wood, D. A. (2005). Improving multiple-cmp systems using token coherence, *11th Int'l Symp. on High-Performance Computer Architecture (HPCA)*, pp. 328–339.

Mukherjee, S. S. & Hill, M. D. (1994). An evaluation of directory protocols for medium-scale shared-memory multiprocessors, *8th Int'l Conference on Supercomputing (ICS)*, pp. 64–74.

Owner, J. M., Hummel, M. D., Meyer, D. R. & Keller, J. B. (2006). *System and method of maintaining coherency in a distributed communication system*, U.S. Patent 7069361.

Puente, V., Gregorio, J. A. & Beivide, R. (2002). SICOSYS: An integrated framework for studying interconnection network in multiprocessor systems, *10th Euromicro Workshop on Parallel, Distributed and Network-based Processing*, pp. 15–22.

Ros, A., Acacio, M. E. & García, J. M. (2008a). DiCo-CMP: Efficient cache coherency in tiled cmp architectures, *22nd Int'l Parallel and Distributed Processing Symp. (IPDPS)*.

Ros, A., Acacio, M. E. & García, J. M. (2008b). Scalable directory organization for tiled cmp architectures, *Int'l Conference on Computer Design (CDES)*, pp. 112–118.

Shah, M., Barreh, J., Brooks, J., Golla, R., Grohoski, G., Gura, N., Hetherington, R., Jordan, P., Luttrell, M., Olson, C., Saha, B., Sheahan, D., Spracklen, L. & Wynn, A. (2007). UltraSPARC T2: A highly-threaded, power-efficient, SPARC SoC, *IEEE Asian Solid-State Circuits Conference*, pp. 22–25.

Taylor, M. B., Kim, J., Miller, J., Wentzlaff, D., Ghodrat, F., Greenwald, B., Hoffman, H., Lee, J.-W., Johnson, P., Lee, W., Ma, A., Saraf, A., Seneski, M., Shnidman, N., Strumpen, V., Frank, M., Amarasinghe, S. & Agarwal, A. (2002). The raw microprocessor: A computational fabric for software circuits and general purpose programs, *IEEE Micro* **22**(2): 25–35.

Thoziyoor, S., Muralimanohar, N., Ahn, J. H. & Jouppi, N. P. (2008). Cacti 5.1, *Technical Report HPL-2008-20*, HP Labs.

Wang, H., Peh, L.-S. & Malik, S. (2003). Power-driven design of router microarchitectures in on-chip networks, *36th IEEE/ACM Int'l Symp. on Microarchitecture (MICRO)*, pp. 105–111.

Woo, S. C., Ohara, M., Torrie, E., Singh, J. P. & Gupta, A. (1995). The SPLASH-2 programs: Characterization and methodological considerations, *22nd Int'l Symp. on Computer Architecture (ISCA)*, pp. 24–36.

Zhang, M. & Asanovic, K. (2005). Victim replication: Maximizing capacity while hiding wire delay in tiled chip multiprocessors, *32nd Int'l Symp. on Computer Architecture (ISCA)*, pp. 336–345.

7

Using hardware resource allocation to balance HPC applications

Carlos Boneti, Roberto Gioiosa, Francisco J. Cazorla and Mateo Valero
Barcelona Supercomputing Center
Spain

1. Introduction

High Performance Computing (HPC) applications are usually *Single Process-Multiple Data* (SPMD) and are implemented using an MPI or an OpenMP library. In MPI applications, all the processes execute the same code on different data sets and use synchronization primitives (such as barriers or collective operations) to coordinate their work. Since the processes execute the same code, they are supposed to reach their synchronization points roughly at the same time.

However, this is not always the case, as many applications suffer from *imbalance*, where a parallel application has multiple inter-dependent tasks[1] and these tasks have to wait for others to complete in order to continue their execution (in Section 2 we will see some causes of applications' imbalance). During this waiting time, the CPUs of the waiting tasks are idle, thus, not performing any useful job. If one process has to complete its execution while all the other processes are waiting for it to reach the synchronization point; then several processors may be idle, resulting in a significant loss of performance and waste of resources. In fact, imbalance is a very common problem that has been studied by many researchers. Since there are several different factors that may create or make variable imbalance, there is no trivial solution and no solution solves all application's imbalance. A more detailed survey about solutions for the problem of imbalance is presented at Section 5.

Most of the current Supercomputers use processors with some multi-threaded features (TOP500, 2007). In the last years, the performance achievable by traditional super-scalar processor designs has almost saturated due to the limitation imposed by Instruction-Level Parallelism (ILP). As a consequence, Thread-Level Parallelism (TLP) has become a common strategy for improving processor performance. Since it is difficult to extract more Instruction-Level Parallelism from a single program, MultiThreaded (MT) processors, that is, processors that execute multiple threads at the same time, obtain more parallelism by simultaneously executing several tasks. This strategy has led to a wide range of MT processor architectures, from Simultaneous Multi-Threaded processors (SMT) (Serrano et al., 1993; Tullsen et al., 1995; Marr et all, 2002), in which most processor resources are shared

[1]In this chapter, the term *task* refers to a software entity representing an MPI process, a *software thread* or simply a *process*.

among hardware threads[2], to Chip Multi-Processors (CMP) (Bossen et al, 2002), in which every hardware thread has its own dedicated processor resources, only sharing the highest levels of the memory hierarchy (for example the L2 cache), and a combination of both (Sinharoy et al., 2005; IBM et al. 2006; Le et al, 2007). Resource sharing makes multi-threaded processors have good performance/cost and performance/power consumption ratios (Alpert, 2003), two desirable characteristics for a supercomputer.

Usually, software has no control over how processor resources are distributed among the active hardware threads in multi-threaded processors. For example, in an SMT processor the *instruction fetch policy*, decides how instructions are fetched from the threads, thereby implicitly determining the way internal processor resources are allocated to the threads. This is an undesirable characteristic that makes the execution time of programs unpredictable (Cazorla et al., 2006). In order to alleviate this problem, recently, some processor vendors have equipped their MT processors with mechanisms that allow the software to control processor's internals resource allocation, and thus, control application's speed.

There are several ways to reassign hardware resources in multi-threaded processors. In theory, every shared resource in a system can be partitioned or biased to satisfy a load-balancing target. For instance, cache replacement policy, processor fetch or decode cycles, power and several other split or shared resources can be controlled to improve the execution of a set of critical tasks in order to balance a parallel application.

In practice, currently, not every system allows such control over its hardware resources. For instance, dynamic voltage scaling can be used to save power for the slower tasks without sacrificing the performance of the critical tasks (the ones that limit the application's execution time), but it will not provide performance speedup. In cases where it is possible to give more resources to the critical tasks, increasing its speed, there is potential to decrease the overall program's execution time. These mechanisms open new opportunities to improve the performance of parallel applications.

The work presented in this chapter is a first step toward the use of hardware resource allocation to improve software targets: re-assigning hardware resources in a multi-threaded processor can reduce the imbalance in parallel applications, and hence improve their performance. In particular, this work presents a way to regain balance assigning more hardware resources to processes that compute the longer. The solution is transparent to the users and is implemented at the Operating System (OS) or run-time levels. In order to use it, users do not need to adapt their programming model or to know specific processor's implementation details when writing or compiling their applications.

In this chapter, the idea of load balancing through smart hardware resource allocation is explored experimentally on a real system with an MT processor, the IBM POWER5™ (Kalla et al., 2004). The POWER5 is a dual-core, 2-way SMT processor that allows us to change the way hardware resources are assigned to the core's SMT contexts by means of a *software-controlled hardware priority* (or hardware thread priority[3]) that controls the number of resources each context receives. This machine runs a Linux kernel that we modified in order to allow the HPC application to exploit the advantage of assigning the processor's resources.

---

[2]The terms *thread, hardware thread* and *context* are employed interchangeably to refer to a *hardware context* of an SMT processor.

[3]The hardware thread priorities mentioned here are independent of the operating system's concept of software thread priority.

As case studies, we performed several experiments with MPI applications, focused on the IBM POWER5. We present them in increasing order of complexity, that is, when their imbalance becomes more and more variable:

1. We started from a micro-benchmark (Metbench), developed at the Barcelona Supercomputing Center (BSC), where we introduce some artificial imbalance.
2. In the second experiment, we ran the widely used the NAS BT-MZ (NASA, 2009) benchmark; this version suffers of load imbalance, as shown in Section 4.2.
3. We demonstrate the effect of the proposal on a dynamic application (MetbenchVar), motivating the push for dynamic mechanisms that use hardware resource allocation, effectively using resource redistribution to perform load balancing.
4. Finally, we present a real application running on MareNostrum, SIESTA (SIESTA, 2009; Soler et al., 2002). With this specific input, SIESTA exhibits a very unpredictable imbalance.

Our results show that controlling hardware resources is a powerful tool that can significantly decrease applications' execution time. However, if used incorrectly, it may lead to significant performance loss. Moreover, non-HPC applications may benefit differently from re-assigning hardware resources.

The rest of this chapter is organized as follows: Section 2 shows the imbalance problem in HPC applications, classifying and discussing its sources; Section 3 introduces the concept of load-balancing based on smart allocation of hardware resources; we present the POWER5 processor and its prioritization mechanism, and the Linux kernel interface required to use the prioritization system. Section 4 shows our case-studies; Section 5 presents similar works in the same area; finally Section 6 provides our conclusion and future work.

2. Imbalance in HPC applications

HPC applications are usually SPMD, which means that every process executes the same code on different data. For example, let's assume that an HPC application is performing a matrix-vector multiplication and that each process receives a sub-matrix and the part of the vector required to compute the sub-matrix by vector multiplication. If the matrix can be divided into homogeneous parts (i.e., they require the same amount of time to be processed), all the processes in the parallel application would finish, ideally, at the same time.

However, the data set could be very different: let's suppose that, in the previous example, the matrix is sparse or triagonal, hence, the time required to process the data sub-set could vary as well. In this scenario the amount of time required to complete the sub-matrix by vector multiplication depends on the number of non-zero values present in the sub-matrix. In the extreme case, one process could receive a full sub-matrix while another gets an empty one. The former process requires much more time to reach the synchronization point than the latter.

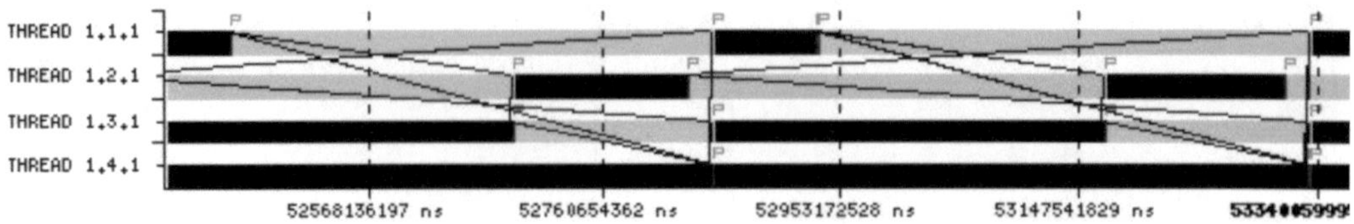

Fig. 1. Two iterations of NAS BT-MZ showing the message exchanges. In this trace, black areas represent computation, grey areas represent waiting time.

The NAS BT-MZ benchmark, explained in Section 4.2, is a clear example of an imbalanced application due to data distribution. As shown in Figure 1, each MPI process communicates with its two neighborhoods, exchanging data after each iteration. The processes get different amount of work and the process *P4* gets to perform the largest part of the computations. At the end, because of the communications, all other processes are slowed down by *P4* and have to wait for most of their time in order to allow *P4* to complete its job.
We classify the sources of imbalance in two main classes: *intrinsic* and *extrinsic* factors of imbalance. Bellow we detail issues and possible reasons for both of the classes.

2.1. Intrinsic imbalance

We refer to *intrinsic imbalance* as the imbalance an application experiences because of data (for example a sparse matrix) or algorithm (as for instance, a branch and bound implementation where some branches may be cut much earlier than others and each task gets a set of branches). The causes for the intrinsic imbalance are internal to the application's code, input set or both. It could be caused by several factors; here we point some of them out:
Input set: As we already said, this scenario happens when a process has a small input set to work on while another has a large amount of data to process. One example of application that is strongly dependent on the input set is SIESTA (Soler et al., 2002) (described in better details in Section 4.4).
SIESTA analyzes materials at the atom level. Depending on the distribution and density of the atoms across the material, some processes may perform more work than others. Very homogeneous materials tend to be well balanced, although SIESTA may also present imbalance caused by the algorithm. Figure 2 shows the trace of SIESTA when processing atoms of graphite (C6). In this case, the four MPI processes execute, respectively for 92.82%, 91.44%, 91.81% and 91.68% of the time. In fact, if we discard the initialization phase, they all have more than 98.80% of CPU utilization.
In another case, shown in Figure 3, when processing PTCDA molecules (perylene-3,4,9,10-tetracarboxylic-3,4,9,10-dianhydride), it exhibits a highly imbalanced execution: the MPI processes show respectively 92.94%, 21.79%, 96.60%, 21.71% of utilization.
Domain: Iterative methods approximate the solution of a problem (for example, Partial Differential Equations, PDE) with a function in some domain starting from an initial condition. The domain is divided in several sub-domains and each process computes its part of the solution. At the end of every iteration, the error made in the approximation is computed and, eventually, another iteration is to be started. If the function in some part of the domain is smooth, only few iterations are required to converge to a good approximation. Conversely, if the function has several peaks in the sub-domain, more

iterations are necessary to find a good solution and/or more points in the domain have to be considered during the computing phase.

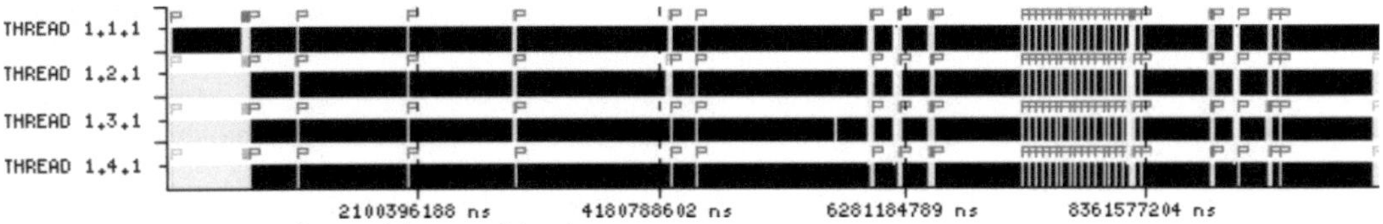

Fig. 2. Siesta execution with graphite input.

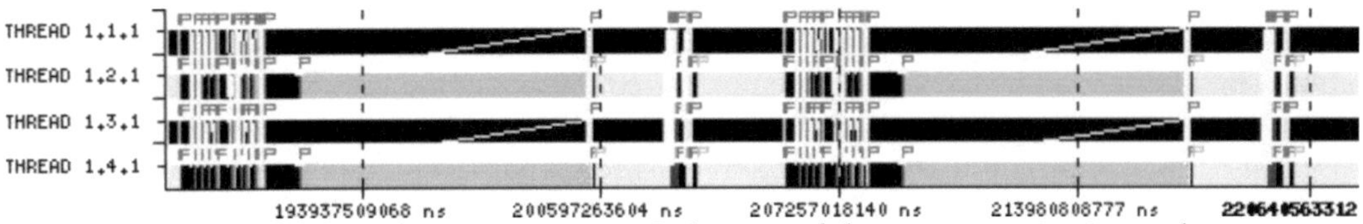

Fig. 3. Siesta execution with PTCDA input. Only part of the execution is pictured.

Data exchanging: During their execution, processes may require to exchange data among themselves. If the two peers are on the same node, the latency of the communication is small; if a process needs to exchange data with a neighbor on another node the latency is large, even larger if the destination process is far away in the network.
In all the previous cases, the application may result to be imbalanced.

2.2. Extrinsic imbalance

Even if both the application's algorithm and the input set are balanced, the execution of the parallel application can still be imbalanced. This is caused by external factors that slow some processes down (but not others). For example, the Operating System (OS) might decide to run another process (say a kernel daemon) in place of the MPI process running on one CPU. Since that MPI process is not able to run all the time while the others are running, it takes longer to complete, making all the other processes wait for it. Those external factors are the sources of *extrinsic imbalance*. There may be several causes for the imbalance:
OS noise: The CPU is used by the OS to perform services such as handling interrupts, page reclaiming, assigning memory on demand, etc. The OS noise has been recognized as one of the major source of extrinsic imbalance (Gioiosa et al., 2004; Petrini et al., 2003; Tsafrir et al., 2005). A classical example is the interrupt annoyance problem present in Intel processors: all the interrupts coming from external devices are routed to CPU0; therefore, the OS noise caused by executing the interrupt handlers on CPU0 is higher than the noise on the other CPUs.
User daemons: HPC systems often run profile or statistic collectors together with the HPC applications. These activities could steal computing power from one process, delaying its execution.
Network topology: Exchanging data between processes in the same sub-network is faster than exchanging data between processes in different sub-networks. In general, if the job scheduler has placed processes that need to communicate ``far away'', their communication latency could increase so much that the whole application will be affected.

Memory management: Even inside a single node, it is common to have NUMA (Non-Uniform Memory Access). A process that requests a large amount of memory may have it allocated in a memory region that is comparably slower than the memory allocated to the other processes of a parallel application (maybe because there is not enough memory close enough to this processor). In this case, the performance of this process will be significantly impacted and, depending on the application, this process may delay the execution of the entire program, making the others wait for its results.

An expert programmer could reduce the intrinsic imbalance in the application. However, this is not an easy task, as the imbalance can be caused by the algorithm, but it can also be caused by the input data set, changing distribution and intensity according to different inputs. Balancing a HPC application by hand is a time-consuming task and may require quite a lot of effort. In fact, the programmer has to distribute the data among the processes considering the way the algorithm has been implemented and the correctness of the application. Moreover, on many applications this work has to be done every time the input or the machine change.

Even worse is the case of extrinsic imbalance, as those factors are neither under the control of the application nor of the programmer and there is no straightforward way to solve this problem. Thus, it is clear that a mechanism that aims to solve the imbalance of an application should be transparent to the user, dynamic and independent from the programming model, libraries or input set. As we will see later, the proposal presented in this chapter is both transparent and independent from the programming model, libraries and input set.

3. Hardware Resource Allocation

With the arrival of MT architectures, and in particular those that allow the software to control processor's resource allocation, new opportunities arise to mitigate the problem of imbalance in HPC applications. This is mainly due to the fact that the software is allowed to exercise a fine control over the progress of tasks, by allocating or deallocating processor resources to them. Such a fine-grain control cannot be achieved by previous solutions for load imbalance; in fact, even if a lot of processors with shared resources have been introduced in the market since early 90s, very few of them allow the software to control how internal resources are allocated. Allowing the software to control how to assign shared resources is a key factor for HPC systems. In this view, having MT processors able to provide such mechanism will be essential for improving the performance of HPC systems.

The solution presented in this chapter for balancing HPC applications, consists of assigning more hardware resources to the most compute-intensive processes (the bottleneck). Giving this process more hardware resource shall decrease its execution time and, since this process is the bottleneck of the application, the execution time of the whole MPI application.

Clearly the underlying processor has to support the capability of re-assigning processor resources among running contexts. Currently, multi-threaded processors like the IBM POWER5 (Kalla et al., 2004), the POWER6 (Le et al., 2007) or the Cell processor (IBM et al., 2006; IBM, 2008) provide such a capability with their hardware thread priority mechanisms. More details about the POWER5 prioritization mechanism are available in Section 3.1.

Even if in this chapter we focus on the IBM POWER5, the idea presented is general and can be applied to other MT processors that allow the OS to the control or influence the allocation of processor's resources (for example, partitioning a shared L2 cache in a multi-core CPU

(Moreto et al., 2008; Qureshi and Patt, 2006). The IBM POWER5 processor is used, among others, by ASC Purple, installed at the Lawrence Livermore National Laboratory[4].

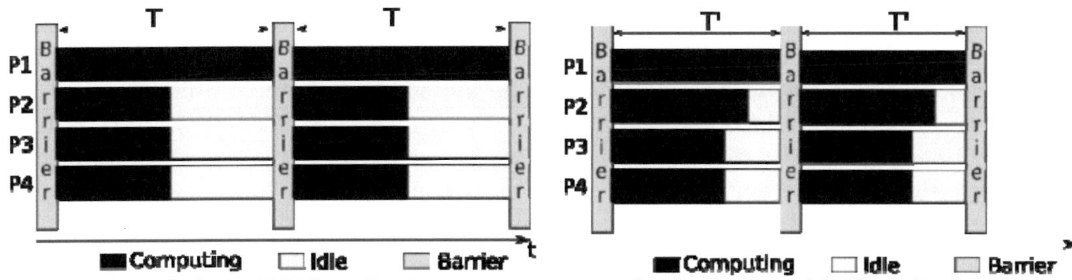

(a) Imbalanced HPC application (b) More balanced HPC application

Fig. 4. Expected effect of the proposed solution ($T' < T$).

We should point out that increasing the performance of one process by giving it more hardware resources, does not come for free. In fact, at the same time, the performance of the other process running on the same core, therefore sharing the resources with the former process, may reduce. Figure 4 shows a synthetic example that illustrates this case: in Figure 4(a), process *P1* shares resources with *P2*, while *P3* shares them with *P4*; *P2*, *P3* and *P4* take the same amount of time to reach their synchronization point but *P1* takes much longer. As a result, *P2*, *P3* and *P4* are idle for a long time. In Figure 4(b), we increase the priority of *P1*, so it uses more hardware resources and its execution time decreases; *P2*'s execution time, instead, increases since it runs with less hardware resources. Since *P2* is not the bottleneck and has enough "spare time", its slowdown does not affect the application's performance. On the other hand, the performance improvement of *P1* directly translates into a performance improvement for the whole application, as it is possible to see comparing Figures 4(a) and 4(b).

No assumption is made on what kind of application, programming model or input set the programmer has to use. The only assumption made is that the underlying processor must provide a mechanism, visible at software level, to control the hardware shared resources. The solution for load balancing through hardware resource allocation works at OS level and is completely transparent to the users, who are free to use the MPI, OpenMP or any other programming model or library they wish. Moreover, the approach can be adjusted so the amount of resources assigned to a process can change according to the input set provided to the application.

It is important to notice that not all the POWER5 priorities are available from the user-level and a special kernel patch was needed to enable the use of the full spectrum of software-controlled hardware priorities. For the technique presented in the current chapter, we employ the same patch developed to perform the characterization in (Boneti et al., 2008a). The patch only provides a mechanism to set all the priorities (available at OS level) from user applications. It is the responsibility of the user applications (or run time systems) to balance the system load using this interface.

[4]The 3rd supercomputer in the Top500 list of 06/2006, the 11th at the list of 11/2007.

3.1. The IBM POWER5 processor

The IBM POWER5 (IBM, 2005a; IBM, 2005b; IBM, 2005c; Sinharoy et al., 2005) processor is a dual-core chip where each core is a 2-way SMT core (Kalla et al., 2004). Each core has its own private first-level data and instruction caches. The unified second- and third-level caches are shared between cores.

The forms of Multi-Threading implemented in the POWER5 are Simultaneous Multi-threading and Chip-Multiprocessing. The main characteristic of SMT processors is their ability to issue instructions from different threads in the same cycle. As a result, SMTs not only can switch to a different thread to use the idle issue cycles in a long-latency operation, like coarse-grain multi-threading, or in a short-latency operation, like in a fine-grain multi-threaded, but also fill unused issue slots in a given cycle.

What makes the IBM POWER5 ideal for testing our proposal is the capability that each core has to assign some hardware resources to one context rather than to the other. Each context in a core has a *hardware thread priority* (Boneti et al, 2008a; Gibbs et al., 2005; Kalla et al., 2003), an integer value in the range of 0 (the context is off) to 7 (the other context is off and the core is running in Single Thread (ST) mode), as illustrated in Table 1. As the hardware thread priority of a context increases (keeping the other constant) the amount of hardware resources assigned to that context increases too.

Priority	Priority level	Privilege level	or-nop inst.
0	Thread shut off	Hypervisor	-
1	Very low	Supervisor	`or 31,31,31`
2	Low	User	`or 1,1,1`
3	Medium-Low	User	`or 6,6,6`
4	Medium	User	`or 2,2,2`
5	Medium-high	Supervisor	`or 5,5,5`
6	High	Supervisor	`or 3,3,3`
7	Very high	Hypervisor	`or 7,7,7`

Table 1. Hardware thread priorities in the IBM POWER5 processor

3.1.1. Thread priorities implementation

The way each core assigns more hardware resources to a given hardware thread is by decoding more instructions from that thread than from the other. In other words, the number of decode cycles assigned to each thread depends on its hardware priority. In general, the higher the priority, the higher the number of decode cycles assigned to the thread (and, therefore, the higher the number of shared resources held by the thread).

Let's assume two threads (ThreadA and ThreadB) are running on a POWER5 core with priorities X and Y, respectively. In POWER5 the decode time is divided in time-slices of R cycles: the lower priority thread receives 1 of those cycles, while the higher priority thread receives (R-1) cycles. R is computed as:

$$R = 2^{|X-Y|+1} \tag{1}$$

Table 2 shows the possible values of R and how many decode slots are assigned to the two threads as the difference between ThreadA's and ThreadB's priority moves from 0 to 4. In fact, the amount of resources assigned to a thread is determined using the difference between the thread priorities, X and Y. For example, assuming that ThreadA has hardware priority 6 and ThreadB has hardware priority 2 (the difference is 4), then the core fetches 31 times from context0 and once from context1 (more details on the hardware implementation are provided in (Gibbs et al., 2005). It is clear that the performance of the process running on Context0 shall increase to the detriment of the one running on Context1. When any of the threads has priority 0 or 1, the behavior of the hardware prioritization mechanism is different, as shown in Table 3.

Priority difference (X-Y)	R	Decode cycles for A	Decode cycles for B
0	2	1	1
1	4	3	1
2	8	7	1
3	16	15	1
4	32	31	1

Table 2. Decode cycle allocation in the IBM POWER5 with different priorities.

Thread A	Thread B	Action
>1	>1	Decode cycles are given to the two threads as according with the thread's priorities.
1	>1	ThreadB gets all the execution resources; ThreadA takes what is left over.
1	1	Power save mode; both ThreadA and ThreadB receive 1 of 64 decode cycles.
0	>1	Processor in ST mode. ThreadB receives all the resources.
0	1	1 of 32 cycles are given to ThreadB.
0	0	Processor is stopped.

Table 3. Resource allocation in the IBM POWER5 when the priority of any of the threads is 0 or 1.

3.1.2. Hardware interface for priority management

The IBM POWER5 provides two different interfaces to change the priority of a thread: issuing an `or`-nop instruction or using the *Thread Status Register* (TSR). We used the former interface, in which case a thread has to execute an instruction like `or X,X,X`, where `X` is an specific register number (see Table 1). This operation does not do anything but changing the hardware thread priority. Table 1 also shows the privilege level required to set each priority and how to change priority using this interface. The second interface consists of writing the hardware priority into the local (i.e., per-context) TSR by means of a `mtspr` operation. The actual thread priority can be read from the local TSR using a `mfspr` instruction.

3.2. The Linux kernel interface to hardware priorities

By default, users can only set three hardware priorities: MEDIUM (4), MEDIUM-LOW (3) and LOW (2). This basically means that users are only allowed to reduce their priority, since the MEDIUM priority is the default case. If the user reduces the thread priority when a process does not require lot or resources (for example because the process is waiting for a lock), the overall performance might increase (because the other thread receives more resources and, therefore, may go faster). Thus, it is recommended that the user reduces the thread priority whenever the thread processor is executing a low-priority operation (such as spinning for a lock, polling, etc.).

Modern Linux kernels running on IBM POWER5 processors make use of the hardware priority mechanism the chip provides. In this Section we will first explore the standard behavior of the Linux kernel when dealing with hardware priorities, and then present how we modified the standard kernel in order to solve the imbalance problem by means of the IBM POWER5 hardware prioritization mechanism.

3.2.1. The use of priorities in the standard Linux Kernel

The Linux kernel only exploits hardware priorities in a limited number of cases: the general idea is to reduce the priority of a process that is not performing any useful operation and to give more resources to the process running on the other context.

The standard Linux kernel makes use of the thread priorities in three cases:

1. The processor is spinning for a lock in kernel mode. In this case the priority of the spinning process is reduced (the process is not really advancing in its job).
2. The kernel is waiting for some operations to complete. This happens, for example, when the kernel wants a specific CPU to perform some operation by means of a `smp_call_function()` (for example, invalidating its TLB) and cannot proceed until the operation has completed. In this case the priority of the CPU is decreased until the operation completes.
3. The kernel is running the idle process because there is no other process ready to run. In this case the kernel reduces the priority of the idle CPU and, eventually, put the core in Single Thread (ST) mode.

In all these cases the kernel reduces the priority of the context, restoring the priority to MEDIUM when there is some job to perform. The hardware thread priority is also reset to MEDIUM as soon as the kernel executes an interrupt or an exception handler as well as a system call. In fact, since the kernel does not keep track of the current priority, it cannot restore the process' priority. Therefore, the kernel simply resets the priority to MEDIUM every time it starts to execute an interrupt handler (or a system call), so that it can be sure that those critical operations will be performed with enough resources.

3.2.2. Modification to the Linux kernel

In order to use the hardware prioritization for balancing the HPC application, we modified the original kernel code for two reasons:

1. Every time the CPU receives an interrupt, the interrupt handler sets the priority back to MEDIUM, regardless of the current priority. We want to maintain the given priority even after an interrupt is received or during the interrupt handler itself; thus, we removed the code that makes use of the hardware thread priority capabilities from the handlers.
2. Only hardware priorities 2 (LOW), 3 (MEDIUM-LOW) and 4 (MEDIUM) can be set by a user-level program. Priorities 1 (VERY LOW), 5 (MEDIUM-HIGH) and 6 (HIGH) can only be set by the Operating System (OS). Priorities 0 (context off) and 7 (VERY HIGH, ST mode) can only be set by the Hypervisor. We developed an interface that allows

the user to set all the possible priorities available in kernel mode. A user who wants to set priority `N` to process `<PID>` shall simply write to a `proc` file, like:

```
echo N > /proc/<PID>/hmt_priority
```

This patch provides a mechanism to set all the priorities from user applications. It is developed for several standard kernel versions (2.6.19, 2.6.24, 2.6.28, etc) in a way that it is not intrusive and has no impact on the performance of our experiments. With this patch, it is the responsibility of the user applications, system scheduler or run time systems to balance the system load. It is the building block that can be used for other mechanisms, like the transparent load balancer proposed in (Boneti et al., 2008b).

4. Case Studies on the IBM POWER5 processor

In this section, we present some experiments on an IBM OpenPower 710 server, with one POWER5 processor. Since MPI is the most common protocol, the test cases in this section are MPI applications (in the experiments we used the MPI-CH 1.0.4p1 implementation of MPI protocol).

We present four different cases: Section 4.1 shows how the IBM POWER5 priority mechanism works using our micro-benchmark (Metbench); Section 4.2 provides details on how the hardware priorities can be used to balance a widely used benchmark (NAS BT-MZ) and improve its performance. Section 4.3 presents a different version of Metbench that presents dynamic behavior and, thus, variable imbalance. Finally, 4.4 shows how the hardware prioritization improves the performance of a real application frequently executed on MareNostrum (SIESTA). In this case, SIESTA receives an input that makes it exhibit a variable behavior and imbalance.

In order to present experiments in a simple way, we use as metric the total execution time of the application. We use PARAVER (Labarta et al., 1996), a visualization and performance analysis tool developed at CEPBA, to collect data and statistics and to show the trace of each process during the tests.

4.1. Metbench

Metbench (Minimum Execution Time Benchmark) is a suite of MPI micro-benchmarks developed at BSC whose structure is representative of the real applications running on MareNostrum. Metbench consists of a *framework* and several *loads*. The framework is composed by a *master* process and several *workers*: each worker executes its assigned load and then waits for all the others to complete their task. The role of the master is to maintain a strict synchronization between the workers: once all the workers have finished their tasks, the master eventually starts another iteration (the number of iterations to perform is a run-time parameter). The master and the workers only exchange data during the initialization phase and use an `mpi\_barrier()` to get synchronized. In the traces shown in this section, the master process corresponds to the first process and is not balanced as it will be always idle, waiting for the conclusion of all worker processes.

One of the goals of Metbench is to allow researchers at BSC to understand the performance and capabilities of a processor or a cluster. In order to do that, we developed several loads, each one stressing a different processor resource (for example, the Floating Point Unit, the L2 cache, the branch predictor, etc) for a given amount of time.

In this experiment we introduce imbalance in the MPI application by assigning to a worker a larger load than the one assigned to the worker on the same core. In this way, the faster worker will spend most of its time waiting for the slower worker to process its load. As we will see in Section 4.2 this scenario is quite common for both standard benchmarks and real applications. Figure 5 shows the effect of the hardware resource allocation on Metbench. Each horizontal line represents the activity of a process and each color represents a different state: dark bars show computing time while grey bars show waiting time. In this example, processes *P*1 (the master), *P*2, and *P*3 are mapped to the first core of the POWER5, while processes *P*4 and *P*5 are mapped to the other core. The x-axis represents time.

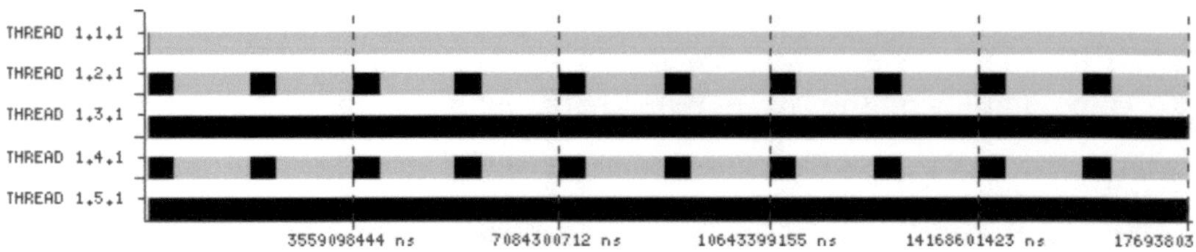

(a) Metbench Case A

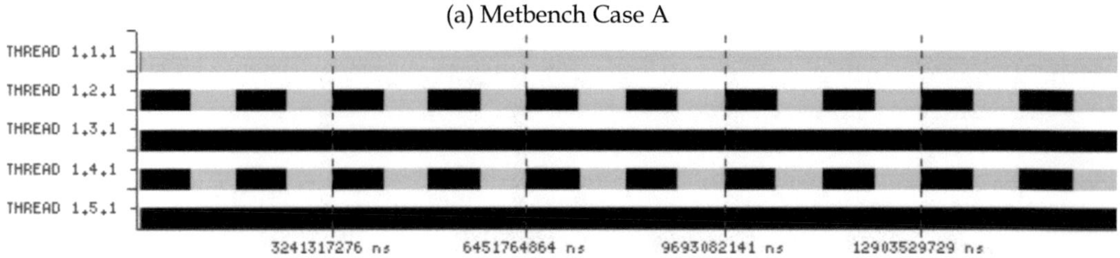

(b) Metbench Case B

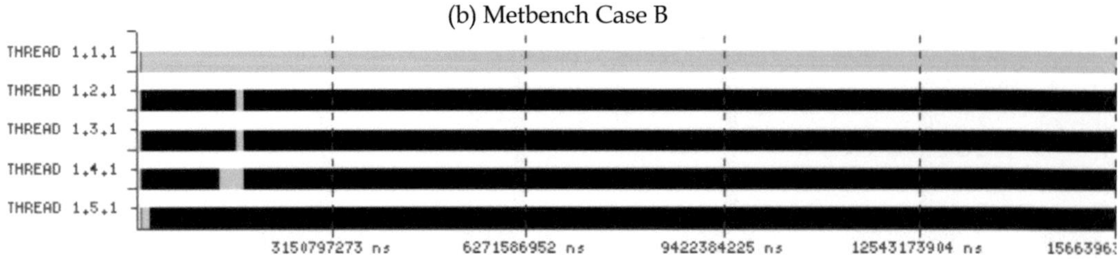

(c) Metbench Case C

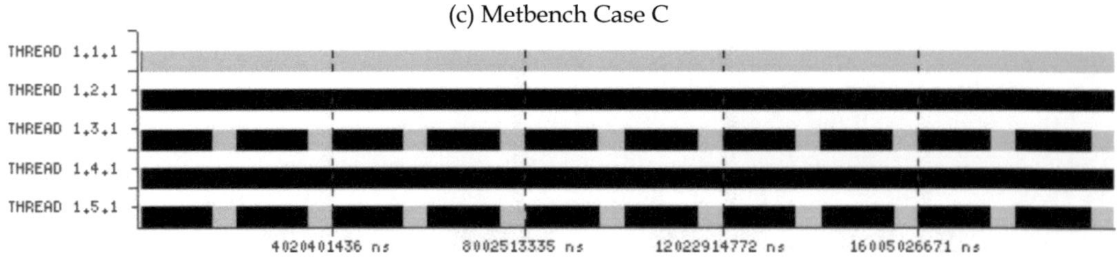

(d) Metbench Case D

Fig. 5. Effect of the hardware thread prioritization on Metbench. Each trace represents only some iterations of the application.

Case A: Figure 5(a) represents our reference case, i.e., the MPI application is running with default priorities (4). As we can see from Figure 5(a) Metbench shows a great imbalance:

more specifically, processes *P*2 and *P*4 spend about 75.6% of their time waiting for processes *P*3 and *P*5 to complete their computing phase.

Case B: Using the software-controlled hardware prioritization, we increased the priority of *P*3 and *P*5 (the most computing intensive processes) up to 6, while the priority of *P*2 and *P*4 are set to 5 (remember that what really matters is the difference between the thread priorities, here *P*2 and *P*4 are running with less priority than in Case A).

Figure 5(b) shows how the imbalance has been reduced, also reducing the total execution time (from 81.64 sec to 76.98 sec, 5.71% of improvement).

Case C: We increased again the amount of hardware resources assigned to *P*3 and *P*5 in order to speed them up.

Indeed, we obtained an even more balanced situation where all the processes compute for (roughly) the same amount of time. The total execution time reduces to 74.90 sec (8.26% of improvement over Case A).

Case D: Next, we increased again the amount of resources given to *P*3 and *P*5. As we can see from Figure 5(d) we reversed the imbalance, i.e., now *P*3 and *P*5 are much faster than *P*2 and *P*4 and spend most of their time waiting. As a result the execution time (95.71 sec) increases.

Test	Proc	Core	% Comp	Priority	Exec. Time
A	P1	1	0.02	4	81.64s
	P2	1	24.32	4	
	P3	1	98.99	4	
	P4	2	24.31	4	
	P5	2	99.99	4	
B	P1	1	0.02	4	76.98s
	P2	1	51.16	5	
	P3	1	99.82	6	
	P4	2	51.18	5	
	P5	2	99.98	6	
C	P1	1	0.03	4	74.90s
	P2	1	98.96	4	
	P3	1	98.56	6	
	P4	2	97.01	4	
	P5	2	98.37	6	
D	P1	1	0.02	4	95.71s
	P2	1	99.87	3	
	P3	1	73.25	6	
	P4	2	99.72	3	
	P5	2	73.25	6	

Table 4. Metbench balanced and imbalanced characterization

Case D shows an interesting property of the IBM POWER5 hardware priority mechanism: the hardware thread priority implementation is a powerful tool but the performance of the penalized process can be reduced more than linearly (in fact, exponentially) (Boneti et al. 2008a), thus, *P*2 and *P*4 can become the new bottlenecks.

4.2. BT-MZ

Block Tri-diagonal (BT) is one of the NAS Parallel Benchmarks (NPB) suite. BT solves discretized versions of the unsteady, compressible Navier-Stokes equations in three spatial dimensions, operating on a structured discretization mesh. BT Multi-Zone (BT-MZ) (Jin and der Wijngaart, 2006) is a variation of the BT benchmark which uses several meshes (named *zones*) for, in realistic applications, a single mesh is not enough to describe a complex domain.

Besides the complexity of the algorithm, BT-MZ shows a behavior very similar to our Metbench benchmark: every process in the MPI application performs some computation on its part of the data set and then exchanges data with its neighbors asynchronously (using `mpi_isend()` and `mpi_irecv()`); after this communication phase (which lasts for a very short time, around 0.10% of the total execution time) each process waits (with a `mpi_waitall()` function) for its neighbors to complete their communication phases. In this way, each process gets synchronized with its neighbors (note that this does not mean that each process gets synchronized with all the other processes). Once a process has exchanged all the data it had to exchange, a new iteration can start and the previous behavior repeats again until the end of the application (in our experiments we used BT-MZ with default values: class A with 200 iterations).

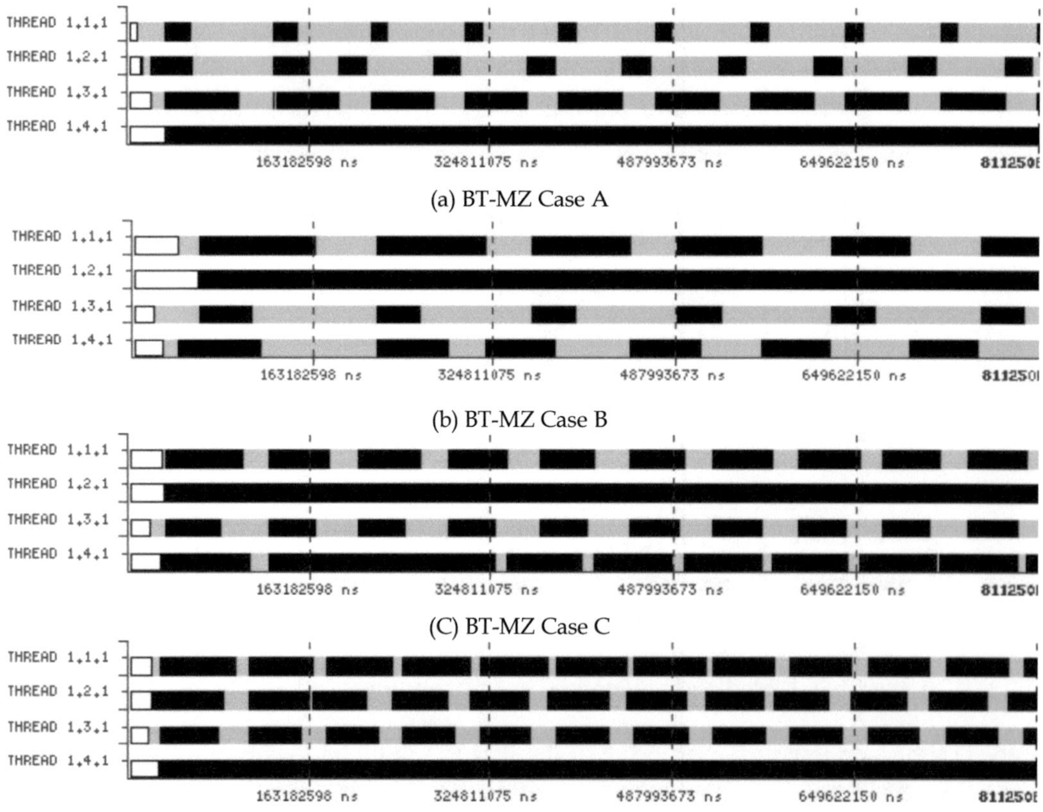

(a) BT-MZ Case A

(b) BT-MZ Case B

(C) BT-MZ Case C

(D) BT-MZ Case D

Fig. 6. Effect of the hardware thread prioritization on BT-MZ. Each trace represents only some iterations of the application. Communication has been removed to increase clearness

Case A: Figure 6(a) shows the BT behavior in the reference case, i.e. when process P_i is assigned to CPU_i and the priority of all the processes is 4. After an initialization phase (white bars at the beginning of the execution of each task), all the processes reach a barrier (synchronization point). From this point on, the real algorithm starts: during every iteration, each process alternate computing phases (black) with synchronization phases (grey).
It is easy to see from Figure 6(a) that BT-MZ shows a great imbalance[5]. The imbalance is caused by the fact that some processes (for example process *P1*) have a small part of the data to work on, while other processes (for example, processes *P4*) have a large amount of data to take care of. It is also clear that process *P4* is the bottleneck of the application and that speeding up this process will improve overall performance.

Test	Proc	Core	% Comp	Priority	Exec. Time
ST	P1	1	49.33	7	108.32s
	P2	2	99.46	7	
A	P1	1	17.63	4	81.64s
	P2	1	28.91	4	
	P3	2	66.47	4	
	P4	2	99.72	4	
B	P1	1	52.33	3	127.91s
	P2	2	99.64	3	
	P3	2	28.87	6	
	P4	1	46.26	6	
C	P1	1	65.32	4	75.62s
	P2	2	99.68	4	
	P3	2	53.78	6	
	P4	1	85.88	6	
D	P1	1	82.73	4	66.88s
	P2	2	73.68	4	
	P3	2	66.40	5	
	P4	1	99.72	6	

Table 5. BT-MZ balanced and imbalanced characterization

Case B: In order to solve the imbalance introduced by data repartition in BT-MZ, we ran process *P1* and *P4* on the same core and assigned more hardware resources to the latter, improving its performance while decreasing *P1*'s performance. This mapping seems reasonable, as our goal is to increase the performance of *P4* (the most computing intensive process) and we know that, with this operation, we will reduce the performance of the process running on the same core with *P4*. We chose *P1* because it is the process with the shortest computation phase.
In our first attempt to reduce the imbalance we assigned priority 3 to processes *P1* and *P2* and priority 6 to processes *P3* and *P4*. Figure 6(b) shows how the imbalance has been inverted: process *P1* now takes longer than *P4* and the new bottleneck is now process *P2*, which is also running with priority 3. As a consequence, the total execution time increases

[5]Even if the goal of this chapter is not to show whether SMT processors are useful in HPC or not, the table also shows the ST mode performance (only one process per core) of the application.

(127.91 sec instead of 81.62 sec), which means the new bottleneck runs for much longer than the previous one.

Case C: In order to restore the original relative behavior between process *P*1 and *P*4 we incremented the resources assigned to process *P*1 and *P*2. Figure 6(c) shows that *P*1 now runs for less time than *P*4, as in Case A. In addition, giving more resource to *P*2 (which is again the bottleneck) reduced the total execution time to 75.62 sec, with a 7.37% of improvement with respect to Case A.

Case D: Finally, we can argue that *P*2 and *P*3 execute their operation on a similar amount of data, therefore the amount of resources given to each process should not be as different as for *P*1 and *P*4. In our last test, we still assigned priority 4 to *P*1 and 6 to *P*4, as in the previous case, but we assigned priority 5 to *P*2 and 6 to *P*3, sharing resources between these two processes running on the same core more equally. Figure 6(d) shows that the imbalance has been reduced again with respect to Case C, in fact, now *P*2 and *P*3 compute more or less for the same amount of time. Also the new bottleneck is *P*4, which is much shorter than *P*2 in Case C. Table 5 shows how the total execution time has also been reduced to 66.88 sec, with an 18.08% of improvement over the reference Case A.

4.3. MetbenchVar

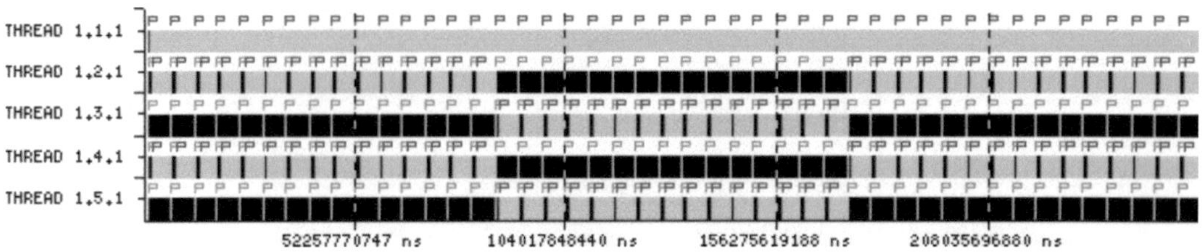

(a) MetbenchVar Case A

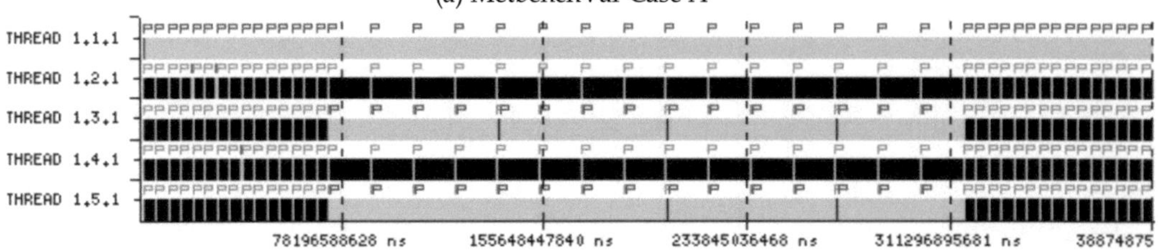

(b) MetbenchVar Case B

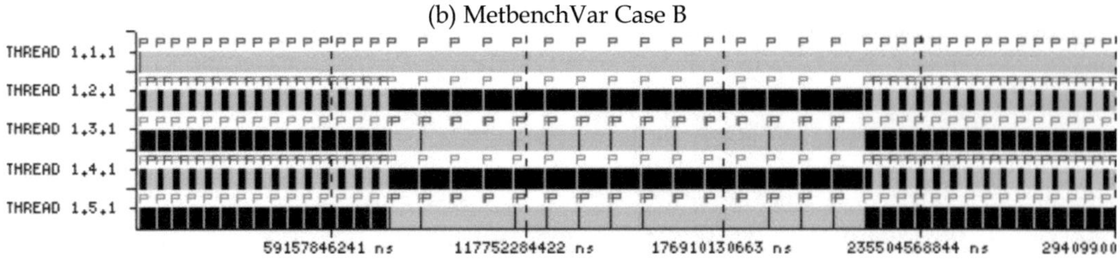

(c) MetbenchVar Case C

Fig. 7. Effect of the hardware thread prioritization on MetbenchVar

MetbenchVar is a slightly modified version of Metbench where the workers change their behavior after *k* iteration. Figure 7(a) shows the standard execution of MetbenchVar with *k*=15: at the beginning *P*2 and *P*4 execute a small load while *P*3 and *P*5 a large load. At the 15th iteration, *P*2 and *P*4 start to execute the large load while *P*3 and *P*5 perform their task on the small load. In this way, we reverse the load imbalance at run time making the application's behavior dynamic. At the 30th iteration, we switch again the behavior of the tasks. Recall that, as it was the case for Metbench (Section 4.1), *P*1 does not perform any job and presents no significant impact on performance, as it only waits for *P*2 to *P*5 to finish their execution.

Figure 7(b) shows how the static prioritization works in this case: the application is perfectly balanced in the first (iterations 1-15) and third period (iteration 31-45) but the imbalance is reversed in the second period (iterations 16-30), as a result, in the second period the application performs worst than in the standard case. Furthermore, for this workload, the negative impact of applying the wrong prioritization is extremely high and, although for two thirds of the cases the benchmark runs with the right priorities (4,6), the performance degradation of running with the wrong priorities is by far more important. Overall, for this program, the static prioritization presents 50% of performance degradation when compared to the standard case of this benchmark.

Figure 7(c) shows that trying to decrease the priority difference between *P*2 and *P*3, and between *P*4 and *P*5 does not improve the baseline either. In this case, when comparing to the standard execution, statically applying a hardware prioritization still degrades performance by 13.20%.

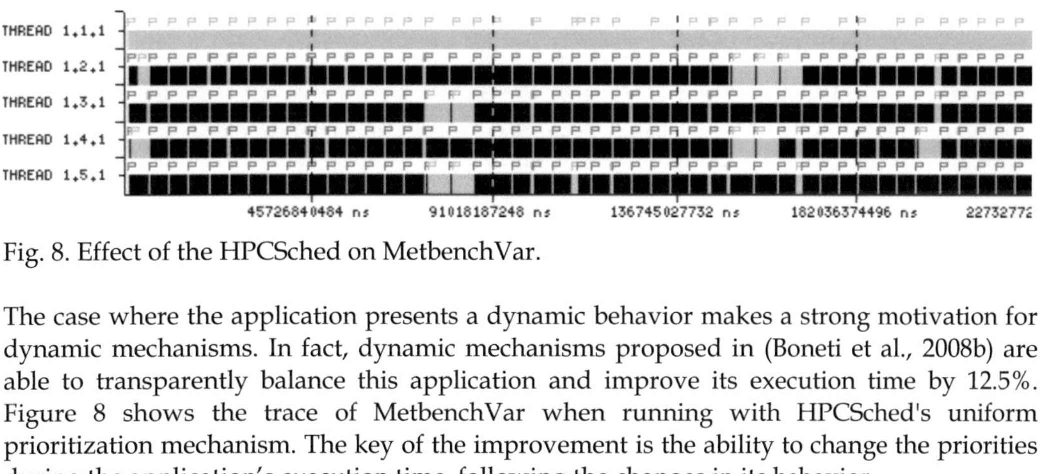

Fig. 8. Effect of the HPCSched on MetbenchVar.

The case where the application presents a dynamic behavior makes a strong motivation for dynamic mechanisms. In fact, dynamic mechanisms proposed in (Boneti et al., 2008b) are able to transparently balance this application and improve its execution time by 12.5%. Figure 8 shows the trace of MetbenchVar when running with HPCSched's uniform prioritization mechanism. The key of the improvement is the ability to change the priorities during the application's execution time, following the changes in its behavior.

Another very interesting point is that, for applications with very variable behavior, using the overall relative computational time (or utilization) of a task can be tricky. For instance, if we refer to the case A in Table 6, we can see that process *P*2 computes for 49.34% of the time, while *P*3 processed for 74.65% of the time. It becomes intuitive that we should always prioritize *P*2. However, let's take a look at the utilization per phase: during the first phase, the utilizations are 24.17%, 100.00%, 24.16%, 99.97%, during the second, they are 100%, 23.65%, 99.94%, 23.65%, finally, the third iteration has the same behavior as the first one. It becomes clear why a constant prioritization is not good, and furthermore, that the overall utilization is not a good indicator of imbalance for this application.

On Case B of Table 6, the measured overall utilization is also misleading. We may believe that the imbalance is not so different from the baseline Case A, however, for initial and final phases the utilizations are: 99.63%, 99.90%, 98.52%, 99.94% and for the middle phase: 99.95%, 4.90%, 99.87%, 4.89%. On the previous cases, as the imbalance was constant, it was not necessary to use per-phase utilization. Clearly, in the case of MetbenchVar, if the utilization is used as a metric, it must be evaluated for each of the phases of the program.

Test	Proc	Core	% Comp	Priority	Exec. Time
A	P1	1	0.01	4	259.79s
	P2	1	49.34	4	
	P3	1	74.65	4	
	P4	2	49.31	4	
	P5	2	76.63	4	
B	P1	1	0.00	4	388.75s
	P2	1	99.43	4	
	P3	1	40.65	6	
	P4	2	99.35	4	
	P5	2	40.64	6	
C	P1	1	0.01	4	294.10s
	P2	1	75.36	4	
	P3	1	56.34	5	
	P4	2	75.32	4	
	P5	2	56.35	5	
HPCSched	P1	1	0.01	-	227.33s
	P2	1	90.11	-	
	P3	1	93.95	-	
	P4	2	89.28	-	
	P5	2	93.75	-	

Table 6. MetbenchVar balanced and imbalanced characterization

4.4. Siesta

Our last experiment consists of running SIESTA as an example of real application. SIESTA (SIESTA, 2009; Soler et al., 2002) is a method for *ab initio order-N materials simulation*, specifically it is a self-consistent density functional method that uses standard norm-conserving pseudo-potentials and a flexible, numerical linear combination of atomic orbitals basis set, which includes multiple-zeta and polarization orbitals.

The application presents an imbalance caused by both the algorithm and the input set. For this very interesting input set, a nanoparticle of barium titanate, SIESTA behavior is not constant during each iteration, as can be seen in Figure 9(a); this makes our static balancing solution not as good as for the BT-MZ case. Yet, we achieved an improvement of 8.1% of execution time reduction with respect to the reference case (Case A).

Case A: Like for BT-MZ, Case A is the reference case, i.e., where process P_i is assigned to CPU_i and the priority of all the processes is set to 4. Figure 9(a) shows the trace for this reference case. The program starts with an initialization phase (11.99% of the total time) at the end of which each process in the application must reach a barrier. The initialization phase already presents some little imbalance, which evidences how the input set makes

SIESTA imbalanced. In the internal parts, each process exchanges data only with a subset of the other processes in the application, and then reaches a synchronization point (`WaitAll()`), waiting for all the others to complete their jobs. In the last part, the processes finalize their work (13.41% of the total time): after the last barrier, each process computes its function on its sub-set of data and then ends. A complete execution of the program in this configuration takes 858.57 secs.

Case B: As we can see from the trace in Figure 9(a) is not easy to understand how to balance the application and whether our balancing approach is worth. However, Table 7 shows some more information about SIESTA (hard to retrieve from the trace): processes *P*1 and *P*2 spend a considerable amount of time waiting for *P*3 and *P*4 to reach the barrier. Thus, the first hint would be to put *P*1 and *P*3 on one core and *P*2 and *P*4 on the other and then play with priority. We tried this case but then we realized that *P*2 and *P*3 have almost the same amount of data to work on. Thus, in Case B we put *P*2 and *P*3 on the first core and *P*1 and *P*4 on the second one and increased the priority of *P*3 and *P*4 to 5. In this case we achieved a little improvement of 1.24% (the total execution time is 847.91 sec). Figure 9(b) shows that, in this new configuration, *P*2 is the new bottleneck of the finalization part.

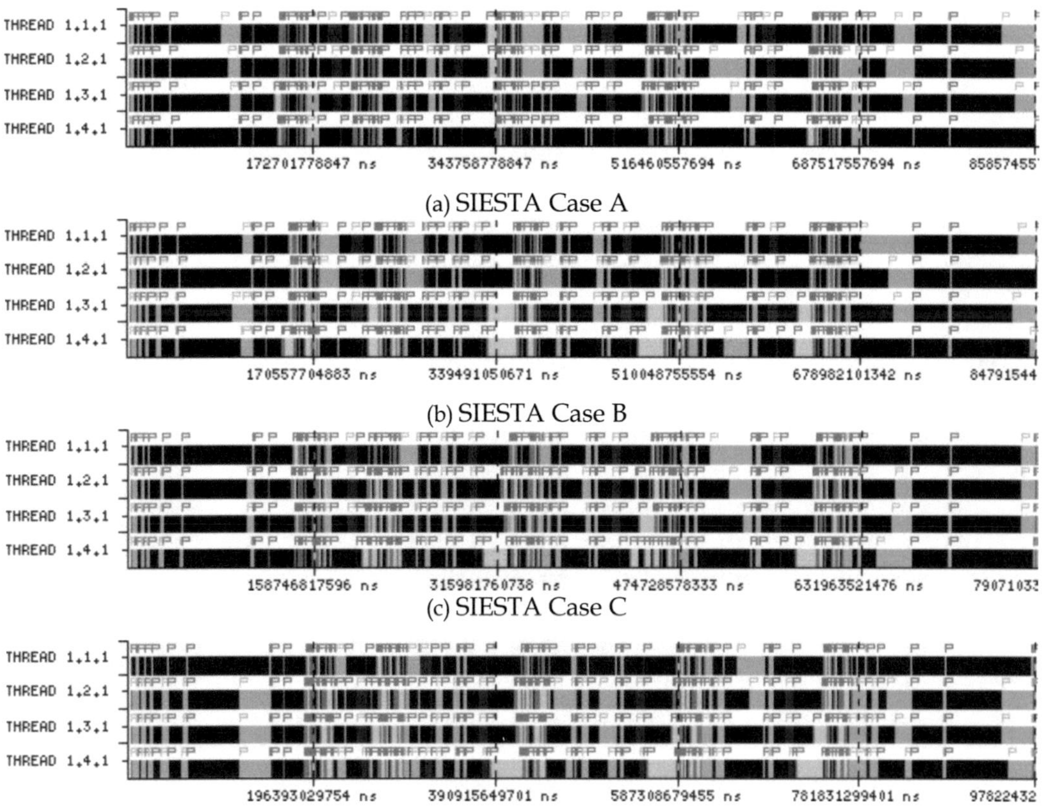

(a) SIESTA Case A

(b) SIESTA Case B

(c) SIESTA Case C

(d) SIESTA Case D

Fig. 9. Effect of the hardware thread prioritization on SIESTA

Case C: In the previous case we obtained a little improvement, still the application results quite imbalanced. We realized that, since *P2* and *P3* work, more or less, on the same amount of data, using a different priority for these two processes may introduce even more imbalance. Figure 9(b) shows that, indeed, this is the case. In Case C we restored the original relative behavior between process *P2* and *P3* setting both their priority to 4 (i.e., the difference is 0). Figure 9(c) shows how the application is now more balanced. For example, looking at the initialization and the finalization part, it is possible to see that the processes are much more balanced than in Case A and Case B. In fact, re-balancing SIESTA reduces the total execution time to 798.20 sec, an improvement of 8.1% with respect to the reference case.

Case D: Following the same idea of the previous case (i.e., leave *P2* and *P3* with the same priority and play with *P1* and *P4*), we increased the amount of resources assigned to *P4*, penalizing *P1*. Figure 9(d) shows how we reverse the imbalance: SIESTA is again imbalanced, though in a different way than in the reference case. In Case D, *P1* (the process with less hardware resources) is the bottleneck (in the initialization, finalization and most of the internal phases) and the total execution time increases to 976.35 sec, with a loss of 13.72%.

Test	Proc	Core	% Comp	Priority	Exec. Time
ST	P1	1	81.79	7	1236.05s
	P2	2	93.72	7	
A	P1	1	75.94	4	858.57s
	P2	1	75.24	4	
	P3	2	82.08	4	
	P4	2	93.47	4	
B	P1	2	79.57	4	847.91s
	P2	1	87.06	4	
	P3	1	72.04	5	
	P4	2	77.73	5	
C	P1	2	83.04	4	789.20s
	P2	1	79.66	4	
	P3	1	80.78	4	
	P4	2	78.74	5	
D	P1	2	90.76	4	976.35s
	P2	1	65.74	4	
	P3	1	68.08	4	
	P4	2	63.95	6	

Table 7. SIESTA balanced and imbalanced characterization

BT-MZ and SIESTA are two cases of non-balanced HPC applications, though their imbalance is quite different. BT-MZ executes several iterations, all of them similar from the execution time, CPU utilization and imbalance point of view. SIESTA also executes several iterations, but each iteration is not necessarily similar to the previous or the next one. In particular, the process that computes the most is not the same across all the iterations. For example, in the *i*-th iteration *P1* could be the bottleneck while in the *(i+1)*-th the most computing process could be *P4*. This behavior suggests that a good balancing mechanism would prioritize *P1* in the *i*-th and *P4* in the *i+1*-th iteration. Our static approach does not allow us to play in this way as we assign the priority at the beginning of the execution and never change them during the execution. We argue that a dynamic mechanism is required to correctly set priorities for applications that change their behavior throughout their execution.

5. Related work

Traditional solutions to attack the problem of load imbalance in HPC applications typically use dynamic data re-distribution. For OpenMP applications load balancing may be performed using some of the existing loop scheduling algorithms that assigns iterations to software threads dynamically (Aygade et al., 2003). MPI applications are much more complex because data communications are defined explicitly in the algorithm by programmers. Static approaches for distributing data using sophisticated tools have been proposed: for example, METIS (METIS, 2009) analyzes data and tries to find the best data distribution. These approaches achieve good performance results but have the drawback that they must be repeated for each input data set and architecture. Dynamic approaches have also been proposed in the literature (Schloegel et al., 2000) and (Walshaw and Cross, 2002). The authors try to solve the load-balancing problem of irregular applications by proposing mesh repartitioning algorithms and evaluating the convenience of repartitioning the mesh or adjusting it.

Processing re-distribution is another approach that consists of assigning more resources to those processes that compute for longer. In the case of OpenMP, this can be useful when using nested parallelism, assigning more software threads to those groups with high load (Duran et al., 2005). The case of MPI is much more complex because the number of processes is statically determined when starting the job (in case of malleable jobs), or when compiling the application (in case of rigid jobs). This problem has been also approached through hybrid programming models, combining MPI and OpenMP. Huang and Tafti (Huang and Tafti, 1999) balance irregular applications by modifying the computational power rather than using the typical mesh redistribution. In their work, the application detects the overloading of some of its processes and tries to solve the problem by creating new software threads at run time. They observe that one of the difficulties of this method is that they do not control the operating system decisions which could oppose their own ones.

Concerning the use of SMT architectures for HPC applications, several studies (Curtis-Maury and Wang, 2005; Celebioglu et al, 2004) show that Hyper-Threading (the SMT implementation of Intel Processors) improve performance for some workloads. However, for other workloads there are many conflicts when accessing shared resources, creating a negative impact on the performance. In (Curtis-Maury and Wang, 2005) the study is performed for MPI applications while in (Celebioglu et al, 2004) the study focuses in OpenMP applications. In (Celebioglu et al, 2004) the authors propose a mechanism that, given a multiprocessor machine with Hyper-Threading processors, dynamically deactivates the Hyper-Threading in some processors in order to improve the performance of the workload under study.

The solution presented in this chapter is orthogonal to both the software thread re-distribution and the dynamically activating Hyper-Threading. Let's assume that we want to run an HPC application on a cluster having several IBM POWER5 processors. The proposal in (Celebioglu et al, 2004) can be used to determine in which cores SMT has to be deactivated. For those cores with the SMT feature active, hardware prioritization can be used to select the appropriate hardware priority to reduce imbalance. Compared with software thread-distribution, hardware prioritization can be seen as low level solution for load balancing.

6. Summary

In this chapter we present the problem of imbalance in HPC applications. In fact, some applications show an imbalanced behavior, i.e., some processes require more time to complete their computing phase while all the other processes are waiting at some synchronization point and cannot move forward. We show the reasons for imbalance and some examples where the application is imbalanced because of data distribution (NAS BT-MZ), or because of the application's input (SIESTA).

We also present the idea of using software controlled allocation of the hardware resources to perform load-balance of HPC applications. Experimental cases show how using a modified Linux kernel to control a processor capable to dynamically assign processor resources to running contexts (the IBM POWER5 in this case), reduces the application imbalance and, therefore, improves overall performance. The experiments performed show an improvement up to 18% for a widely used BT-MZ benchmark and up to 8.1% for a real application (SIESTA). These results do not require putting the burden of balancing the application on the programmer and are independent from the used programming model. In addition, we show cases where the application presents variable behavior. We discuss on why it motivates the use of automatic load-balancers based on software-controlled hardware resource allocation.

From the case studies presented, it is possible to conclude that the hardware resource allocation in multithreaded processors is an important tool that allows to load-balance HPC applications, improving significantly their performance.

7. References

Alpert, D. (2003). Will microprocessor become simpler? *Microprocessor Report.*

Ayguade, E., Blainey, B., Duran, A., Labarta, J., Martinez, F., Martorell, X., and Silvera, R. (2003). Is the schedule clause really necessary in openMP? *In Proceedings of the 4th International Workshop on OpenMP Applications and Tools (WOMPAT'03)*, volume 2716 of Lecture Notes in Computer Science (LNCS), pages 147–159, Toronto, Canada. Springer-Verlag (New York).

Boneti, C., Cazorla, F. J., Gioiosa, R., Buyuktosunoglu, A., Cher, C.-Y., and Valero, M. (2008a). Software-controlled priority characterization of POWER5 processor. *In Proceedings of the 35th International Symposium on Computer Architecture (ISCA'08)*, Beijing. ACM SIGARCH.

Boneti, C., Gioiosa, R., Cazorla, F. J., and Valero, M. (2008b). A dynamic scheduler for balancing HPC applications. *In Proceedings of the International Conference for High Performance Computing, Networking, Storage and Analysis (SC'08)*, Austin, TX. IEEE/ACM.

Bossen, D. C., Tendler, J. M., and Reick, K. (2002). Power4 system design for high reliability. *IEEE Micro*, 22(2):16–24.

Cazorla, F. J., Knijnenburg, P. M. W., Sakellariou, R., Fernandez, E., Ramirez, A., and Valero, M. (2006). Predictable performance in SMT processors: Synergy between the OS and SMTs. *IEEE Transactions on Computers*, 55(7):785- 799.

Celebioglu, O., Saify, A., Leng, T., Hsieh, J., Mashayekhi, V., and Rooholamini, R. (2004). The performance impact of computational efficiency on HPC clusters with hyper-threading technology. *In Proceedings of the 3rd International Workshop on Performance Modeling, Evaluation, and Optimization of Parallel and Distributed Systems (PMEOPDS'04)*, Santa Fe, New Mexico, USA. IEEE Computer Society (Los Alamitos, CA).

Curtis-Maury, M. and Wang, T. (2005). Integrating multiple forms of multithreaded execution on multi-SMT systems: A study with scientific applications. *In Proceedings of the 2nd International Conference on the Quantitative Evaluation of Systems (QEST'05)*, pages 199–209, Torino, Italy. IEEE Computer Society.

Duran, A., Gonzalez, M., Corbalan, J., Martorell, X., Ayguade, E., Labarta, J., and Silvera, R. (2005). Automatic thread distribution for nested parallelism in OpenMP. *In Proceedings of the 19th ACM International Conference on Supercomputing (ICS'05)*, pages 121–130, Cambridge, Massachusetts, USA.

Gibbs, B., Atyam, B., Berres, F., Blanchard, B., Castillo, L., Coelho, P., Guerin, N., Liu, L., Maciel, C. D., Sosa, C., and Thirumalai, R. (2005). *Advanced POWER Virtualization on IBM eServer p5 Servers: Architecture and Performance Considerations*. IBM Redbook. IBM, International Technical Support Organization, Austin, TX, USA.

Gioiosa, R., Petrini, F., Davis, K., and Lebaillif-Delamare, F. (2004). Analysis of system overhead on parallel computers. *In Proceedings of the 4th IEEE International Symposium on Signal Processing and Information Technology (ISSPIT'04)*, pages 387–390, Rome, Italy.

Huang, W. and Tafti, D. (1999). A parallel computing framework for dynamic power balancing in adaptive mesh refinement applications. *In Proceedings of the Parallel Computational Fluid Dynamics (PCFD'99)*.

IBM (2005a). *User Instruction Set Architecture version 2.02*. Number 1 in PowerPC Architecture books.

IBM (2005b). *PowerPC Operating Environment Architecture version 2.02*. Number 3 in PowerPC Architecture books.

IBM (2005c). *PowerPC Virtual Environment Architecture version 2.02*. Number 2 in PowerPC Architecture books.

IBM (2008). *Cell broadband engine programming handbook v1.11*.

IBM, Sony, and Toshiba (2006). *Cell broadband engine architecture v1.01*.

Jin, H. and der Wijngaart, R. F. V. (2006). Performance characteristics of the multi-zone NAS parallel benchmarks. *Journal of Parallel and Distributed Computing*, 66(5):674- 685.

Kalla, R. N., Sinharoy, B., and Tendler, J. M. (2003). SMT implementation in POWER5. *In Hot Chips*, volume 15.

Kalla, R. N., Sinharoy, B., and Tendler, J. M. (2004). IBM POWER5 Chip: a dual-core multithreaded processor. *IEEE Micro*, 24(2):40–47.

Labarta, J., Girona, S., Pillet, V., Cortes, T., and Gregoris, L. (1996). DiP: A parallel program development environment. *In Proceedings of the 2nd International Conference on Parallel Processing (Euro-Par'96)*, volume II of Lecture Notes in Computer Science, pages 665–674, Lyon, France. Springer.

Le, H. Q., Starke, W. J., Fields, J. S., O'Connell, F. P., Nguyen, D. Q., Ronchetti, B. J., Sauer, W., Schwarz, E. M., and Vaden, M. T. (2007). *IBM POWER6 microarchitecture. IBM Journal of Research and Development*, 51(6):639- 662.

Marr, D. T., Binns, F., Hill, D. L., Hinton, G., Koufaty, D. A., Miller, J. A., and Upton, M. (2002). *Hyper-threading technology architecture and microarchitecture*. Intel Technology Journal, 6(1):4–15.

Metis - family of multilevel partitioning algorithms (2009). http://glaros.dtc.umn.edu/gkhome/views/metis.

Moreto, M., Cazorla, F. J., Ramirez, A., and Valero, M. (2008). MLP-aware dynamic cache partitioning. *In Proceedins of the 3rd International Conference on High Performance Embedded Architectures and Compilers (HiPEAC'08)*, volume 4917 of Lecture Notes in Computer Science, pages 337–352, Goteborg, Sweden. Springer.

NASA. NAS parallel benchmarks (2009). http://www.nas.nasa.gov/Resources/Software/npb.html

Petrini, F., Kerbyson, D. J., and Pakin, S. (2003). The case of the missing supercomputer performance: Achieving optimal performance on the 8, 192 processors of ASCI Q. *In International Conference for High Perfromance Computing, Networking, Storage and Analysis (SC'03)*, page 55. IEEE/ACM SIGARCH.

Qureshi, M. K. and Patt, Y. N. (2006). Utility-based cache partitioning: A low-overhead, high-performance, runtime mechanism to partition shared caches. *In Proceedings of the 39th International Symposium on Microar- chitecture (MICRO'06)*, pages 423–432. IEEE Computer Society.

Schloegel, K., Karypis, G., and Kumar, V. (2000). Parallel multilevel algorithms for multi-constraint graph partitioning. *In Proceedings of the 6th International Conference on Parallel Processing (Euro-Par'00)*, volume 1900 of LNCS, pages 296–310. Springer-Verlag, Berlin.

Serrano, M. J., Wood, R. C., and Nemirovsky, M. (1993). A study on multistreamed superscalar processors. *Technical Report 93-05*, University of California Santa Barbara.

SIESTA: A linear-scaling density-functional method (2009). http://www.uam.es/siesta/

Sinharoy, B., Kalla, R. N., Tendler, J. M., Eickemeyer, R. J., and Joyner, J. B. (2005). POWER5 system microarchitecture. *IBM Journal of Research and Development*, 49(4/5):505- 521.

Soler, J. M., Artacho, E., Gale, J. D., Garcia, A., Junquera, J., Ordejon, P., and Sanchez-Portal, D. (2002). The SIESTA method for ab initio order-n materials simulation. *Journal of Physics: Condensed Matter*, 14(11).

The TOP500 Supercomputing Sites (2007). http://www.top500.org/lists/2007/06.

Tsafrir, D., Etsion, Y., Feitelson, D. G., and Kirkpatrick, S. (2005). System noise, os clock ticks, and fine- grained parallel applications. *In Proceedings of the 19th International Conference on Supercomputing (ICS '05)*, pages 303–312, New York, NY, USA. ACM Press.

Tullsen, D. M., Eggers, S. J., and Levy, H. M. (1995). Simultaneous multithreading: Maximizing on-chip parallelism. *Proceedings of the 22nd Annual International Symposium on Computer Architecture (ISCA'95)*, pages 392–403.

Walshaw, C. H. and Cross, M. (2002). Dynamic mesh partitioning and load-balancing for parallel computational mechanics codes. *In Computational Mechanics Using High Performance Computing*, pages 79–94. Saxe-Coburg Publications, Stirling

8

A Fixed-Priority Scheduling Algorithm for Multiprocessor Real-Time Systems

Shinpei Kato
The University of Tokyo
Japan

1. Introduction

Major chip manufacturers have adopted multicore technologies in recent years, due to the thermal problems that distress traditional single-core chip designs in terms of processor performance and power consumption. Nowadays, multiprocessor platforms have proliferated in the marketplace, not only for servers and personal computers but also for embedded machines. The research on real-time systems has been therefore renewed for those multiprocessor platforms, especially in the context of real-time scheduling.

Real-time scheduling techniques for multiprocessors are mainly classified into *partitioned scheduling* and *global scheduling*. In the partitioned scheduling class, tasks are first assigned to specific processors, and then executed on those processors without migrations. In the global scheduling class, on the other hand, all tasks are stored in a global queue, and the same number of the highest priority tasks as processors are selected for execution.

The partitioned scheduling class has such an advantage that can reduce a problem of multiprocessor scheduling into a set of uniprocessor one, after tasks are partitioned. In addition, it does not incur runtime overhead as much as global scheduling, since tasks never migrate across processors. However, there is a disadvantage in theoretical scheduling performance, i.e., schedulability a likelihood of a system being schedulable. Specifically, the worst-case leads to that a periodic task system can cause deadline misses in partitioned scheduling, if the system utilization exceeds 50% (Lopez et al., 2004).

The global scheduling class is meanwhile attractive in the worst-case schedulability. In this class, Pfair (Baruah et al., 1996) and LLREF (Cho et al., 2006) are known to be optimal algorithms. Any task sets are scheduled successfully by those algorithms, if the processor utilization does not exceed 100%. However, the number of migrations and context switches is often criticized. This scheduling class also provides concise and efficient algorithms, such as EDZL (Cho et al., 2002) and EDCL (Kato & Yamasaki, 2008a), which perform with less preemptions than the optimal ones, but the absolute worst-case processor utilization is still 50%.

For the purpose of finding a balance point between partitioned scheduling and global scheduling, recent work have made available a new class, called *semi-partitioned scheduling* in this paper. In this scheduling class, most tasks are fixed to specific processors as partitioned scheduling to reduce the number of migrations, while a few tasks may migrate across processors to improve available processor utilization as much as possible.

In addition to scheduling classes, the real-time systems community often argue priority-driven scheduling policies. Commodity operating systems for practical use usually prefer fixed-priority algorithms in terms of implementation simplicity and priority-based predictability. The most well-known fixed-priority algorithm is Rate Monotonic (RM) (Liu & Layland, 1973). Andersson et al. showed that RM based on global scheduling offers the bound on system utilization no greater than 33% (Andersson et al., 2001), while RM based on partitioned scheduling offers the one up to 50% (Andersson & Jonsson, 2003). So if we restrict our attention to fixed-priority algorithms, partitioned scheduling may be more efficient than global scheduling.

This chapter presents a new fixed-priority algorithm based on semi-partitioned scheduling. The presented algorithm has two major contributions. First, it allows tasks to migrate across processors only if they cannot be assigned (fixed) to any individual processors, to strictly dominate the previous algorithms based on classical partitioned scheduling. Second, its scheduling policy conforms Deadline Monotonic (DM) (Leung & Whitehead, 1982), which is a generalization of RM for arbitrary-deadline tasks, to make available the prior analytical results of DM (and RM). The contents of this chapter are based on the paper in (Kato & Yamasaki, 2009).

The reminder of this chapter is organized as follows. The next section reviews prior work on semi-partitioned scheduling. The system model is defined in Section 3. Section 4 then presents a new algorithm based on semi-partitioned scheduling. Section 5 evaluates the effectiveness of the new algorithm. This chapter is concluded in Section 6.

2. Related Work

The concept of semi-partitioned scheduling was originally introduced by EDF-fm (Anderson et al., 2005). EDF-fm assigns the highest priority to migratory tasks in a static manner. The fixed tasks are then scheduled according to EDF, when no migratory tasks are ready for execution. Since EDF-fm is designed for soft real-time systems, the schedulability of a task set is not tightly guaranteed, while the tardiness is bounded.

EKG (Andersson & Tovar, 2006) is designed to guarantee all tasks to meet deadlines for implicit-deadline periodic task systems. Here, a deadline is said to be implicit, if it is equal to a period. EKG differs from EDF-fm in that migratory tasks are executed in certain time slots, while fixed tasks are scheduled according to EDF. The achievable processor utilization is traded with the number of preemptions and migrations by a parameter. The optimal parameter configuration leads to that any task sets are scheduled successfully with more preemptions and migrations.

In the later work (Andersson & Bletsas, 2008), EKG is extended for sporadic task systems. Here, a task is said to be sporadic, if its job arrivals are separated at least length equal to its period. The extended algorithm is also parametric with respect to the length of the time slots reserved for migratory tasks. EDF-SS (Andersson et al., 2008) is a further extension of the algorithm for arbitrary-deadline systems. Here, a deadline is said to be arbitrary, if it is not necessarily equal to a period. It is shown by simulations that EDF-SS offers a significant improvement on schedulability over EDF-FFD (Baker, 2005), the best performer among partitioned scheduling algorithms.

EDDHP (Kato & Yamasaki, 2007) is designed in consideration of reducing preemptions, as compared to EKG. In EDDHP, the highest priority is assigned to migratory tasks, and other fixed tasks have the EDF priorities, though it differs in that the scheduling policy guarantees all tasks to meet deadlines unlike EDF-fm. It is shown by simulations that EDDHP outperforms partitioned EDF-based algorithms, with less preemptions than EKG. EDDP (Kato & Yamasaki, 2008b) is an extension of EDDHP in that the priority ordering is fully dynamic. The worst-case processor utilization is then bounded by 65% for implicit-deadline systems.

RMDP (Kato & Yamasaki, 2008c) is a fixed-priority version of EDDHP: the highest priority is given to migratory tasks, and other fixed tasks have the RM priorities. It is shown by simulations that RMDP improves schedulability over traditional fixed-priority algorithms. The worst-case processor utilization is bounded by 50% for implicit-deadline systems. To the best of our knowledge, no other algorithms based on semi-partitioned scheduling consider fixed-priority assignments.

We have several concerns for the previous algorithms mentioned above. First, tasks migrate across processors, even though they can be assigned to individual processors. Hence, we are not sure that those algorithms are truly more effective than classical partitioned scheduling approaches. Then, such tasks may migrate in and out of the same processor many times within the same period, which is likely to cause the cache hit ratio to decline. The number of context switches is also problematic due to repetition of migrations. In addition, optional techniques for EDF and RM, such as synchronization and dynamic voltage scaling, may not be easily available, since the scheduling policy is more or less modified from EDF and RM. In this chapter, we aim at addressing those concerns.

3. System Model

The system is composed of m identical processors P_1, P_2, ..., P_m and n sporadic tasks $T_1, T_2, ..., T_n$. Each task T_i is characterized by a tuple (c_i, d_i, p_i), where c_i is a worst-case computation time, d_i is a relative deadline, and p_i is a minimum inter-arrival time (period). The utilization of T_i is denoted by $u_i = c_i / p_i$. We assume such a constrained task model that satisfies $c_i \leq d_i \leq p_i$ for any T_i. Each task T_i generates an infinite sequence of jobs, each of which has a constant execution time c_i. A job of T_i released at time t has a deadline at time $t + d_i$. Any inter-arrival intervals of successive jobs of T_i are separated by at least p_i.

Each task is independent and preemptive. Any job is not allowed to be executed in parallel. Jobs produced by the same task must be executed sequentially, which means that every job of T_i is not allowed to begin before the preceding job of T_i completes. The costs of scheduler invocations, preemptions, and migrations are not modeled.

4. New Algorithm

We present a new algorithm, called **Deadline Monotonic with Priority Migration (DM-PM)**, based on the concept of semi-partitioned scheduling. In consideration of the migration and preemption costs, a task is qualified to migrate, only if it cannot be assigned to any individual processors, in such a way that it is never returned to the same processor within the same period, once it is migrated from one processor to another processor. On uniprocessor platforms, Deadline Monotonic (DM) has been known as an optimal algorithm for fixed-priority scheduling of sporadic task systems. DM assigns a higher priority to a task with a shorter relative deadline. This priority ordering follows Rate Monotonic (RM) for periodic task systems with all relative deadlines equal to periods. Given that DM dominates RM, we design the algorithm based on DM.

4.1 Algorithm Description

As the classical partitioning approaches Andersson & Jonsson (2003); Dhall & Liu (1978); Fisher et al. (2006); Lauzac et al. (1998); Oh & Son (1995), DM-PM assigns each task to a particular processor, using kinds of bin-packing heuristics, upon which the schedulable condition for DM is satisfied. In fact, any heuristics are available for DM-PM. If there are no such processors, DM-PM is going to share the task among more than one processor, whereas a task set is decided to be unfeasible in the classical partitioning approaches. In a scheduling phase, such a shared task is qualified to migrate across those multiple processors.

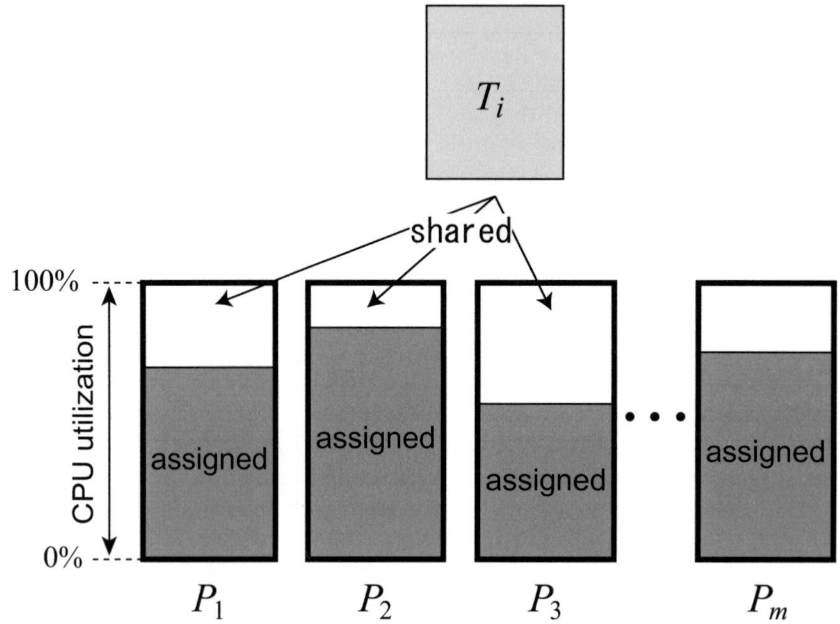

Fig. 1. Example of sharing a task.

Figure 1 demonstrates an example of sharing a task among more than one processor. Let us assume that none of the m processors has spare capacity enough to accept full share of a task T_i. According to DM-PM, T_i is for instance shared among the three processors P_1, P_2, and P_3. In terms of utilization share, T_i is "split" into three portions. The share is always assigned to processors with lower indexes. The execution capacity is then given to each share so that the corresponding processors are filled to capacity. In other words, the processors have no spare capacity to receive other tasks, once a shared task is assigned to them. However, only the last processor to which the shared task is assigned may still have spare capacity, since the execution requirement of the last portion of the task is not necessarily aligned with the remaining capacity of the last processor. Thus, in the example, no tasks will be assigned to P_1 and P_2, while some tasks may be later assigned to P_3. In a scheduling phase, T_i migrates across P_1, P_2 and P_3. We will describe how to compute the execution capacity for each share in Section 4.2.

Here, we need to guarantee that multiple processors never execute a shared task simultaneously. To this end, DM-PM simplifies the scheduling policy as follows.

- A shared task is scheduled by the highest priority within the execution capacity on each processor.

- Every job of the shared task is released on the processor with the lowest index, and it is sequentially migrated to the next processor when the execution capacity is consumed on one processor.
- Fixed tasks are then scheduled according to DM.

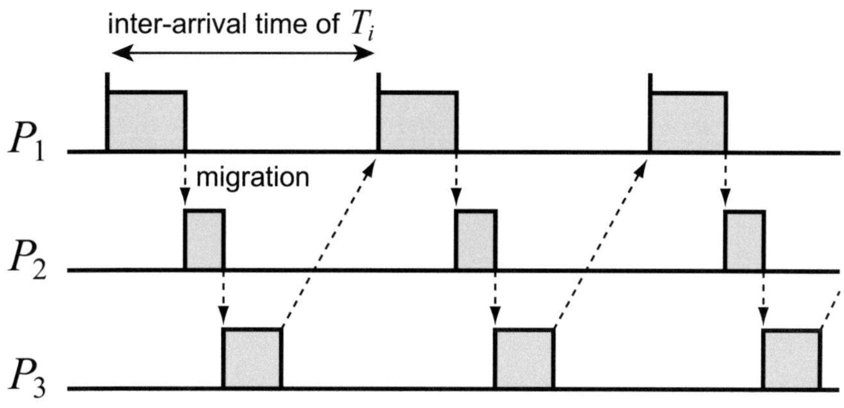

Fig. 2. Example of scheduling a shared task

Figure 2 illustrates an example of scheduling a shared task T_i whose share is assigned to three processors P_1, P_2, and P_3. Let $c'_{i,1}$, $c'_{i,2}$, and $c'_{i,3}$ be the execution capacity assigned to T_i on P_1, P_2, and P_3 respectively. Every job of T_i is released on P_1 that has the lowest index. Since T_i is scheduled by the highest priority, it is immediately executed until it consumes $c'_{i,1}$ time units. When $c'_{i,1}$ is consumed, T_i is migrated to the next processor P_2, and then scheduled by the highest priority again. T_i is finally migrated to the last processor P_3 when $c'_{i,2}$ is consumed on P_2, and then executed in the same manner.

The scheduling policy of DM-PM above implies that the execution of a shared task T_i is repeated exactly at its inter-arrival time on every processor, because it is scheduled by the highest priority on each processor until the constant execution capacity is consumed. A shared task T_i can be thus regarded as an independent task with an execution time $c'_{i,k}$ and a minimum inter-arrival time p_i, to which the highest priority is given, on every processor P_k. As a result, all tasks are scheduled strictly in order of fixed-priority, though the scheduling policy is slightly modified from DM.

We next need to consider the case in which one processor executes two shared tasks. Let us assume that another task T_j is shared among three processors T_3, T_4, and T_5, following that a former task T_i has been assigned to three processors P_1, P_2, and P_3, i.e. P_3 is not filled to capacity yet as explained in the previous example with Figure 3. We here need to break a tie between two shared tasks T_i and T_j assigned to the same processor P_3, since they both have the highest priority. DM-PM is for this designed so that ties are broken in favor of the one assigned later to the processor. Thus, in the example, T_j has a higher priority than T_i on P_3 in a scheduling phase.

Figure 4 depicts an example of scheduling two shared tasks T_i and T_j, based on the tie-breaking rule above, that are assigned to processors as shown in Figure 3. Jobs of T_i and T_j are generally executed by the highest priority. However, the second job of T_i is blocked by the second job of T_j, when it is migrated to P_3 from P_2, because T_j has a higher priority. The

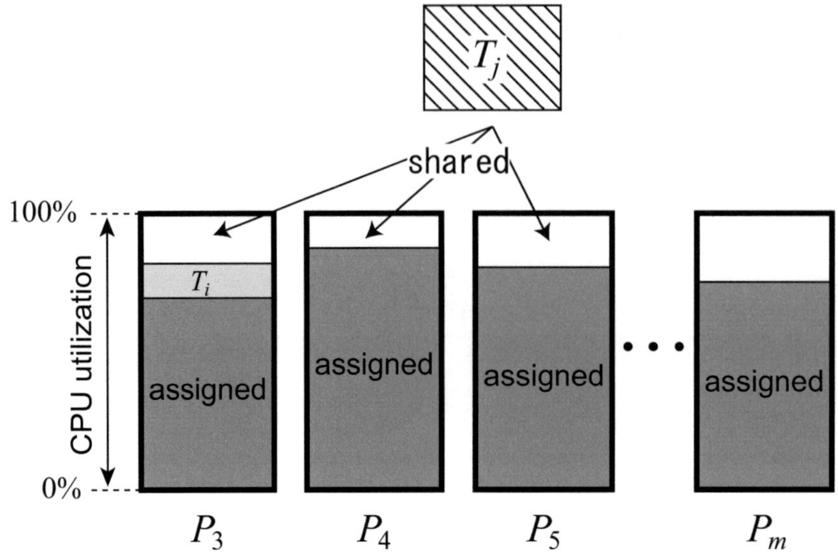

Fig. 3. Example of assigning two shared tasks to one processor.

third job of T_i is also preempted and blocked by the third job of T_j. Here, we see the reason why ties are broken between two shared tasks in favor of the one assigned later to the processor. The execution of T_i is not affected very much, even if it is blocked by T_j, since P_3 is a last processor for T_i to execute. Meanwhile, P_3 is a first processor for T_j to execute, and thus the following execution would be affected very much, if it is blocked on P_3.

Implementation of DM-PM is fairly simplified as compared to the previous algorithms based on semi-partitioned scheduling, because all we have to renew implementation of DM is to set a timer, when a job of a shared task T_i is released on or is migrated to a processor P_k at time t, so that the scheduler will be invoked at time $t + c'_{i,k}$ to preempt the job of T_i for migration. If P_k is a last processor for T_i to execute, we do not have to set a timer. On the other hand, many high-resolution timers are required for implementation of the previous algorithms Andersson & Bletsas (2008); Andersson & Tovar (2006); Kato & Yamasaki (2007; 2008b;c).

4.2 Execution Capacity of Shared Tasks

We now describe how to compute the execution capacity of a shared task on each processor. The amount of execution capacity must guarantee that timing constraints of all tasks are not violated, while processor resource is given to the shared task as much as possible to improve schedulability. To this end, we make use of response time analysis.

It has been known Liu & Layland (1973) that the response time of tasks is never greater than the case in which all tasks are released at the same time, so-called *critical instant*, in fixed-priority scheduling. As we mentioned before, DM-PM guarantees that all tasks are scheduled strictly in order of priority, the worst-case response time is also obtained at the critical instant. Henceforth, we assume that all the tasks are released at the critical instant t_0.

Consider two tasks T_i and T_j, regardless of whether they are fixed tasks or shared tasks. T_i is assigned a lower priority than T_j. Let $I_{i,j}(d_i)$ be the maximum interference (blocking time) that T_i receives from T_j within a time interval of length d_i. Since we assume that all tasks meet

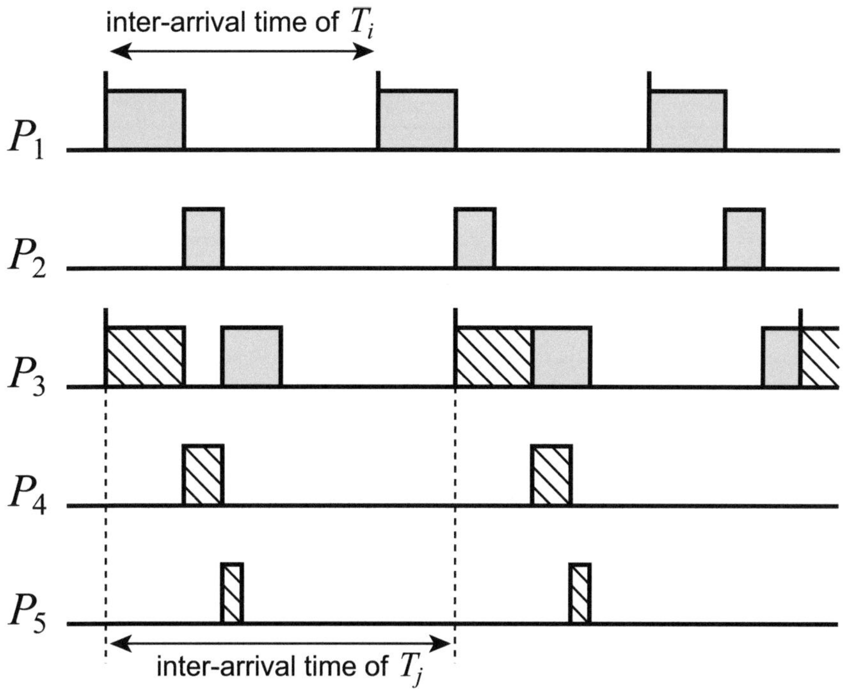

Fig. 4. Example of scheduling two shared tasks on one processor.

deadlines, a job of T_i is blocked by T_j for at most $I_{i,j}(d_i)$. Given the release at the critical instant t_0, it is clear that the total amount of time consumed by a task within any interval $[t_0, t_1)$ is maximized, when the following two conditions hold.

1. The task is released periodically at its minimum inter-arrival time.
2. Every job of the task consumes exactly c_i time units without being preempted right after its release.

The formula of $I_{i,j}(d_i)$, the maximum interference that T_i receives from T_j within d_i, is derived as follows. According to Buttazzo (1997), the maximum interference that a task receives from another task depends on the relation among execution time, period, and deadline. Hereinafter, let $F = \lfloor d_i / p_j \rfloor$ denote the maximum number of jobs of T_j that complete within a time interval of length d_i.

We first consider the case of $d_i \geq Fp_j + c_j$, in which the deadline of T_i occurs while T_j is not executed, as shown in Figure 5. In this case, $I_{i,j}(d_i)$ is obtained by Equation (1).

$$I_{i,j}(d_i) = Fc_j + c_j = (F+1)c_j \tag{1}$$

We next consider the case of $d_i \leq Fp_j + c_j$, in which the deadline of T_i occurs while T_j is executed, as shown in Figure 6. In this case, $I_{i,j}(d_i)$ is obtained by Equation (2).

$$I_{i,j}(d_i) = d_i - F(p_j - c_j) \tag{2}$$

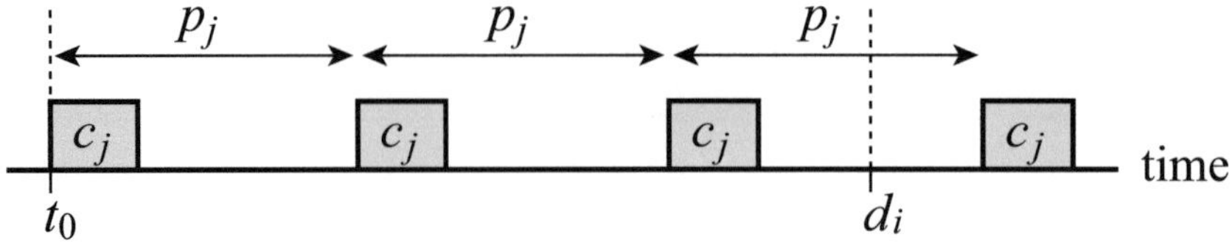

Fig. 5. Case 1: $d_i \geq Fp_j + c_j$.

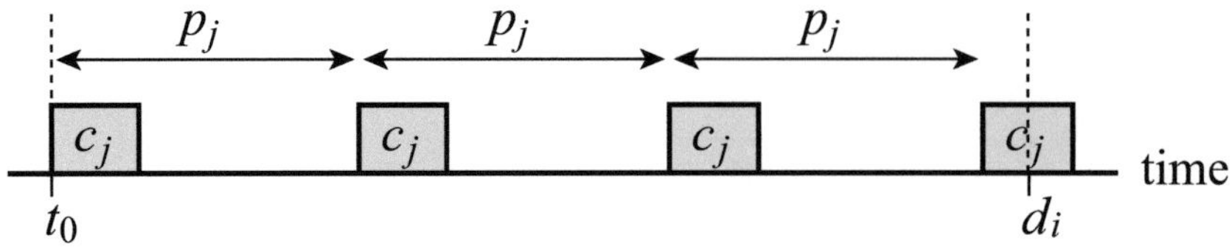

Fig. 6. Case 2: $d_i \leq Fp_j + c_j$.

For the sake of simplicity of description, the notation of $I_{i,j}(d_i)$ unifies Equation (1) and Equation (2) afterwards. The worst-case response time $R_{i,k}$ of each task T_i on P_k is then given by Equation (3), where $\mathcal{P}_k$ is a set of tasks that have been assigned to P_k, and $\mathcal{H}_i$ is a set of tasks that have priorities higher than or equal to T_i.

$$R_{i,k} = \sum_{T_j \in \mathcal{P}_k \cap \mathcal{H}_i} I_{i,j}(d_i) + c_i \tag{3}$$

We then consider the total amount of time that a shared task competes with another task. Let T_s be a shared task, and P_k be a processor to which the share of T_s is assigned. As we mention in Section 4.1, a shared task T_s can be regarded as an independent task with an execution time $c'_{s,k}$ and a minimum inter-arrival time p_s, to which the highest priority is given, on every processor P_k. The maximum total amount $W_{s,k}(d_i)$ of time that T_s competes with a task T_i on P_k within a time interval of length d_i is therefore obtained by Equation (4).

$$W_{s,k}(d_i) = \left\lceil \frac{d_i}{p_s} \right\rceil c'_{s,k} \tag{4}$$

In order to guarantee all tasks to meet deadlines, the following condition must hold for every task T_i on every processor P_k to which a shared task T_s is assigned.

$$R_{i,k} + W_{s,k}(d_i) \leq d_i \tag{5}$$

It is clear that the value of $c'_{s,k}$ is maximized for $R_{i,k} + W_{s,k}(d_i) = d_i$. Finally, $c'_{s,k}$ is given by Equation (6), where $G = \lceil d_i / p_s \rceil$.

$$c'_{s,k} = \min \left\{ \frac{d_i - R_{i,k}}{G} \;\middle|\; T_i \in \mathcal{P}_k \right\} \tag{6}$$

In the end, we describe how to assign tasks to processors. As most partitioning algorithms Dhall & Liu (1978); Fisher et al. (2006); Lauzac et al. (1998); Oh & Son (1995) do, each task is

1. **for each** $P_k \in \Pi$
2. $c_{req} := c_s;$
3. $c'_{s,k} := 0;$
4. **for each** $T_i \in \mathcal{P}_k$
5. **if** T_i is a shared task **then**
6. $x := (d_i - c_i)/\lceil d_i/p_s \rceil;$
7. **else**
8. $x := (d_i - R_{i,k})/\lceil d_i/p_s \rceil;$
9. **end if**
10. **if** $x < c'_{s,k}$ **then**
11. $c'_{s,k} := \max(0, x);$
12. **end if**
13. **end for**
14. **if** $c'_{s,k} \neq 0$ **then**
15. $\mathcal{P}_k := \mathcal{P}_k \cup \{T_s\}:$
16. $c_{req} := c_{req} - c'_{s,k}:$
17. **if** $c_{req} = 0$ **then**
18. $\Pi := \Pi \setminus \{P_k\}:$
19. return *SUCCESS*:
20. **else if** $c_{req} < 0$ **then**
21. $c'_{s,k} := c'_{s,k} + c_{req}:$
22. return *SUCCESS*:
23. **else**
24. $\Pi := \Pi \setminus \{P_k\}:$
25. **end if**
26. **end if**
27. **end for**
28. return *FAILURE*:

Fig. 7. Pseudo code of splitting T_s.

assigned to the first processor upon which a schedulable condition is satisfied. The schedulable condition of T_i for P_k here is defined by $R_{i,k} \leq d_i$. If T_i does not satisfy the schedulable condition, its utilization share is going to be split across processors.

Figure 7 shows the pseudo code of splitting T_s. Π is a set of processors processors that have spare capacity to accept tasks. c_{req} is a temporal variable that indicates the remaining execution requirement of T_s, which must be assigned to some processors. For each processor, the algorithm computes the value of $c'_{s,k}$ until the total of those $c'_{s,k}$ reaches c_s. The value of each $c'_{s,k}$ is based on Equation (6). Notice that if T_i is a shared task that has been assigned to P_k before T_s, the temporal execution capacity is not denoted by $(d_i - c'_{i,k})/\lceil d_i/p_i \rceil$ but by $(d_i - c_i)/\lceil d_i/p_i \rceil$ (line 6), because a job of T_i released at time t always completes at time $t + c_i$ given that T_i is assigned the highest priority. Otherwise, it is denoted by $(d_i - R_{i,k})/\lceil d_i/p_s \rceil$ (line 8). The value of $c'_{s,k}$ must be non-negative (line 11). If $c'_{s,k}$ is successfully obtained, the share of T_s is assigned to P_k (line 15). Now c_{req} is reduced to $c_{req} - c'_{s,k}$ (line 16). A non-positive value of c_{req} means that the utilization share of T_s has been entirely assigned to some processors. Thus, it declares success. Here, a negative value of c_{req} means that the execution capacity has been excessively assigned to T_s. Therefore, we need to adjust the value of $c'_{s,k}$ for the last portion (line 21). If c_{req} is still positive, the same procedure is repeated.

4.3 Optimization

This section considers optimization of DM-PM. Remember again that a shared task T_s can be regarded as an independent task with an execution time $c'_{s,k}$ and a minimum inter-arrival time p_s, to which the highest priority is given, on every processor P_k. We realize from this characteristic that if T_s has the shortest relative deadline on a processor P_k, the resultant scheduling is optimally conformed to DM, though the execution time of T_s is transformed into $c'_{s,k}$.

Based on the idea above, we consider such an optimization that sorts a task set in non-increasing order of relative deadline before the tasks are assigned to processors. This leads to that all tasks that have been assigned to the processors before T_s always have longer relative deadlines than T_s. In other words, T_s always has the shortest relative deadline at this point.

T_s may not have the shortest relative deadline on a processor P_k, if other tasks are later assigned to P_k. Remember that those tasks have shorter relative deadlines than T_s, since a task set is sorted in non-increasing order of relative deadline. According to DM-PM, T_s is assigned to processors so that they are filled to capacity, except for a last processor to which T_s is assigned. Thereby for optimization, we need to concern only such a last processor P_l that executes T_s.

In fact, there is no need to forcefully give the highest priority to T_s on P_l, because the next job of T_s will be released at the beginning of the next period, regardless of its completion time, whereas it is necessary to give the highest priority to T_s on the preceding processors, because T_s is never executed on the next processor unless the execution capacity is consumed. We thus modify DM-PM for optimization so that the prioritization rule is strictly conformed to DM. As a result, a shared task would have a lower priority than fixed tasks, if they are assigned to the processor later.

The worst case problem. Particularly for implicit-deadline systems where relative deadlines are equal to periods, a set of tasks is scheduled on each processor P_k successfully, if the processor utilization U_k of P_k satisfies the following well-known condition, where n_k is the number of the tasks assigned to P_k, because the scheduling policy of the optimized DM-PM is strictly conformed to DM.

$$U_k \leq n_k(2^{1/n_k} - 1) \tag{7}$$

The worst-case processor utilization is derived as 69% for $n_k \to \infty$. Thus to derive the worst-case performance of DM-PM, we consider a case in which an infinite number of tasks, all of which have very long relative deadlines (close to ∞), meaning very small utilization (close to 0), have been already assigned to every processor. Note that the available processor utilization is at most 69% for all processors.

Let T_s be a shared task with individual utilization ($u_s = c_s/p_s$) greater than 69%, and P_l be a last processor to which the utilization share of T_s is assigned. We then assume that another task T_i is later assigned to P_l. At this point, the worst-case execution capacity that can be assigned to T_i on P_l is $d_s - c_s = d_s(1 - u_s)$, due to $d_i \leq d_s$. Hence, the worst-case utilization bound of T_i on P_l is obtained as follows.

$$u_i = \frac{d_s(1 - u_s)}{d_i} \geq (1 - u_s) \tag{8}$$

Now, we concern a case in which T_s has a very large value of u_s (close to 100%). The worst-case utilization bound of T_i is then derived as $u_i = 1 - u_s \simeq 0$, regardless of the processor utilization of P_l. In other words, even though the processor resource of P_l is not fully utilized at all, P_l cannot accept any other tasks.

In order to overcome such a worst case problem, we next modify DM-PM for optimization so that the tasks with individual utilization greater than or equal to 50% are preferentially assigned to processors, before a task set is sorted in non-increasing order of relative deadline. Since no tasks have individual utilization greater than 50%, when T_s is shared among processors, the worst-case execution capacity of T_i is improved to $u_i = 1 - u_s \geq 50\%$. As a result, the optimized DM-PM guarantees that the processor utilization of every processor is at least 50%, which means that the entire multiprocessor utilization is also at least 50%. Given that no prior fixed-priority algorithms have utilization bounds greater than 50% Andersson & Jonsson (2003), our outcome seems sufficient. Remember that this is the worst case. The simulation-based evaluation presented in Section 5 shows that the optimized DM-PM generally performs much better than the worst case.

4.4 Preemptions Bound

The number of preemptions within a time interval of length L is bounded as follows. Let $N(L)$ be the worst-case number of preemptions within L for DM. Since preemptions may occur every time jobs arrive in DM, $N(L)$ is given by Equation (9), where τ is a set of all tasks.

$$N(L) = \sum_{T_i \in \tau} \left\lceil \frac{L}{p_i} \right\rceil \tag{9}$$

Let $N^*(L)$ then be the worst-case number of preemptions within L for DM-PM. It is clear that there are at most $m-1$ shared tasks. Each shared task is migrated from one processor to another processor once in a period. Every time a shared task is migrated from one processor to another processor, two preemptions occurs: one occurs on the source processor and the other occurs on the destination processor. Hence, $N^*(L)$ is given by Equation (9), where τ' is a set of tasks that are shared among multiple processors.

$$N^*(L) = N(L) + 2(m-1) \left\lceil \frac{L}{\min\{p_s \mid T_s \in \tau'\}} \right\rceil \tag{10}$$

5. Evaluation

In this section, we show the results of simulations conducted to evaluate the effectiveness of DM-PM, as compared to the prior algorithms: RMDP Kato & Yamasaki (2008c), FBB-FDD Fisher et al. (2006), and Partitioned DM (P-DM). RMDP is an algorithm based on semi-partitioned scheduling, though the approach and the scheduling policy are different from DM-PM. FBB-FDD and P-DM are algorithms based on partitioned scheduling. FBB-FDD sorts a task set in non-decreasing order of relative deadline, and assigns tasks to processors based on a first-fit heuristic Dhall & Liu (1978). P-DM assigns tasks based on first-fit heuristic for simplicity without sorting a task set. The tasks are then scheduled according to DM. Note that FBB-FDD uses a polynomial-time acceptance test in a partitioning phase, while P-DM uses a response time analysis presented in Section 4.2.

To the best of our knowledge, FBB-FDD is the best performer among the fixed-priority algorithms based on partitioned scheduling. We are then not aware of any fixed-priority algo-

rithms, except for RMDP, that are based on semi-partitioned scheduling. We thus consider that those algorithms are worthwhile to compare with DM-PM.
The fixed-priority algorithms based on global scheduling, such as Andersson (2008); Andersson et al. (2001); Baker (2006), are not included in a series of simulations, because the previous report Kato & Yamasaki (2008c) on simulation-based evaluation of fixed-priority algorithms testified that their schedulability is in general worse than the ones based on partitioned scheduling.

5.1 Simulation Setup

A series of simulations has a set of parameters: u_{sys}, m, u_{min}, and u_{max}. u_{sys} denotes system utilization. m is the number of processors. u_{min} and u_{max} are the minimum utilization and the maximum utilization of every individual task respectively.
For every set of parameters, we generate 1,000,000 task sets. A task set is said to be successfully scheduled, if all tasks in the task set are successfully assigned to processors. The effectiveness of an algorithm is then estimated by *success ratio*, which is defined as follows.

$$\frac{\textit{the number of successfully-scheduled task sets}}{\textit{the number of submitted task sets}}$$

The system utilization u_{sys} is set every 5% within the range of [0.5,1.0]. Due to limitation of space, we have three sets of m such that $m = 4$, $m = 8$, and $m = 16$. Each task set $\mathcal{T}$ is then generated so that the total utilization $\sum_{T_i \in \mathcal{T}} u$ becomes equal to $u_{sys} \times m$. The utilization of every individual task is uniformly distributed within the range of $[u_{min}, u_{max}]$. Due to limitation of space, we have simulated only the case for $[u_{min}, u_{max}] = [0.1, 1.0]$. The minimum inter-arrival time of each task is also uniformly distributed within the range of [100,10,000]. For every task T_i, once u_i and p_i are determined, we compute the execution time of T_i by $c_i = u_i \times p_i$.
Since RMDP is designed for implicit-deadline systems, for fairness we presume that all tasks have relative deadlines equal to periods. However, DM-PM is also effective to explicit-deadline systems where relative deadlines are different from periods.

5.2 Simulation Results

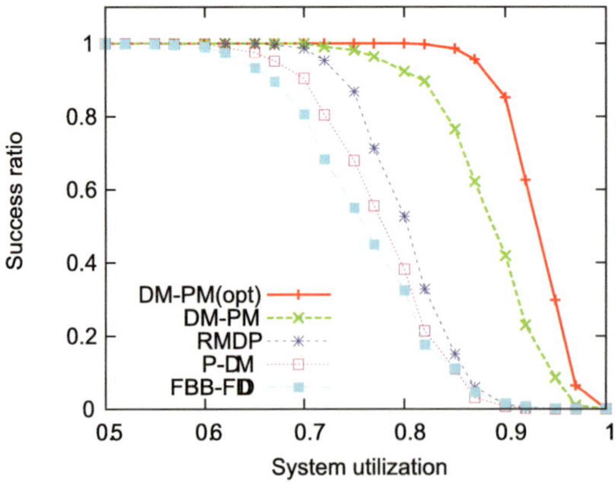

Fig. 8. Results of simulations ($m = 4$ and $[u_{min}, u_{max}] = [0.1, 1.0]$).

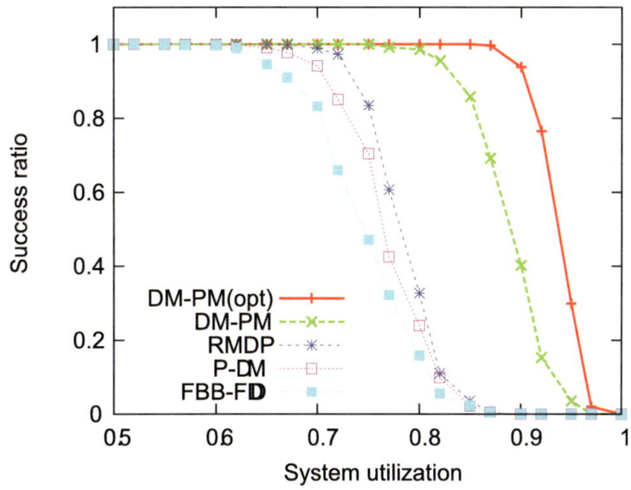

Fig. 9. Results of simulations ($m = 8$ and $[u_{min}, u_{max}] = [0.1, 1.0]$).

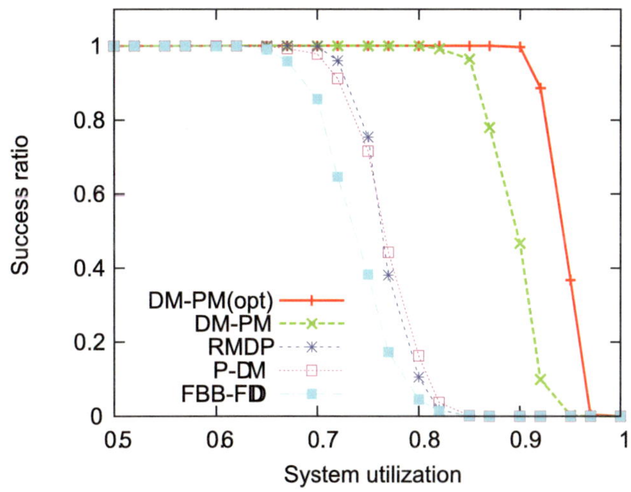

Fig. 10. Results of simulations ($m = 16$ and $[u_{min}, u_{max}] = [0.1, 1.0]$).

Figure 8, 9, and 10 show the results of simulations with $[u_{min}, u_{max}] = [0.1, 1.0]$ on 4, 8, and 16 processors respectively. Here, "DM-PM(opt)" represents the optimized DM-PM. DM-PM substantially outperforms the prior algorithms. Particularly, the optimized DM-PM is able to schedule all task sets successfully, even though system utilization is around 0.9, while the prior algorithms more or less return failure at system utilization around 0.6 to 0.7. It has been reported Lehoczky et al. (1989) that the average case of achievable processor utilization for DM, as well as RM, is about 88% on uniprocessors. Hence, the optimized DM-PM reflects the schedulability of DM on multiprocessors. Even without optimization, DM-PM is able to schedule all task sets when system utilization is smaller than 0.7 to 0.8.

On the whole, the performance of DM-PM is better as the number of processors is greater. That is because tasks are shared among processors more successfully, if there are more processors, when they cannot be assigned to any individual processors. Although RMDP is also able to share tasks among processors, it is far inferior to DM-PM, while it outperforms FBB-FDD and P-DM that are based on classical partitioned scheduling. The difference between DM-PM and RMDP clearly demonstrates the effectiveness of the approach considered in this paper. Note that P-DM outperforms FBB-FDD, because P-DM uses an acceptance test based on the presented response time analysis, while FBB-FDD does a polynomial-time test.

6. Conclusion

A new algorithm was presented for semi-partitioned fixed-priority scheduling of sporadic task systems on identical multiprocessors. We designed the algorithm so that a task is qualified to migrate across processors, only if it cannot be assigned to any individual processors, in such a manner that it is never migrated back to the same processor within the same period, once it is migrated from one processor to another processor. The scheduling policy was then simplified to reduce the number of preemptions and migrations as much as possible for practical use.

We also optimized the algorithm to improve schedulability. Any implicit-deadline systems are successfully scheduled by the optimized algorithm, if system utilization does not exceed 50%. We are not aware of any fixed-priority algorithms that have utilization bounds greater than 50%. Thus, our outcome seems sufficient.

The simulation results showed that the new algorithm significantly outperforms the traditional fixed-priority algorithms regardless of the number of processors and the utilization of tasks. The parameters used in simulations are limited, but we can easily estimate that the new algorithm is also effective to different environments.

In the future work, we will consider arbitrary-deadline systems where relative deadlines may be longer than periods, while we consider constrained-deadline systems where relative deadlines are shorter than or equal to periods. We are also interested in applying the presented semi-partitioned scheduling approach to dynamic-priority scheduling. The implementation problems of the algorithm in practical operating systems are left open.

7. References

Anderson, J., Bud, V. & Devi, U. (2005). An EDF-based Scheduling Algorithm for Multiprocessor Soft Real-Time Systems, *Proceedings of the Euromicro Conference on Real-Time Systems*, pp. 199–208.

Andersson, B. (2008). Global Static-Priority Preemptive Multiprocessor Scheduling with Utilization Bound 38%, *Proceedings of the International Conference on Principles of Distributed Systems*, pp. 73–88.

Andersson, B., Baruah, S. & Jonsson, J. (2001). Static-priority Scheduling on Multiprocessors, *Proceedings of the IEEE Real-Time Systems Symposium*, pp. 193–202.

Andersson, B. & Bletsas, K. (2008). Sporadic Multiprocessor Scheduling with Few Preemptions, *Proceedings of the Euromicro Conference on Real-Time Systems*, pp. 243–252.

Andersson, B., Bletsas, K. & Baruah, S. (2008). Scheduling Arbitrary-Deadline Sporadic Task Systems Multiprocessors, *Proceedings of the IEEE Real-Time Systems Symposium*, pp. 385–394.

Andersson, B. & Jonsson, J. (2003). The Utilization Bounds of Partitioned and Pfair Static-Priority Scheduling on Multiprocessors are 50%, *Proceedings of the Euromicro Conference on Real-Time Systems*, pp. 33–40.

Andersson, B. & Tovar, E. (2006). Multiprocessor Scheduling with Few Preemptions, *Proceedings of the IEEE International Conference on Embedded and Real-Time Computing Systems and Applications*, pp. 322–334.

Baker, T. (2005). An Analysis of EDF Schedulability on a Multiprocessor, *IEEE Transactions on Parallel and Distributed Systems* **16**: 760–768.

Baker, T. (2006). An Analysis of Fixed-Priority Schedulability on a Multiprocessor, *Real-Time Systems* **32**: 49–71.

Baruah, S., Cohen, N., Plaxton, C. & Varvel, D. (1996). Proportionate Progress: A Notion of Fairness in Resource Allocation, *Algorithmica* **15**: 600–625.

Buttazzo, G. (1997). *HARD REAL-TIME COMPUTING SYSTEMS: Predictable Scheduling Algorithms and Applications*, Kluwer Academic Publishers.

Cho, H., Ravindran, B. & Jensen, E. (2006). An Optimal Real-Time Scheduling Algorithm for Multiprocessors, *Proceedings of the IEEE Real-Time Systems Symposium*, pp. 101–110.

Cho, S., Lee, S., Han, A. & Lin, K. (2002). Efficient Real-Time Scheduling Algorithms for Multiprocessor Systems, *IEICE Transactions on Communications* **E85-B**(12): 2859–2867.

Dhall, S. K. & Liu, C. L. (1978). On a Real-Time Scheduling Problem, *Operations Research* **26**: 127–140.

Fisher, N., Baruah, S. & Baker, T. (2006). The Partitioned Multiprocessor Scheduling of Sporadic Task Systems according to Static Priorities, *Proceedings of the Euromicro Conference on Real-Time Systems*, pp. 118–127.

Kato, S. & Yamasaki, N. (2007). Real-Time Scheduling with Task Splitting on Multiprocessors, *Proceedings of the IEEE International Conference on Embedded and Real-Time Computing Systems and Applications*, pp. 441–450.

Kato, S. & Yamasaki, N. (2008a). Global EDF-based Scheduling with Efficient Priority Promotion, *Proceedings of the IEEE International Conference on Embedded and Real-Time Computing Systems and Applications*, pp. 197–206.

Kato, S. & Yamasaki, N. (2008b). Portioned EDF-based Scheduling on Multiprocessors, *Proceedings of the ACM International Conference on Embedded Software*.

Kato, S. & Yamasaki, N. (2008c). Portioned Static-Priority Scheduling on Multiprocessors, *Proceedings of the IEEE International Parallel and Distributed Processing Symposium*.

Kato, S. & Yamasaki, N. (2009). Semi-Partitioned Fixed-Priority Scheduling on Multiprocessors, *Proceedings of the IEEE Real-Time and Embedded Technology and Applications Symposium*, pp. 23–32.

Lauzac, S., Melhem, R. & Mosses, D. (1998). An Efficient RMS Admission Control and Its Application to Multiprocessor Scheduling, *Proceedings of the IEEE International Parallel Processing Symposium*, pp. 511–518.

Lehoczky, J., Sha, L. & Ding, Y. (1989). The Rate Monotonic Scheduling Algorithm: Exact Charaterization and Average Case Behavior, *Proceedings of the IEEE Real-Time Systems Symposium*, pp. 166–171.

Leung, J. & Whitehead, J. (1982). On the Complexity of Fixed-Priority Scheduling of Periodic Real-Time Tasks, *Performance Evaluation, Elsevier Science* **22**: 237–250.

Liu, C. L. & Layland, J. W. (1973). Scheduling Algorithms for Multiprogramming in a Hard Real-Time Environment, *Journal of the ACM* **20**: 46–61.

Lopez, J., Diaz, J. & Garcia, D. (2004). Utilization Bounds for EDF Scheduling on Real-Time Multiprocessor Systems, *Real-Time Systems* **28**: 39–68.

Oh, Y. & Son, S. (1995). Allocating Fixed-Priority Periodic Tasks on Multiprocessor Systems, *Real-Time Systems* **9**: 207–239.

Plagued by Work: Using Immunity to Manage the Largest Computational Collectives

Lucas A. Wilson[1], Michael C. Scherger[2] & John A. Lockman III[1]
[1]*Texas Advanced Computing Center, The University of Texas at Austin*
[2]*Texas A&M University – Corpus Christi*
United States

1. Introduction

Modern computational collectives, ranging from loosely-coupled Grids and Clouds to tightly-coupled clusters, are progressively increasing in both capability and complexity. This has created a need for more efficient methods to schedule tasks to hosts. Typically, system resources in these environments are managed with a combination of simple heuristics and bin-packing algorithms to perform common operations such as backfill. However, as the size and scope of these computational collectives grows ever larger, different approaches must be employed to cope with both the number of resources to manage and the volume of jobs to schedule. One possible avenue is to distribute the task of managing these massive-scale systems across the participants, giving each resource a say in how the final scheduling solution will appear.

The introduction of multi-/many-core architectures has complicated the problem of performing effective scheduling on large-scale systems. The number of allocatable elements per system is now increasing at a staggering rate as hardware manufacturers attempt to keep pace with Moore's Law (Moore 1965). In clusters, for example, the number of "nodes" - standalone physical systems with a network connection - has stabilized due to limitations in current switching technology and power/cooling capacity. However, each node now has more allocatable cores, increasing the cores per node "density" of the system overall. Scheduling algorithms will be required to cope with scheduling quantities of elements increasing by orders of magnitude every few years, while still providing timely decision information.

The Asynchronous Lymphocytic Agent-based Resource Manager (ALARM) was first proposed as a novel method of distributing the task of managing a large set of resources by mimicking the actions of the mammalian immune system (Wilson 2008). Previously reported results demonstrated the viability of using the immune system as a metaphor for distributed resource management and provided a comparison of ALARM to other, more widely-recognized scheduling heuristics (Scherger 2009).

In this chapter we detail how the scheduling problem can be described in terms of the mammalian immune system and provide a description of the ALARM method. We provide comparative results against common scheduling heuristics on large-scale simulations of a tightly-coupled parallel cluster, as well as an analysis of the networking overhead created by using ALARM on the same simulations.

2. Background

As in many tightly or loosely coupled distributed systems, process scheduling is an integral component in determining the efficiency of a high performance computer system. Continuing research in process scheduling algorithms is conducted to ensure that sub-systems in high performance computing will be able to simultaneously maximize utilization and ensure process completion in a specified time period.
Scheduling plays an important role in distributed systems in which it enhances overall system performance metrics such as process completion time and processor utilization (Tel 1998). There are two main classes of distributed process scheduling algorithms: sender-initiated and receiver-initiated algorithms (Chow 1997). A third class of distributed process scheduling algorithms is the hybrid sender-receiver algorithm and is a compromise to overcome the problem from the two algorithms (Ramamritham 2002).
The role of a distributed process scheduler is the same as normal scheduling: improve system performance metrics (Audsley 1994). In distributed systems the existence of multiple processing nodes is a challenging problem for scheduling processes onto processors. One cause for this complex problem is that process scheduling must be performed locally and globally across the whole system. A process created at a node can move to other nodes in the system to redistribute work load as to achieve an improved system performance. Global scheduling performs load sharing between processors. Load sharing allows busy processors to load some of their work to less busy, or even idle, processors (Boger 2001).
Load balancing is a special case of load sharing. In load balancing the global scheduling algorithm is to keep the load even (or balanced) across all processors (Malik 2003). Sender-initiated load sharing occurs when busy processors try to find idle processors to load some work. Receiver-initiated load sharing occurs when idle processors seek busy processors (Stankovic 1999). While load sharing is worthwhile, load balancing is generally not worth the extra effort. Small gains in execution time of tasks are offset by extra effort expended in maintaining a balanced load.
In a distributed system individual nodes have their own policy for determining when to accept or remove tasks. The characteristics of the distributed scheduling algorithm are normally depended on the reason of its existence such as information exchange, resource sharing, and increased reliability through replication and increased performance through parallelization (Boger 2001). Scheduling algorithms have four distinct policies: the transfer policy, the selection policy, the location policy, and the information policy. The transfer policy decides when a node should migrate a particular task, and the selection policy decides which task to migrate. The location policy determines a partner node for the task migration, and the information policy triggers and contains the collection of system state from all nodes: when, what and where (Chaptin 2003).
Scheduling algorithms can also be classified as static or dynamic (Tel 1998). These decisions are based on task characteristics and the current system state. Scheduling algorithms that use a static approach calculates (pre-determine) schedules for the system. It requires a-priori knowledge of the tasks characteristics and does not require any

overhead at run-time. Scheduling algorithms that use a dynamic approach determines schedules at run-time which provide a flexible system that can adapt with non-predicted events. Dynamic scheduling algorithms have a much higher run-time cost overhead but can give greater processor utilization.
Comparison of scheduling algorithms has been researched by (Tel 1998) to evaluate the performance between sender-initiated policy and receiver-initiated policies. Their results prove that sender-initiated policy is better than receiver-initiated policy in light to moderate system loads while receiver-initiated policy is better than sender-initiated policy in high system loads. In addition, (Ramamritham 2002) and (Audsley 1994) have conducted a study towards the performance of sender-initiated and receiver-initiated policies in both homogenous and heterogeneous distributed system with regards to First Come First Serve (FCFS) and Round Robin (RR) scheduling policies. Apart from that, the study also includes the impact of variance in job service times and inter-arrival times. (Boger 2001) provides the explanation on performance sensitivity of the sender-initiated and receiver-initiated policies, to three factors: node-scheduling policy, variance in job inter-arrival, while (Chaptin 2003) has reported the performance of several load sharing policies based on their implementation of both sender-initiated and receiver initiated policies on a five node system connected by a 10Mbps communication network.
Alternatively, (Stankovic 1999) has conducted a study and compared the sender-initiated, receiver-initiated and hybrid (it is called symmetrical-initiated in that literature) policies pertaining to system workload and the effect of probing to overall system performance.

3. Scheduling Tasks on Large-scale Distributed Systems

In general, the scheduling problem is NP-Complete, meaning that a guaranteed optimal solution cannot be found in polynomial time (Cormen 2001). As a result, many resource managers schedule tasks by either building a scheduling matrix (processors x time-window) (Fig. 1) and using an algorithm to solve this packing problem in order to most-efficiently (although not optimally) allocate tasks within that particular time window, by using less expensive heuristics, or through a combination of both. These approaches typically require categorizing tasks into classes of importance.

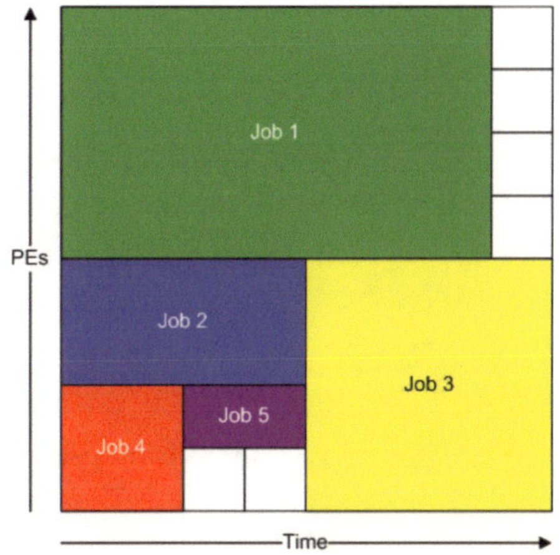

Fig. 1. Example Scheduling Matrix

This is done by either having multiple bins for tasks (e.g. multiple queues on a batch system) or by using a series of priority rules and weighted functions to generate a multi-objective importance factor that can be used to reorder tasks.

3.1 Matrix-based Scheduling Approaches

Managers that use a scheduling matrix have several obvious weaknesses, although they are most likely to generate near-optimal solutions. The primary problem is that they are static in nature. Like many centralized algorithms, solutions to the packing problem can only be performed given the information present when the algorithm begins execution. If new tasks arrive while the algorithm is running, those tasks must either be ignored until the next scheduling period or the algorithm must be restarted. This process can also become extremely expensive both computationally and spatially. Most scheduling algorithms tend to be written with dynamic programming or greedy approaches, the computational costs of which are $O(n)$ (Sadfi 2002) and $O(n^2)$ (Hwang 1991) on small computational sets, respectively. It is important to note, however, that these solutions are pseudo-polynomial in nature, meaning that although they provide solutions in a polynomial fashion for small cases, at extremely large scale they are still NP-Complete (Garey 1979).

Generating complete matrices requires $p*t$ memory locations, where p is the number of processing elements (PEs) in the system and t is the size of the scheduling window. This presents an enormous scaling problem, as the only options when increasing the size of the system (p) is to either increase the amount of memory consumed or reduce the size of the scheduling window (t). As many systems have execution policies that allow for maximum runtimes of 48 hours or more, this typically requires reducing the resolution of the time axis (i.e. changing the smallest time element from 1 minute to 15 minutes). Reducing the resolution will degrade solution quality by creating pockets of idle time on the system, and increasing available memory is a costly alternative, thus limiting the effectiveness of this particular scheduling approach on massive-scale machines exceeding 100,000 or even 1,000,000 PEs.

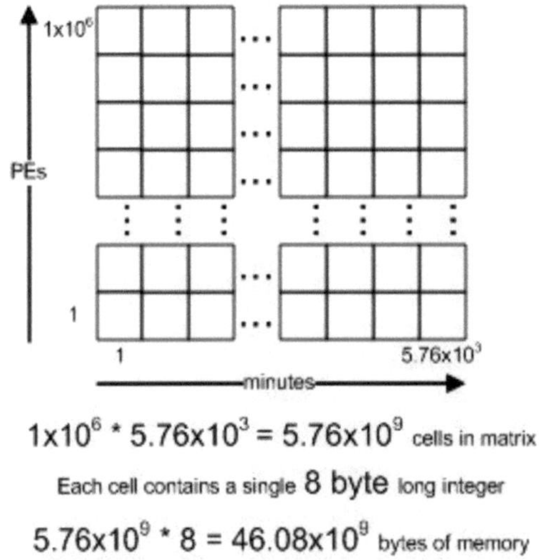

Fig. 2. Memory Requirements for Large-scale Scheduling Matrix

As Fig. 2 demonstrates, scheduling a 1,000,000 PE system using a 96 hr window (which would allow 2 back-to-back 48 hour jobs to be scheduled) with 1 minute resolution would require $1x10^6 * 96 * 60 = 5.76x10^9$ matrix locations. If each matrix location needed to store an 8-byte long integer, such as a job ID, then the scheduling matrix would need to be $5.76x10^9 * 8 = 46.08x10^9$ bytes, or 46.08GB.

3.2 Heuristic-based Scheduling Approaches

Unlike matrix-based scheduling algorithms, heuristic scheduling approaches tend to require less computational and spatial overhead. However, like all other centralized algorithms, they are inherently susceptible to failures in system components that may drastically alter how jobs need to be coordinated. Additionally, many heuristics tend to be static in nature, unable to account for jobs that arrive after the scheduling algorithm has begun. These techniques are typically used in conjunction with matrix-based approaches in batch-processing systems, where weighted functions are used to generate multi-constraint priorities to determine job execution order.

4. Artificial Immune Systems (AIS)

Research into the usability and effectiveness of AIS has been ongoing for the last decade. Although AIS is a relatively new concept in the field of nature-inspired computing, it already shows remarkable ability to adapt to extremely dynamic environments and is well suited to distributed applications (de Castro 2002). Many existing systems are based on the clonal selection model, and very closely resemble other evolutionary computation techniques, most specifically genetic algorithms and genetic programming (Cutello 2002, de Castro 2000).

Because of the noticeable parallels between protecting the body and protecting networks, AIS have been widely used in the field of network security and access management (Boukerche 2004, Kim 2001). Relying heavily on Immune Network Theory (INT), these AIS solutions analyze typical network traffic patterns, determine when abnormal traffic is on the system, then alerts managers to possible security risks. Although some work has been done in automatically protecting network systems from intrusion, many AIS solutions are simply for the detection of abnormal traffic, and not for blocking out the intruder.

4.1 Immune Network Theory

Scientists first believed that the mammalian immune system developed immunities to infection through one process - clonal selection. Clonal selection resembles the evolutionary process, with many thousands of white blood cells created through the act of cloning an existing, activated white blood cell. During the cloning process, called clonal expansion, these cells undergo "hypermutation," making the antibodies on the surface of these cloned cells different from the source. The "affinity" of these clones - the ability of these cells to identify the set of antigens of the infection currently being combated - is then established, and those with the greatest affinity survive while the others are destroyed. By repeating this process again and again when an infection was present, immunity to that infection would eventually be found (Jerne 1955).

The first major theoretical shift in the operation of the immune system came in the 1970's with Immune Network Theory (Jerne 1974). Unlike clonal selection, which creates antibodies through a method of repeated affinity determination and hypermutation, INT attacks new antigens by building up complex antibodies from smaller, more basic antibodies. Like clonal selection, INT relies on linking random combinations of antibody building blocks together to form a single immunity. However, the building blocks in INT are much larger than in clonal selection, reducing the time required to find an appropriate immunity.

4.2 Danger Theory

Danger Theory is a debated concept in immunological research that looks at how the immune system can identify potential problems not by attacking things that are foreign, but by attacking only those things which create "danger." According to danger theory, chemical signals released when a cell is damaged are received by nearby antigen-presenting cells, and then carried to local lymph nodes (Matzinger 1994). The strength of these chemical signals weaken with distance, and because a certain threshold is required for white blood cells to recognize these signals, a set region, or "danger zone," exists around the site of the incident. When antibodies in the lymph nodes "match" antigens collected from within the danger zone, the corresponding B-cells are activated and undergo clonal expansion in order to combat the infection (Aickelin 2002).

5. Applying the Immune System Metaphor to the Scheduling Problem

With all nature-inspired meta-heuristics, a mapping of naturally occurring phenomena to concepts and events in the problem space first must be performed to successfully apply the lessons and processes of the natural system to the target problem. The mammalian immune system consists of myriad chemicals, cells and organs working in concert with one another to perform the task of destroying or preventing infections. (a) Several infections likely occur simultaneously, (b) the immune system must cope with the fact that infections can be spread out over the entirety of the mammalian body, (c) infections cannot all be treated by the same immunological response, and (d) new infections may appear at any time.

The scheduling of tasks in distributed memory environments presents the same type of situational difficulties as dealing with infections in the body. (a) There may be many tasks to be scheduled simultaneously, (b) tasks may be parallel in nature and need resources from many of the distributed memory resources in the system, (c) many tasks have hardware or software dependencies that require the scheduler to act accordingly by ensuring that those tasks are mapped to locations that can accommodate the dependency requirements, and (d) the task space is extremely dynamic, with many new tasks being generated at any given time.

5.1 Defining a Set of Terms for an Immune System-based Resource Manager

Tasks can clearly be seen as infections from the perspective of a distributed-memory system. The job of the resource manager is then to complete as many tasks, or kill as many infections, as possible. This means that the system or environment to be managed can be

likened to the body; each task that is submitted to the system must be executed, just as each infection that enters the body must be destroyed.
To accomplish the goal of destroying infections entering the body, the immune system makes use of special blood cells known as lymphocytes. Although the biological model contains many types of lymphocytes that perform various sets of actions, for the purposes of applying this metaphor to resource management they can all be considered a single type of entity. In a distributed-memory environment, the individual resources that compose the system are responsible for executing tasks.
All infections have a set of chemical "hooks" on their surface called antigens. Conversely, each lymphocyte contains a chemical marker known as an antibody. The job of the immune system is to create an immunological response that properly maps a series of lymphocyte antibodies to the sequence of antigens on the infection. A resource manger, whether controlling a homogeneous or a heterogeneous environment, must similarly map the resource requirements of a task to the appropriate set of resources to effectively execute that task.
Based on these astonishing similarities between the mammalian immune system and the operating requirements of resource managers, we can create a set of terms that frame the distributed-memory environment, its individual resources, and the tasks it executes in the context of the immune system. Table 1 defines the terminology set that will be used.

Immunological Term	**Resource Management Term**
Body	System to be managed
Lymphocyte	Resource in the system
Infection	Task to be executed
Antigen	Resource requirement of task
Antibody	Resource capability

Table 1. Defined terms of immune system metaphor

5.2 Defining Events and Responses for an Immune System-based Resource Manager

Now that a set of terms has been established that places the scheduling problem in the context of the immune system, we must define both the events that occur over the life-cycle of a resource manager, as well as the appropriate responses by the resource manager to those events in the context of the immune system metaphor. Although there are many differing and competing theories on how the immune system both detects malicious activity and responds to that activity, we will use a combination of two theories that fit best with our distributed management environment. Danger Theory provides a simple, distributed method for performing the detection component, while INT gives us a simple method for forming proper responses to those detected events.
Every scheduler must contend with a series of different time-independent events: (a) A task being submitted to the system, (b) a task beginning execution on the system, (c) a task completing execution on the system, either successfully or in error, and (d) resources becoming available or unavailable. Each of these events can be difficult for static, centralized scheduling algorithms to contend with, as they would require the re-execution of the algorithm using a new snapshot of the system.

One of Danger Theory's central concepts is the use of chemical messages to detect the presence of malicious entities. In a biological system, the distance from which an event can be detected is limited due to the decay of these chemical signatures as they travel through the bloodstream. This message-based approach employed in the Danger Theory model can be applied to a system of distributed resources connected via the network. Although a computer network is not limited in the distance it can send messages (through the use of intermediate relays), it would not be beneficial to saturate the network with broadcast messages every time an event occurs.

If one were to use network messages to signal the occurrence of events, it would allow a system to provide dynamic, real-time reactions to those events. Each independent agent in the system (infections and lymphocytes) would be responsible for both transmitting and reacting to various message signals propagated via the network. If each message was transmitted to only a limited subset of the entire network, it would allow many independent events and reactions to occur simultaneously without adversely affecting one another.

In the mammalian immune system, lymphocytes are alerted to the presence of an infection when a victim cell is destroyed and releases a particular chemical signature. Consequently, the infectious agents of an immune system-based resource manger (tasks) would be responsible for the transmission of a message to signal their own presence. Since chemical signatures decay over time and distance, only a limited number of lymphocytes would be close enough to receive that signature and respond to it, or within the "danger zone," as it is referred to in Danger Theory. As a result, only a limited number of lymphocytic agents (system resources) nearby the signaling infectious agent should be privy to this message.

This limited message distance has several interesting side-effects that can be advantageous to a resource manger. If "distance" is measured by some network metric (e.g. hops), then nearby resources will most likely be better localized (such as on the same switch in a switching hierarchy), and therefore provide better communications performance for tightly-coupled parallel codes. Additionally, since only a small number of resources are immediately alerted to the presence of an infection, the likelihood of saturating the network with response messages is reduced. Lastly, because large parallel tasks will be unable to secure enough resources to begin execution immediately, the immune system-based approach provides a natural form of "backfill," which maximizes utilization by squeezing smaller jobs into the slots leftover from scheduling larger jobs. Because large jobs cannot immediately consume available resources, smaller tasks can begin execution while the large jobs are acquiring the resources necessary to execute.

Once a lymphocyte has been alerted to the presence of an infection in the mammalian immune system, it must mount some form of immunological response. In INT, this response would consist of T-cells carrying infection associated antigens back to lymph nodes, which would then begin generating antibodies which match all or part of the antigen pattern. This partial pattern-match allows the immune system to begin the process of mounting a response to infection before a complete, perfect solution is discovered. The generation of partial solutions and iterative construction of solutions is crucial in distributed systems as the individual components do not have the ability to constantly or consistently communicate with one another. In an immune system-based resource manager, lymphocytes which receive a signal from an infection would check to see if any of their antibodies, or resources, match any of the antigens, or resource requirements, presented by the infection. If so, the lymphocyte would respond by binding itself to the infection.

Although immediate response works well when a lymphocyte is idle and unbound, what happens when a lymphocyte is busy or bound to another infection? In the case of a lymphocyte being busy, it should ignore the message. In most cases preemption is not desired on large-scale systems, so there should be no reason to stop executing a task to handle another one. In the case of a lymphocyte being bound to an infection but not running a task, one of two actions could be taken: (1) The lymphocyte could decide that the infection it is currently bound to has higher precedence, and ignore the incoming request, or (2) the lymphocyte could decide that the new infection has higher precedence, and switch from being bound to the first to being bound to the second. By choosing from these actions, a simple priority system can be developed within the resource manager with little computational overhead on the part of the lymphocytes, which are also responsible for executing tasks.

After an infectious agent has received a response from a lymphocyte, it will associate that binding response with a particular antigen subset, indicating that those pieces of the solution have been discovered. When the entire antigen set has been associated with a binding lymphocyte, the infectious agent will signal the lymphocytes associated with that solution to begin execution. When this occurs, the lymphocytes will begin execution of the binary or script associated with that infectious agent.

Unfortunately in many cases an infectious agent cannot receive enough binding responses after the first signaling, either because there are insufficient resources within the danger zone, or those resources are busy executing other tasks. In a biological system, the effect of an insufficient immunological response would be the spreading of the infection to other cells or parts of the body. This has the effect of increasing the size of the danger zone, as more chemical signals are created as the infection spreads. In an immune system-based resource manager, the spreading of an infection can be accomplished not through the replication of the infectious agent, but by increasing the size of the danger zone surrounding the infectious agent. Instead of being able to signal only the most local lymphocytes, an infection would then be able to signal lymphocytes beyond those, up to a certain limit. Theoretically, this limit could expand to the size of the system, if no sufficient response is provided in a timely fashion.

Once a task begins execution, it will continue to execute until "completion," defined as successful or in error, or until an external signal requires that it terminate, such as through user request or the extinguishing of a preset time limit. The completion of a job, regardless of return code, can be considered normal termination. Conversely, the termination of a job through user request, extinguishing of a preset time limit, or by other external means can be considered abnormal termination. Cells in a biological system also terminate in normal and abnormal fashions. Normal cell death is defined as necrosis, whereas abnormal cell death is defined as apoptosis. We shall use the same nomenclature to describe the completion of tasks in the immune system-based resource manager.

When a task completes, the lymphocytes executing that task will transmit a message back to the infectious agent denoting that the task terminated normally, via necrosis. When a task is terminated by external means, the infectious agent will notify the lymphocytes executing that task that the task terminated via apoptosis. The lymphocytes will then respond back to the infectious agent in the same manner that they would for normal termination. In both cases, the lymphocytes will transmit back the return code of the task along with the appropriate signal. When an infectious agent receives termination signals from all associated lymphocytes, the agent will complete and the task will be considered done.

Now that we have a complete picture of the life cycle of an infectious agent, from the moment it appears on the system to the time it terminates, we can see a relatively small set of signals are exchanged between infections and lymphocytes in order to successfully execute tasks. Table 2 and Table 3 define the signals that will be needed for an immune system-based resource manager.

Signal Name	Definition
SIG_INFECT	Indicate the presence of an infection
SIG_ATTACK	Notify lymphocytes that the associated task should be executed
SIG_APOPTOSIS	Notify lymphocytes that a task should be terminated immediately (abnormal termination)

Table 2. List of infection-produced signals

Signal Name	Definition
SIG_BIND	Notify an infectious agent of intent to execute
SIG_DELAY	Notify an infectious agent that it will be binding to another infection
SIG_NECROSIS	Notify an infectious agent that the associated task has completed/terminated

Table 3. List of lymphocyte-produced signals

5.3 Design of Autonomous Agents

With both a working set of terms and a series of events, signals and responses defined, we can begin the process of designing the two types of autonomous agents that form the core of an immune system-based resource manager. Both infections and lymphocytes would be represented as autonomous agents, with each resource having a single lymphocytic agent and each job being "wrapped" in an infectious agent.

Each infectious agent resides on one of the various compute resources in the system, and makes elementary decisions based on response messages received from lymphocytes. Fig. 3 details the design of an infectious agent.

Each resource houses a single lymphocytic agent, which responds to messages from various infectious agents. When a lymphocytic agent receives notification of an infectious agent's presence (via SIG_INFECT), it must also check its antibody list to ensure that is has at least one of the necessary resources to execute that job. Fig. 4 outlines the design of a lymphocytic agent.

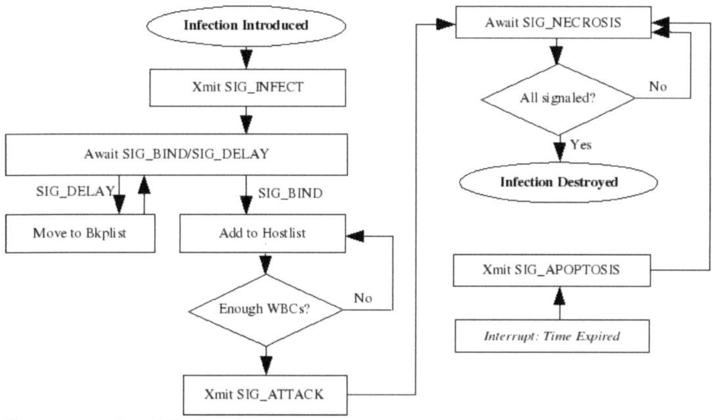

Fig. 3. Control flow graph of infectious agent

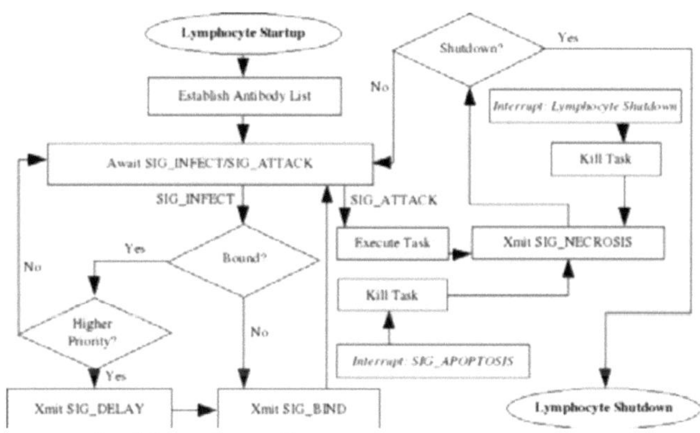

Fig. 4. Control flow graph of lymphocytic agent

5.4 Design of Signal Messages

In order for the various autonomous agents to communicate with each other, they must be able to exchange messages over the network. Each message must be small, so as not to interfere with other user-based network traffic, while containing sufficient information to effectively perform the scheduling operations.

Each message must contain some identifier of the type of signal being transmitted. Additionally, some messages need to send auxiliary information. SIG_INFECT must contain the antigen list in the message, to allow lymphocytes to determine whether or not they should participate in the solution. Also, SIG_NECROSIS must also contain the return code of the task(s) in order to provide that information back to the infectious agent. Each UNIX return code is an integer from 0 to 255, allowing it to be encoded in 8 bits. Additionally, since only 3 bits are required to encode all 6 signal types, the remaining 5 bits of that byte can be used to encode the antigen list, or resource requirements, of an infection. An example message layout is given in Fig. 5.

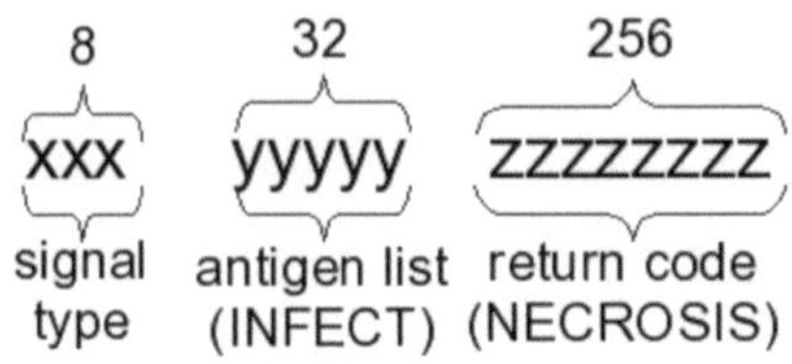

Fig. 5. Example message packet

6. Experimental Validation

To help us evaluate the potential benefits and pitfalls of this immune system-based approach to managing large-scale resource collectives, a series of simulations were performed to help identify performance in two major areas: schedule generation and network congestion.

6.1 Evaluating Schedule Quality

Although it can be difficult to quantify the "quality" of a schedule, there are several metrics that can be used to provide comparisons. By comparing these metrics against schedules generated by other techniques, we can create a picture of the approximate quality of schedules produced. Six metrics (Table 4) were used to compare schedule quality against three basic scheduling heuristics: Smallest Job First (SJF), Largest Job First (LJF), and Best Fit First (BFF).

Metric	Definition
Throughput	Avg. number of jobs completed per hour
Turnaround time	Avg. time between job submission and completion
Wait time	Avg. time between job submission and execution
Load Balance	Std. Dev. in number of jobs per node
Utilization	Ratio of in-use cores to total cores
Makespan	Time from submission of first job to completion of last job

Table 4. Scheduling metrics and definitions used in simulation study

6.2 Evaluating Network Congestion

Although distributing the scheduling problem eases the computational requirements, it can possibly have adverse affects on network performance, either by consuming bandwidth or by overloading the network with excessive small messages. Our tests will examine the aggregate number of signals of each type, in five-minute windows, and then calculate the overall bandwidth and load burdens on two different networking technologies – Gigabit Ethernet and Infiniband (IB).

Ethernet II-based User Datagram Protocol/Internet Protocol ver. 4 (UDP/IPv4) packets consist of a 46 byte message header (IEEE 2005, Braden 1989, Postel 1980) plus a payload section, which for our purposes would house the two byte message illustrated in Fig. 5. This means that each message transmitted using IP over Ethernet would be 48 bytes in length (Fig. 6).

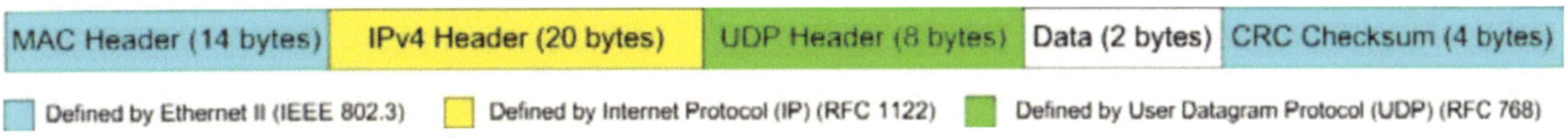

Fig. 6. Ethernet II frame description

In order to send the same UDP/IPv4 message over IB, the IP and UDP packets must be embedded into a native IB frame (known as IP over IB). To have a multi-network, globally addressable IB message, 66 bytes of header and CRC information are required (Infiniband 2007). When combined with the previously described 28 bytes of IP and UDP headers plus the 2 byte message illustrated in Fig. 5, the total size for a UDP/IPv4 over IB message comes to 96 bytes (Fig. 7).

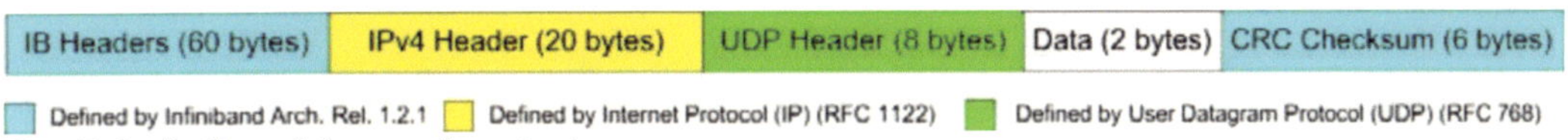

Fig. 7. Infiniband frame description

7. Results

A simulated 4,096-node, single core per node cluster built on a discrete, event-driven engine was tasked with executing 100,000 jobs submitted at a rate of one every sixty seconds. The jobs used in this job deck were taken from the execution logs of the Lonestar Dell-Linux cluster at the Texas Advanced Computing Center (TACC) in Austin, Texas. Each job ranged in size from a single core (serial) job to 1,024 cores and had execution times up to 48 hours.

Each infectious agent simulated had an expansion period of thirty (30) seconds, meaning that every half minute, an infectious agent's danger zone was expanded to include two more resources in a linearly-arranged list of the 4,096 nodes.

7.1 Schedule Quality Comparisons

Fig. 8 shows the results of the previously described simulation runs and how the ALARM method compares to the three basic heuristics (Scherger 2009). Although ALARM was not the top performer, it was able to compete with all three comparison heuristics, placing second in both the turnaround time and wait time. The only significant downside for the immune system-based method was in load balance, although this was most likely caused by persistent saturation of the scheduler with new jobs. With the three comparison heuristics, rate of submission does not affect the resulting schedule generation, while changes in submission rate can affect the binding policies of lymphocytic agents to infectious agents.

7.2 Network Congestion

When offloading computation into the form of communication, latency and bandwidth become a topic of great importance which must be investigated. To validate this method we looked closely at the time period where the largest number of messages were generated by ALARM. Fig. 9(a) shows the results of the previously described simulation runs and focuses on the aggregate number of signals generated by the ALARM technique, spanning 144 simulated days. On the 80th day of this simulation ALARM generated a peak number of signals demonstrating a period of full system saturation where the number of signals sent totaled 51,818,685.

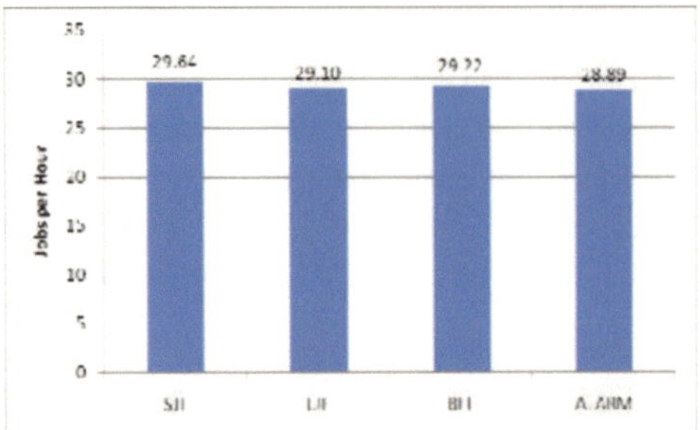

(a) Throughput

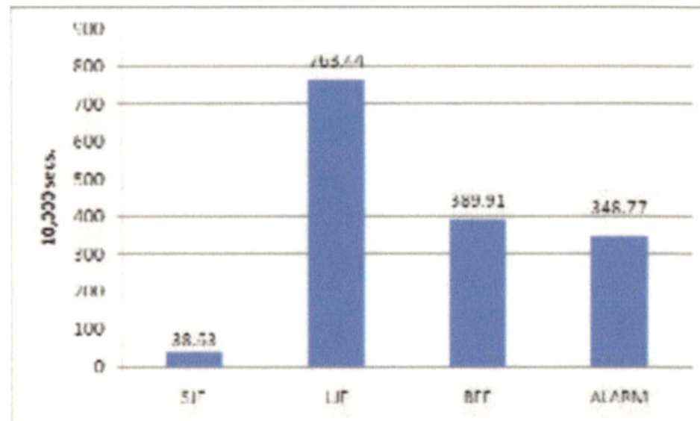

(b) Turnaround Time

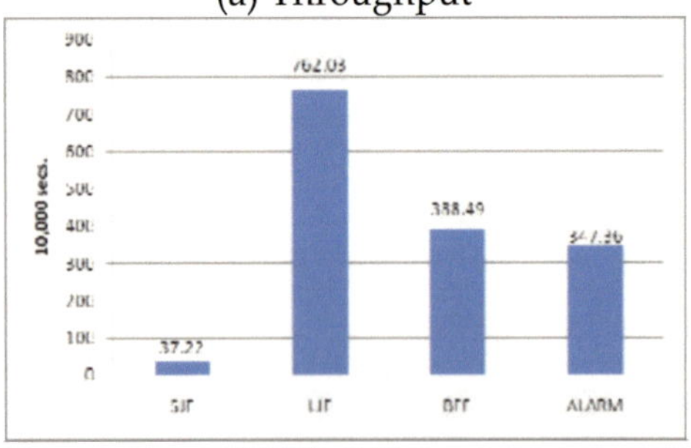

(c) Wait Time

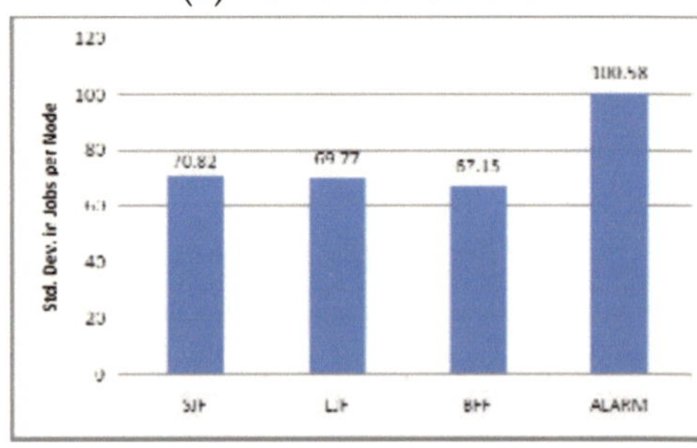

(d) Load Balance

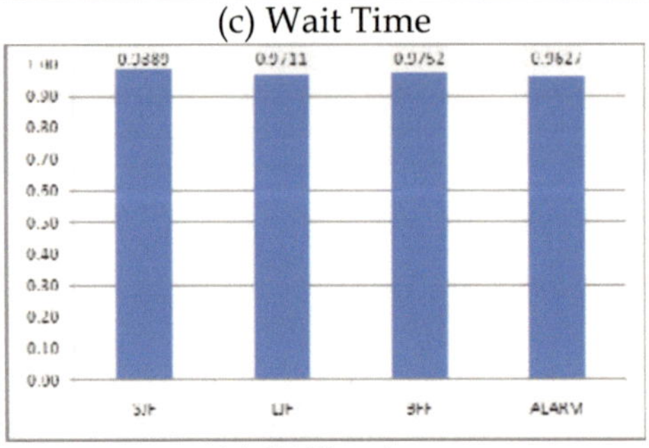

(e) Utilization

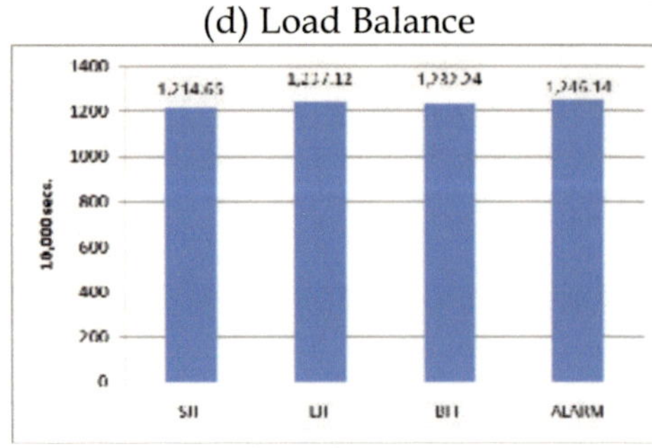

(f) Makespan

Fig. 8. Schedule quality comparisons

Fig. 9(b) provides a closer examination of the 80th day divided into one hour windows, showing that in the 15th hour ALARM generated approximately 6,400 signals per second. Latency of Gigabit Ethernet has been measured between two machines at 135 μsec (Farrell 2000). Using the figures from the peak of our simulation run, the ALARM method would utilize 86.4% of the available network frames, while utilizing 0.2% of theoretical peak bandwidth. InfiniBand, with a latency of 1.5μsec (Koop 2008) , would utilize 0.96% of the available network frames while utilizing 0.05% of theoretical peak bandwidth.

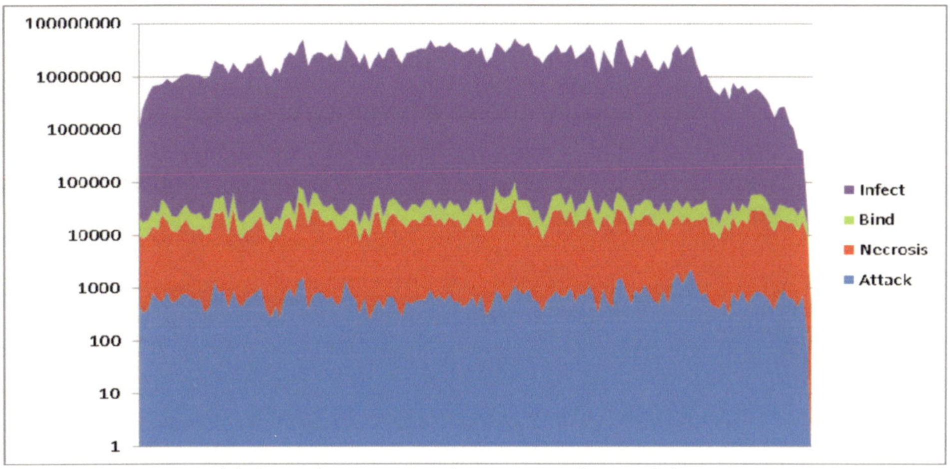

(a) Signals generated over simulation lifetime

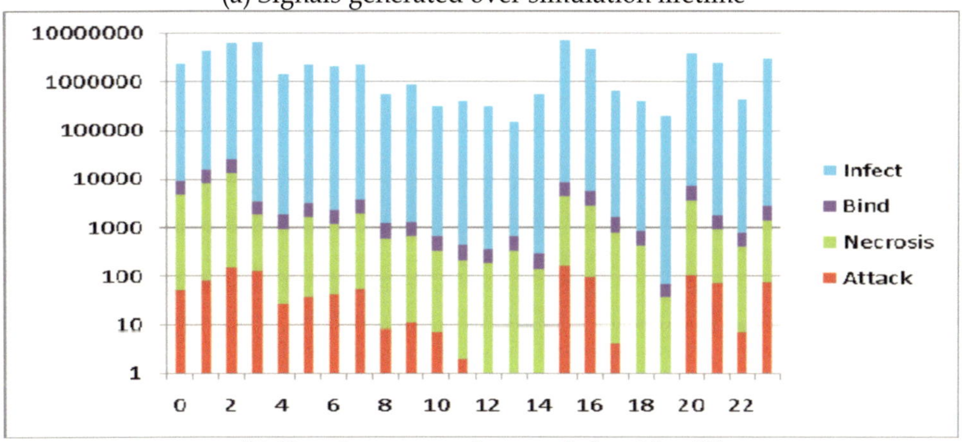

(b) Signals generated on peak day (day 80)

Fig. 9. Network signals produced by ALARM

7.3 Pitfalls of Trivial Decision and Expansion Strategies

ALARM ranked last in nearly all of the metric categories, due mainly to the limitations inherent in the simple heuristic tiebreaker chosen for lymphocytes. Each lymphocyte - or resource on the system - used a job ID-based priority for determining which of many simultaneous SIG_INFECT messages to respond to. In small cases, this can be a very simple and effective tiebreaker, favoring older jobs over newer jobs. However, as the wait time of all jobs increases, the ALARM scheduling method reaches an absolute saturation point where the wait time of each infection submitted exceeds the amount of time necessary for it's influence to expand to the entire system. For example, the simulation system has 4,096 PEs, and each infection increases its danger zone by a radius of 1 PE every 30 seconds, meaning only 61,440 seconds (17 hrs.) are required for an infection's danger zone to encompass the entire system. When this point is reached, lymphocytes that complete jobs are immediately bombarded with SIG_INFECT requests from all currently active infections, and each lymphocyte therefore chooses the infection with the smallest job ID. This makes the entire system behave like the simple heuristic "First Come-First Served" (FCFS), causing large sections of the system to remain idle periodically as resources are allocated to very large jobs without considering smaller jobs behind them. Reducing the expansion rate would alter this behavior temporarily, although a saturation point would eventually be reached that again causes this job ID-based priority heuristic to resort for FCFS. As Fig. **10**10(a) shows, by job 600 the system had already achieved this level of saturation.

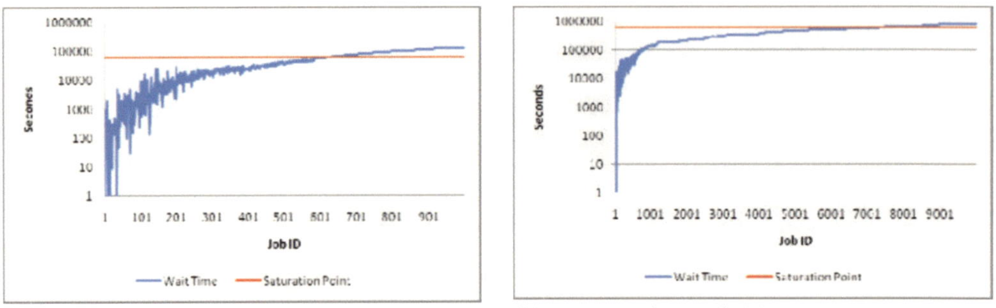

(a) 100,000 jobs with 30 sec. expansion (b) 10,000 jobs with 300 sec. expansion

Fig. 10. Wait time per job approaching saturation point

Additional simulations on the same size system using a reduced expansion rate of once every five minutes (300 seconds) on a smaller instance (10,000 jobs) of the same job deck used for this experiment were done on all four scheduling methods, with ALARM performing significantly better in all 6 categories and generally outperforming all metrics except for SJF (Fig. 11). This reduced expansion rate delayed complete system saturation until jobs maintained a minimum wait time of 307,200 seconds (3.5 days) (Fig. 10(b)). Future investigations into the use of various tiebreaker heuristics and their effects on overall system behavior could be beneficial in improving the performance of ALARM in production settings.

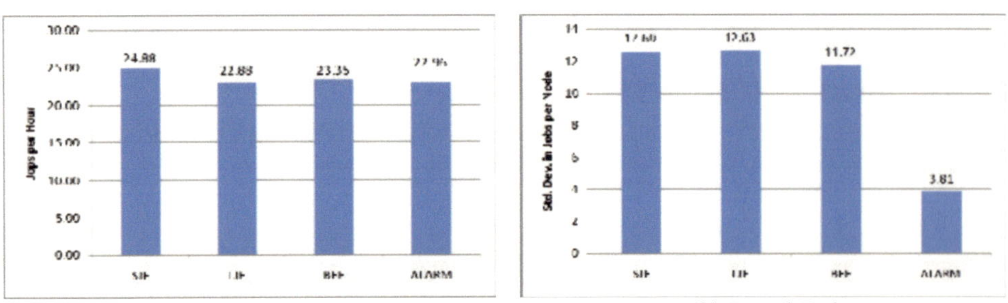

(a) Throughput (b) Load Balance

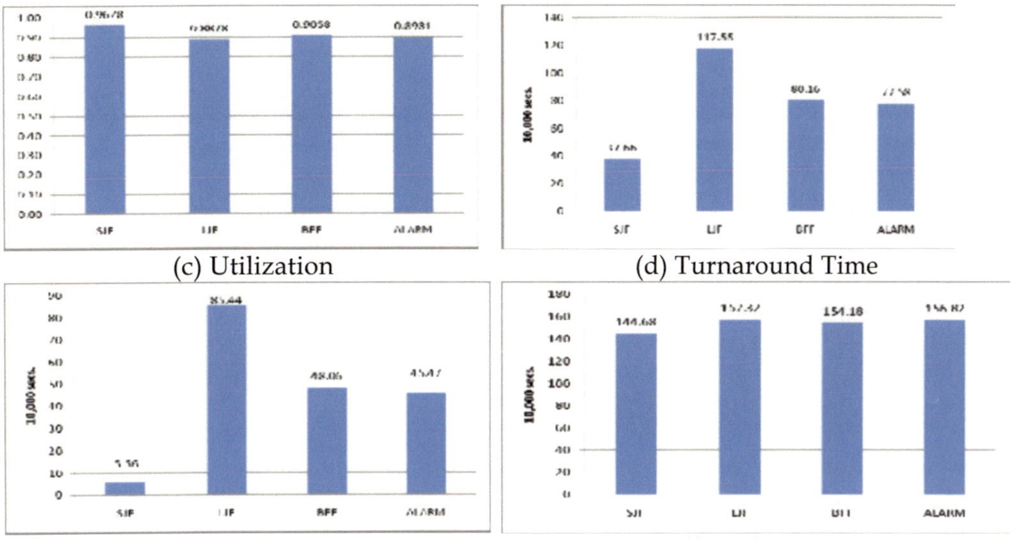

(c) Utilization (d) Turnaround Time

(e) Wait Time (f) Makespan

Fig. 11. Schedule quality comparisons for 10,000 job / 300 sec. expansion case

Additionally, more intelligent signaling and expansion systems for infections could also be explored to determine if more complex network-based algorithms (e.g. back-off algorithm in TCP/IP) could be beneficial in improving the overall performance of ALARM in large-scale production environments.

8. Future Work

As we have demonstrated, a distributed scheduling method - based on the functionality of the mammalian immune system - can indeed be a viable, scalable solution for generating timely scheduling information with limited computational and communications overhead. In our current tests, lymphocytic agents used a trivial decision strategy (lowest job-ID first) for making binding decisions. However, additional investigation into improved decision strategies could lead to more efficient scheduling information without creating additional overhead, thus helping to possibly improve load balance or reduce total makespan. Investigation into improved expansion strategies on the part of infectious agents may also aid in reducing communications overhead.

So far, all investigations have been through simulation in order to verify the feasibility of using an immune system-based scheduling method on large-scale systems. However, the design and development of an actual resource management tool based on this approach should be a primary focus of efforts going forward. Once an initial system has been developed, further research into various decision and expansion strategies can be tested on real-world tasks and hardware. Additionally, development of a real-world system will allow research to concentrate on many of the other components of resource management tools besides the scheduling engine, such as statistics gathering and reporting, administrative control of resources, fault recovery, etc.

9. Conclusions

Historically, increases in computational performance have been achieved by chip manufacturers shrinking transistor scale and increasing clock speed. This meant that although overall performance continued to increase, the number of allocatable elements in a system remained relatively constant. Today, with the ever-increasing popularity of computational collectives ranging from Grids and Clouds to clusters and the increase in unit density with the advent of multi-/many-core architectures, computational performance is achieved by increasing the number of allocatable elements instead of increasing the individual performance of each of those elements. For schedulers and resource managers, this poses a fundamental problem - at what point will traditional, centralized techniques become inadequate for scheduling jobs on massive-scale machines encompassing 100,000 or possibly 1,000,000+ PEs?

As we have seen with high-performance computing in the last decade, the solution to improving performance is to distribute the workload across multiple resources. Meta-heuristics, such as artificial immune systems, have been demonstrated as viable solutions to solving complex computational problems in large-scale, dynamic environments. ALARM, the Asynchronous Lymphocytic Agent-based Resource Manager, uses this immune-system metaphor to create a distributed, dynamic solution to scheduling jobs on large scale computational collectives, whether loosely- or tightly-coupled.

Results presented here and in other works (Wilson 2008, Scherger 2009) demonstrate the viability of this approach and suggest that implementation of a real-world system based on this technique would be a reasonable near-term goal. Additional investigation into lymphocyte decision strategies and infection expansion strategies may also yield higher quality results without significant additional computational or communications cost.

10. References

Aickelin, U. and Cayzer, S. (2002). The danger theory and its application to artificial immune systems. *Proceedings of the 1st International Conference on Artificial Immune Systems*, pp. 141-148.

Audsley, N. and A. Burns, 1994, Real -Time Scheduling, in Department of Computer Science, University of York.

Boger, M., 2001, *Java in Distributed Systems*, Wiley.

Boukerche, A, Juca, K., Sobral, J.B. and Notare, M. (2004). An artificial immune based intrusion detection model for computer and telecommunications systems. *Parallel Comput.*, 30(5-6), pp. 629-646.

Braden, R. (ed.) (1989). Requirements for Intenet Hosts -- Communication Layers, *Network Working Group Request for Comments (RFC) 1122*, Internet Engineering Task Force, October 1989.

de Castro, L.N. and von Zuben, F.J. (2000). The clonal selection algorithm with engineering applications. *Artificial Immune Systems*, pp. 36-39.

de Castro, L.N. and Timmis, J. (2002). *Artificial Immune Systems: A New Computational Approach*. Springer-Verlag, London, U.K.

Chaptin, S.J., 2003, Distributed and Multiprocessor Scheduling, University of Minnesota.

Chow, R. and T. Johnson, 1997, *Distributed Operating Systems and Algorithms*, Addison-Wesley.

Cormen, Thomas H., Leiserson, Charles E., Rivest, Ronald L. and Stein, Clifford (2001). *Introduction to Algorithms*, Second Edition. MIT Press. 2001.

Cutello, V. and Nicosa, G. (2002). An immunilogical approach to combinatorial optimization problems. *Proceedings of the 8th Ibero-American Conference on AI*, pp. 361-370.

Farrell, P.A. and Ong, H. (2000). Communication performance over a gigabit Ethernet network, *Proceedings of the Performance, Computing, and Communications Conference*, pp. 181-189.

Garey, M.R. and Johnson, D.S. (1979). *Computers and Intractability: A Guide to the Theory of NP-Completeness*. W.H. Freeman and Company, 1979.

Hwang, Cheng-Tsung, Lee, Jiang-Humg and Hsu, Yu-Chin. (1991). A Formal Approach to the Scheduling Problem in High Level Synthesis. *IEEE Transactions on Computer-Aided Design*, 10:4, 1991.

IEEE (2005). IEEE Std 802.3-2005, IEEE, 2005.

Infiniband (2007). *Infiniband Architecture Specification*, 1, rel. 1.2.1, November 2007.

Jerne, N. K. (1955). The natural selection theory of antibody formation. *Proceedings of the National Academy of Science*, USA. 41, 1955, 849-857.

Jerne, N.K. (1974). Towards a network theory of the immune system. *Ann Immunol (Paris)*, 125C(1-2), 1974, 373-389.

Kim, J. and Bentley, P.J. (2001). An evalutation of negative selection in an artificial immune system for network intrusion detection. *Proceedings of the Genetic and Evolutionary Computation Conference (GECCO-2001)*, pp. 1330-1337.

Koop, M.J., Jones, T., and Panda, D.K. (2008). MVAPICH-Aptus: Scalable high-performance multi-transport MPI over Infiniband, *Proceeding of the International Parallel and Distributed Processing Symposium (IPDPS)*, pp. 1-12.

Malik, S., 2003, *Dynamic Load Balancing in a Network Workstations*, Prentice-Hall.

Matzinger, P. (1994). Tolerance, danger and the extended family. *Annu. Rev. Immun.*, 12:991, 1994.

Moore, G. E. (1965). Cramming more components onto integrated circuits. *Electronics*, 38(8), April 1965.

Postel, J. (ed.) (1980). User Datagram Protocol, *Request for Comments (RFC) 768*, USC/Information Sciences Institute, August 1980.

Ramamritham, K. and Stankovic, J.A. (2002). Dynamic Task Scheduling in Hard Real-Time Distributed Systems, *IEEE Software*, 2002. 1(3): p. 65-75.

Sadfi, C., Penz, B. and Rapine, C. (2002). A dynamic programming algorithm for the single machine total completion time scheduling problem with availability constraints. *Eighth international workshop on project management and scheduling*, 2002.

Scherger, M. and Wilson, L. A. (2009). Task Scheduling Using an Artificial Immune System in a Tightly Coupled Parallel Computing Environment. *The 2009 International Conference on Genetic and Evolutionary Methods (GEM'09)*, July 2009.

Stankovic, J.A. (199). Simulations of three adaptive, decentralized controlled, job scheduling algorithms. *Computer Networks*, 1999. 8(3): p. 199-217.

Tel, G.,(1998), *Introduction to Distributed Process Scheduling*, University of Cambridge.

Wilson, L. A. (2008). Distributed, Heterogeneous Resource Management Using Artificial Immune Systems. *Proceedings of the International Parallel and Distributed Processing Symposium, NIDISC*, Apr. 2008.

10

Scheduling of Divisible Loads on Heterogeneous Distributed Systems

Abhay Ghatpande[1]*, Hidenori Nakazato[1] and Olivier Beaumont[2]
[1]*GITI, Waseda University, Tokyo 169-0051*
[2]*LaBRI, France 33405*

1. Introduction

Divisible loads are a special class of applications that have regular linear structure, and which if given a large enough volume, can be partitioned into independently- and identically-processable *load fractions* (parts). Examples of applications that satisfy this divisibility property include image processing and rendering, signal processing, computation of Hough transforms, tree and database search, Monte Carlo simulations, computational fluid dynamics, and matrix computations.

The partitioning of a divisible load, the allocation (mapping) of the parts to appropriate processors for execution, and the sequencing (ordering) the transfer of the parts to and from the processors, is together known as *Divisible Load Scheduling* (DLS). *Divisible Load Theory* (DLT) is the framework that studies the optimization of DLS (Bharadwaj et al., 1996). Beaumont, Casanova, Legrand, Robert & Yang (2005) recently published a review of the work done to date in DLT. An exhaustive listing of papers regarding DLT and DLS is available on (Robertazzi, 2008).

1.1 Shortcomings of Traditional DLT

The basic principle of DLT to determine an optimal schedule for a master-slave system is the AFS (All slaves Finish Simultaneously) policy (Barlas, 1998). The AFS policy implies that after the nodes finish computing their individual load fractions, no results are returned to the source. This is an unrealistic assumption for many applications, as the result collection phase can contribute significantly to the total execution time. This is a serious shortcoming of traditional DLT. Along with the AFS policy, the presence of idle time in the optimal schedule has been overlooked in DLT work on result collection and heterogeneity. It is a very important issue because it may sometimes be possible to improve a schedule by inserting idle time.

A few papers that have dealt with DLS on heterogeneous systems to date (Beaumont, Marchal, Rehn & Robert, 2005; Beaumont et al., 2006; Beaumont, Marchal & Robert, 2005; Bharadwaj et al., 1996; Comino & Narasimhan, 2002; Rosenberg, 2001) proved that the sequence of allocation of data to the processors is important in heterogeneous networks. Without considering result collection, they proved that for optimum performance, (a) when processors have equal computation capacity, the optimal schedule results when the fractions are allocated in the order of decreasing communication link capacity, and (b) when communication capacity

*Corresponding author: abhay.ghatpande@ieee.org

is equal, the data should be allocated in the order of decreasing computation capacity. As far as can be judged, no paper has given a satisfactory solution to the scheduling problem where both the network bandwidth and computation capacities of the slaves are different, and the result transfer to the master is explicitly considered.

Cheng & Robertazzi (1990) and Bharadwaj et al. (1996, Chap. 3) addressed the issue of result collection with a simplistic constant result collection time, which is possible only for a limited number of applications on homogeneous networks. All other papers that have addressed result collection to date, advocated FIFO (First In, First Out) and LIFO (Last In, First Out) type of schedules. In FIFO, results are collected in the same order as that of load allocation, while in LIFO, the order of result collection is reversed. Barlas (1998) addressed the result collection phase for single-level and arbitrary tree networks, but the optimal sequences derived were essentially LIFO or FIFO. Rosenberg (2001) too proposed the LIFO and FIFO sequences for result collection. He concluded through simulations that FIFO is better when the network is homogeneous with a large number of processors, while LIFO is advantageous when the network is heterogeneous with a small number of processors.

For the first time, it was shown in (Beaumont, Marchal & Robert, 2005) that the LIFO and FIFO orderings are not always optimal for a given set of processors. In (Beaumont, Marchal, Rehn & Robert, 2005; Beaumont et al., 2006), it was proved that all processors from a given set of processors may not be used in the optimal solution. For the unidirectional single-port communication model (see Section 2), (Beaumont, Marchal, Rehn & Robert, 2005; Beaumont et al., 2006; Beaumont, Marchal & Robert, 2005) proved several interesting features in optimal schedules.

1.2 Chapter Organisation

Section 2 explains the choices made to represent the communication and computation speeds, the model used for size of result data, the assumptions and reasons regarding continuous delivery of data, the unidirectional one-port communication model, and the decision to use linear models of computation and communication time. Sections 2.3 and 3 provide a detailed derivation of the DLSRCHETS problem definition. After first laying the theoretical basis, the DLSRCHETS problem is defined in terms of a linear program. Section 4 lays the foundation of the two-slave system that forms the basis for the SPORT algorithm. Section 5 introduces the SPORT algorithm as a solution to the DLSRCHETS problem. Given a set of processors sorted in the order of decreasing communication speed, the complexity of SPORT is $O(m)$. Section 6 summarizes the chapter and ideas for future work.

2. The System Model

The execution of a divisible job on each slave comprises of three distinct phases in the following order — the allocation phase, where data is sent to the slave from the master, the computation phase, where the data is processed, and the result collection phase, where the slave sends the result data back to the source. The computation phase begins only after the entire load fraction allocated to that slave is received from the source. Similarly, the result collection phase begins only after the entire load fraction has been processed, and is ready for transmission back to the master. This is known as the *non-preemptive*, *atomic*, or *block based* model, and each phase forms a block on the time line as shown in Fig. 1.

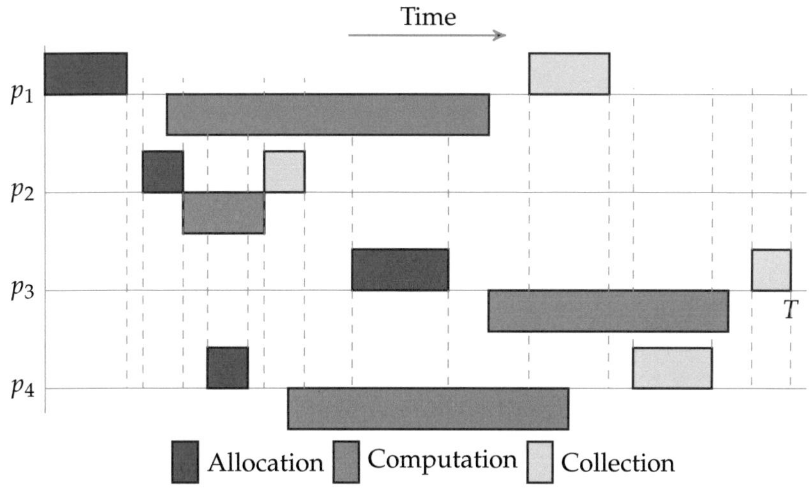

Fig. 1. A general schedule for DLSRCHETS. Processors can do only one thing at a time — either compute or communicate. There are three phases for each processor — allocation, computation, and result collection, in that order. However, phases of different processors may be interleaved. Each phase is *atomic*, i.e., continues to its end without interruption. Communication phases (either allocation or collection) cannot overlap as shown by the dashed lines. Computation phases are independent of each other.

2.1 Communication and Computation Model

The non-preemptive communication and computation phases necessitate that the slaves are continuously and exclusively available during the course of execution of the divisible load. The master and slaves can do only any one thing at a time — either communicate or compute (the no-overlap model), and if communicating, then either send data or receive data (the unidirectional one-port model).

A heterogeneous master-slave (sometimes called as *star* or *single-level tree*) system $\mathcal{H} = (\mathcal{P}, \mathcal{L})$ is as shown in Fig. 2, where $\mathcal{P} = \{p_0, \ldots, p_m\}$ is the set of $m+1$ processors, and $\mathcal{L} = \{l_1, \ldots, l_m\}$ is the set of m network links that connect the master scheduler (source) p_0 at the center of the star (root of the tree), to the slave processors $p_1, \ldots, p_m$ at the points of the star (leaves of the tree). $\mathcal{E} = \{E_1, \ldots, E_m\}$ is the set of unit computation times of the slave processors, and $\mathcal{C} = \{C_1, \ldots, C_m\}$ is the set of unit communication times of the network links, i.e., p_k takes E_k time units to process a unit load transmitted to it from p_0 in C_k time units over the link l_k. It follows that $E_k, C_k > 0$, $k \in \{1, \ldots, m\}$. The values in $\mathcal{E}$ and $\mathcal{C}$ are assumed to be deterministic and available at the master.

The master holds a divisible load (job) $\mathcal{J}$ that is to be distributed and processed on $\mathcal{H}$. Based on the unit communication and computation time values of the slaves, the master p_0 splits $\mathcal{J}$ into parts (fractions) $\alpha_1, \ldots, \alpha_m$ and sends them to the respective slave processors $p_1, \ldots, p_m$ for computation. Each such set of m fractions is known as a *load distribution* $\alpha = \{\alpha_1, \ldots, \alpha_m\}$. The source does not retain any part of the load for computation. Since the job $\mathcal{J}$ is assumed to be arbitrarily divisible, $\alpha_k \in \mathbb{R}_0^+$, $\alpha_k \geq 0$, $k \in \{1, \ldots, m\}$. The unit communication and computation times are conditional upon the job $\mathcal{J}$ under consideration. So ideally, the values should be indexed as $C_k^{\mathcal{J}}$ and $E_k^{\mathcal{J}}$, to indicate that the values are valid only for the job $\mathcal{J}$. This index is omitted as the context is clear to be the job $\mathcal{J}$.

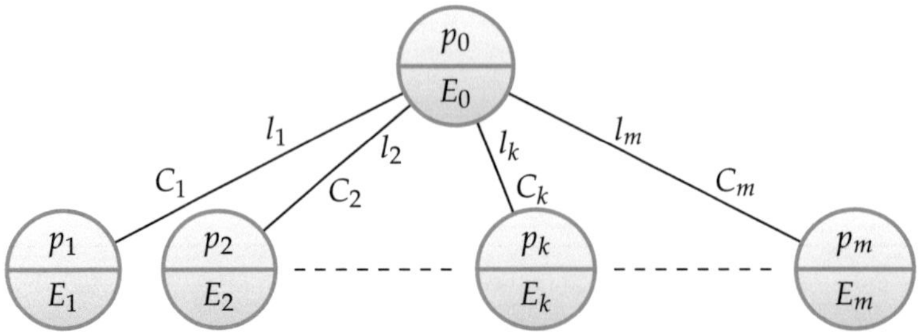

Fig. 2. The heterogeneous master-slave system $\mathcal{H}$. The processors have different computation speeds and network bandwidths.

2.2 Result Data Model

For the divisible loads under consideration, the computation phase usually involves simple linear transformations on the input data, and the volume of returned results can be considered to be proportional to the amount of load received in the allocation phase. If the allocated load fraction is α_k, then the returned result is equal to $\delta\alpha_k$, $0 \leq \delta \leq 1$. The constant δ is application specific, and is the same for all processors for a particular load $\mathcal{J}$. This is the accepted model for returned results in literature to date (Adler et al., 2003; Barlas, 1998; Beaumont, Marchal, Rehn & Robert, 2005; Beaumont et al., 2006; Beaumont, Marchal & Robert, 2005; Bharadwaj et al., 1996; Comino & Narasimhan, 2002; Rosenberg, 2001; Yu & Robertazzi, 2003).

2.3 Communication and Computation Time

The time taken for communication and computation is assumed to be a linearly increasing function of the size of load fraction. For a load fraction α_k, $\alpha_k C_k$ is the transmission time from p_0 to p_k, $\alpha_k E_k$ is the time it takes p_k to perform the requisite processing on α_k, and $\delta\alpha_k C_k$ is the time it takes p_k to finally transmit the results back to p_0. Though a linear model is considered for computation and communication times for the sake of simplicity, all results can be easily extended to other models.

In the DLSRCHETS problem, the master has to partition the load $\mathcal{J}$ into fractions $\alpha_1, \ldots, \alpha_m$, and manage the allocation of these fractions to, and collection of the results from the processors $p_1, \ldots, p_m$ in the minimum possible time. Let $\mathcal{T} = \{1, \ldots, m\}$ be the set of *tasks* corresponding to the m fractions that are allocated to, and $\mathcal{R} = \{1, \ldots, m\}$ be the set of *results* that are collected from the processors $p_1, \ldots, p_m$ respectively.

Though the load fractions (tasks) can be processed independently of each other on the respective processors, the single-port communication model implicitly induces a *precedence order* on the distribution of the tasks and collection of the results. Let $\prec_a$ and $\prec_c$ be *total orders* on the sets $\mathcal{T}$ and $\mathcal{R}$ respectively, such that $\prec_a$ represents the sequence (order) in which processors are allocated tasks, and $\prec_c$ is the sequence in which results are collected from the processors at the master. Then, $i \prec_a j$ implies that task i *precedes* task j (or equivalently task j *succeeds* task i) in the allocation sequence $\prec_a$, and $i \prec_c j$ signifies that result i precedes result j in the collection sequence $\prec_c$. If $\{k \in \mathcal{T} : i \prec_a k \prec_a j\} = \emptyset$, then task i is the *immediate predecessor* of task j in $\prec_a$, and is denoted as $i \lessdot_a j$. Similarly, if $\{k \in \mathcal{R} : i \prec_c k \prec_c j\} = \emptyset$, then result j is the *immediate successor* of result i in $\prec_c$, and is denoted as $i \lessdot_c j$. Define $B^i_{\prec_a} := \{j \in \mathcal{T} : j \prec_a i\} \cup \{i\}$ and $F^i_{\prec_a} := \{j \in \mathcal{T} : i \prec_a j\} \cup \{i\}$, i.e., $B^i_{\prec_a}$ is the set of task i and the tasks *before* i (*predecessors* of i) in $\prec_a$, while $F^i_{\prec_a}$ is the set of task i and the *followers* (*successors*) of task i in $\prec_a$. $B^i_{\prec_c}$ and $F^i_{\prec_c}$ are defined accordingly for $\prec_c$. The *minimal element* of $\prec_a$ is defined as $\prec_a^+ := \exists!\, i \in \mathcal{T} : B^i_{\prec_a} = \{i\}$ and the *maximal element* of $\prec_a$ is defined as, $\prec_a^- := \exists!\, i \in \mathcal{T} : F^i_{\prec_a} = \{i\}$, i.e., $\prec_a^+$ and $\prec_a^-$ are

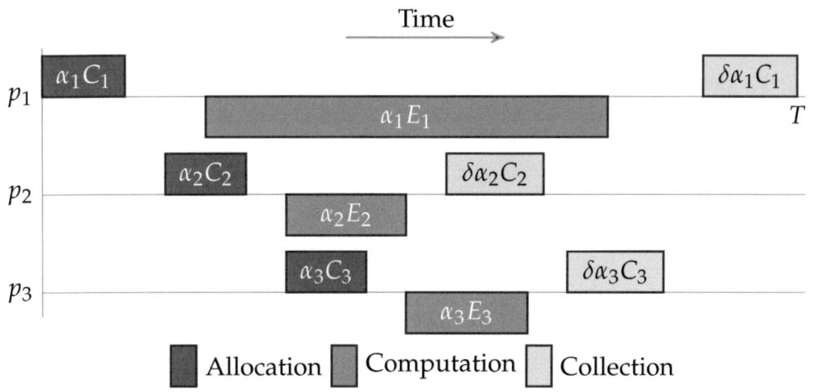

Fig. 3. A possible schedule with $m = 3$. The three phases of each processor are atomic and satisfy the constraints (1) to (9).

the first and last tasks allocated in $\prec_a$. $\prec_c^+$ and $\prec_c^-$ are similarly defined as the first and last results returned in $\prec_c$.

For a given load $\mathcal{J}$, the objective is to minimize the total processing time T, which is defined as the time taken from the point when the master first initiates the allocation of tasks, to the point when the master completes reception of all the results. The *schedule* $\mathcal{S}$ of DLSRCHETS for a given load distribution α, is a pair (t, r), where, $t : \mathcal{T} \mapsto \mathbb{R}_0^+$ is the task allocation start time function, and $r : \mathcal{R} \mapsto \mathbb{R}_0^+$ is the result collection start time function. In a *feasible* schedule, the start times in t and r must satisfy the following constraints:

$$t_j - t_i \geq \alpha_i C_i \qquad \forall\, i \in \{1, \ldots, m\}, i \preccurlyeq_a j \tag{1}$$

$$t_i \geq \sum_{j \in B^i_{\prec_a} \setminus \{i\}} \alpha_j C_j \qquad \forall\, i \in \{1, \ldots, m\} \tag{2}$$

$$r_j - r_i \geq \delta\alpha_i C_i \qquad \forall\, i \in \{1, \ldots, m\}, i \preccurlyeq_c j \tag{3}$$

$$T - r_i \geq \sum_{j \in F^i_{\prec_c}} \delta\alpha_j C_j \qquad \forall\, i \in \{1, \ldots, m\} \tag{4}$$

$$r_i - t_i \geq \alpha_i C_i + \alpha_i E_i \qquad \forall\, i \in \{1, \ldots, m\} \tag{5}$$

$$t_i \neq r_j \qquad \forall\, i, j \in \{1, \ldots, m\} \tag{6}$$

$$r_j - t_i \geq \alpha_i C_i \qquad \forall\, j \in \{1, \ldots, m\}, \forall\, t_i < r_j \tag{7}$$

$$t_i - r_j \geq \delta\alpha_j C_j \qquad \forall\, i \in \{1, \ldots, m\}, \forall\, r_j < t_i \tag{8}$$

$$t_i, r_j \geq 0 \qquad \forall\, i, j \in \{1, \ldots, m\} \tag{9}$$

The precedence constraints of $\prec_a$ are enforced by (1) and (2), while inequalities (3) and (4) impose the precedence constraints of $\prec_c$ and define the processing time T. The fact that the result collection cannot begin before the execution of the entire load fraction is complete is shown by (5). Constraints (6), (7), and (8) impose the single-port model so that no allocation and collection phase can overlap. The non-negativity of the start times is ensured by (9).

Figure 3 shows the timing diagram for a feasible schedule with $m = 3$. The time spent in communication with the master p_0 is shown above the horizontal axes, and time spent in computation by the individual processors below the horizontal axes. Since p_0 does not retain any part of the load for itself, there is no p_0 axis.

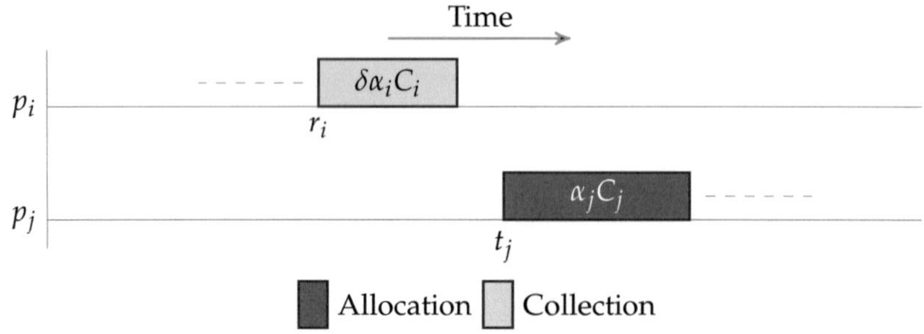

Fig. 4. Interleaved result collection. There exists at least one pair of r_i and t_j that immediately follow each other.

Condition 1 (Allocation Precedence Condition). The master should first allocate the entire load to the processors before receiving any results from the processors.

Lemma 1 (Allocation Precedence Lemma). *There exists an optimal schedule for DLSRCHETS that satisfies the allocation precedence condition. (There may exist other optimal schedules that do not satisfy the allocation precedence condition.)*

Proof. Consider a feasible schedule with processing time T, that satisfies (1) to (9) for a load distribution α, and an arbitrary order of allocation and collection $\prec_a$ and $\prec_c$, such that some results are collected before the load is completely allocated first.
Then, there exists at least one pair (i, j) with $i \prec_a j$, such that the result collection starting at r_i is followed by a task allocation at t_j, without any other intermediate communication phase as shown in Fig. 4.
Suppose that all load fractions in α, and all other start times in t and r are maintained the same, and only the order of collection of result i and allocation of task j is exchanged, such that the new allocation start time of task j is $t'_j = r_i$, and the new collection start time of result i is $r'_i = r_i + \alpha_j C_j$.
Since the above exchange does not alter the order of allocation of different tasks, the precedence constraints of $\prec_a$ defined by (1) and (2) still hold. Similarly, the precedence constraints of $\prec_c$, imposed by (3) and (4) also hold after the exchange. The constraints (6), (7), and (8) are valid after the exchange because the single-port model is not violated by the exchange.
Only the conditions expressed by (5) require verification. Before the exchange, the conditions $r_i - t_i \geq \alpha_i C_i + \alpha_i E_i$ and $r_j - t_j \geq \alpha_j C_j + \alpha_j E_j$ are satisfied. After the exchange, the constraints (5) are still valid because $r'_i - t_i = r_i + \alpha_j C_j - t_i > r_i - t_i$, and $r_j - t'_j = r_j - r_i > r_j - t_j$.
From the above observations, it is clear that after the reordering, all conditions for feasibility are still satisfied. Moreover, the orders $\prec_a$ and $\prec_c$ are unchanged, and no additional processing time is required for the reordering.
If a similar reordering is carried out for all such pairs (i, j), then the allocation precedence condition is satisfied with no addition in total processing time T.
Now if there is an optimal schedule for DLSRCHETS that does not satisfy the allocation precedence condition, then a reordering can be performed as mentioned above so that the schedule satisfies the allocation precedence condition without an increase in the total processing time. That is, there always exists an optimal schedule that satisfies the allocation precedence condition, and only such schedules need be considered in the search for the optimal schedule. ■

Two other basic lemma are stated before the DLSRCHETS problem is defined.

Lemma 2. *There exists an optimal schedule for DLSRCHETS that has no idle time between any two consecutive allocation phases and any two consecutive result collection phases. (There may exist other optimal schedules that do not satisfy this condition.)*

Proof. Assume that a feasible schedule that obeys (1) to (9), and in addition also satisfies the allocation precedence condition, has idle time between the consecutive communication phases (see Fig. 3). Let the processing time be T, the load distribution be α, and $(\prec_a, \prec_c)$ be the orders of allocation and collection.
According to the assumptions in the system model, all processors are available continuously and exclusively during the entire execution process, and the master can only communicate with one processor at a time. For any $i \preccurlyeq_a j$, when processor p_i completes the reception of its allocated task at time $t_i + \alpha_i C_i$, processor p_j is already available and can start receiving data immediately at $t_j = t_i + \alpha_i C_i$. Because the schedule satisfies the allocation precedence condition, load is first distributed to all the processors sequentially before result collection begins. Thus the start time of each task $i \in \mathcal{T}$ can be brought forward so that $t_i = t_{\prec_a^+} + \sum_{j \in B^i_{\prec_a} \setminus \{i\}} \alpha_j C_j$, and the inequalities (1) and (2) are reduced to equalities without exceeding T.
Following a similar logic to the one above, the result collection of each result $i \in \mathcal{R}$ can be delayed to the extent necessary to make the result collection start time $r_i = T - \sum_{j \in F^i_{\prec_c}} \delta \alpha_j C_j$, with inequalities (3) and (4) reduced to equalities and no extra time added to T.
Since any feasible schedule can be reordered in this manner to eliminate the idle time between communication phases, it follows that an optimal schedule to DLSRCHETS also has no idle time between any two consecutive allocation and result collection phases. ■

Lemma 3. *There exists an optimal schedule for DLSRCHETS that has no idle time between the allocation and computation phases of each processor. (There may exist other optimal schedules that do not satisfy this condition.)*

Proof. Following an argument similar to the one used in Lemma 2, since all processors are always available, they can begin computing immediately upon receiving their load fractions in the allocation phase without affecting the schedule.
Any processor p_i begins computing its allocated task at time $t_{\prec_a^+} + \sum_{j \in B^i_{\prec_a}} \alpha_j C_j$ without crossing the time interval T. Since any feasible schedule can be reordered in this manner, an optimal schedule to DLSRCHETS too has no idle time between the allocation and computation phases of each processor. ■

Theorem 1 (Feasible Schedule Theorem). *There exists an optimal schedule for DLSRCHETS that satisfies Lemmas 1 to 3.*

Proof. If there exists an optimal schedule that does not satisfy any or all of the Lemmas 1 to 3, it can always be reordered as explained in the respective proofs to satisfy the same. ■

From Theorem 1, it follows that only those schedules that satisfy Lemmas 1 to 3 need be considered in the search for the optimal solution to DLSRCHETS. A possible timing diagram for such a schedule is shown in Fig. 5.
From the preceding discussion, it can be concluded that the start times t and r in the optimal schedule for DLSRCHETS can be determined from the sequences $\prec_a$ and $\prec_c$, and the load distribution α that minimize the processing time T. Hence instead of finding t and r as in traditional scheduling practice, the DLSRCHETS problem is formulated as a linear programming

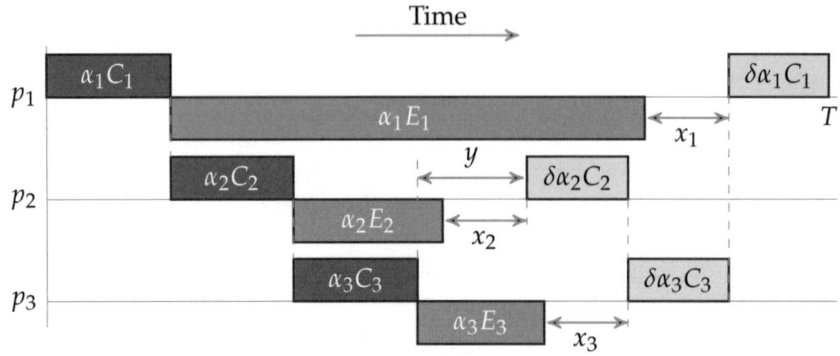

Fig. 5. A schedule for $m = 3$ that satisfies the Feasible Schedule Theorem. Result collection begins only after the entire load is distributed. Each allocation and result collection phase follows its predecessor without delay. The computation phase of each processor follows its allocation phase without delay. Idle time may be present in each processor between the end of its computation phase and the start of the result collection phase.

problem, to find $\prec_a$, $\prec_c$, and α that minimize T. Once the optimal values of these variables are known, it is straightforward to find the optimal schedule.
The constraints (1) to (9) and the allocation precedence condition are combined into a unified form, and for each processor p_i, constraints on T are written in terms of $B^i_{\prec_a}$ and $F^i_{\prec_c}$. The DLSRCHETS problem is defined in terms of a linear program as follows.

Definition 1 (Divisible Load Scheduling with Result Collection on HETerogeneous Systems).

Given a heterogeneous network $\mathcal{H} = (\mathcal{P}, \mathcal{L})$, a divisible load $\mathcal{J}$, unit communication and computation times $\mathcal{C}$, $\mathcal{E}$, find the sequence pair $(\prec^*_a, \prec^*_c)$, and load distribution $\alpha^* = \{\alpha^*_1, \ldots, \alpha^*_m\}$ that

Minimize T
Subject To:

$$\sum_{j \in B^k_{\prec_a}} \alpha_j C_j + \alpha_k E_k + \sum_{j \in F^k_{\prec_c}} \delta\alpha_j C_j \leq T \qquad k = 1, \ldots, m \tag{10}$$

$$\sum_{j=1}^{m} \alpha_j C_j + \sum_{j=1}^{m} \delta\alpha_j C_j \leq T \tag{11}$$

$$\sum_{j=1}^{m} \alpha_j = \mathcal{J} \tag{12}$$

$$T \geq 0, \quad \alpha_k \geq 0 \qquad k = 1, \ldots, m \tag{13}$$

In the above formulation, for a sequence pair $(\prec_a, \prec_c)$, and a load distribution α, the LHS (Left Hand Side) of constraint (10) indicates the total time spent in transmission of tasks to all the processors that must receive load before the processor p_i can begin processing its allocated task, the computation time on the processor p_i itself, and the time for transmission back to the master of results of processor p_i, and all its subsequent result transfers. For the no-overlap model to be satisfied, the processing time T should be greater than or equal to this time for all the m processors. The single-port communication model is enforced by (11) since its LHS represents the lower bound on the time for distribution and collection under this model. The fact that the entire load is distributed amongst the processors is imposed by (12). This is the *normalization equation*. The non-negativity of the decision variables is ensured by constraint (13).

3. Analysis of Optimal Solution

Processors that are allocated load are called *participating processors* or *participants*.

Theorem 2 (Idle Time Theorem). *There exists an optimal solution to the DLSRCHETS problem, in which irrespective of whether load is allocated to all available processors, at the most one of the participating processors has idle time, and the idle time exists only when the result collection begins immediately after the completion of load distribution.*

Proof. For a pair $(\prec_a, \prec_c)$, the DLSRCHETS problem defined by (10) to (13) always has a feasible solution. This is because, for any load distribution α that satisfies (12), T can be made arbitrarily large to satisfy the inequalities (10) and (11). It implies that the polyhedron formed by the constraints of the DLSRCHETS problem, $P := \{x \in \mathbb{R}^{m+1} : Ax \leq b, x \geq 0\} \neq \emptyset$. According to the theory of linear programming, the optimal solution to DLSRCHETS is obtained at some vertex of this polyhedron (Dantzig, 1963; Vanderbei, 2001). As the DLSRCHETS problem has $m+1$ decision variables and $2m+3$ constraints, in a *non-degenerate* optimal solution, at the optimal vertex, $m+1$ constraints out of these must be *tight*, i.e., satisfied with equality. In a *degenerate* optimal solution, more than $m+1$ constraints are tight.
It is clear that in an optimal solution, the normalization constraint (12) will always be tight, and T will always be greater than zero. This means that m constraints out of the remaining $2m+1$ constraints will be tight in a non-degenerate optimal solution. There are two possible ways to proceed with the analysis at this point depending on the allocated load fractions in the optimal solution.

1. $\forall k \in \{1, \ldots, m\} : \alpha_k > 0$.
   In this case, all the load fractions are assumed to be always greater than zero, i.e. number of participants is m. Since all decision variables are positive, there can be no degeneracy (Vanderbei, 2001, Chapter 3).
   It leaves only $m+1$ constraints (10) and (11), out of which m will be tight in the optimal solution. Hence, in the optimal solution, either,
   (a) the m constraints (10) are tight, and the (11) constraint is not, or
   (b) the (11) constraint is tight and one of the (10) constraints is not.

   If any constraint from (10) and (11) is not tight in the optimal solution, it implies a *shortfall* in the LHS as compared to the optimal processing time. In constraints (10) this shortfall represents idle time in a processor, while in (11) it represents the intervening time interval between completion of load distribution from the master and the start of result transfer to the master.
   Thus, if the option (a) above is true, then none of the processors have any idle time in the optimal solution. If the option (b) is true, then one of the processors has idle time, and since this happens only when constraint (11) is tight, it means that idle time in a processor exists only when result transfer to the master begins immediately after completion of load allocation is completed. This is similar to the analysis in Beaumont, Marchal, Rehn & Robert (2005); Beaumont et al. (2006).

2. $\exists\, k \in \{1,\ldots,m\} : \alpha_k = 0$.
   In this case, some of the processors can be allocated zero load in the optimal solution. The analysis has two parts — one for non-degenerate and the other for degenerate optimal solutions.
   Non-degenerate Optimal Solution
   If there are p $(p \leq m)$ participants in the optimal solution,then $m - p$ constraints of (13) are necessarily tight. This means that out of the $m + 1$ constraints (10) and (11), only p constraints will be tight in the optimal solution. Hence, in an optimal solution, either,
   (a) p of the (10) constraints are tight, $m - p$ of the (10) constraints are not tight, and the (11) constraint is not tight, or
   (b) the (11) constraint is tight, $p - 1$ of the (10) constraints are tight, and $m - p + 1$ of the (10) constraints are not tight.

   In the optimal solution, if the option (a) is true, then $m - p$ processors have idle time, while if the option (b) is true, then $m - p + 1$ processors have idle time.
   Since $m - p$ processors are not allocated load, it is obvious that they are idle throughout in either of the above two options. The additional processor with idle time if the option (b) is true has to be one of the participating processors. This means that idle time in a participating processor exists only when the result collection begins immediately upon completion of load allocation.
   Degenerate Optimal Solution
   Similar to the non-degenerate case, if there are p $(p \leq m)$ participants in the optimal solution, then $m - p$ constraints of (13) are necessarily tight. Since the optimal solution is degenerate, *more than* p constraints out of the $m + 1$ constraints (10) and (11) will be tight.
   This means that in the optimal solution, irrespective of whether the (11) constraint is tight, *at least* p of the (10) constraints are tight, and *less than* $m - p$ of the (10) constraints are not tight. Since $m - p$ processors are necessarily idle, some of the (10) constraints corresponding to the processors allocated zero load are tight in the degenerate solution.
   Since $\forall\, k \in \{1,\ldots,m\}$, $B^k_{\prec_a}, F^k_{\prec_c} \subseteq \{1,\ldots,m\}$, it implies that,

$$\sum_{j \in B^k_{\prec_a}} \alpha_j C_j \leq \sum_{j=1}^{m} \alpha_j C_j \qquad k \in \{1,\ldots,m\}$$

and

$$\sum_{j \in F^k_{\prec_c}} \delta\alpha_j C_j \leq \sum_{j=1}^{m} \delta\alpha_j C_j \qquad k \in \{1,\ldots,m\}$$

It follows that,

$$\sum_{j \in B^k_{\prec_a}} \alpha_j C_j + \sum_{j \in F^k_{\prec_c}} \delta\alpha_j C_j \leq \sum_{j=1}^{m} \alpha_j C_j + \sum_{j=1}^{m} \delta\alpha_j C_j \qquad k \in \{1,\ldots,m\} \tag{14}$$

If (11) is not tight, then the RHS (Right Hand Side) of (14) is strictly less than T. That is,

$$\sum_{j \in B^k_{\prec_a}} \alpha_j C_j + \sum_{j \in F^k_{\prec_c}} \delta\alpha_j C_j < T \quad k \in \{1,\ldots,m\} \tag{15}$$

If $\exists\, k \in \{1, \ldots, m\} : \alpha_k = 0$, then $\alpha_k E_k = 0$, and from (15), it immediately follows that the corresponding constraint from (10) can never be tight.
Thus, a constraint corresponding to a processor p_k allocated zero load is tight in the optimal solution only if

$$\sum_{j \in B^k_{\prec_a}} \alpha_j C_j + \sum_{j \in F^k_{\prec_c}} \delta \alpha_j C_j - T = 0 \tag{16}$$

or equivalently if (14) is satisfied with an equality, *and* the RHS of (14) is equal to T, i.e, the (11) constraint is tight.
It is now clear that a degenerate optimal solution exists only when the (11) constraint is tight, and the condition (16) is satisfied. To find when the condition is satisfied, consider the case where for some pair $(\prec_a, \prec_c)$, one or more of the processors allocated zero load follow each other at the end of the allocation sequence and the start of the result collection sequence in the optimal solution.
For example, if $\alpha_i, \alpha_j, \alpha_k = 0$, and one or more of the following occur (the list is not exhaustive):

- $\prec_a^- = i$ and $\prec_c^+ = i$
- $i \preccurlyeq_a j$, $\prec_a^- = j$ and $\prec_c^+ = i$
- $i \preccurlyeq_a j$, $\prec_a^- = j$, $\prec_c^+ = k$ and $k \preccurlyeq_c i$

Only if such tail-end zero-load processors exist, then (14) is satisfied with an equality. Finally, if constraint (11) is tight in the optimal solution, then it follows that the constraints corresponding to these processors are tight.
The linear program obtained after eliminating the redundant constraints corresponding to the tail-end zero-load processors has a non-degenerate optimal solution. This is because, the feasible region defined by the constraints of the non-degenerate problem does not change after addition of the redundant constraints. Hence only a single participant processor has idle time in the degenerate optimal solution.

From the preceding discussion on the optimal solution to the linear program for a pair $(\prec_a, \prec_c)$, it follows that in the optimal solution to the DLSRCHETS problem, $(\prec_a^*, \prec_c^*, \alpha^*)$, at the most one participating processor can have idle time. The idle time occurs *only when* the result collection from processor $\prec_c^+$ starts immediately after completion of load allocation to processor $\prec_a^-$. ■

There are $m!$ possible permutations each of $\prec_a$ and $\prec_c$, and the linear program has to be evaluated $(m!)^2$ times to determine the globally optimum solution $(\prec_a^*, \prec_c^*, \alpha^*)$ for DLSRCHETS. Since the solution to the linear program is completely determined by the values of δ, $\mathcal{C}$ and $\mathcal{E}$, along with the pair $(\prec_a, \prec_c)$, it is not possible to predict which of the processors or how many processors will be allocated zero load.

4. Analysis of Two-Slave System

For a sequence pair (σ_a, σ_c) and load distribution $\alpha = \{\alpha_1, \ldots, \alpha_m\}$, a slave processor p_i, may have idle time x_i because it may have to wait for another processor to release the communication medium for result transfer (ref. Fig. 5). In the optimal solution to DLSRCHETS, $\forall i \in \{1 \ldots m\}$, $x_i = 0$, if and only if $y > 0$, and that there exists a unique $x_i > 0$ if and only if $y = 0$, where y is the intervening time interval between the end of allocation phase of processor $\sigma_a[m]$ and the start of result collection from processor $\sigma_c[1]$. For the FIFO schedule in

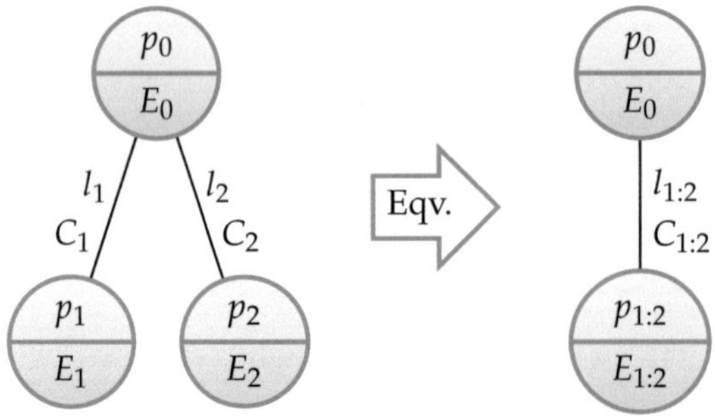

Fig. 6. The heterogeneous two-slave system. The two processors p_1 and p_2 are replaced by an equivalent virtual processor $p_{1:2}$ on the right. The two network links l_1 and l_2 are replaced by an equivalent virtual link $l_{1:2}$. As far as the master p_0 is concerned, there is no difference in the time it takes for the equivalent processor to execute a task.

particular, processor $\sigma_a[m]$ can always be selected to have idle time when $y = 0$, i.e., in the FIFO schedule, $x_{\sigma_a[m]} > 0$ if and only if $y = 0$. In the LIFO schedule, since $y > 0$ always, no processor has idle time, i.e., $\forall i \in \{1 \ldots m\}$, $x_i = 0$ always (Beaumont, Marchal, Rehn & Robert, 2005; Beaumont et al., 2006; Beaumont, Marchal & Robert, 2005).

Let the allocation sequence be represented by σ_a, and the collection sequence by σ_c, both of which are permutations of the index set $K = \{1, \ldots, m\}$ of slave processors in the heterogeneous system $\mathcal{H}$. For a pair (σ_a, σ_c), the solution to the linear program defined by (10) to (13) is completely determined by the values of δ, $\mathcal{E}$, $\mathcal{C}$, and it is not possible to predict which processor is the one that has idle time in the optimal solution. In fact, it is possible that not all processors are allocated load in the optimal solution, in which case some processors are idle throughout.

The heterogeneous system $\mathcal{H} = (\mathcal{P}, \mathcal{L})$ with $m = 2$ is shown in Fig. 6. It is defined by $\mathcal{P} = \{p_0, p_1, p_2\}$ and $\mathcal{L} = \{l_1, l_2\}$. The unit computation and communication times are defined by the sets $\mathcal{E} = \{E_1, E_2\}$, and $\mathcal{C} = \{C_1, C_2\}$. Without loss of generality, it is assumed that the total load to be processed available at the master is $\mathcal{J} = 1$. Also it is assumed that $C_1 \leq C_2$. No assumptions are possible regarding the relationship between E_1 and E_2, or $C_1 + E_1 + \delta C_1$ and $C_2 + E_2 + \delta C_2$.

An important parameter, ρ_k, known as the *network parameter* is introduced, which indicates for a slave p_k, how fast (or slow) its computation parameter E_k is with respect to the communication parameter C_k of its network link:

$$\rho_k = \frac{E_k}{C_k} \qquad k = 1, \ldots, m \tag{17}$$

The master p_0 distributes the load $\mathcal{J}$ between the two slave processors p_1 and p_2 so as to minimize the processing time T. Depending on the values of δ, $\mathcal{E}$ and $\mathcal{C}$, there are three possibilities:

1. **Entire load is distributed to p_1 only.**
   The total processing time is given by

$$T^1 = C_1 + E_1 + \delta C_1 = C_1(1 + \delta + \rho_1) \tag{18}$$

2. **Entire load is distributed to p_2 only.**

The total processing time in this case is

$$T^2 = C_2 + E_2 + \delta C_2 = C_2(1 + \delta + \rho_2) \tag{19}$$

3. **Load is distributed to both p_1 and p_2.**
   It can be proved that as long as $C_1 \le C_2$, only the schedules in Figs. 7, 8, and 9 can be optimal for a two-slave system. These schedules are the FIFO schedule, the LIFO schedule, and the FIFO schedule with idle time in p_2.
   These schedules are referred to as Schedule f, Schedule l, and Schedule g respectively. Superscripts f, l, and g are used to distinguish the three schedules. The equations for load fractions, processing times, and the conditions for optimality of Schedules f, l, and g are not derived on account of space constraints. The interested reader is directed to (Ghatpande, Nakazato, Beaumont & Watanabe, 2008) for details.

4.1 Optimal Schedule in Two-Slave System

A few lemmas and theorems to determine the optimal schedule for a two-slave system are now stated without proof. Please refer to Ghatpande, Nakazato, Beaumont & Watanabe (2008) for the proofs.

Lemma 4. *It is always advantageous to distribute the load to both the processors, rather than execute it on the individual processors (for the system model under consideration).*

Lemma 5 (Idle Indicator Lemma). $\rho_1\rho_2 \le \delta$ *is a necessary and sufficient condition to indicate the presence of idle time in the FIFO schedule (i.e. Schedule g).*

The simplicity of the condition to detect the presence of idle time in the FIFO schedule is both pleasing and surprising, and has been derived for the first time ever. Further confirmation of this condition is obtained in Sect. 4.2.

Theorem 3 (Optimal Schedule Theorem). *The optimal schedule for a two-slave system can be found as follows:*

1. *If $\delta C_2 > C_1(1 + \delta + \rho_1)$, then Schedule l is optimal.*
2. *Else If $\delta C_2 \le C_1(1 + \delta + \rho_1)$, $\rho_1\rho_2 \le \delta$ and $C_2 \le C_1\left(1 + \frac{(1+\rho_1)\rho_2}{\delta(1+\delta+\rho_2)}\right)$, then Schedule g is optimal.*
3. *Else if $\delta C_2 \le C_1(1 + \delta + \rho_1)$, $\rho_1\rho_2 \le \delta$ and $C_2 > C_1\left(1 + \frac{(1+\rho_1)\rho_2}{\delta(1+\delta+\rho_2)}\right)$, then Schedule l is optimal.*
4. *Else If $\delta C_2 \le C_1(1 + \delta + \rho_1)$, $\rho_1\rho_2 > \delta$, and $T^f \le \frac{C_1C_2}{(C_2-C_1)}$, then Schedule f is optimal.*
5. *Else if $\delta C_2 \le C_1(1 + \delta + \rho_1)$, $\rho_1\rho_2 > \delta$, and $T^f > \frac{C_1C_2}{(C_2-C_1)}$, then Schedule l is optimal.*

The optimal solution to DLSRCHETS, $(\sigma_a^*, \sigma_c^*, \alpha^*)$, for a system with two slave processors is a function of the system parameters and the application under consideration, because of which, no particular sequence of allocation and collection can be defined *a priori* as the optimal sequence. The optimal solution can only be determined once all the parameters become known.

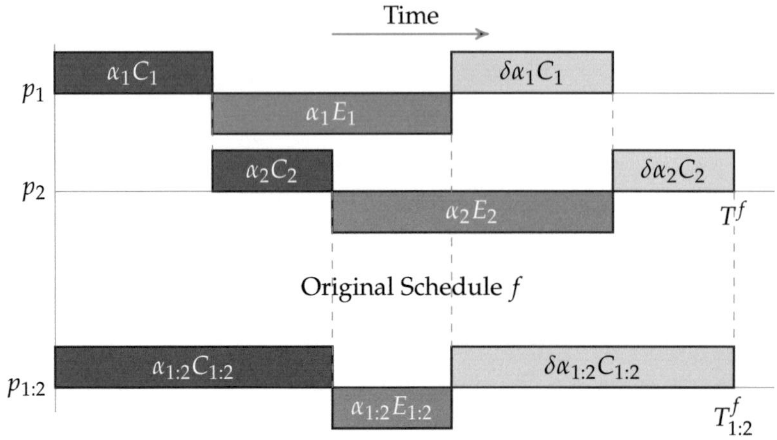

Fig. 7. Equivalent processor in Schedule f. The total communication time remains the same as the original two processors. The equivalent computation time is equal to the interval between the end of allocation to p_2 and the start of result collection from p_1.

4.2 The Concept of Equivalent Processor

To extend the above result to the general case with m slave processors, the concept of an *equivalent processor* is introduced. Consider the system in Fig. 6. The processors p_1 and p_2 are replaced by a single equivalent processor $p_{1:2}$ with computation parameter $E_{1:2}$, connected to the root by an equivalent link $l_{1:2}$ with communication parameter $C_{1:2}$. The resulting system is called the *equivalent system* and the resulting schedule is known as the *equivalent schedule*. The values of the parameters for the three equivalent schedules are defined below.

If the initial load distribution is $\alpha = \{\alpha_1, \alpha_2\}$, and the processing time is T, then the equivalent system satisfies the following properties:

- The load processed by $p_{1:2}$ is $\alpha_{1:2} = \alpha_1 + \alpha_2 = 1$.
- The processing time is unchanged and equal to T.
- The time spent in load distribution and result collection is unchanged, i.e., for all three schedules,
  - $\alpha_{1:2}C_{1:2} = \alpha_1 C_1 + \alpha_2 C_2$, and
  - $\delta\alpha_{1:2}C_{1:2} = \delta\alpha_1 C_1 + \delta\alpha_2 C_2$.
- The time spent in load computation is equal to the intervening time interval between the end of allocation phase and the start of result collection phase, i.e.,
  - For Schedule f, $\alpha_{1:2}E^f_{1:2} = \alpha_1 E_1 - \alpha_2 C_2 = \alpha_2 E_2 - \delta\alpha_1 C_1$.
  - For Schedule l, $\alpha_{1:2}E^l_{1:2} = \alpha_2 E_2 = \alpha_1 E_1 - \alpha_2 C_2 - \delta\alpha_2 C_2$.
  - For Schedule g, $\alpha_{1:2}E^g_{1:2} = 0$.

4.3 The Equivalent Processor Theorem

This leads to the following theorem: (refer to (Ghatpande, Nakazato, Beaumont & Watanabe, 2008) for proof.)

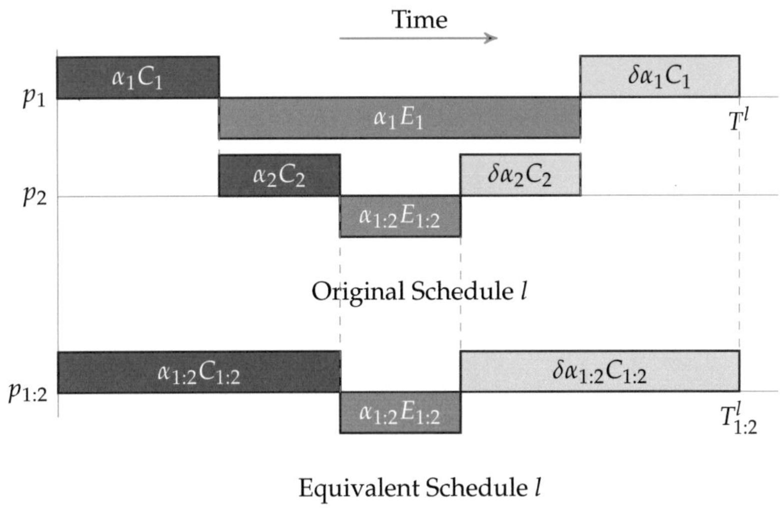

Fig. 8. Equivalent processor in Schedule l. The total communication time remains the same as the original two processors. The equivalent computation time is equal to the computation time of p_2.

Theorem 4 (Equivalent Processor Theorem). *In a heterogeneous system $\mathcal{H}$ with $m = 2$, the two slave processors p_1 and p_2 can be replaced without affecting the processing time T, by a single (virtual) equivalent processor $p_{1:2}$ with equivalent parameters $C_{1:2}$ and $E_{1:2}$, such that $C_1 \leq C_{1:2} \leq C_2$ and $E_{1:2} \leq E_1, E_2$.*

The equivalent processor enables replacement of two processors by a single processor with communication parameter with a value that lies between the values of communication parameters of the original two links. Because of this property, if the processors are arranged so that $C_1 \leq C_2 \leq \ldots \leq C_m$, and two processors are combined at a time sequentially starting from the fastest two, then the resultant equivalent processor does not disturb the order of the sequence.

The equivalent processor for Schedule f provides additional confirmation of the condition for the presence of idle time in a FIFO schedule. It is known that idle time can exist in a FIFO schedule only when the intervening time interval $y = 0$. According to the definition of equivalent processor, this interval corresponds to the equivalent computation capacity $E^f_{1:2}$. This value becomes zero only when $\rho_1\rho_2 - \delta = 0$. Thus, if $\rho_1\rho_2 < \delta$, then idle time must exist in the FIFO schedule.

5. The SPORT Algorithm

Algorithm 1 (SPORT).

arrange $p_1, \ldots, p_m$ *such that* $C_1 \leq C_2 \leq \ldots \leq C_m$

$\sigma_a \leftarrow 1, \sigma_c \leftarrow 1, \alpha_1 \leftarrow 1$

for $k := 2$ *to* m **do**

$C_1 \leftarrow C_{1:k-1}, E_1 \leftarrow E_{1:k-1}, C_2 \leftarrow C_k, E_2 \leftarrow E_k$

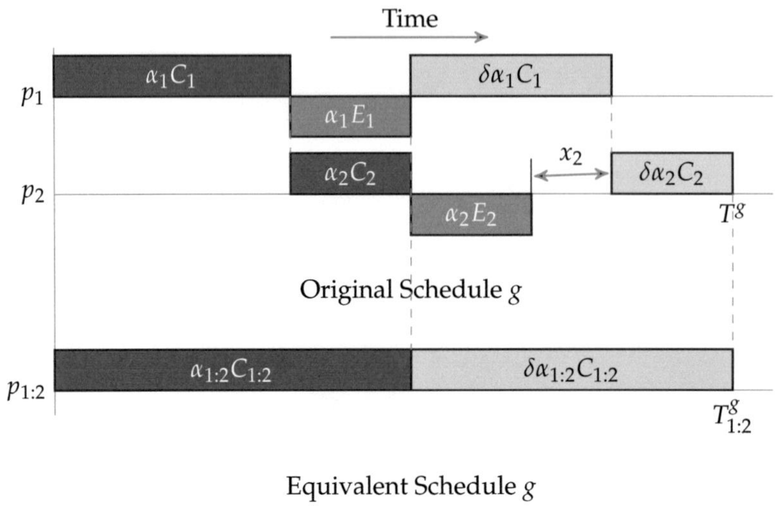

Fig. 9. Equivalent processor in Schedule g. The total communication time remains the same as the original two processors. The equivalent computation time is equal to zero as the result collection begins immediately after the allocation phase ends.

if $\delta C_2 > C_1(1 + \delta + \rho_1)$ **then**

/ $T^l < T^f, T^g$, use Schedule l */*

call `schedule_lifo`

else

/ Need to check other conditions */*

if $\rho_1\rho_2 \leq \delta$ **then**

/ Possibility of idle time */*

if $C_2 \leq C_1\left(1 + \frac{(1+\rho_1)\rho_2}{\delta(1+\delta+\rho_2)}\right)$ **then**

/ $T^g < T^l$, use Schedule g */*

call `schedule_idle`

break for

else

/ $T^l < T^g$, use Schedule l */*

call `schedule_lifo`

end if

else

/ No idle time present */*

if $T^f \leq \dfrac{C_1 C_2}{C_2 - C_1}$ **then**

/ $T^f < T^l$, use Schedule f */*

call `schedule_fifo`

else

/ $T^l < T^f$, use Schedule l */*

call `schedule_lifo`

end if

end if

end if

end for

$n \leftarrow$ `numberOfProcessorsUsed`

/ Update load fractions from stored values */*

$$\alpha_k \leftarrow \begin{cases} \alpha_k \cdot \prod_{j=2}^{n} \alpha_{1:j} & \text{if } k = 1 \\ \alpha_k \cdot \prod_{j=k}^{n} \alpha_{1:j} & \text{if } k = 2, \ldots, n \end{cases}$$

$T \leftarrow C_{1:n} + E_{1:n} + \delta C_{1:n}$

The procedures in the algorithm are given below:

procedure `schedule_idle`

$\alpha_{1:k-1} \leftarrow \dfrac{C_2}{C_1\rho_1 + C_2}$

$\alpha_k \leftarrow \dfrac{C_1\rho_1}{C_1\rho_1 + C_2}$

/ Update sequences for FIFO */*

$\sigma_a \leftarrow \{\sigma_a,\ k\}$

$\sigma_c \leftarrow \{\sigma_c,\ k\}$

/ Compute equivalent processor parameters */*

$C_{1:k} \leftarrow \dfrac{C_1 C_2 (1 + \rho_1)}{C_1\rho_1 + C_2}$

$E_{1:k} \leftarrow 0$

`numberOfProcessorsUsed` $\leftarrow k$

return

procedure `schedule_lifo`

$r_1^l \leftarrow \rho_1$

$r_2^l \leftarrow 1 + \delta + \rho_2$

$\alpha_{1:k-1} \leftarrow \dfrac{C_2 r_2^l}{C_1 r_1^l + C_2 r_2^l}$

$\alpha_k \leftarrow \dfrac{C_1 r_1^l}{C_1 r_1^l + C_2 r_2^l}$

/* *Update sequences for LIFO* */

$\sigma_a \leftarrow \{\sigma_a, k\}$

$\sigma_c \leftarrow \{k, \sigma_c\}$

/* *Compute equivalent processor parameters* */

$C_{1:k} \leftarrow \dfrac{C_1 C_2 (r_1^l + r_2^l)}{C_1 r_1^l + C_2 r_2^l}$

$E_{1:k} \leftarrow \dfrac{C_1 C_2 \rho_1 \rho_2}{C_1 r_1^l + C_2 r_2^l}$

`numberOfProcessorsUsed` $\leftarrow k$

return

procedure `schedule_fifo`

$r_1^f \leftarrow \delta + \rho_1$

$r_2^f \leftarrow 1 + \rho_2$

$\alpha_{1:k-1} \leftarrow \dfrac{C_2 r_2^f}{C_1 r_1^f + C_2 r_2^f}$

$\alpha_k \leftarrow \dfrac{C_1 r_1^f}{C_1 r_1^f + C_2 r_2^f}$

/* *Update sequences for FIFO* */

$\sigma_a \leftarrow \{\sigma_a, k\}$

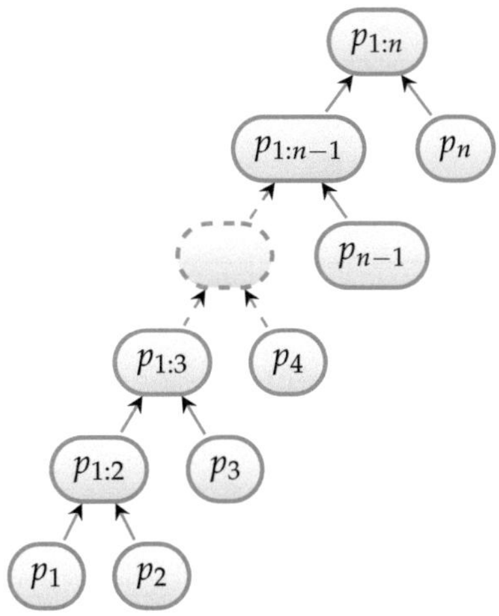

Fig. 10. The building of SPORT solution. At each step only two processors are involved (the state space remains constant). The optimal schedule for two processors can be easily computed in constant time using simple if-then-else statements in Theorem 3.

$\sigma_c \leftarrow \{\sigma_c, k\}$

/ Compute equivalent processor parameters */*

$C_{1:k} \leftarrow \dfrac{C_1 C_2 (r_1^f + r_2^f)}{C_1 r_1^f + C_2 r_2^f}$

$E_{1:k} \leftarrow \dfrac{C_1 C_2 (\rho_1 \rho_2 - \delta)}{C_1 r_1^f + C_2 r_2^f}$

`numberOfProcessorsUsed` $\leftarrow k$

return

5.1 Algorithm Explanation

At the start, the processors are arranged so that $C_1 \leq C_2 \leq \ldots \leq C_m$, and two processors with the fastest communication links are selected. The optimal schedule and load distribution for the two processors are found according to Theorem 3. If Schedule f or l is found optimal, then the two processors are replaced by their equivalent processor. In either case, since $C_1 \leq C_{1:2} \leq C_2$, the ordering of the processors does not change. In the subsequent iteration, the equivalent processor and the processor with the next fastest communication link are selected and the steps are repeated until either all processors are used up, or Schedule g is found to be optimal. If Schedule g is found to be optimal in any iteration, then the algorithm exits after finding the load distribution for that iteration.

The computation of the allocation and collection sequences is straightforward. The allocation sequence σ_a is maintained in the order of decreasing communication link bandwidth of the processors. Irrespective of the schedule found optimal in iteration k, k is always appended to σ_a. The collection sequence σ_c is constructed as follows:

- If Schedule f or g is found optimal in iteration k, k is appended to σ_c.

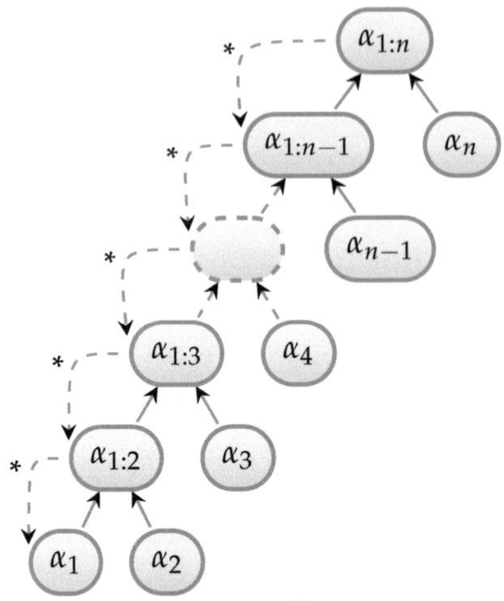

Fig. 11. Calculating the load fractions in SPORT. α_1' is the initial value of α_1. It is multiplied by the product term in (20) to get the final value of $\alpha_1 = \alpha_{1:n} \cdot \alpha_{1:n-1} \cdots \alpha_{1:2} \cdot \alpha_1'$. This is equivalent to traversing the binary tree from the root to the leaf nodes and taking the product of all nodes (values) encountered. This calculation can be implemented in $O(m)$ time by starting with α_m and storing the intermediate values.

- If Schedule l is found optimal in iteration k, k is prepended to σ_c.

The calculation of load distribution to the processors occurs simultaneously with the search for the optimal schedule. As shown in Fig. 11, the algorithm creates a *one-sided binary tree* of load fractions. If the number of processors participating in the computation is n, $2 \leq n \leq m$, the root node of the binary tree is $\alpha_{1:n}$ and the leaf nodes represent the final load fractions allocated to the processors. The value of the root node need not be calculated as it is equal to one. The individual load fractions, α_k, are initially assigned value α_k' (say), and then updated at the end as:

$$\alpha_k = \begin{cases} \alpha_k' \cdot \prod_{j=2}^{n} \alpha_{1:j} & \text{if } k = 1 \\ \alpha_k' \cdot \prod_{j=k}^{n} \alpha_{1:j} & \text{if } k = 2, \ldots, n \end{cases} \quad (20)$$

This is equivalent to traversing the binary tree from the root to each leaf node and taking the product of the nodes encountered (see Fig. 11). This calculation can be easily implemented in $O(m)$ time by starting with the computation of α_n, and storing the values of the product terms (i.e. $\prod \alpha_{1:j}$) for each processor and then using that value for the next processor.

Once the sequences (σ_a, σ_c) and load distribution α are found, calculating the processing time is straightforward. The processing time is simply the sum of the (equivalent) parameters of the equivalent processor $p_{1:n}$, i.e., $T = C_{1:n} + E_{1:n} + \delta\, C_{1:n}$.

In SPORT, defining the allocation sequence by sorting the values of C_k requires $O(m \log m)$ time, while finding the collection sequence and load distribution requires $O(m)$ time in the worst case. Thus, if sorted values of C_k are given, then the overall complexity of the algorithm is polynomial in m and is equal to $O(m)$.

5.2 Simulations and Analysis

The performance of SPORT was compared to four algorithms, viz. OPT, FIFOC, LIFOC, and ITERLP. The globally optimal schedule OPT is obtained after evaluation of the linear pro-

Table 1. Minimum statistics for SPORT simulations. In sets 1 and 2, the minimum errors in LIFOC are 2 orders of magnitude higher than SPORT, ITERLP, and FIFOC. In sets 3 and 4, FIFOC error is 2 to 3 orders of magnitude higher than the other three algorithms.

Set	m	$\delta = 0.2$				$\delta = 0.5$			
		SPORT	ITERLP	LIFOC	FIFOC	SPORT	ITERLP	LIFOC	FIFOC
1	4	5.73e-03	4.32e-03	8.08e-01	5.76e-03	2.20e-02	1.06e-02	1.07e+00	2.21e-02
	5	7.89e-04	6.90e-04	7.21e-01	7.89e-04	5.40e-03	4.21e-03	9.63e-01	5.30e-03
2	4	1.01e-02	5.78e-03	8.41e-01	1.01e-02	2.37e-02	1.43e-02	1.15e+00	2.40e-02
	5	3.34e-03	2.10e-03	7.93e-01	3.34e-03	1.06e-02	8.92e-03	1.10e+00	1.07e-02
3	4	2.03e-01	1.80e-03	1.05e-01	1.61e+00	1.12e-01	5.13e-03	9.59e-02	4.43e+00
	5	3.96e-01	1.90e-01	8.90e-02	1.75e+00	5.34e-02	9.32e-02	5.13e-02	4.74e+00
4	4	4.95e-06	1.97e-16	4.92e-06	1.05e+00	3.09e-02	2.77e-15	3.09e-02	3.23e+00
	5	1.08e-02	5.81e-04	2.75e-06	1.15e+00	5.84e-02	2.18e-03	5.84e-02	3.74e+00

Table 2. Maximum statistics for SPORT simulations. In sets 1 and 2, the maximum errors in LIFOC are 2 orders of magnitude higher than SPORT, ITERLP, and FIFOC. In sets 3 and 4, FIFOC error is 2 to 3 orders of magnitude higher than the other three algorithms.

Set	m	$\delta = 0.2$				$\delta = 0.5$			
		SPORT	ITERLP	LIFOC	FIFOC	SPORT	ITERLP	LIFOC	FIFOC
1	4	5.34e-02	3.09e-02	3.11e+00	5.61e-02	1.84e-01	7.57e-02	4.20e+00	2.02e-01
	5	8.24e-02	4.87e-02	3.00e+00	8.79e-02	2.26e-01	1.19e-01	3.91e+00	2.30e-01
2	4	3.03e-02	1.69e-02	1.83e+00	3.06e-02	9.35e-02	4.93e-02	3.10e+00	1.10e-01
	5	3.66e-02	2.61e-02	2.24e+00	3.68e-02	1.15e-01	8.34e-02	2.75e+00	1.26e-01
3	4	4.01e-01	3.42e-01	4.66e-01	2.02e+00	4.03e-01	2.22e-01	4.03e-01	5.44e+00
	5	5.31e-01	3.86e-01	4.84e-01	2.30e+00	5.45e-01	3.80e-01	4.16e-01	6.05e+00
4	4	1.32e+00	6.50e-01	8.84e-01	4.47e+00	8.02e-01	7.11e-01	4.00e-01	1.12e+01
	5	1.56e+00	7.66e-01	4.34e-01	4.85e+00	9.35e-01	8.97e-01	4.24e-01	1.15e+01

gram for all possible $(m!)^2$ permutations of (σ_a, σ_c). In FIFOC, processors are allocated load and result are collected in the order of decreasing communication link bandwidth of the processors. In LIFOC, load allocation is in the order of decreasing communication link bandwidth of the processors, while result collection is the reverse order of increasing communication link bandwidth of the processors. ITERLP (Ghatpande, Beaumont, Nakazato & Watanabe, 2008) is a near-optimal algorithm for DLSRCHETS. To explore the effects of system parameter values on the performance of the algorithms, several sets of simulations were carried out:

Set 1 Homogeneous network and homogeneous processors
Set 2 Homogeneous network and heterogeneous processors
Set 3 Heterogeneous network and homogeneous processors
Set 4 Heterogeneous network and heterogeneous processors

The error values with respective to the optimal are calculated. Over 500,000 simulation runs are carried out. Further details can be obtained in (Ghatpande, Beaumont, Nakazato & Watanabe, 2008; Ghatpande, Nakazato, Beaumont & Watanabe, 2008). The minimum and maximum

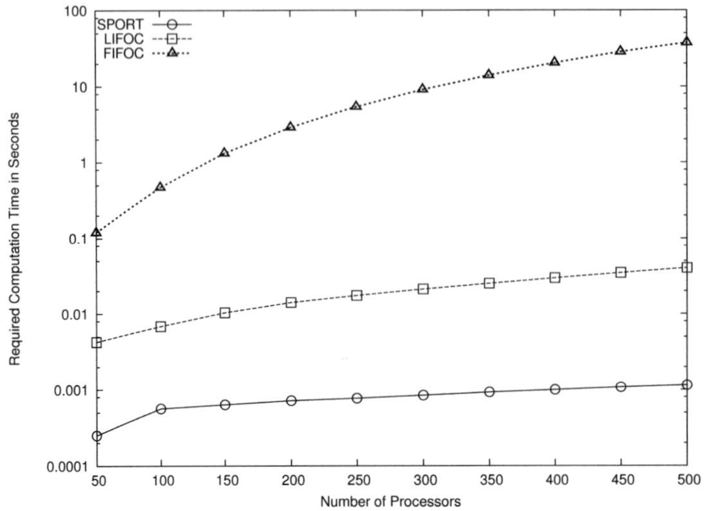

Fig. 12. Comparison of wall-clock time for SPORT, LIFOC, and FIFOC. SPORT is two orders of magnitude faster than LIFOC and almost four orders of magnitude faster than FIFOC. This figure appears in (Ghatpande, Nakazato, Beaumont & Watanabe, 2008).

mean error values of each algorithm are tabulated in Tables 1 and 2. It can be observed that in sets 1 and 2, the minimum and maximum errors in LIFOC are 2 orders of magnitude higher than SPORT, ITERLP, and FIFOC. On the other hand in sets 3 and 4, FIFOC error is 2 to 3 orders of magnitude higher than the other three algorithms.

There is a significant downside to LIFOC because of its property to use all available processors — the time required to compute the optimal solution (wall-clock time) is almost two orders of magnitude greater than that of SPORT as seen in Fig. 12. These values were obtained by averaging the wall-clock time to compute a solution over 1000 runs. The results show that though both SPORT and LIFOC are $O(m)$ algorithms given a set of processors sorted by decreasing communication bandwidth, clearly SPORT is the better performing algorithm, with the best cost-performance ratio for large values of m. The values for FIFOC are almost four orders of magnitude larger than SPORT. The extensive simulations show that:

- If network links are homogeneous, then LIFOC performance is affected for both homogeneous and heterogeneous computation speeds.
- If network links are heterogeneous, then FIFOC performance is affected for both homogeneous and heterogeneous computation speeds.
- SPORT performance is also affected to a certain degree by the heterogeneity in network links and computation speeds, but since SPORT does not use a single predefined sequence of allocation and collection, it is able to better adapt to the changing system conditions.
- ITERLP performance is somewhat better than SPORT, but is computationally expensive. SPORT generates similar schedules at a fraction of the cost.

6. Conclusion

In this chapter, the DLSRCHETS problem for the scheduling of divisible loads on heterogeneous master-slave systems and considering the result collection phase was formulated and analysed. A new polynomial-time algorithm, SPORT was proposed and tested. Future work can proceed in the following main directions:

Theoretical Analysis The complexity of DLSRCHETS is still an open issue. It makes for an interesting research topic. Is it at all possible that DLSRCHETS can be solved in polynomial time? Does imposition of some additional constraints make it tractable? What are those conditions?

Extending the System Model This area has a large number of possibilities for future work. Scheduling purists may consider the system model used in this thesis to be quite simplistic. As future work, the conditions (constraints on values of E_k and C_k), that minimize the error need to be found. An interesting area would be the investigation of the effect of affine cost models, processor deadlines and release times. Another important area would be to extend the results to multi-installment delivery and multi-level processor trees.

Modification of DLSRCHETS The ways in which DLSRCHETS may be modified are — dynamism and uncertainty in the system parameters, non-clairvoyance, non-omniscience of the master, node (slave) turnover (failure), slave sharing, multiple jobs on one master, multiple masters, multiple jobs on several masters, decentralization of scheduling decision (P2P model), QoS requirements, buffer, bandwidth, and computation constraints on slaves.

Application Development All the testing in this work has been carried out using simulations. It will be interesting to see how the algorithms perform in practice. New and different applications apart from the number of possible scientific applications mentioned in the introduction, need to be developed that use the results in this work. This may require development of new libraries and middleware to support the computation models considered.

7. References

Adler, M., Gong, Y. & Rosenberg, A. L. (2003). Optimal sharing of bags of tasks in heterogeneous clusters, *SPAA '03: Proceedings of the fifteenth annual ACM symposium on Parallel algorithms and architectures*, ACM, New York, NY, USA, pp. 1–10.

Barlas, G. D. (1998). Collection-aware optimum sequencing of operations and closed-form solutions for the distribution of a divisible load on arbitrary processor trees, **9**(5): 429–441.

Beaumont, O., Casanova, H., Legrand, A., Robert, Y. & Yang, Y. (2005). Scheduling divisible loads on star and tree networks: Results and open problems, **16**(3): 207–218.

Beaumont, O., Marchal, L., Rehn, V. & Robert, Y. (2005). FIFO scheduling of divisible loads with return messages under the one-port model, *Research Report 2005-52*, LIP, ENS Lyon, France.

Beaumont, O., Marchal, L., Rehn, V. & Robert, Y. (2006). FIFO scheduling of divisible loads with return messages under the one port model, *Proc. Heterogeneous Computing Workshop HCW'06*.

Beaumont, O., Marchal, L. & Robert, Y. (2005). Scheduling divisible loads with return messages on heterogeneous master-worker platforms, *Research Report 2005-21*, LIP, ENS Lyon, France.

Bharadwaj, V., Ghose, D., Mani, V. & Robertazzi, T. G. (1996). *Scheduling Divisible Loads in Parallel and Distributed Systems*, IEEE Computer Society Press, Los Alamitos, CA.

Cheng, Y.-C. & Robertazzi, T. G. (1990). Distributed computation for a tree network with communication delays, **26**(3): 511–516.

Comino, N. & Narasimhan, V. L. (2002). A novel data distribution technique for host-client type parallel applications, **13**(2): 97–110.

Dantzig, G. B. (1963). *Linear Programming and Extensions*, Princeton Univ. Press, Princeton, NJ.

Ghatpande, A., Beaumont, O., Nakazato, H. & Watanabe, H. (2008). Divisible load scheduling with result collection on heterogeneous systems, *Proc. Heterogeneous Computing Workshop (HCW 2008) held in the IEEE Intl. Parallel and Distributed Processing Sysmposium (IPDPS 2008)*, Miami, FL.

Ghatpande, A., Nakazato, H., Beaumont, O. & Watanabe, H. (2008). SPORT: An algorithm for divisible load scheduling with result collection on heterogeneous systems, *IEICE Transactions on Communications* **E91-B**(8).

Robertazzi, T. (2008). Divisible (partitionable) load scheduling research.
URL: *http://www.ece.sunysb.edu/ tom/dlt.html#THEORY*

Rosenberg, A. (2001). Sharing partitionable workload in heterogeneous NOWs: Greedier is not better, *IEEE International Conference on Cluster Computing*, Newport Beach, CA, pp. 124–131.

Vanderbei, R. J. (2001). *Linear Programming: Foundations and Extensions*, Vol. 37 of *International Series in Operations Research & Management*, 2nd edn, Kluwer Academic Publishers.
URL: *http://www.princeton.edu/ rvdb/LPbook/online.html*

Yu, D. & Robertazzi, T. G. (2003). Divisible load scheduling for grid computing, *Proc. International Conference on Parallel and Distributed Computing Systems (PDCS 2003)*, Vol. 1, Los Angeles, CA, USA.

11

On the Role of Helper Peers in P2P Networks

Shay Horovitz and Danny Dolev
Hebrew University of Jerusalem
Israel

1. Introduction

Recent studies in peer-to-peer (P2P) networks present surprising new designs that rely on helper peers. Helper peers, sometimes named as Feeders or Support peers are nodes that do not function as direct consumers or providers of content but are used to collaborate with other peers in the network for a growing variety of benefits.

In File Sharing networks for instance, due to frequent joins, leaves and the characteristic fluctuating throughput of source peers, clients usually download at an unstable rate. In addition, existing P2P protocols tend to ignore source peers that have relatively low bandwidth to offer and practically miss a potentially huge resource. By employing helper peers that are optimal for availability and throughput stability with the downloading client, it is possible to provide a maximal stable throughput even with extremely weak and unstable sources.

Other interesting examples of helper peers in file sharing demonstrated how to integrate helper peers in order to increase the number of sources under flash crowds situations, how to solve the last chunk problem and how to bypass fairness rules for better download rates.

In P2P streaming networks such as live IPTV and VOD, helper peers can contribute in preventing glitches and expanding the dissemination of packets, as well as synchronizing and ordering frames for the clients.

In this chapter we present novel architectures that embed helper peers in order to solve key problems in P2P networks. We discuss the implications and key techniques in each proposal and point the weaknesses and limitations of mentioned architectures.

We present different selection criteria for choosing the optimal helper peers based on theoretic simulations, practical measurements and experiments with popular protocols such as eMule and BitTorrent.

We propose an advanced Machine Learning based design that actively learns the behavioural patterns of peers and leverages the performance of clients by collaborating with the "right" helper peers at the right time.

Though helper peers gained popularity in P2P research, different works in this field term the same ideas differently and in some cases do not mention each other; this chapter presents the current state of the art in helper-supported P2P networks. Finally, we present future research directions in this field.

2. Background

P2P technology earned its fame throughout the last decade as a result of the wide deployment of P2P file sharing applications over the Internet in the late 1990s. Among the early releases, the popular ones were Napster, Scour Exchange, iMesh and Gnutella which were followed by improved designs such as KaZaA, eDonkey and BitTorrent. Following the increased popularity of online video content, new designs of P2P streaming networks were proposed by Joost, PPLive and others. In parallel, the research community introduced some promising designs in order to overcome the major challenges that relates to P2P networks – mainly dealing with the Lookup problem but also with security, scalability and performance. The potential of P2P for the end user in a P2P network is obvious – the ability to receive content (in some cases free of charge) easily, backed by an efficient search and an active community that continuously update the shared content.

While the above seems promising, recent measurements of broadband usage patterns in ISPs reveal a surprising rising trend that should concern the P2P research community: new server based services are growing in traffic at the expense of P2P traffic. While P2P is still responsible for more than 60% of all upstream data in ISPs, it is claimed that subscribers are increasingly turning to alternatives such as File Hosting web sites like RapidShare and MegaUpload, since they enable much faster download speed compared to P2P networks (see e.g. Sandvide 2008 Global Broadband Phenomena (2008)). RapidShare is already ranked as the 17th web site in global traffic rankings according to Alexa.Com web traffic rating. Another study (see e.g. IPoque Internet Study (2007)) supports the above and claims that web sites like RapidShare are already responsible for nearly 9% of the Internet traffic in the Middle East and over 4% in Germany. BitTorrent (see, e.g. Cohen (2003)) for example – the most popular P2P protocol, suffers from unstable download rates and hardly exploits the available download capacity (see e.g. Bindal and Cao (2006), Andrade et al. (2007)).

One of the most promising P2P streaming networks was Joost, which suffered from severe QOS problems such as connection loss, hiccups (see, e.g. VentureBeat report (2008)) and degraded throughput (see, e.g. DailyIPTV report (2007)). Joost also failed in broadcasting live events (see, e.g. NewTeeVee report (2008)) and recently Joost finally abandoned P2P completely for a server based solution (see, e.g. TechCrunch report (2008)). PPLive - Another highly popular P2P streaming network is also reported to suffer from occasional glitches, re-buffering and broken streams (see, e.g. All-Streaming-Media report (2008)). While in server based streaming services it is possible to solve QOS problems with buffering, the instability of peers' upload in P2P streaming networks requires a much larger buffer, which puts QOS in question again for the latency - as even though PPLive offers only modest low-quality narrow-band P2P video streaming (see, e.g. Horvath et al. (2008)), its subscribers experience a latency between tens of seconds (see, e.g. Vu et al. (2006)) to two minutes (see, e.g. Hei et al. (2006)).

The above problems put P2P technologies in question for commercial system designers. As most P2P systems already run a best effort approach by prioritizing peers with minimized infrastructure problems like delay and packet loss, they still miss a key factor in degrading P2P performance – the user behaviour. In addition, this approach is blind to a large number of weak sources that remain unused, while the small group of strong sources are exploited and overused (see, e.g. Horvath et al. (2008)).

In Collabory (see, e.g. Horovitz and Dolev (2008)) we analyzed the factors for the instability of source peers in P2P networks and found that the aspect that has the greatest impact is the behaviour of users at source peers. The most obvious occurrence is the case where the user at the source peer invokes applications that heavily use bandwidth such as Email clients, online games or other P2P applications. By doing so, the bandwidth available for the client connected to that machine may be drastically reduced and becomes significantly unstable. Studies confirm that the major factor that has direct impact on QOS in P2P networks is the behaviour of users at the source peers (see, e.g. Do et al. (2004), Rejaie et al. (2003)). This behaviour leads to fluctuating rate of packets for the client peer that might be reflected by a reduced download rate in file sharing networks or high latencies, delays, hiccups and freezes in streaming P2P networks.

As the existing model of P2P networks failed to provide a stable download speed both in file sharing and streaming, some research papers proposed the idea of employing Helper peers, sometimes named as Feeders or Support peers - peers that do not function as direct consumers or providers of content but are used to collaborate with other peers in the network. In the following sections we will survey different implementations of Helper peers for different applications in P2P networks. We focus on designs that aim to solve the stability problem– as we believe that Helpers will play a crucial role in creating future P2P networks that are competitive with old school's centralized file hosting and streaming systems.

3. Helpers for Service Availability

3.1 Increasing Sources in File Sharing & Multicast

The concept of employing helper peers in a P2P networks was first proposed by Wong (see, e.g. Wong (2004)). In his work, which was limited to file sharing based on a swarming mechanism, Wong offered to utilize the free upload capacity of a helper peer for the benefit of client peers, simply by joining helper peers to an existing swarm (See Fig. 1). The helper aims to upload each file piece (portion) it downloads at least u times, where u is a heuristically predetermined number called upload factor. Thus, helpers can guarantee to upload more than they download and contribute to the system. To make sure each piece it downloads is uploaded at least u times, a helper keeps track of the number of times each piece has been uploaded and considers a piece unfulfilled if the piece has not been uploaded u times. The helper downloads a new piece when the number of unfulfilled pieces is below a certain predetermined limit. Its objective was to increase the total amount of available bandwidth in the P2P network, by voluntarily contributing the helper peer's bandwidth resources. It was shown that this strategy is wasteful because the longer a peer/helper stays in the system, the more pieces it will download, which is unnecessary for helpers to keep their upload bandwidth fully utilized (see, e.g. Wang et al. (2007)). It was also shown that the inherent assumption of sufficient altruism in the network without any incentives makes the approach impractical in real world environments (see, e.g. Pouwelse et al. (2006)). While Wong presented a new mechanism for increasing the available bandwidth at the network level, the performance at the client's side was still in question as the proposed mechanisms did not address the problem of bandwidth stability of a helper peer - which is a major factor for the performance of the download process. In addition, the whole design is not generic but is based solely on swarming that is managed by a tracker; this limits the potential of the solution to BitTorrent based systems only.

Following Wong's work, Wang et. al. (see, e.g. Wang et. al. (2007)) proposed a mechanism where the helpers need to download only small portions of a file to be "busy" enough for serving other peers in the long term. This work is also limited to BitTorrent protocol. Yet, it is claimed that the increased upload contribution only marginally improves download rates in BitTorrent (see, e.g. Piatek (2008)). In addition, it is considered that the network environment is homogeneous - where users have the same link capacities. This is clearly an unrealistic assumption given Internet's heterogeneity.
In a recent work (see, e.g. Wang et al. (2008)) it is proposed to employ helper peers in a hybrid network for streaming video content at a speed that is higher than the average upload bandwidth of peers. The authors discuss the term helpers as peers that are not participating in the multicast. Unlike the case of file sharing where users tend to leave their machine running for predefined downloads, in streaming the user has no motivation for leaving the application up and running when not used for streaming. Other works that proposed similar ideas of using helpers for multicast are De Asis Lopez-Fuentes and Steinbach's (see, e.g. De Asis Lopez-Fuentes and Steinbach (2008)) and DynaPeer (see, e.g. Souza et. al (2007)), where helpers take part in a collaboration process for a specific video stream that is managed by a virtual server.

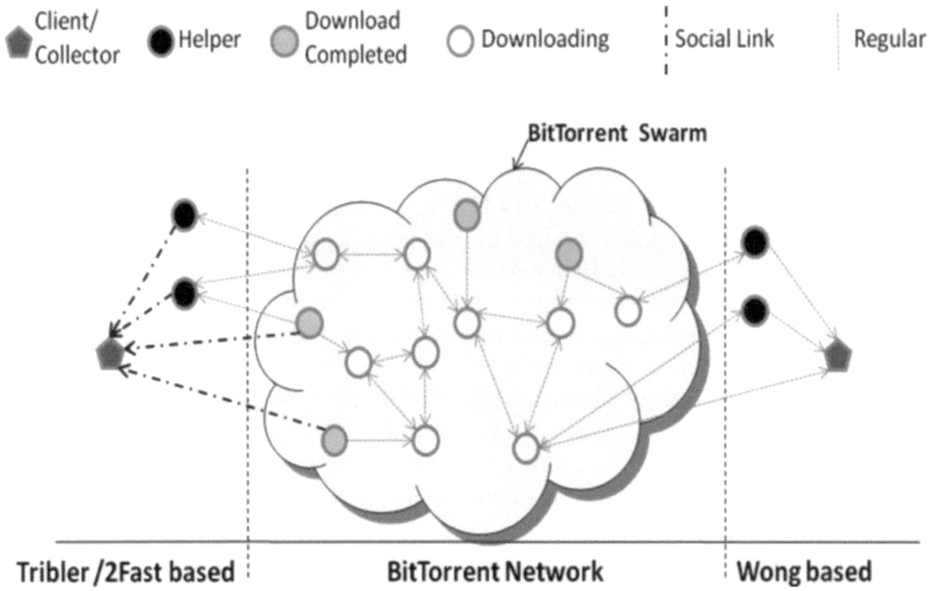

Fig. 1. Wong and Tribler's additions to a BitTorrent swarm-based network

3.2 Social Helpers

In Tribler (see, e.g. Pouwelse et al. (2006)) it was proposed to associate the helpers' contribution with social phenomena such as friendship and trust. In their 2Fast file sharing protocol (see, e.g. Garbacki et al. (2006)), a peer trying to download a file actively recruits its "friends", such as other peers in the same social network, to help exclusively with its download. 2Fast was originally offered to overcome the problem of free-riding in P2P networks. Peers from a social group that decide to participate in a cooperative download take one of two roles: they are either collectors or helpers. A collector is the peer that is interested in obtaining a complete copy of a particular file - like a typical client in a P2P network, and a helper is a peer that is recruited by a collector to assist in downloading that file. Both collector and helpers start downloading the file using the classical BitTorrent tit-for-tat and cooperative download extensions (See Fig. 1). Before downloading, a helper asks the collector what chunk it should download. After downloading a file chunk, the helper sends the chunk to the collector without requesting anything in return.

In addition to receiving file chunks from its helpers, the collector also optimizes its download performance by dynamically selecting the best available data source from the set of helpers and other peers in the Bittorrent network. Helpers give priority to collector requests and are therefore preferred as data sources. Specifically, a peer will assign a list of pieces to obtain for each of its helpers; these are the pieces that it has not started downloading. The helpers will try to obtain these pieces just like regular leechers and upload these pieces only to the peer they are helping. In such a scheme, peers with more friends can indeed benefit greatly and enjoy a much reduced file download time. However, it was shown that the constraint that helpers only aim to help a single peer requires the helpers to download much more than necessary to remain helpful to this peer (see, e.g. Wang et al. (2007)). The fact that the help is served only by social linked helpers is a limit for the success of the solution as some peers might not have any social links and others might have but the "friends" are not online or running the Tribler client when required. As Wong's work, Tribler did not address the problem of bandwidth stability of a helper peer either. Again, this work's contribution is also limited to BitTorrent-like swarming architectures.

In between Wong's work and Tribler, Guo et al. (see, e.g. Guo et al. (2005)) proposed a different mechanism of inter-torrent collaboration, where peers may download pieces of a file in which they are not interested in exchange for pieces of a file they want to download. Yet, it was shown that this approach will not necessarily provide any performance gain (see, e.g. Wang (2008)).

The main contribution of the above mentioned works is in enabling a multicast download system which circumvents bandwidth asymmetry restrictions by recognising peers for their contribution of idle bandwidth, thus - increasing service availability.

3.3 Fairness and Free-Riding

In addition to the anti free-riding solution that was proposed in 2Fast and Tribler, it was shown (see, e.g. Izhak-Ratzin (2009)) that pairs of peers can collaborate as helpers for the benefit of fairness and anti free-riding. Yet, this work assumes that the collaboration is possible only between peers that have similar upload bandwidth. This requirement is problematic as the available upload bandwidth in a typical peer is subject to change over time.

3.4 Key Lookup

In P-Grid (see, e.g. Crainiceanu (2004)) - an index structure for P2P systems that is based on the concept of Chord, entries are owned by peers within strict bounds. The peers that do not take part in the structure are termed in the paper as helper peers; those peers are obliged to "help" a peer that is already in the ring by managing some part of the range indexed by it - this is done for load balancing of requests in a P2P ring structure. This resembles the previous mentioned works in the idea that a peer assists other peers even though it does not ask for a service for its user.

4. Helpers for Service Performance

While the availability of content in a P2P network can be increased by employing the techniques mentioned in the previous section, the performance of a peer's service is still directly influenced by the user that operates this peer.

While working on Collabory (see, e.g. Horovitz and Dolev (2008)), we found that the greatest impact on download rate stability is the behaviour of users at source peers. More specifically, actions that the user of the uploading peer machine occasionally takes might directly affect the upload rate of the machine. The most obvious occurrence is the case where the user at the source peer invokes applications that heavily use bandwidth such as Email clients, online games or other P2P applications; by doing so, the bandwidth available for the client connected to that machine may be drastically reduced and becomes significantly unstable.

4.1 Feeders

For addressing this problem, we proposed Collabory (see, e.g. Horovitz and Dolev (2008)), where we defined a new type of helper peers that serve as a proxy cache for the benefit of a client peers that wish to download a file; we named these helpers as Feeders. The Feeder stores the file's pieces from several unstable sources and offers the pieces to the client in a stable fashion. In order to guarantee the stability, we matched a given client with potential feeders that have good connectivity with the client like minimal packet loss, small delay, low jitter and are likely to stay online while the client is downloading. In order to guarantee the long service of a suitable feeder, we relied on historical statistics of overlapping online time periods between the client and the feeder. Unlike previous works, Collabory intentionally selects the helpers to be optimal for availability and throughput stability with the client by constantly measuring stability factors. The Feeders negotiate with potential source peers and aggregate the downloads from multiple unstable sources into a single, stable stream served to the downloading peer. Unlike normal helper peers that only assist content delivery, Feeders are employed exclusively as a means of delivering data to the client.

We'd like the potential feeder peers to be online and have limited network and CPU consumption when the consumer is about to start a new download process. Therefore, we look for feeders that have a matching pattern of availability, meaning that they are likely to stay online and have low network and CPU consumption while the consumer is downloading. We'll use the term *fit* to address the above demands. In order to find fitting feeders, we log feeders' online periods (sessions) and the relevant network use and CPU utilization measurements within these sessions. We term *Feedability* as the ability of a feeder to feed a consumer peer at a specific point in time i.e., the feeder is online and has low network use and CPU consumption.

Denote a Feedability function *FA* of feeder *f*, in session *s* at time *t* (time units after session initiation time) as:

$$FA_{f,s}(t) = \begin{cases} 1 & f_{S_{cpu}}(t) < Th_{cpu} \wedge f_{S_{bw}}(t) < Th_{bw} \\ 0 & otherwise \end{cases} \quad (1)$$

where $f_{S_{cpu}}(t)$ and $f_{S_{bw}}(t)$ are the measurements of cpu utilization and consumed upload bandwidth after t time units from the beginning of session s (when the feeder went online). Th_{cpu} and Th_{bw} are the thresholds of cpu utilization and consumed bandwidth enabling the feeder to serve a consumer peer.

A potential feeder p is the most fitting feeder to a consumer peer (among all online feeders that have small RTT and low jitter with the consumer peer) if the average of its Feedability function $FA_{f,s}(t)$ over all of its sessions and a given time period (when the consumer requested to start a new download) is maximized over all other feeders:

$$p = \operatorname*{argmax}_{f} \int_{t}^{t+k} \sum_{i=1}^{n_f} \frac{FA_{f,s}(t)}{n_f} \quad (2)$$

where n_f is the number of sessions that were logged by feeder *f*. We choose *k* as the length of a minimal time period for feeding before looking for alternative feeders.

In Fig. 2, $C_{regular}$ represents the case of normal file transfer - downloading from *m* sources, each supplyin$\frac{MaxD}{m}$ bps g where *MaxD* is the maximum download rate of the client peer. In $C_{feeder-based}$ however, the client downloads a file from *m* feeders, each of them downloads from two sources: the 1st source supplies $\frac{MaxD}{m}$ bps and the second source up to ε *bps*. We use the sources that supply ε as for short-term caching to ensure that the feeder peer can always supply $\frac{MaxD}{m}$ bps for its client.

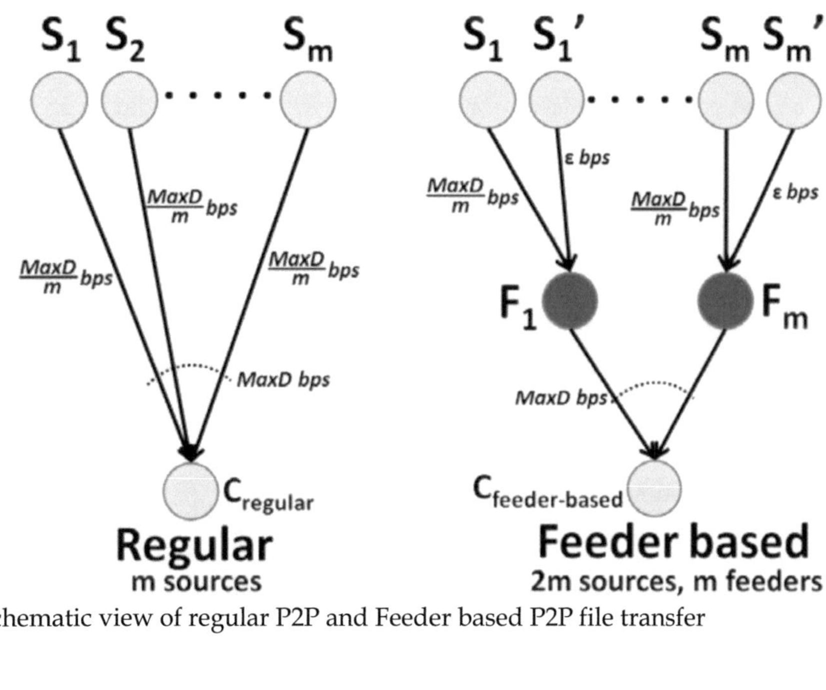

Fig. 2. Schematic view of regular P2P and Feeder based P2P file transfer

In a working system, ε will dynamically change during the download process depending on the bandwidth supplied by the source peer. Following is the analysis of the simple model described above, comparing the Effective Download Rate (*EDR*) of each case, where p_x is the probability that a peer *x* (source or feeder) will deliver packets at full speed (Internet link capacity):

$$EDR(C_{regular}) = m(EUB\ of\ each\ \mathbf{source}) = mp_s(capacity\ of\ each\ source) \\ = mp_s\frac{MaxD}{m} = p_sMaxD \tag{3}$$

where *EUB* is the effective upload bandwidth.

$$EDR(C_{feeder-based}) = m(EUB\ of\ each\ \mathbf{feeder}) \\ = m(p_f(UB\ of\ feeder\ depended\ on\ its'sources)) \\ = m(p_f\min(\frac{MaxD}{m}, \sum EUB(feeder's\ sources))) \\ = \min(p_fMaxD, p_fp_sMaxD + mp_fp_s\varepsilon) \tag{4}$$

where *UB* is the upload bandwidth and *EUB* is the effective upload bandwidth. Thus:

$$\frac{EDR(C_{feeder-based})}{EDR(C_{regular})} = \frac{\min(p_fMaxD, p_fp_sMaxD + mp_fp_s\varepsilon)}{p_sMaxD} = \min(\frac{p_f}{p_s}, p_f + \frac{mp_f\varepsilon}{MaxD}) \tag{5}$$

meaning that $C_{feeder-based}$ will download at higher speed than $C_{regular}$ if $p_f + \frac{mp_f\varepsilon}{MaxD} > 1$, which means that $\varepsilon > \frac{(1-p_f)\text{MaxD}}{p_fm}$. Notice that as *m* grows, a smaller ε will satisfy the benefit of the feeder-based solution. Likewise, if we allow a bigger ε we can use less feeders to gain the same results.

This shows a great benefit of the feeder-based model over the regular model as it is possible to move the "risk" of a non-stable download bandwidth from the client to the feeder - that has potentially much more available download bandwidth than the client.

Upon selecting stable feeders it is possible to reach better download stability while using even less stable sources, since the feeder has available download bandwidth that can be used for short-term caching - meaning that we use a bigger ε to make sure that the feeder will be able to supply the requested bandwidth to the supplier. The asymmetric upload and download bandwidth does not affect our solution, since a feeder can theoretically download at full download speed to ensure the small upload bandwidth that it should supply the source.

Since we can adjust ε dynamically during the download phase, we can afford using extremely weak and unstable sources from the P2P network and still not influence the stability of the download rate at the client, as long as the feeder manages to gather enough cache to be able to provide the requested rate by the consumer. Since it's possible to employ weak sources we estimate that Collabory enhances existing networks' scalability as it increases the total number of potential sources because nowadays existing P2P applications tend to neglect weak sources.

In Fig. 3, we set the maximum download throughput of all peers to 20Kb/Sec and the upload is bounded by 10Kb/Sec. This was chosen to show the benefit of Collabory on extremely weak peers that are hardly being used in existing networks because of their unstable nature and low bandwidth.
We examine different values of ε to see how it affects the performance of feeders. We set all source peers to behave in a repeating pattern of sending at 80% of their maximal upload bandwidth for 10 seconds followed by additional 10 seconds of sending at full speed. Sources that transmit ε repeatedly transmit 0.8 ε Kb/Sec for 10 seconds and then ε Kb/Sec for the following 10 seconds accordingly. Given larger values of ε allows the feeders to hold a cache for a longer period of time and this way be able to transmit the cache content to the client accordingly.
Notice that when we set ε to 2.2 the cache content was increasing consistently thus allows the feeder to transmit the client as if it was a stable source.
In this scenario the client received stable download rate of 18.9Kb/Sec.

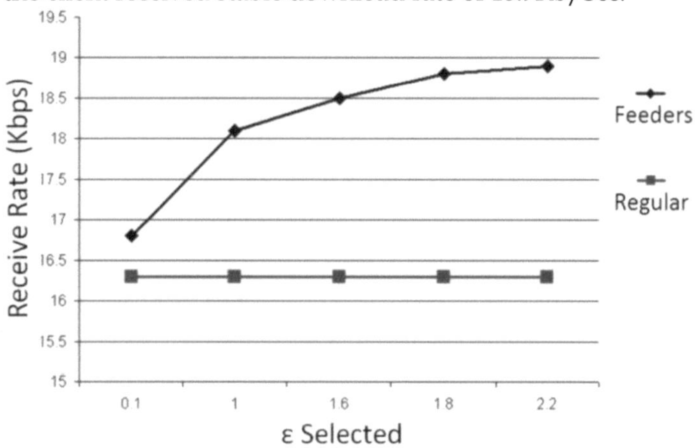

Fig. 3. Feeder-based P2P versus regular P2P with different ε values

We also tested the case of using weak source peers for the feeder (See Fig. 4). For the regular method we set 2 sources of 10Kb/Sec with the behaviour of 80% mentioned above. For the feeder method we set the following different test settings- *A*: 4 sources of 6.0Kb/Sec under 80% behaviour as mentioned above. *B*: 8 sources of 3.0Kb/Sec under 80% behaviour. *C*: 8 sources of 4.0Kb/Sec under 50% behaviour. In all of our tests we gained stable increased rate in the feeder case compared to unstable rate in the regular case.

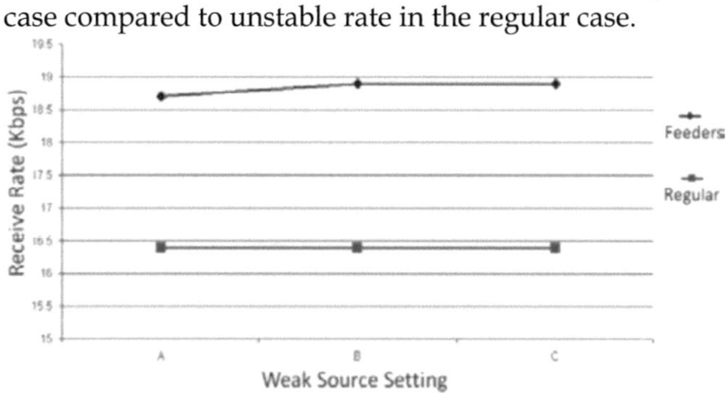

Fig. 4. Feeder-based P2P versus regular P2P with different settings of weak sources

5. Helpers and Machine Learning

In order to guarantee the long service of a suitable feeder, Collabory relied on historical statistics of overlapping online time periods between the client and the feeder. Yet, this strategy misses many potential feeders and sources that have good quality connection with the client but weren't selected since the overlapping online time periods were not long enough to provide confidence that the feeder won't disconnect while the client is downloading from it. If we were able to predict that a potential feeder's uplink is about to be dropped, we could alert the client to select an alternative feeder prior to that drop. This will significantly increase the amount of potential feeders as we will no longer be restricted to bounds dictated by historical statistics of overlapping time periods.
Collabory's problems were discussed and addressed in Collabrium (see, e.g. Horovitz and Dolev (2009a)) and Maxtream (see, e.g. Horovitz and Dolev (2009b)). Collabrium is a collaborative solution based on a machine learning approach, that employs SVM - Support Vector Machines (See, Vapnik (1995)) to actively predict load in the upload link of source/feeder peers and accordingly alert the client to select alternative source/feeder peers. Collabrium discerns patterns of communications with no prior knowledge about any protocol which allows it to predict new protocols as well. We reinforce our solution with an optional agent that monitors process executions and file system events that improve the prediction even more.

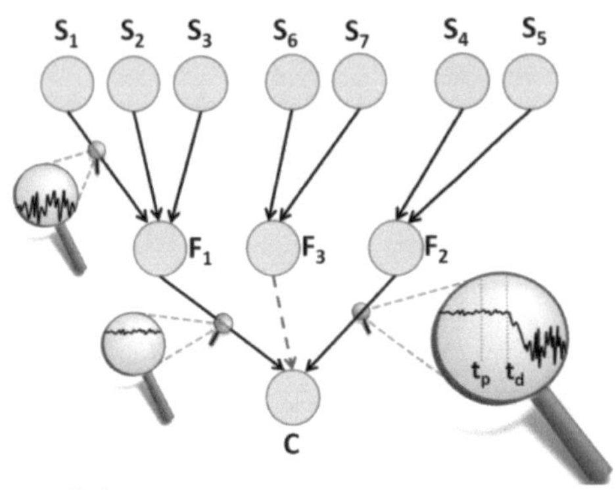

Fig. 5. Learning Feeders in Collabrium

Fig. 5 illustrates the concept of user behaviour aware feeders. C represents the client that downloads a file or a streamed media content. S_i represents the sources in a regular P2P network and F_1, F_2, F_3 represent the feeders. Notice that the throughput between S_1 and F_1 is low and unstable, we assume the same for all of the connections between sources and feeders. Yet, the throughput between F_1 and C is high and stable, as we mentioned above that feeders are selected as peers with good connectivity with the client. Now let's assume that C begins using F_1 and F_2. F_1 has enough available upload bandwidth to supply C a stable throughput. As for F_2, notice that at the beginning it provided stable throughput to C as well, but at time $t_p - \varepsilon$ the user at F_2 opened another P2P software or any other process that consume upload bandwidth. A few seconds later, at time t_d, the throughput between F_2 and C dropped and became unstable due to the new software/process. Collabrium's agent that runs on F_2 predicts at time t_p that it will soon have to share its upload bandwidth with another process, therefore it immediately notifies C to replace a feeder. C connects to F_3 and by t_d, C no longer communicates with F_2, thus C didn't experience any drop in its download rate. Collabrium can be implemented over any P2P existing protocol as the sources in Fig. 5 can be sources of any P2P network and we don't manage them, but only request for file portions.

Following, we discuss the structure of Collabrium that is composed of 3 modules: Monitoring, Learning and Prediction.

5.1 Monitoring Module

The monitoring module is responsible for collecting data for the learning module. It acts as a packet sniffer for both inbound and outbound links and logs packet arrival time, header and payload. Though we found the network collected data alone to provide sufficient prediction accuracy, we log additional data for file system activity and active process list as in some cases it can further improve the prediction. The file system information is logged by a Win32 IFS (Installable File System) hook - a DLL that monitors file system events such as read, seek, write etc.

While the monitoring is done as a background process, we only log information in a database for a limited time - while we actually try to learn. This time should be sufficient to gain enough information so that the user behaviour can be predicted in the future, given a set of measurements. For the average user, our experience showed that logging along one full day is enough. We recommend re-running the learning process from time to time, in order to adapt to the user's new habits and trends.

5.2 Learning Module Design

The learning process extracts the data that was collected by the monitoring module into sets of features and values for the learning algorithm. The core of this module is based on a Support Vector Machines classification algorithm, yet the assembly of *feature:value* pairs is not straightforward as we elaborate here.

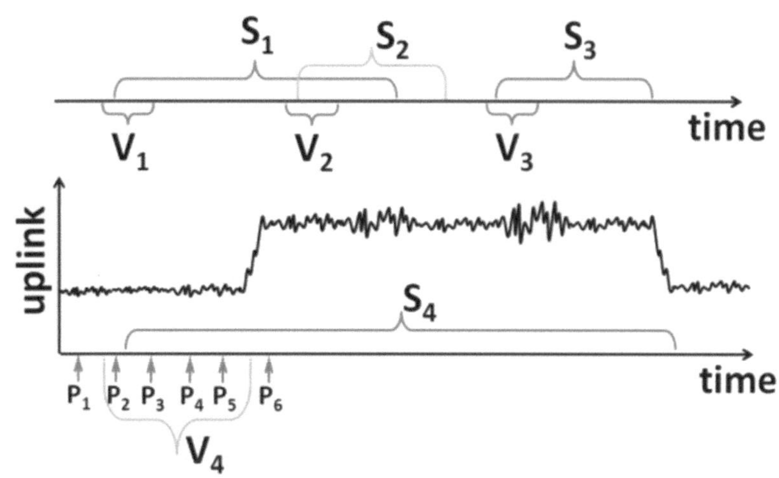

Fig. 6. Load Vicinity Pattern Prediction Concept

We wish our learning algorithm to link the collected data to the occurrences of traffic load in the uplink. As illustrated in Figure 6, S_1, S_2 and S_3 are sessions. A session is identified by source IP and port, and destination IP and port, thus it begins with the first packet that was sent between our peer *i* on port *x* and a peer *j* on port *y* and ends with the last message that was sent between the same peers on the same ports. If the time between 2 sequential messages is larger than a specific predefined threshold, we see it as 2 sessions. Notice that sessions might overlap as in sessions S_1 and S_2 but still we can identify the session of a packet using the key of IPs and ports. V_1, V_2 and V_3 are the vicinities of S_1, S_2 and S_3 respectively.

A *vicinity* is a collection of packets that were collected around a predefined time period at the beginning of each session. Notice that the vicinity begins a few milliseconds before the beginning of a session. In session S_4 and its vicinity V_4 we show the change in uplink utilization due to that session. Notice that typically, the load in the uplink begins a few seconds after the beginning of a session and not immediately, as in most P2P algorithms the very first messages are used for preliminary negotiation, thus we can use the packet P_3 and its neighbors to predict the upcoming load and still have enough time to notify the client about it. In some protocols, packets that are in the vicinity but precede the session like P_2 can tell us about the upcoming load due to some negotiation between the peers or between a peer to its supernode.

Collabrium's key strategy is that we can predict a traffic load by examining the properties of packets that precede the load - meaning the packets in the vicinity of sessions that loaded the uplink. Following we present different properties that proved to be significant for prediction and their extraction techniques.

5.2.1 Load Vicinity Pattern Prediction

In this method we look at the first bytes (15 bytes were found to be effective) of the payload of each packet that is in the vicinity and extract *feature:value* pairs for SVM so it can learn specific patterns. For example, in eMule's client-client protocol, the 1st byte is always *0xE3* and in the handshake message the 6th is always *0x01;* we mark them as *byte:value* pairs that form a pattern: *1:0xE3, 6:0x01*. We'd like SVM to realize these patterns out of the messages in the vicinity. Since close values such as *1:0xE3* and *1:0xE4* might belong to completely different protocols or different messages of the same protocol, we can't present SVM these values directly as it will not relate them as discrete values. Therefore, we collect the most popular *byte:value* instances of packets in the vicinities of all sessions while giving priority to *byte:value* pairs that appear in different sessions, as shown in Figure 7.

Finally, we supply the training set for SVM; Each item in the training set contains the following features: Source IP, Source port, Destination IP and Destination port. Then we create a feature per each of the top popular items in *ByteValueList*, i.e. if the most popular *byte:value* pair is *5:0xE3* and the value of the 5th byte of the packet we examine is *0xE3* then we insert *1:1* as a *feature:value* pair for the training item; if the second most popular *byte:value* pair is *3:0xB6* and the value of the 3rd byte of the packet we examine is *0xC2* then we insert *2:0* in the training set since the values are different and so forth for the next popular *byte:value* items, up to a certain amount of features (we found that the top 100 popular yield satisfactory results). We label as *+1* training items that represent packets in the vicinity that contain at least one instance of the top popular *byte:value* pairs. We supply the training set also packets that are not in the vicinity and label them as *-1*. When we run the prediction module to look for upcoming loads in the uplink, we simply propose recent captured packets' properties to SVM with the appropriate features and SVM classifies the packet as leading to uplink load or not.

```
For each packet p in PacketLog do
   SessionList[p.SrcIP,p.SrcPort,p.DstIP,p.DstPort].ByteCount += p.ByteCount
For each session s in SessionsList do
   If s.ByteCount < BYTE_COUNT_THRESHOLD then
      SessionsList.Delete(s)
For each packet p in PacketLog do
{
   s = SessionsList.GetNearestSession(p.TimeStamp)
   If SecondsBetween(s.StartTime, p.TimeStamp) < VICINITY_THRESHOLD then
      For i = 1 .. MAX_PATTERN_SIZE do
         If Not ( s.ID in ByteValueList[ i, p[i].Value].Sessions ) then
         {
            ByteValueList[ i, p[i].Value].Count += 1
            ByteValueList[ i, p[i].Value].Sessions.Add( s.ID)
         }
}
ByteValueList.SortByCount
```

Fig. 7. Algorithm for extracting popular *byte_value* pairs

5.2.2 Packet Size Sequence Prediction

While looking at the data we captured in the beginning of sessions, we noticed an interesting phenomenon in P2P protocols - the byte count of the first packets form a sequence that repeats itself with minor differences for nearly all sessions of the same protocol. For example, a typical packet size sequence for eMule is *{0,0,0,125,108,11,11,41,83,77,55,55,22}*. Since we noticed some slight differences in the sequence, we can't use it as a serial set of features for SVM as in some cases the value of *108* in eMule might appear as the byte count of the 5th packet while in other cases it will be the byte count of the 6th packet due to an extra packet. Therefore, we relate these values as a histogram, and simply define a predefined number of features (we found 30 to yield good results) for the most popular byte count values in a similar manner to the previous algorithm. For example, if the most popular byte count is *125*, we supply the training set a feature with a value of *1* if the vicinity of the examined packet contains at least one packet with this byte count or *0* if not.

5.3 Prediction Module

In the prediction module, while packets are being captured, the properties mentioned above are extracted and served to the SVM algorithm. In case that SVM classified the packet as leading for load and the uplink used bandwidth is larger than a predefined threshold, we notify the client to select an alternative feeder.

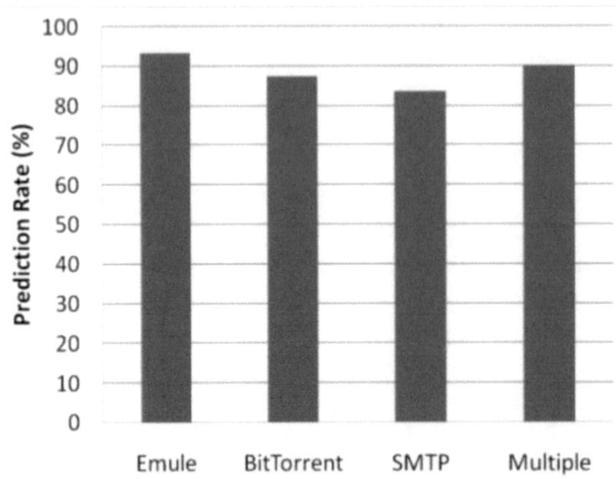

Fig. 8. Prediction success rate of popular protocols

In Figure 8, we examined various protocols that use the upstream and the ability to predict an upcoming load per each protocol. We captured 5 hours of activity on each of these protocols separately. Then we mapped all large sessions (more than *1MB*) and counted the cases where we predicted a large session successfully. Notice that in the fourth case, we ran all protocols on the same machine for 5 hours, to examine the case where the vicinity contains messages of multiple protocols.
In Figure 9, we measured the time between the prediction and the beginning of the load in upstream per each of the leading protocols.

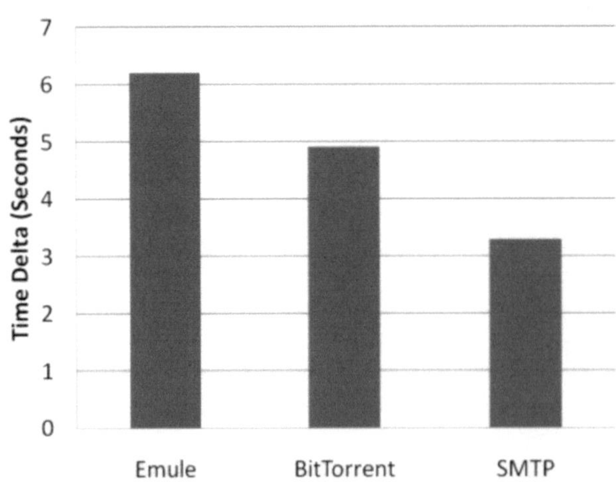

Fig. 9. Time difference between prediction and load (seconds)

Notice that we have between 3 and 6 seconds to alert a client for replacing a source - which enables it to completely evade the upcoming load before it begins.

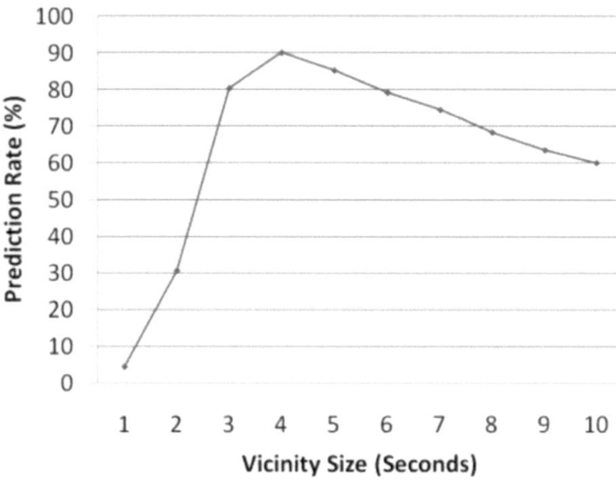

Fig. 10. Prediction success rate per vicinity size

In Figure 10, we experimented different vicinity sizes and measured the appropriate prediction success rate. The leading part of the vicinity (3rd of its size) is placed before the beginning of a session - to allow prediction using packets that might lead to a session (like an interaction between a peer and a supernode prior to the file transfer between peers). Notice that small vicinities of between 1 and 2 seconds do not cover enough information to predict an upcoming load with high success rate. In addition, vicinities larger than 4 seconds begin to create more noise than useful information for prediction and accordingly the prediction success rate degrades.

6. Summary and Future Work

In this chapter, we presented the evolution of helper peers in P2P file sharing and streaming networks.

We presented advanced designs of helpers that integrate machine learning for reaching stability in throughput.

We believe that helpers will play a crucial role in the design of future P2P networks, as it enables P2P to compete with both service availability and stability of traditional client-server systems but with much larger scalability. The next required step is to embed and adapt the mentioned ideas onto large scale P2P networks and measure their benefits under different scenarios.

In addition, it will be interesting to analyze different topologies of networks of helper peers. For example, a two-tier helper network might manage 2 different classes of helpers, a hash ring of helpers, a tree of helpers and other topologies.

7. References

All-Streaming-Media report (2008) – PPLive glitches. *http://all-streaming-media.com/peerto-peer-tv/p2p-streaming-internet-tv-pplive.htm*

Andrade, N.; Santana, J.; Brasileiro, F. & Cirne, W. On the efficiency and cost of introducing qos in BitTorrent. *In CCGRID '07: Proceedings of the Seventh IEEE International*

Symposium on Cluster Computing and the Grid, pages 767–772, Washington, DC, USA, 2007. IEEE Computer Society

Bindal, R. & Cao, P. (2006). Can self-organizing p2p file distribution provide qos guarantees? *SIGOPS Oper. Syst. Rev.*,40(3):22–30

Cohen, B. (2003). Incentives Build Robustness in BitTorrent. *Workshop on Economics of Peer-to-Peer Systems, 6, 2003*

Crainiceanu, A.; Linga, P. ; Machanavajjhala, A. ; Gehrke, J. ; Shanmugasundaram, J. (2004), P-Ring: An Index Structure for Peer-to-Peer Systems, *Technical Report, Cornell University, 2004*

DailyIPTV report - Joost bandwidth problems (2007), *http://www.dailyiptv.com/features/joostb andwid thproblem-082007/*

De Asis Lopez-Fuentes, F.; Steinbach, E. (2008), Multi-source video multicast in peer-to-peer networks, *IEEE International Symposium on Parallel and Distributed Processing, IPDPS 2008*

Do, T. ; Hua, K. A. & Tantaoui, M. (2004). P2VoD: Providing fault tolerant video-on-demand streaming in peer-to-peer environment. *In Proc. of the IEEE Int. Conf. on Communications (ICC 2004), june 2004*

Garbacki, P.; Iosup, A.; Epema, D. & van Steen, M. (2006). 2fast: Collaborative downloads in p2p networks. *p2p, 2006*

Guo, L.; Chen, S.; Xiao, Z.; Tan, E.; Ding, X. & Zhang, X. (2005). Measurements, Analysis, and Modeling of BitTorrent-like Systems. *Internet Measurement Conference, 2005*

Hei, X.; Liang, C.; Liang, J.; Liu, Y. & Ross, K.W. (2006). Insights into pplive: A measurement study of a large-scale p2p iptv system, *Proceedings of IPTV Workshop, International World Wide Web Conference*

Horovitz, S. & Dolev, D. (2008). Collabory: A Collaborative Throughput Stabilizer & Accelerator for P2P Protocols, *Proceedings of the 2008 IEEE 17th Workshop on Enabling Technologies: Infrastructure for Collaborative Enterprises*, pp.115-120, 2008, IEEE Computer Society

Horovitz, S. & Dolev, D. (2009a). Collabrium: Active Traffic Pattern Prediction for Boosting P2P Collaboration, *Proceedings of the 2009 IEEE 18th Workshop on Enabling Technologies: Infrastructure for Collaborative Enterprises*, 2009, IEEE Computer Society

Horovitz, S. & Dolev, D. (2009b). Maxtream: Stabilizing P2P Streaming by Active Prediction of Behavior Patterns, *Proceedings of the 2009 Third International Conference on Multimedia and Ubiquitous Engineering*, pp.546-553, 2009, IEEE Computer Society

Horvath, A.; Telek, M. ; Rossi, D. ; Veglia, P. ; Ciullo, D.; Garcia, M. A. ; Leonardi, E. & Mellia, M. (2008). Dissecting PPLive, Sopcast, TVants, *Technical report, Politecnico di Torino*

IPoque Internet Study – The Impact of P2P File Sharing (2007), *http://www.ipoque.com/userfil es/file/internet_study_2007.pdf*

Izhak-Ratzin, R. (2009), Collaboration in BitTorrent Systems, *Networking 2009: 8th International IFIP-TC 6 Networking Conference*

NewTeeVee report - Joost bandwidth problems (2008), *http://newteevee.com/2008/03/20/wher e-to-watch-marchmadness/*

Piatek, M.; Isdal, T.; Krishnamurthy, A. & Anderson, T. (2008), One hop reputations for peer to peer file sharing workloads, NSDI'08: *Proceedings of the 5th USENIX Symposium on Networked Systems Design and Implementation*

Pouwelse, J.; Garbacki, P.; Wang, J.; Bakker, A.; Yang, J.; Iosup, A.; Epema, D.; Reinders, M.; van Steen, M. & Sips, H. (2006). Tribler: A social-based peer-to-peer system. *IPTPS06*

Rejaie, R. & Ortega, A. (2003). Pals: Peer-to-peer adaptive layered streaming. *NOSSDAV'03 Monterey, CA*

Sandvide 2008 Global Broadband Phenomena (2008), *http://www.sandvine.com/general/documents/2008-global-broadband -phenomena - executive summary.pdf*

Schlosser, D.; Hossfeld, T. & Tutschku, K. (2006). Comparison of Robust Cooperation Strategies for P2P Content Distribution Networks with Multiple Source Download, *Proceedings of the Sixth IEEE International Conference on Peer-to-Peer Computing, pages 31–38, 2006*

Souza, L.; Cores, F.; Yang, X. & Ripoll, A. (2007), DynaPeer: A Dynamic Peer-to-Peer Based Delivery Scheme for VoD Systems. *Euro-Par 2007 Parallel Processing, ISBN 978-3-540-74465-8, 2007*

TechCrunch report - Joost abandons p2p (2008), *http://www.techcrunch.com/2008/12/17/joost-just-gives-upon-p2p/*

Vapnik, V. N. (1995), The nature of statistical learning theory. *Springer-Verlag New York, Inc., 1995.*

VentureBeat report - Joost playback problems (2008), *http://venturebeat.com/2008/11/2 8/joost-is-loosed-onthe-iphone-if-only-it-worked/*

Vu, L. ; Gupta, I. ; Liang, J. & Nahrstedt, K. (2006), Mapping the PPLive network: Studying the impacts of media streaming on p2p overlays, *Technical report, August 2006*

Wang, J. (2008). Robust video transmission over lossy channels and efficient video distribution over peer-to-peer networks, *Technical Report, University of California at Berkeley, 2008*

Wang, J.; Yeo, C.; Prabhakaran, V.& Ramchandran, K. (2007). On the role of helpers in peer-to-peer file download systems: Design, analysis and simulation. *IPTPS07*

Wang, J. & Ramchandran, K. (2008), Enhancing peer-to-peer live multicast quality using helpers, *Image Processing, 2008, ICIP 2008*

Wong, J. (2004), Enhancing collaborative content delivery with helpers. *Master's thesis, Univ of British Columbia, 2004*

12

Parallel and Distributed Immersive Real-Time Simulation of Large-Scale Networks

Jason Liu
Florida International University
United States

1. Introduction

Network researchers need to embrace the challenge of designing the next-generation high-performance networking and software infrastructures that address the growing demand of distributed applications. These applications, particularly those potential "game changers" or "killer apps", such as voice-over-IP (VoIP) and peer-to-peer (P2P) applications surfaced in recent years, will significantly influence the way people conduct business and go about their daily lives. These distributed applications also include platforms that facilitate large-scale scientific experimentation through remote control and visualization. Many large-scale science applications—such as those in the field of astronomy, astrophysics, climate and environmental science, material science, particle physics, and social science—depend on the availability of high performance facilities and advanced experimental instruments. Extreme networking capabilities together with effective high-end middleware infrastructures are of great importance to interconnecting these applications, computing resources and experimental facilities. "When all you have is a hammer, everything looks like a nail." The success of advancing critical technologies, to a large extent, depends on the available tools that can help effectively prototype, test, and analyze new designs and new ideas. Traditionally, network research has relied on a variety of tools. Physical network testbeds, such as WAIL (Barford and Landweber, 2003) and PlanetLab (Peterson et al., 2002), provide physical network connectivity; these testbeds are designed specifically for studying network protocols and services under real network conditions. However, the network condition of these testbeds is by and large constrained by the physical setup of the system and therefore inflexible for network researchers to explore a wide spectrum of the design space.

To allow more flexibility, some of these testbeds, such as EmuLab (White et al., 2002) and VINI (Bavier et al., 2006), also offer emulation capabilities by modulating network traffic according to configuration and traffic condition of the target network. Physical and emulation testbeds currently are the mainstream for experimental networking research, primarily due to their capability of achieving desirable realism and accuracy. These testbeds, however, are costly to build. Due to limited resources available, conducting prolonged large-scale experiments on these platforms is difficult. Another solution is to use analytical models. Although analytical models are capable of bringing us important insight to the system design, dealing with a system as complex as the global network requires significantly simplified assumptions to be made to keep the models tractable. These simplified assumptions often exclude implementation details, which are often crucial to the validity of the system design.

Simulation and emulation play an important role in network design and evaluation. While both refer to the technique of mimicking network operations in software, one major distinction is that simulation is purely virtual, whereas emulation focuses on interactions with real applications. A network simulation consists of software implementation of network protocols and various network entities, such as routers and links. Network operations (e.g., packet forwarding) are merely logical operations. As a result, the simulation time advancement bears no direct relationship to the wall-clock time. Emulation, on the other hand, focuses on interactions with real applications, such as distributed network services and distributed database systems. These real applications generate traffic; an emulator provides traffic shaping functions by adding appropriate packet delays and sometimes dropping packets. Emulation delivers more realism as it interacts with the physical entities. Comparatively, simulation is effective at capturing high-level design issues, answering what-if questions, and therefore can help us understand complex system behaviors, such as multi-scale interactions, self-organizing characteristics, and emergent phenomena. Unfortunately, simulation fairs poorly in many aspects, including notably the absence of operational realism. Further, simulation model development is both labor-intensive and error-prone; reproducing realistic network topology, representative traffic, and diverse operational conditions in simulation is known to be a substantial undertaking (Floyd and Paxson, 2001).

Real-time simulation combines the advantages of both simulation and emulation: it can run simulation and simultaneously interact with the physical world. Real-time network simulation, sometimes called immersive network simulation, can be defined as the technique of simulating computer networks and communication systems in real time so that the simulated network can interact with real implementations of network protocols, network services, and distributed applications. The word "immersive" suggests that the virtual network behavior should not be distinguishable from a physical network for conducting network traffic. That is, simulation should capture important characteristics of the target network and support seamless interactions with the real applications. Real-time network simulation is based on simulation, and therefore is fast in execution and flexible at answering what-if questions. It allows high-level mathematical models (such as stochastic network traffic models) to be incorporated into the system with relative ease. The system interacts with real applications and real network traffic. Not only does it allow us to study the impact of real application traffic on the virtual network, but also supports studying the behavior of real applications under diverse simulated network conditions.

The challenge is to keep it in real time. Since real applications operate in real time, real-time network simulation must meet real-time requirements. Especially, the performance of a large-scale network simulation must be able to keep up with the wall-clock time and allow real-time interactions with potentially a lot of real applications. A real-time simulator must also be able to characterize the behavior of a network, potentially with millions of network entities and with realistic traffic load at commensurate scale—all in real time. To speed up simulation, on the one hand, we need to apply parallel and distributed discrete-event simulation techniques to harness the computing resources of parallel computers so as to physically increase the event-processing power; on the other hand, we need to resort to multi-resolution modeling techniques using models at high-level of abstraction to reduce the computational demand. We also need to create a scalable emulation infrastructure, through which real applications can interact with the simulated network and sustain high-level emulation traffic intensity. In this chapter, we review the techniques that allow real-time simulation to model large-scale networks and interact with many real applications under the real-time constraint. We discuss advanced modeling and simulation techniques supporting real-time execution. We describe the emulation infrastructure and machine virtualization techniques supporting the network immersion of a large number of real applications. Through case studies, we show the potentials of real-time simulation in various areas of network science.

2. Background

2.1 Existing Network Testbeds

We classify available network testbeds into physical, emulation, and simulation testbeds. We can further divide physical testbeds into production testbeds and research testbeds (Anderson et al., 2005). Production testbeds, such as CAIRN and Internet2, support network experiments directly on the network itself and thus with live traffic; however, they are very restrictive allowing only certain types of experiments that do not disrupt normal network operations. Comparatively, research testbeds, such as WAIL and PlanetLab, provide far better flexibility. WAIL (Barford and Landweber, 2003) is a research testbed consisting of a large set of commercial networking components (including router, switches, and end hosts) connected to form an experimental network capable of representing typical end-to-end configurations found on the Internet. PlanetLab (Peterson et al., 2002) is a well-known research facility consisting of machines distributed across the Internet and shared by researchers conducting experiments. Most research testbeds, however, can only provide an iconic view of the Internet at large. Also, the underlying facility is typically overloaded due to heavy use, which potentially affects their availability as well as accuracy (Spring et al., 2006).

Many research testbeds are based on emulation. Network emulation adds packet delays and possibly drops packets when conducting traffic between real applications. Examples of emulation testbeds include Ahn et al. (1995); Carson and Santay (2003); Herrscher and Rothermel (2002); Zheng and Ni (2003) and Huang et al. (1999). The traffic modulation function can be implemented at the sender or receiver side, or both. For example, in dummynet (Rizzo, 1997), each virtual network link is represented as a queue with specific bandwidth and delay constraints; packets are intercepted at the protocol stack of the sender and pushed through a finite queue to simulate the time it takes to forward the packet.

Emulation testbeds can be built on a variety of computing infrastructures. For example, ModelNet (Vahdat et al., 2002) extends dummynet, where a large number of network applications can run unmodified on a set of edge nodes and communicate via a virtual network emulated on parallel computers at the core. EmuLab (White et al., 2002) is an experimentation facility consisting of a compute cluster integrated and coordinated to present a diverse virtual network environment. DETER (Benzel et al., 2006) extends EmuLab to support research and development of cyber security applications. Some of the emulation testbeds are built for distributed environments, such as X-Bone (Touch, 2000), VIOLIN (Jiang and Xu, 2004), VNET (Sundararaj and Dinda, 2004), and VINI (Bavier et al., 2006). Other emulation testbeds may require special programmable devices. For example, the Open Network Laboratory (DeHart et al., 2006) uses embedded processors and configures them to represent realistic network settings for experimentation and observation. ORBIT

(Raychaudhuri et al., 2005) is an open large-scale wireless network emulation testbed that supports experimental studies using an array of real wireless devices. The CMU Wireless Emulator (Judd and Steenkiste, 2004) is a wireless network testbed based on a large Field-Programmable Gate Array (FPGA) that can modify wireless signals sent by real wireless devices according to signal propagation models. A major distinction between simulation and emulation is that simulation contains only software modules representing network protocols and network entities, such as routers and links, and mimicking network transactions as pure logic operations to the state variables. Examples of network simulators include Barr et al. (2005); Tyan and Hou (2001) and Varga (2001). The ns-2 simulator (Breslau et al., 2000) is one of the most popular simulators with a rich collection of network algorithms and protocols for both wired and wireless networks. To scale up network simulation, a number of parallel and distributed simulators have also been developed, which include SSFNet (Cowie et al., 1999), GTNets (Riley, 2003), ROSSNet (Yaun et al., 2003), and GloMoSim (Bajaj et al., 1999). Next, we describe parallel and distributed simulation as the enabling technique for real-time simulation.

2.2 Parallel and Distributed Simulation

Parallel and distributed simulation, also known as parallel simulation or parallel discrete-event simulation (PDES), is concerned with executing a single discrete-event simulation program on parallel computers (Fujimoto, 1990). By exploiting the concurrency of a simulation model, parallel simulation can overcome the limitations of sequential simulation in both execution time and memory space. The critical issue of allowing a discrete-event simulation program to run in parallel is to maintain the causality constraint, which means that simulation events in the system must be processed in a non-decreasing timestamp order. This is because an event with a smaller timestamp has the potential to change the state of the system and affect events that happen later (with larger timestamps). Most parallel simulation adopts spatial decomposition: a model is divided into sub-models called logical processes (LPs), each of which maintains its own local simulation clock and can run on a different processor. For network simulation, a simulated network can be partitioned into smaller sub-networks, each handled by a different processor.

The way how the causality constraint is enforced divides parallel simulation into conservative and optimistic approaches. The conservative approach strictly prohibits out-of-order event execution: a processor must be blocked from processing the next event in its event queue until it is safe to do so. That is, it must ensure that no event will arrive from another processor with a timestamp earlier than the local simulation clock. In contrast, the optimistic approach allows events to be processed out of order. Once a causality error is detected—an event arrives at a logical process with a timestamp in the simulated past—the simulation will be rolled back to a state before the error occurs. In order for the simulation to retract and recover from an erroneous execution path, state saving and recovery mechanisms are typically provided. The seminal work for the conservative approach is the CMB algorithm, an asynchronous algorithm proposed independently by Chandy and Misra (1979), and Bryant (1977). The CMB algorithm provides several important observations that epitomize the fundamentals of conservative synchronization. One important concept is lookahead. To avoid deadlock, an LP must determine a lower bound on the timestamp of messages it will send to another LP. In essence, Lookahead is the amount of simulation time that an LP can predict into the simulated future. Extensive performance studies emphasize the importance of extrapolating lookahead from the model (Fujimoto, 1988,1989; Reed et al., 1988). Nicol (1996) gave a classification of lookahead based on different levels of knowledge that can be extracted from the model. The use of different dimensions of lookahead underscores conservative synchronization protocols. Several models have been shown to exhibit good lookahead properties, such as first-come-first-serve stochastic queuing networks (Nicol, 1988) and continuous-time Markov chains (Nicol and Heidelberger, 1995). In addition, several synchronization protocols have been developed to exploit lookahead for general applications, such as the conditional event approach by Chandy and Sherman (1989), the YAWNS protocol by Nicol (1991), the bounded lag algorithm by Lubachevsky (1988), the distance-between-objects algorithm by Ayani (1989), and the TNE algorithm by Groselj and Tropper (1988).

The first optimistic synchronization protocol is the Time Warp algorithm (Jefferson, 1985). Since the optimistic approach allows events to be processed out of timestamp order, Time Warp provides mechanisms to "roll back" erroneous event processing. An LP is able to save and later restore the state of the LP and "unsend" any messages it sends to other LPs during an erroneous execution. Since Time Warp requires state saving during event processing, the algorithm must be able to reclaim the memory resource; otherwise, the simulation would soon run out of memory. To accomplish this, the concept of global virtual time (GVT) is introduced as a timestamp lower-bound of all unprocessed or partially processed events at any given time. It serves as a "moving commitment horizon": any message and state with a timestamp less than GVT can be reclaimed and any irrevocable operations (such as I/O) that happen before GVT can be committed. Time Warp needs to overcome several problems in order to maintain good efficiency. These problems have prompted a flood of research in areas of state saving (e.g., Gomes et al., 1996; Lin and Lazowska, 1990; Lin et al., 1993; Ronngren et al., 1996), rollback (e.g., Gafni, 1988; Reiher et al., 1990; West, 1988), GVT computation (e.g., Fujimoto and Hybinette, 1997; Mattern, 1993; Samadi, 1985), memory management (e.g., Jefferson, 1990; Lin and Preiss, 1991; Preiss and Loucks, 1995), and alternative optimistic execution (e.g., Dickens and Reynolds, 1990; Sokol et al., 1988; Steinman, 1991, 1993).

The jury is out on which of the two approaches is a better choice. This is because parallel simulation performance largely depends on the characteristics of the simulation model. For network simulation, conservative synchronization is generally preferred as it requires a smaller memory footprint as opposed to the optimistic counterpart that generally needs additional memory for state saving and rollback. An interesting exception is the reverse computation technique (Carothers et al., 1999). Instead of applying state saving, one performs reverse computation to re-create the original state when rollback happens. Recent study shows that, with careful implementation, reverse computation achieves great memory efficiency in simulating large networks (Yaun et al., 2003).

3. Real-Time Network Simulation

Real-time simulation combines the advantages of simulation and emulation by conducting network simulation in real time and interacting with real applications and real network traffic. It allows us to study the impact of real application traffic on the virtual network and study real application behavior under a diverse set of simulated network conditions. Specifically, real-time network simulation provides the following capabilities:

- Accuracy. Real-time network simulation is based on simulation; thus, it is able to efficiently capture detailed packet-level transactions in the network. This is particularly true for simulating packet forwarding on wired infrastructure networks as it is relatively straightforward to calculate the link state with sufficient accuracy (such as the delay for a packet being forwarded from one router to the next). Real-time network simulation can also increase the fidelity of simulation since it can create real traffic conditions generated by real applications. Furthermore, existing implementations, such as routing protocols, can be incorporated directly in simulation rather than using a separate implementation just for simulation purposes. The design and implementation of network protocols, services, and applications is complex and labor-intensive. Maintaining code separately for simulation and for real deployment would have to include costly procedures for verification and validation.
- Repeatability. Repeatability is important to both protocol development and evaluation. In real-time network simulation, an experiment may or may not be repeatable, depending on whether interaction with the applications is repeatable or not. The virtual network in real-time network simulation is controlled by simulation events, and thus can be used to produce repeatable network conditions to test real network applications.
- Scalability. Emulation typically implements packet transmission by really directing a packet across a physical link, although in some cases this process can be accelerated by using special programmable devices (e.g., DeHart et al., 2006). In comparison, network operations in real-time network simulation are handled in software; each packet transmission involves only a few changes to the state variables in simulation that are computationally insignificant compared to the I/O overhead. Furthermore, since packet forwarding operations are relatively easy to parallelize, the simulated network can be scaled up far beyond what could be supported by emulation.
- Flexibility. Simulation is both a tool for analyzing the performance of existing systems and a tool for evaluating new design alternatives potentially under various operating settings. Once a simulation model is in place, it takes little effort to conduct simulation experiments, for example, to explore a wide spectrum of design space. We can also incorporate different analytical models in real-time network simulation. For example, we can use low-resolution models to describe aggregate Internet traffic behavior, which can significantly increase the scale of the network being simulated.

Most real-time network simulators are based on existing network simulators added with emulation capabilities in order to interact with real applications. Examples include NSE (Fall, 1999), IP-TNE (Bradford et al., 2000), MaSSF (Liu et al., 2003), and Maya (Zhou et al., 2004). NSE is an emulation extension of the popular ns-2 simulator with support for connecting with real applications and scheduling real-time events. ns-2 is built on a sequential discrete-event simulation engine, which severely limits the size of the network it is capable of simulating; for real-time simulation, this means that the size of the network has to be kept small to allow realtime processing. IP-TNE is an emulation extension of an existing parallel network simulator. It is the first simulator we know that applies parallel simulation to large-scale network emulations. MaSSF is built on our parallel simulator DaSSF with support for the grid computing environment. Maya is an emulation extension of a simulator for wireless mobile networks. Our real-time network simulator is called PRIME, which stands for Parallel Real-time Immersive network Modeling Environment. The implementation of PRIME inherits most of our previous efforts in the development of DaSSF, a process-oriented and conservatively synchronized parallel simulation engine designed for multi-protocol communication networks. DaSSF can run on most platforms, including shared-memory multiprocessors and clusters of distributed-memory machines. The DaSSF simulation engine is ultra fast and has been demonstrated capable of handling large network models, including simulation of infrastructure networks, cellular systems, wireless ad hoc networks, and wireless sensor networks. In order to support large-scale simulation, PRIME applies advanced parallel simulation techniques. For example, to achieve good performance on distributed-memory machines, PRIME adopts a hierarchical synchronization scheme to address the discrepancy in the communication cost between distributed-memory and shared-memory platforms (Liu and Nicol, 2001). Further, PRIME implements the composite synchronization algorithm (Nicol and Liu, 2002), which combines the traditional synchronous and asynchronous conservative parallel simulation algorithms. Consequently, PRIME is able to efficiently simulate diverse network scenarios, including those that exhibit large variability in link types (particularly with the existence of low-latency connections), and node types (especially for those with a large degree of connectivity).

PRIME extends DaSSF with emulation capabilities, where unmodified implementations of real applications can interact with the network simulator that operates in real time. Traffic originated from the real applications is captured by PRIME's emulation facilities and forwarded to the simulator. The real network packets are treated as simulation events as they are "carried" on the virtual network and experience appropriate delays and losses according to the run-time state of the simulated network.

4. Supporting Real-Time Performance

Real-time network simulation needs to resolve two important and related issues: responsiveness and timeliness. Responsiveness dictates that the real-time simulator must be able to interact with real applications in time. That is, the system interface must be able to receive and respond to real-time events promptly according to proper real-time deadlines. Timeliness refers to the system's ability to keep up with the wall-clock time. That is, the simulation must be able to characterize the behavior of the networks, potentially with millions of network entities and with a large amount of network traffic flows, in real time. Failing to do so will introduce timing faults, where the simulation fails to process events before the designated deadlines. An elevated occurrence of timing faults will cause the simulator to become less responsive when interacting with real applications. In this section we briefly describe the techniques we developed so far to factor out these issues.

4.1 Hybrid Traffic Modeling

Large-scale real-time network simulation requires simulation be able to characterize the network behavior in real time. To speed up simulation, on the one hand, we apply parallel and distributed simulation techniques to harness the computing resources of parallel computers to physically increase the event-processing power; on the other hand, we resort to multi-resolution modeling techniques mixing models with high level of abstraction (and low resolution) to reduce the computational demand.

Our solution to this problem is to use a hybrid network traffic model that combines a fluid-based analytical model using ordinary differential equations (ODEs) with the traditional packet-oriented discrete-event simulation (Liu, 2006). The model extends the fluid model by Liu et al. (2004) where ODEs are used to predict the mean behavior of the dynamic TCP congestion windows, the network queue lengths, and packet loss probabilities, as traffic flows through a set of network queues. These network queues are augmented with functions to handle both fluid flows and individual packets, as well as the interaction between them. We briefly describe the functions of these equations below. A detailed discussion of the hybrid model can be found in Liu (2006). We first define the variables in Table 1.

$$\frac{dW_i(t)}{dt} = \frac{1}{R_i(t)} - \frac{W_i(t)}{2} \cdot \lambda_i(t) \tag{1}$$

$$\frac{dq_l(t)}{dt} = \xi_l(t)(1 - p_l(t)) - C_l \tag{2}$$

$$\frac{dx_l(t)}{dt} = \frac{\ln(1-\alpha)}{\delta} x_l(t) - \frac{\ln(1-\alpha)}{\delta} q_l(t) \tag{3}$$

ni	number of (homogeneous) flows in fluid class i
W (t)	congestion window size of fluid class i at time t
Ri (t)	round trip time of fluid class i at time t
Xi (t)	loss rate of fluid class i at time t
qi (t)	instantaneous queue length at link I at time t
pi (t)	packet loss rate at link I at time t
xi (t)	average queue length at link I at time t
11 (t)	aggregate arrival rate at link I at time t
A (t) 4 (t)	arrival rate of fluid class i at link I at time t
D (t)	average packet arrival rate at link I at time t
	departure rate of fluid class i at link I at time t
d\ (t)	cumulative delay of fluid class i at link I at time t
Yl (t)	cumulative loss rate of fluid class i at link I at time t
h	first network queue (traversed by flow class i)
fn	last network queue (traversed by flow class i)
gi (l)	next queue of I for fluid class i
bi (l)	predecessor queue of I for fluid class i
al	propagation delay of link I
Ci	bandwidth of link I
Ni	set of fluid classes passing through link I
qa, qb, Px	RED queue parameters
a	weight used for RED EWMA calculation
	one-way path propagation delay for fluid class i

Table 1. Variables defined in the hybrid model.

$$p(x) = \begin{cases} 0 & 0 \le x < q_a \\ \dfrac{x - q_a}{q_b - q_a} px & q_a \le x < q_b \\ 1 & \text{otherwise} \end{cases} \tag{4}$$

$$A_i^{f_1}(t) = \frac{n_i W_i(t)}{R_i(t)} \tag{5}$$

$$A_i^{g_i(l)}(t + a_l) = D_i^l(t) \tag{6}$$

$$\xi_l(t) = \sum_{i \in N_l} A_i^l(t) + A_P^l(t) \tag{7}$$

$$t_f = t + q_l(t) / C_l \tag{8}$$

$$D_i^l(t_f) = \begin{cases} A_i^l(t)(1 - p_l(t)) & \text{if } \xi_l(t)(1 - p_l(t)) \le C_l \\ \dfrac{A_i^l(t)}{\xi_l(t)} C_l & \text{otherwise} \end{cases} \tag{9}$$

$$d_l^i(t_f) = \begin{cases} \dfrac{q_l(t)}{C_l} & \text{if } l = f_1 \\ d_{b_i(l)}^i(t - a_{b_i(l)}) + a_{b_i(l)} + \dfrac{q_l(t)}{C_l} & \text{otherwise} \end{cases} \tag{10}$$

$$\gamma_l^i(t_f) = \begin{cases} A_i^l(t) p_l(t) & \text{if } l = f_1 \\ \gamma_{b_i(l)}(t - a_{b_i(l)}) + A_i^l(t) p_l(t) & \text{otherwise} \end{cases} \tag{11}$$

$$R_i(t) = d_{f_n}^i(t - \pi_i) + \pi_i \tag{12}$$

$$\lambda_i(t) = \gamma_{f_n}^i(t - \pi_i) / n_i \tag{13}$$

Equation (1) models the additive-increase-multiplicative-decrease (AIMD) behavior of a TCP congestion window during the congestion avoidance stage. The window size and the round-trip time determine the arrival rate at the first router in Equation (5). For UDP flows, we use a constant send rate instead. The arrival rate at subsequent routers is the same as the departure rate at the predecessor router only postponed by the link's propagation delay, as prescribed in Equation (6). Equation (7) sums up the arrivals of both fluid and packet flows. The total arrival rate, together with the loss probability and the link's bandwidth, are used to determine the instantaneous queue length in Equation (2). An average queue length is then calculated in Equation (3), which is derived from the Exponential Weighted Moving Average (EWMA) calculation in network queues with RED (Random Early Detection) queue management. The calculated average queue length contributes to the loss probability as dictated by the RED policy in Equation (4). The loss probability for drop-tail queues can be calculated directly from projected buffer overflows. Equation (9) describes the departure rate as a function of the arrival rate postponed by the queuing delay calculated using Equation (8). Equations (10) and (11) calculate the cumulative delay and loss since the beginning when the segment of flow is originated from the traffic source. The cumulative delay and loss are used to calculate the round-trip time and the total loss rate in Equations (12) and (13), which in turn are used to calculate the congestion window size.

With proper performance optimization (Liu and Li, 2008), this hybrid traffic model can achieve significant performance improvement, in certain cases, over three orders of magnitude. The hybrid model can also be parallelized to achieve even greater performance.

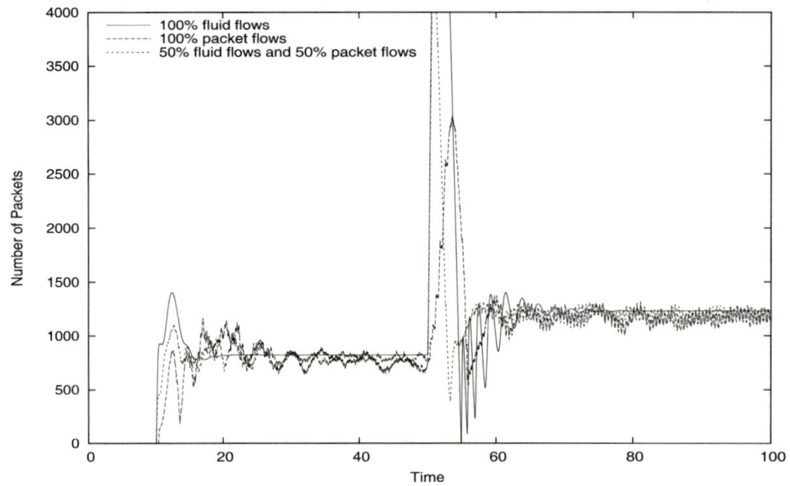

Fig. 1. Instantaneous queue length.

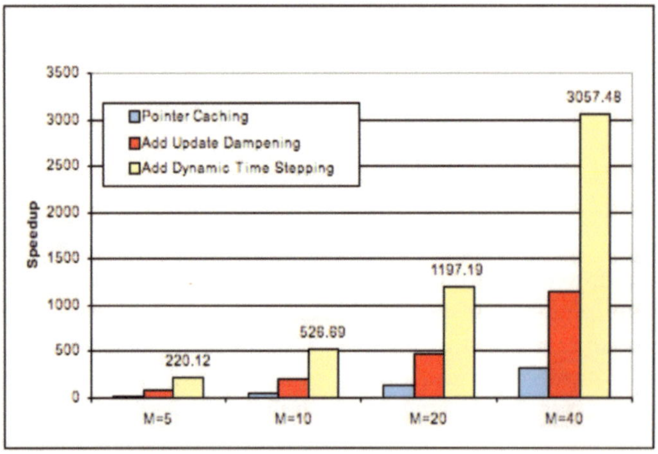

Fig. 2. Speedup over packet simulation.

To illustrate the potential of this approach, here we examine the accuracy and performance of the hybrid model using a simple dumbbell network model. In the experiment, the dumbbell network contains two routers in the middle connecting N server nodes on one side and N client nodes on the other side. Each server node directs M simultaneous TCP flows to the corresponding client node. All links are set with a propagation delay of 5 ms. The experiments were run sequentially on an Apple Mac Pro with two 3 GHz dual-core Intel Xeon processors and 9 GB of memory. We first set N – 10 and M – 30. Half of the connections are established at time 10 and the rest at time 50. We set the bandwidth of the bottleneck link to be 20 Mb/s. Each server or client node connects to its adjacent router over a 10 Mb/s link.

Figure 1 compares the instantaneous queues lengths at the bottleneck router as predicted by fluid-based and packet-oriented simulations, as well as a hybrid of the two. The result from the fluid-based simulation matches well with that of the packet-oriented simulation in terms of averaged behavior. The hybrid model (with 50% fluid flows and 50% packet flows) produces similar results.

To show the overall performance benefit of our hybrid approach, we use the same dumbbell topology but change the parameters, such as the bandwidth at the bottleneck link, so that the cost of the simulation may increase proportionally as we increase the number of TCP sessions. Specifically, we vary M, the number of simultaneous TCP sessions between each pair of client-server nodes. We set the bandwidth of the link between each client or server node and its adjacent router to be (10 x M) Mb/s. The network queues at both ends of the link has a buffer size of M MB. The link between the two routers has a bandwidth of (10 ×M × N) Mb/s. The corresponding network queues in the two routers have a buffer size of (M × N) MB. All TCP sessions start at time 0 and the experiments are run for 100 simulated seconds. The rest of the parameters are the same as in the previous experiment. Figure 2 shows the speedup of the fluid model over the pure packet simulation with different performance improvement techniques enabled one at a time (see Liu and Li, 2008 for more details about these performance improvement techniques). Here we set N – 100 and M – {5,10,20,40}. We see that, as we turn on all improving techniques in the case of M – 40, we can obtain a speedup as much as 3,057 over packet-oriented simulation. The effective packet-event rate actually reaches over 566 million packet-event per second.

We further extend the hybrid model to represent network background traffic (Li and Liu, 2009a). In real-time network simulation, we can make a distinction between foreground traffic, which is generated by the real applications we intend to study with high fidelity, and background traffic, which represents the bulk of the network traffic that is of secondary interest and does not necessarily require significant accuracy. Nevertheless, background traffic interferes with foreground traffic as they both compete for network resources, and thus determines (and also is determined by) the behavior of network applications under investigation (Vishwanath and Vahdat, 2008).

Our enhanced model enables bi-directional flows and uses heavy-tail distributions to describe the flow durations. To enable bi-directional flows, we assume that the forwarding path of the TCP flows in the fluid class *i* (from the source to the destination) consists of n queues: $f_1, f_2, \ldots, f_n$, and the reverse path (from the destination to the source) consists of m queues: $r_1, r_2, \ldots, r_m$. We use Equation (5) to calculate the arrival rate at the first queue f1. For subsequent queues except r_1, i.e., $l \in \{f_2, \ldots, f_n, r_2, \ldots, r_m\}$, we use Equation (6) to calculate the arrival rate from the departure rate at the predecessor queue. For queue r_1 (the first queue on the reverse path), we have:

$$A_i^{r_1}(t) = \alpha_i D_i^{f_n}(t) / \beta_i, \tag{14}$$

where α_1 is the average ACK packet size, and β_i is the average data packet size in fluid class *i*. This equation represents the conversion from the data flows on the forwarding path to the corresponding ACK flows on the reverse path.

To capture traffic burstness, we use the Poisson Pareto Burst process (PPBP) model to predict the aggregate Internet traffic. PPBP is a process based on multiple overlapping bursts, with Poisson arrival and burst lengths following a heavy-tail distribution (Zukerman et al., 2003). We schedule TCP session arrivals using the exponential distribution with a mean arrival rate μ. The durations of the TCP sessions d are independent and identically distributed Pareto random variables with parameters $\delta > 0$ and $1 < \gamma < 2$:

$$P_r(d > x) = \begin{cases} (x/\delta)^{-\gamma} & \text{if } x \geq \delta \\ 1 & \text{otherwise} \end{cases} \tag{15}$$

With the Pareto distributed flow duration, we can regenerate the long range dependence (LRD) characteristic of realistic background traffic in our model, which can be evaluated by a parameter called the Hurst parameter:

$$H = \frac{3-\gamma}{2}. \tag{16}$$

When $0.5 < H < 1$, it implies that the traffic exhibits LRD and is self-similar. In our fluid model, we replace the constant number of homogeneous fluid flows ni with the PPBP process, $N_i(t)$. Specifically, we redefine the equations for calculating the arrival rate at the first queue f_1 (Equation 5), and the end-to-end packet loss rate (Equation 13) as follows:

$$A_i^{f_1}(t) = \frac{N_i(t) W_i(t)}{R_i(t)} \tag{17}$$

$$\lambda_i(t) = \gamma_{r_m}^i(t) / N_i(t) \tag{18}$$

Figure 3 shows the result of an experiment using the same dumbbell model measuring the number of packets per second sent over time for both packet simulation (left plots) and the fluid background traffic model (right plots). From top down we progressively decreasing the sampling time scale, while maintaining the number of samples to be 300. The starting time scale is 1 second; each subsequent plot is obtained from the previous one by concentrating on a randomly chosen sub-interval with a length being one tenth of the previous one.

That is, the time resolution is increased by a factor of 10. To a large extent, the results from the packet-oriented simulation and from the fluid-based simulation are similar, except for the 10 ms timescale (bottom plots). The fluid model does not capture packet details at sub-RTT level; the RTT for the dumbbell model is at least 10 ms.

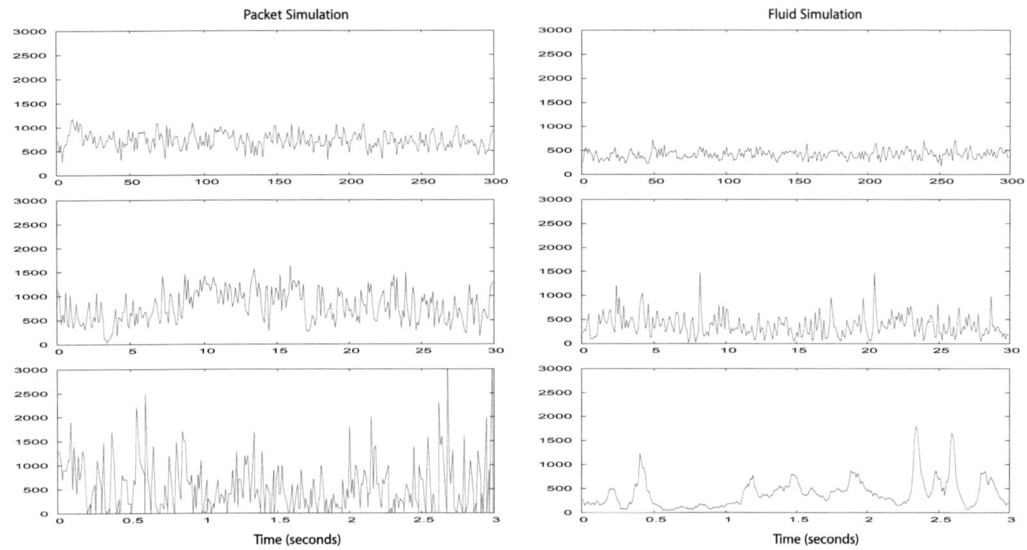

Fig. 3. Traffic burstness.

4.2 Scalable Emulation Infrastructure

A large-scale network simulation must be able to interact with a large number of real applications. The emulation infrastructure, which connects the simulator to the applications, must be able to embed real applications easily in the real-time simulation. There are several ways to incorporate real applications into a simulation environment, the decision of which to use largely depends on where the interactions take place. Several techniques exist that allow running unmodified software, which include using packet capturing techniques (such as libpcap, IP table, and IP tunnel), preloading dynamic libraries, and modifying the binary executables. In certain cases, moderate software modifications are necessary to allow efficient direct execution.

Our first attempt follows an open system approach (Liu et al., 2007). The emulation infrastructure is built on the Virtual Private Network (VPN), which is customized to function as a gateway that bridges traffic between the physical entities and the simulated network (see Figure 4). Client machines run real applications. They establish connection to the simulation gateway as VPN clients (by running an automatically generated VPN configuration scripts). Traffic generated by the applications running on the client machines and destined for the virtual network is directed by the emulation infrastructure to the real-time network simulator. We use an example to show how it works. Suppose two client machines are connected to the simulation gateway (not necessarily the same one) and want to communicate with each other. One client is assigned with the IP address `10.0.0.14` and the other with `10.0.1.2`. Packets

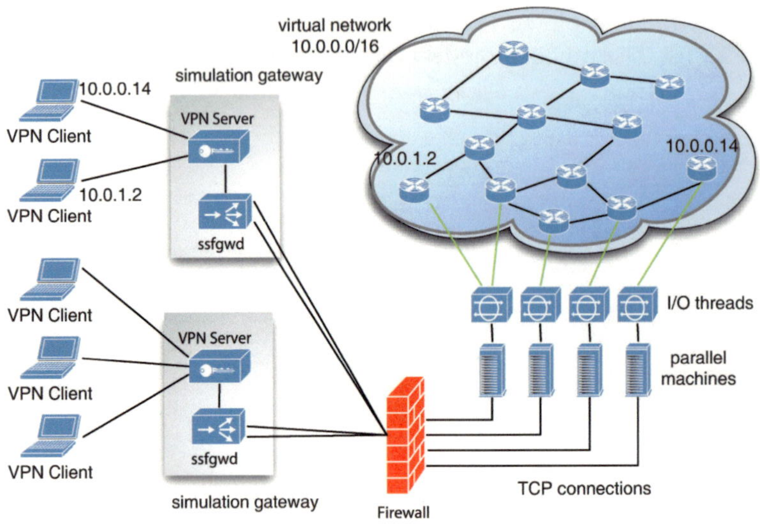

Fig. 4. VPN emulation infrastructure.

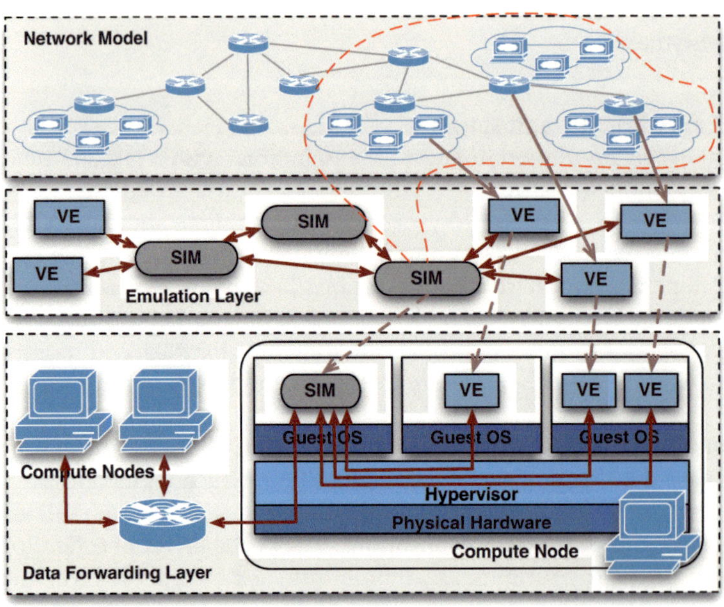

Fig. 5. VM emulation infrastructure.

sent from `10.0.0.14` to `10.0.1.2` are forwarded to the VPN server at the simulation gateway. The VPN server has been altered to forward the packets to a daemon process (ssfgwd), which then sends the packets to the real-time simulator via a dedicated TCP connection. At the simulator, the packets are injected into the simulation event list; the simulator simulates the packets being forwarded on the virtual network as if they were created by the virtual node with the same IP address `10.0.0.14`. Upon reaching the virtual node `10.0.1.2`, the packets are exported from simulation and travel in the reverse direction via the simulation gateway back to the client machine assigned with the IP address `10.0.1.2`.

One distinct advantage of this approach is that the emulation infrastructure does not require special hardware to set up. It is also secure and scalable, which are merits inherited directly from the underlying VPN implementation. Multiple simulation gateways can run simultaneously. In order to produce accurate results, however, the emulation infrastructure needs a tight coupling between the emulated entities (i.e., the client machines) and the real-time simulator. In particular, the segment between the client machines and the real-time network simulator should consist of only low-latency links. To maintain high throughput, the segment must also provide sufficient bandwidth to carry the emulation traffic. With these constraints, the physical latency between the clients and the simulator can actually be made transparent in the network model (Liljenstam et al., 2005). The idea is to allow an emulation packet in simulation to preempt other simulated packets in the network queues so that the packet can be delivered ahead of its schedule in order to compensate for the physical delays.

We also inspect machine virtualization solutions for an accurate environment of running real applications. Machine virtualization has found a number of interesting applications, including resource management in data centers, security, virtual desktop environments, and software distribution. Recently, researchers have also proposed using virtualization techniques for building network emulation testbeds. We follow the method proposed by Maier et al. (2007) to classify virtual machine (VM) solutions for network emulation. Classical virtual machines, such as VMWare Workstation and User-Mode Linux (Dike, 2000), provide full machine virtualization and can therefore run unmodified guest operating systems. These solutions offer complete transparency (with a complete abstraction of a computer system) to the guest operating system, but in doing so incur a large performance overhead. Light-weight virtual machines, such as Xen (Barham et al., 2003), VMWare ESX Server, and Denali (Whitaker et al., 2002), implement partial virtualization for greater efficiency, but require slight modification of guest OSes.

In addition to virtualizing an entire operating system instance, researchers have proposed virtual network stacks (Bavier et al., 2006; Huang et al., 1999; OpenVZ; Soltesz et al., 2007; Zec, 2003) and virtual routers (Maier et al., 2007; VRF) as alternative solutions. With virtual network stacks, applications running on the same OS instance are presented with multiple independent network stacks, which can be managed individually and control distinct physical devices. With virtual routers, a single OS instance can maintain multiple routing table instances, thereby allowing the co-execution of multiple router software. Since these two techniques only virtualize the network resource, they provide greater efficiency than light-weight VMs. They do not, however, provide a complete isolation of resources (such as CPU); they are also invasive, sometimes requiring substantial modification to the guest OS.

Our work so far has explored the use of light-weight virtual machines and virtual network stacks as candidate emulated elements in a real-time simulation infrastructure. We have built a real-time simulation infrastructure that can seamlessly use light-weight virtual machines to emulate arbitrary network elements including routers and application end-points. We looked into four types of network resources that may be provided by a virtual machine: network sockets, network interfaces, forwarding table, and loopback device. Network sockets (TCP, UDP, and raw sockets) are used by applications to establish connectivity and exchanging information. Network interfaces and the forwarding table are used by routing protocols to conduct network forwarding. A network loopback device is sometimes used by separate processes to communicate on the same machine. We investigated four popular virtualization technologies: Xen, OpenVZ, Linux-VServer and VRF and found that, while all four types of network resources are provided in Xen and OpenVZ, Linux-VServer and VRF have only partial network virtualization support.

Figure 5 shows a high-level view of our VM-based emulation infrastructure. We view each physical machine as a basic scaling unit, where emulated hosts are mapped to independent virtual machines (or virtual environments) so that they can run unmodified applications. Each instance of the real-time simulator runs on a separate virtual machine of the same physical machine, and processes events associated with a designated sub-network. The simulator instances on different physical machines are synchronized using conservative parallel simulation techniques. Real network traffic generated by the applications is intercepted by the hypervisor (or VM manager) and sent to the virtual machine where the corresponding realtime simulator instance is located. The simulator then processes these packets applying packet delays and losses according to the simulated network conditions.

5. Applications and Case Studies

We have been able to successfully apply real-time simulation to study many applications, including routing algorithms, transport protocols, content distribution services, web services, multimedia streaming, and peer-to-peer networks. In this section, we select several case studies to demonstrate the potentials of real-time simulation.

5.1 Large-Scale Routing Experiments

The availability of open-source router platforms, such as XORP, Zebra, and Quagga, has simplified the task of researchers, who can now prototype and evaluate routing protocols with relative ease. To support experiments on a large-scale network consisting of many routers with multiple traffic sources and sinks, we need to integrate the open-source router platforms with the real-time network simulator.

Since the routers are emulated outside the real-time simulator on client machines where they can run the real routing software directly, every packet traveling along its path from the source to the destination needs to be exported to each intermediate router for forwarding decisions, and subsequently imported back into the simulation engine. Thus, the forwarding operation for each packet at each hop would incur substantial I/O overhead. Consequently, the overall overhead would significantly impact the performance of the emulation infrastructure, especially in large-scale routing experiments. To avoid this problem, we propose a forwarding plane offloading approach, which moves the packet forwarding functions from the emulated router software to the simulation engine so that we can eliminate the I/O overhead associated with communicating bulk-traffic back and forth between the router software and the real-time simulator (Li et al., 2008).

In our current implementation, we combine XORP with PRIME to provide a scalable platform for conducting routing experiments. We create a forwarding plane plug-in in XORP, which maintains a command channel with the PRIME simulator for transferring forwarding information updates and network interface configuration requests between the XORP instance and the corresponding simulated router.

We carried out several experiments using the scalable routing platform. These experiments include an intra-domain routing experiment consisting of a realistic Abilene network model (Li et al., 2008) with the objective of observing the convergence of OSPF and its effect on data traffic. We injected a link failure followed by a recovery between two routers on the network. We were able to measure their effect on the round-trip time and data throughput of end applications. We also conducted realistic large-scale inter-domain routing experiments consisting of major autonomous systems connecting Swedish Internet users with realistic routing configurations derived from the routing registry (Li and Liu, 2009b). We ran a series of real-time security exercises on this routing system to study the consequence of intentionally propagating false routing information on interdomain routing and the effectiveness of corresponding defensive measures.

5.2 Large-Scale TCP Evaluation

The TCP congestion control mechanism, which limits the rate of data entering the network, is essential to the overall stability of the network under traffic congestion and important to the protocol's performance. It has been widely documented that the traditional TCP congestion control algorithms (such as TCP Reno and TCP SACK) have serious problems preventing TCP from reaching high data throughput over high-speed long-latency links. Consequently, quite a number of TCP variants have been proposed to directly tackle these problems. Compared with the traditional methods, these TCP variants typically adopt more aggressive congestion control methods in order to address the under-utilization problem of TCP over networks with a large bandwidth-delay product.

The ability to establish an objective comparison between these high-performance TCP variants under diverse networking conditions and to obtain a quantitative assessment of their impact on the global network traffic is essential to a community-wide understanding of various design approaches. Small-scale experiments are insufficient for a comprehensive study of these TCP variants. We developed a TCP performance evaluation testbed, called SVEET, based on real-time simulation technique using real implementations of the TCP variants, which are evaluated under diverse network configurations and workloads in large-scale network settings (Erazo et al., 2009).

In order for SVEET to accommodate data communications with multi-gigabit throughput performance, we apply time dilation, proportionally slowing down the virtual machines and the network simulator. Using time dilation allows us to provide much higher bandwidths than what can be provided by the physical system and the network simulator at the cost of increased experiment time. We adopt the time dilation technique developed by Gupta et al. (2006), which can uniformly slow the passage of time from the perspective of the guest operating system (XenoLinux). This is achieved primarily by enlarging the interval between timer interrupts delivered to the virtual machines from the Xen hypervisor by a specified factor, called the Time Dilation Factor (TDF). Time dilation can scale the perceived I/O rate and processing power on the virtual machines by the same factor. For instance, if a virtual machine has a TDF of 10, it means that the time, as perceived by the applications running on the virtual machine, will be advanced at a pace 10 times slower than the true wall-time clock. Similarly, the applications would experience a tenfold increase in both network capacity and CPU cycles.

We ported several TCP congestion control algorithms from the ns-2 simulator consisting of thirteen TCP variants originally implemented for Linux. In doing so we are able to conduct large-scale experiments using simulated traffic generated by these TCP variants. We also customized the Linux kernel on the virtual machines to include these TCP variants so that we can test them using real applications running on the virtual machines to communicate via the TCP/IP stack. We conducted extensive experiments to validate our testbed and investigated the impact of TCP variants on web applications, multimedia streaming, and peer-to-peer traffic.

5.3 Large-Scale Peer-to-Peer Content Distribution Network

We design one of the largest network experiments that involve a real implementation of a peer-to-peer content distribution system under HTTP traffic from a public-domain empirical workload trace and using a realistic large network model (Liu et al., 2009). The main idea behind the content distribution network (CDN) is to replicate content at the edge of the Internet closer to the clients. In doing so, CDN can alleviate both the workload at the server and the traffic load at the network core. We choose to use an open-source CDN system called CoralCDN (Freedman et al., 2004), which is a peer-to-peer web-content distribution network that consists of three parts: 1) a network of cooperative web proxies for handling HTTP requests, 2) a network of domain name servers (DNS) to map clients to nearby web proxies, and 3) an underlying clustering mechanism and an indexing infrastructure to facilitate DNS mapping and content distribution. We statically mapped the clients to nearby Coral nodes to send HTTP requests. Thus we ignore CoralCDN's DNS redirection function and only focus on web-content distribution for the experiment.

We extend the Rocketfuel to build the network model for our study. Rocketfuel (Spring et al., 2004) contains the topology of 13 tier-1 ISPs, derived from information obtained from traceroute paths, BGP routing tables, and DNS. Previously, we created a best-effort Internet topology for large-scale network simulation studies using the Rocketfuel dataset (Liljenstam et al., 2003). Based on this study, we further process the Rocketfuel network topology to improve accuracy and reduce data noise. We choose to use one of the tier-1 ISP networks for our study, which contains 637 routers (out of which 235 are backbone routers) connected by 1,381 links. Attached to the backbone network are medium-sized stub networks, called the campus network. Each campus network consists of 504 end hosts, organized into 12 local area networks (LANs) connected by 18 routers. Four extra end hosts are designated to form a server cluster. Each LAN consists of a gateway router and 42 end-hosts. The entire campus network is divided into four OSPF areas. The campus network is connected to the outside world through a BGP router. We attach 84 such campus networks to the tier-1 ISP network. The entire network thus contains 42,672 end hosts and 3,157 routers.

We place one CoralCDN node within each of the 12 LANs of the 84 campus network (at one of the 42 end hosts in each LAN), thus making a total of 1,008 CoralCDN nodes overall. Each CoralCDN node is emulated in a separate OpenVZ container. The web clients are simulated; they send HTTP requests to the CoralCDN node within the same LAN and subsequently receive data objects from the Coral proxy. PRIME implements a full-fledged TCP model that allows simulated nodes to interact with real TCP counterparts. We attach a stub network to a backbone router in the tier-1 ISP network (located in Paris, France) to run a web server, emulated on a separate compute node.

We select the HTTP trace at the 1998 World Cup web site, which is publicly available (Arlitt and Jin, 1998). The trace is collected with all HTTP requests made to the 1998 World Cup Web site. We select a 24-hour period of this trace (from June 5,1998, 22:00:01 GMT to June

6,1998, 22:00:00 GMT). The segment consists of 5,452,684 requests originated from 40,491 clients. We pre-process the trace to filter out the sequence of requests sent from each client and randomly map the 40,491 clients to the end hosts in our network model for a complete daily pattern of the caching behavior. Through the experiment, we were able to successfully collect three important metrics to analyze the performance the peer-to-peer content distribution network: cache hit rate, web server load, and response time.

6. Conclusions and Future Work

In this chapter we describe real-time simulation of large-scale networks and compare it against other major tools for networking research. We discuss the problems that may prevent simulation from achieving real-time performance and subsequently present our current solutions. We conduct large-scale network experiments incorporating real-time simulation to demonstrate its capabilities.

Future work includes efficient background traffic models for large-scale networks, high-performance communication conduit for connecting virtual machines and the real-time simulator, and effective methods for configuring, running and visualizing network experiments.

Acknowledgments

This chapter significantly extends our previous work (Liu, 2008) with a high-level summary of published results thereafter. Our research reported in this chapter is supported in part by National Science Foundation grants CNS-0546712, CNS-0836408 and HRD-0833093.

7. References

Jong Suk Ahn, Peter B. Danzip, Zhen Liu, and Limin Yan. Evaluation of TCP Vegas: emulation and experiment. In Proceedings of the 1995 ACM SIGCOMM Conference, pages 185-195, August 1995.

Thomas Anderson, Larry Peterson, Scott Shenker, and Jonathan Turner. Overcoming the Internet impasse through virtualization. Computer, 38(4):34—41, 2005.

Martin Arlitt and Tai Jin. 1998 World Cup web site access logs. Available at: http://www.acm.org/sigcomm/ITA/, August 1998.

Rassul Ayani. A parallel simulation scheme based on the distance between objects. Proceedings of the 1989 SCS Multiconference on Distributed Simulation, 21(2):113-118, March 1989.

Lokesh Bajaj, Mineo Takai, Rajat Ahuja, Ken Tang, Rajive Bagrodia, and Mario Gerla. GloMoSim: a scalable network simulation environment. Technical Report 990027, Department of Computer Science, UCLA, May 1999.

Paul Barford and Larry Landweber. Bench-style network research in an Internet instance laboratory. ACM SIGCOMM Computer Communication Review, 33(3):21-26, 2003.

Paul Barham, Boris Dragovic, Keir Fraser, Steven Hand, Tim Harris, Alex Ho, Rolf Neugebauer, Ian Pratt, and Andrew Warfield. Xen and the art of virtualization. In Proceedings of the 19th ACM Symposium on Operating Systems Principles (SOSP'03), 2003.

Rimon Barr, Zygmunt Haas, and Robbert van Renesse. JiST: An efficient approach to simulation using virtual machines. Software Practice and Experience, 35(6):539-576, May 2005.

Andy Bavier, Nick Feamster, Mark Huang, Larry Peterson, and Jennifer Rexford. In VINI veritas: realistic and controlled network experimentation. ACMSIGCOMMComputer Communication Review, 36(4):3-14, 2006.

Terry Benzel, Robert Braden, Dongho Kim, Clifford Neuman, Anthony Joseph, Keith Sklower, Ron Ostrenga, and Stephen Schwab. Experience with DETER: A testbed for security research. In Proceedings of 2nd International Conference on Testbeds and Research Infrastructures for the Development of Networks and Communities (TRIDENTCOM'06), March 2006.

Russell Bradford, Rob Simmonds, and Brian Unger. A parallel discrete event IP network emulator. In Proceedings of the 8th International Symposium on Modeling, Analysis and Simulation of Computer and Telecommunication Systems (MASCOTS'00), pages 315-322, August 2000.

Lee Breslau, Deborah Estrin, Kevin Fall, Sally Floyd, John Heidemann, Ahmed Helmy, Polly Huang, Steven McCanne, Kannan Varadhan, Ya Xu, and Haobo Yu. Advances in network simulation. IEEE Computer, 33(5):59-67, May 2000.

Randal E. Bryant. Simulation of packet communication architecture computer systems. Technical Report MIT-LCS-TR-188, MIT, 1977.

Christopher D. Carothers, Kalyan S. Perumalla, and Richard M. Fujimoto. Efficient optimistic parallel simulations using reverse computation. ACM Transactions on Modeling and Computer Simulation, 9(3):224-253, July 1999.

Mark Carson and Darrin Santay. NIST Net: a Linux-based network emulation tool. SIGCOMM Computer Communication Review, 33(3):111-126, 2003.

K. M. Chandy and R. Sherman. The conditional event approach to distributed simulation. Proceedings ofthe 1989 SCS Multiconference on Distributed Simulation, 21(2):93-99, March 1989.

K. Mani Chandy and Jayadev Misra. Distributed simulation: A case study in design and verification of distributed programs. IEEE Transactions on Software Engineering, SE-5 (5):440^52, May 1979.

James Cowie, David Nicol, and Andy Ogielski. Modeling the global Internet. Computing in Science and Engineering, 1(1):42-50, January 1999. DaSSF. Dartmouth Scalable Simulation Framework. http://users.cis.fiu.edu/^liux/research/projects/dassf/index.html.

John DeHart, Fred Kuhns, Jyoti Parwatikar, Jonathan Turner, Charlie Wiseman, and Ken Wong. The open network laboratory. ACM SIGCSE Bulletin, 38(1):107-111, 2006.

Phillip M. Dickens and Paul F. Reynolds. SRADS with local rollback. Proceedings of the 1990 SCS Multiconference on Distributed Simulation, 22(1):161-164, January 1990.

Jeff Dike. A user-mode port of the Linux kernel. In Proceedings of the 4th Annual Linux Showcase & Conference, 2000.

Miguel Erazo, Yue Li, and Jason Liu. SVEET! A scalable virtualized evaluation environment for TCP. In Proceedings of the 5th International Conference on Testbeds and Research Infrastructures for the Development of Networks and Communities (TridentCom'09), April 2009.

Kevin Fall. Network emulation in the Vint/NS simulator. In Proceedings of the 4th IEEE Symposium on Computers and Communications (ISCC'99), pages 244-250, July 1999.

Sally Floyd and Vern Paxson. Difficulties in simulating the Internet. IEEE/ACM Transactions on Networking, 9(4):392-403, August 2001.

Michael J. Freedman, Eric Freudenthal, and David Mazieres. Democratizing content publication with Coral. In Proceedings of the 1st USENIX Symposium on Networked Systems

Design and Implementation (NSDI 04), pages 239-252, 2004.

Richard M. Fujimoto. Lookahead in parallel discrete event simulation. In Proceedings of the 1988 International Conference on Parallel Processing, pages 34-41, August 1988.

Richard M. Fujimoto. Performance measurements of distributed simulation strategies. Transactions of the Society for Computer Simulation, 6(2):89-132, April 1989.

Richard M. Fujimoto. Parallel discrete event simulation. Communications ofthe ACM, 33(10): 30-53, October 1990.

Richard M. Fujimoto and Maria Hybinette. Computing global virtual time in shared memory multiprocessors. ACM Transactions on Modeling and Computer Simulation, 7(4):425-446, October 1997.

A. Gafni. Rollback mechanisms for optimistic distributed simulation systems. Proceedings of the 1988 SCS Multiconference on Distributed Simulation, 19(3):61-67, July 1988.

Fabian Gomes, Brian Unger, and John Cleary. Language based state saving extensions for optimistic parallel simulation. In Proceedings of the 1996 Winter Simulation Conference (WSC'96), pages 794-800, December 1996.

Bojan Groselj and Carl Tropper. The time of next event algorithm. Proceedings ofthe 1988 SCS Multiconference on Distributed Simulation, 19(3):25-29, July 1988.

Diwaker Gupta, Kenneth Yocum, Marvin McNett, Alex Snoeren, Amin Vahdat, and Geoffrey Voelker. To infinity and beyond: time-warped network emulation. In Proceedings of the 3rd USENIX Symposium on Networked Systems Design and Implementation (NSDI 06), 2006.

Daniel Herrscher and Kurt Rothermel. A dynamic network scenario emulation tool. In Proceedings of the 11th International Conference on Computer Communications and Networks (ICCCN'02), pages 262-267, October 2002.

X. W. Huang, R. Sharma, and S. Keshav. The ENTRAPID protocol development environment. In Proceedings of the 1999 IEEE INFOCOM, pages 1107-1115, March 1999.

David R. Jefferson. Virtual time. ACM Transactions on Programming Languages and Systems, 7 (3):404^25, July 1985.

David R. Jefferson. Virtual time II: Storage management in distributed simulation. In Proceeings ofthe 9th Annual ACM Symposium on Principles ofDistributed Computing, pages 75-89, August 1990.

Xuxian Jiang and Dongyan Xu. VIOLIN: Virtual internetworking on overlay infrastructure.

In Proceedings of the 2nd Internattonai Symposium on Paraiiei and Distributed Processing and Appiications (ISPA'04), pages 937-946, 2004.

Glenn Judd and Peter Steenkiste. Repeatable and realistic wireless experimentation through physical emulation. ACM SIGCOMM Computer Communication Review, 34(1):63-68, 2004.

Ting Li and Jason Liu. A fluid background traffic model. In Proceedings of the 2009 IEEE Internationai Conference on Communications (ICC'09), June 2009a.

Yue Li and Jason Liu. Real-time security exercises on a realistic interdomain routing experiment platform. In Proceedings of the 23rd Workshop on Principies of Advanced and Distributed Simuiation (PADS 09), June 2009b.

Yue Li, Jason Liu, and Raju Rangaswami. Toward scalable routing experiments with real-time network simulation. In Proceedings of the 22nd Workshop on Principies of Advanced and Distributed Simuiation (PADS'08), pages 23-30, June 2008.

Michael Liljenstam, Jason Liu, and David M. Nicol. Development of an Internet backbone topology for large-scale network simulations. In Proceedings of the 2003 Winter Simu-iation Conference, pages 694-702, 2003.

Michael Liljenstam, Jason Liu, David M. Nicol, Yougu Yuan, Guanhua Yan, and Chris Grier. RINSE: the real-time interactive network simulation environment for network security exercises. In Proceedings of the 19th Workshop on Paraiiei and Distributed Simuiation (PADS'05), pages 119-128, June 2005.

Yi-Bing Lin and Edward D. Lazowska. Reducing the state saving overhead for Time Warp parallel simulation. Technical Report 90-02-03, Department of Computer Science, University of Washington, February 1990.

Yi-Bing Lin and Bruno R. Preiss. Optimal memory management for Time Warp parallel simulation. ACM Transactions on Modeiing and Computer Simuiation, 1(4):283-307, October 1991.

Yi-Bing Lin, Bruno Richard Preiss, Wayne Mervin Loucks, and Edward D. Lazowska. Selecting the checkpoint interval in Time Warp simulation. In Proceedings of the 7th Workshop on Paraiiei and Distributed Simuiation (PADS 93), pages 3-10, May 1993.

Jason Liu. Packet-level integration of fluid TCP models in real-time network simulation. In Proceedings of the 2006 Winter Simuiation Conference (WSC'06), pages 2162-2169, December 2006.

Jason Liu. A primer for real-time simulation of large-scale networks. In Proceedings ofthe 41st Annuai Simuiation Symposium (ANSS'08), April 2008.

Jason Liu and Yue Li. On the performance of a hybrid network traffic model. Simuiation Modeiiing Practice and Theory, 16(6):656-669, 2008.

Jason Liu and David M. Nicol. Learning not to share. In Proceedings of the 15th Workshop on Paraiiei and Distributed Simuiation (PADS'01), pages 46-55, May 2001.

Jason Liu, Scott Mann, Nathanael Van Vorst, and Keith Hellman. An open and scalable emulation infrastructure for large-scale real-time network simulations. In Proceedings of 2007 IEEE INFOCOM MiniSymposium, pages 2471-2475, May 2007.

Jason Liu, Yue Li, and Ying He. A large-scale real-time network simulation study using PRIME. In Proceedings ofthe 2009 Winter Simuiation Conference (WSC 09), December

2009. To appear.

Xin Liu, Huaxia Xia, and Andrew A. Chien. Network emulation tools for modeling grid behavior. In Proceedings of3rd IEEE/ACM International Symposium on Cluster Computing and the Grid (CCGrid'03), May 2003.

Yong Liu, Francesco Presti, Vishal Misra, Donald Towsley, and Yu Gu. Scalable fluid models and simulations for large-scale IP networks. ACM Transactions on Modeling and Computer Simulation (TOMACS), 14(3):305-324, July 2004.

Boris D. Lubachevsky. Bounded lag distributed discrete event simulation. Proceedings ofthe 1988 SCS Multiconference on Distributed Simulation, 19(3):183-191, July 1988.

Steffen Maier, Daniel Herrscher, and Kurt Rothermel. Experiences with node virtualization for scalable network emulation. Computer Communications, 30(5):943-956, 2007.

Friedemann Mattern. Efficient distributed snapshots and global virtual time approximation. Journal of Parallel and Distributed Computing, 18(4):423-434, August 1993.

David M. Nicol. Parallel discrete-event simulation of FCFS stochastic queueing networks. ACM SIGPLAN Notices, 23(9):124-137, September 1988.

David M. Nicol. Performance bounds on parallel self-initiating discrete-event simulations. ACM Transactions on Modeling and Computer Simulation, 1(1):24-50, January 1991.

David M. Nicol. Principles of conservative parallel simulation. In Proceedings ofthe1996 Winter Simulation Conference (WSC 96), pages 128-135, December 1996.

David M. Nicol and Philip Heidelberger. A comparative study of parallel algorithms for simulating continuous time Markov chains. ACM Transactions on Modeling and Computer Simulation, 5(4):326-354, October 1995.

David M. Nicol and Jason Liu. Composite synchronization in parallel discrete-event simulation. IEEE Transactions on Parallel and Distributed Systems, 13(5):433-446, May 2002. OpenVZ. http://openvz.org/.

Larry Peterson, Tom Anderson, David Culler, and Timothy Roscoe. A blueprint for introducing disruptive technology into the Internet. HotNets-I, October 2002.

Bruno Richard Preiss and Wayne Mervin Loucks. Memory management techniques for Time Warp on a distributed memory machine. In Proceedings ofthe 9th Workshop on Parallel and Distributed Simulation (PADS 95), pages 30-39, June 1995.

PRIME. http://www.primessf.net/.

Quagga. http://www.quagga.net/.

D. Raychaudhuri, I. Seskar, M. Ott, S. Ganu, K. Ramachandran, H. Kremo, R. Siracusa, H. Liu, and M. Singh. Overview of the ORBIT radio grid testbed for evaluation of next-generation wireless network protocols. In Proceedings ofthe IEEE Wireless Communications and Networking Conference (WCNC 05), March 2005.

Daniel A. Reed, Allen D. Malony, and Bradley McCredie. Parallel discrete event simulation using shared memory. IEEE Transactions on Software Engineering, 14(4):541-53, April 1988.

P. L. Reiher, R. M. Fujimoto, S. Bellenot, and D. Jefferson. Cancellation strategies in optimistic execution systems. Proceedings ofthe 1990 SCS Multiconference on Distributed Simulation, 22(1):112-121, January 1990.

George F. Riley. The Georgia Tech network simulator. In Proceedings ofthe ACM SIGCOMM Workshop on Models, Methods and Tools for Reproducible Network Research (MoMe-Tools 03), pages 5-12, August 2003.

Luigi Rizzo. Dummynet: a simple approach to the evaulation of network protocols. ACM SIGCOMM Computer Communication Review, 27(1):31-41, January 1997.

Robert Ronngren, Michael Liljenstam, Rassul Ayani, and Johan Montagnat. Transparent incremental state saving in Time Warp parallel discrete event simulation. In Proceedings of the 10th Workshop on Parallel and Distributed Simulation (PADS'96), pages 70-77, May 1996.

Behrokh Samadi. Distributed simulation, algorithms and performance analysis. PhD thesis, Department of Computer Science, UCLA, 1985.

L. M. Sokol, D. P. Briscoe, and A. P. Wieland. MTW: A strategy for scheduling discrete simulation events for concurrent execution. Proceedings of the 1988 SCS Multiconference on Distributed Simulation, 19(3):34^2, July 1988.

Stephen Soltesz, Herbert Potzl, Marc E. Fiuczynski, Andy Bavier, and Larry Peterson.

Container-based operating system virtualization: A scalable, high-performance alternative to hypervisors. In Proceedings of the 2nd ACM SIGOPS/EuroSys European Conference on Computer Systemsof (EuroSys'07), March 2007.

Neil Spring, Ratul Mahajan, David Wetherall, and Thomas Anderson. Measuring isp topologies with rocketfuel. IEEE/ACM Transactions on Networking, 12(1):2-16, 2004.

Neil Spring, Larry Peterson, Andy Bavier, and Vivek Pai. Using PlanetLab for network research: myths, realities, and best practices. ACM SIGOPS Operating Systems Review, 40(1):17-24, 2006.

Jeff S. Steinman. SPEEDES: Synchronous parallel environment for emulation and discrete event simulation. Proceedings of the SCS Multiconference on Advances in Parallel and Distributed Simulation, SCS Simulation Series, 23(1):95-103, January 1991.

Jeff S. Steinman. Breathing Time Warp. In Proceedings of the 7th Workshop on Parallel and Distributed Simulation (PADS'93), pages 109-118, May 1993.

Ananth I. Sundararaj and Peter A. Dinda. Towards virtual networks for virtual machine grid computing. In Proceedings of the 3rd USENIX Conference on Virtual Machine Technology (VM'04), pages 14-14, 2004.

Joe Touch. Dynamic Internet overlay deployment and management using the X-Bone. In Proceedings of the 2000 International Conference on Network Protocols (ICNP'00), pages 59-68, 2000.

Hung-ying Tyan and Jennifer Hou. JavaSim: A component based compositional network simulation environment. In Proceedings of the Western Simulation Multiconference, January 2001.

Amin Vahdat, Ken Yocum, Kevin Walsh, Priya Mahadevan, Dejan Kostic, Jeff Chase, and David Becker. Scalability and accuracy in a large scale network emulator. In Proceedings of the 5th Symposium on Operating Systems Design and Implementation (OSDI'02), pages 271-284, December 2002.

Andrs Varga. The OMNeT++ discrete event simulation system. In Proceedings of the European Simulation Multiconference (ESM 01), June 2001.

Kashi Venkatesh Vishwanath and Amin Vahdat. Evaluating distributed systems: Does background traffic matter. In Proceedings of the 2008 USENIX Technical Conference, pages 227-240, May 2008.

VMWare ESX Server. http://www.vmware.com/products/vi/esx/.

VMWare Workstation. http://www.vmware.com/products/desktop/workstation.html.

VRF. Linux Virtual Routing and Forwarding. http://sourceforge.net/projects/ linux-vrf/.

Darrin West. Optimizing Time Warp: Lazy rollback and lazy re-evaluation. Master's thesis, Department of Computer Science, University of Calgary, January 1988.

A. Whitaker, M. Shaw, and S. Gribble. Denali: Lightweight virtual machines for distributed and networked applications. In Proceedings of the USENIX Annual Technical Conference,

June 2002. Brian White, Jay Lepreau, Leigh Stoller, Robert Ricci, Shashi Guruprasad, Mac Newbold, Mike Hibler, Chad Barb, and Abhijeet Joglekar. An integrated experimental environment for distributed systems and networks. In Proceedings of the 5th Symposium on Operating Systems Design and Implementation (OSDI 02), pages 255-270, December 2002.

XORP. http://www.xorp.org/.

Garrett Yaun, David Bauer, Harshad Bhutada, Christopher Carothers, Murat Yuksel, and Shiv-kumar Kalyanaraman. Large-scale network simulation techniques: examples of TCP and OSPF models. ACM SIGCOMM Computer Communication Review, 33(3):27-41, 2003.

Zebra. http://www.zebra.org/.

Marko Zec. Implementing a clonable network stack in the FreeBSD kernel. In Proceedings of the 2003 USENIX Annual Technical Conference, June 2003.

Pei Zheng and Lionel M. Ni. EMPOWER: a network emulator for wireline and wireless networks. In Proceedings of the 2003 IEEE INFOCOM, volume 3, pages 1933-1942, March/April 2003.

Junlan Zhou, Zhengrong Ji, Mineo Takai, and Rajive Bagrodia. MAYA: integrating hybrid network modeling to the physical world. ACM Transactions on Modeling and Computer Simulation (TOMACS), 14(2):149-169, April 2004.

Moshe Zukerman, Timothy D. Neame, and Ronald G. Addie. Internet traffic modeling and future technology implications. In Proceedings ofthe2003 IEEE INFOCOM, 2003.

13

A parallel simulated annealing algorithm as a tool for fitness landscapes exploration

Zbigniew J. Czech
Silesia University of Technology and University of Silesia
Poland

1. Introduction

Solving a discrete optimization problem consists in finding a solution which maximizes (or minimizes) an objective function. The function is often called the fitness and the corresponding landscape the fitness landscape. We are concerned with statistical measures of a fitness landscape in the context of the vehicle routing problem with time windows (VRPTW). The measures are determined by using a parallel simulated annealing algorithm as a tool for exploring a solution space. This chapter summarizes our experience in designing parallel simulated annealing algorithms and investigating fitness landscapes of a sample NP-hard bicriterion optimization problem.

Since 2002 we have developed several versions of the parallel simulated annealing (SA) algorithm (11)-(19). Each of these versions comprises a number of parallel SA processes which co-operate periodically by passing and exploiting the best solutions found during the search. For this purpose a specific scheme of co-operation of processes has been devised. The methods of parallelization of simulated annealing are discussed in Aarts and van Laarhoven (2), Aarts and Korst (1), Greening (20), Abramson (3), Boissin and Lutton (8), and Verhoeven and Aarts (35). Parallel simulated annealing to solve the VRPTW is applied by Arbelaitz et al. (4). Onbaşoğlu and Özdamar (26) present the applications of parallel simulated annealing algorithms in various global optimization problems. The comprehensive study of parallelization of simulated annealing is given by Azencott et al. (5)

The parallel SA algorithm allowed us to discover the landscape properties of the VRPTW benchmarking tests (33). This knowledge not only increased our understanding of processes which happen during optimization, but also helped to improve the performance of the parallel algorithm. The usage of the landscape notion is traced back to the paper by Wright (37). The more formal treatments of the landscape properties are given by Stadler (32), Hordijk and Stadler (22), Reidys and Stadler (31). Statistical measures of a landscape are proposed by Weinberger (36). The reviews of the landscape issues are given by Reeves (30) and Reeves and Rowe (29).

Section 2 of this chapter formulates the optimization problem which is solved. Section 3 describes a sequential SA algorithm. In section 4 two versions of the parallel SA algorithm, called independent and co-operating searches, are presented. Section 5 is devoted to the statistical measures of the fitness landscapes in the context of the VRPTW. In subsections 5.1-5.2 some basic notions are introduced, and in subsection 5.3 the results of the experimental study are discussed. Section 6 concludes the chapter.

2. Problem formulation

The VRPTW is an extension to the capacitated vehicle routing problem (CVRP) which is formulated as follows (34). There is a central depot of goods and n customers (nodes) geographically scattered around the depot. The locations of the depot ($i = 0$) and the customers ($i = 1, 2, \ldots, n$), as well as the shortest distances d_{ij} and the corresponding travel times t_{ij} between any two customers i and j are given. Each customer asks for a quantity q_i of goods which has to be delivered (or picked up from) by a vehicle of capacity Q. Because of this capacity limit, the vehicle after serving a subset of customers has to return to the depot for reloading. The vehicle effects the whole service on a number of routes. Each route starts and terminates at the depot. A solution to the CVRP is a set of routes of minimum travel distance (or travel time) which visits each customer i, $i = 1, 2, \ldots, n$, exactly once. The total demand for each route cannot exceed Q.
The CVRP is extended into the VRPTW by introducing for each customer and the depot a service time window $[e_i, f_i]$ and a service time s_i ($s_0 = 0$). The values e_i and f_i determine, respectively, the earliest and the latest time for start servicing. The customer i has to be served within the time window $[e_i, f_i]$ and the service of all customers should be accomplished within the time window of the depot $[e_0, f_0]$. The vehicle can arrive to the customer before the time window but then it has to wait until time e_i, when the service can begin. The latest time for arrival of the vehicle to customer i is f_i. It is assumed that the routes are traveled simultaneously by a fleet of K homogeneous vehicles (i.e. of equal capacity), each vehicle assigned to a single route. A solution to the VRPTW is the set of routes which guarantees the delivery of goods to all customers and satisfies the time window and vehicle capacity constraints. Furthermore, the size of the set equal to the number of vehicles needed (primary objective) and the total travel distance (secondary objective) should be minimized.
More formally, there are three types of decision variables in this two-objective optimization problem. The first decision variable, $x_{i,j,k}$, $i, j \in \{0,1,\ldots,n\}, k \in \{1,2,\ldots,K\}, i \neq j$, is 1 if vehicle k travels from customer i to j, and 0 otherwise. The second decision variable, t_i, denotes the time when a vehicle arrives at customer i, and the third decision variable, b_i, denotes the waiting time at that customer. The aim is to:

$$\text{minimize} \qquad K, \quad \text{and then} \tag{1}$$

$$\text{minimize} \qquad \textstyle\sum_{i=0}^{n} \sum_{j=0, j\neq i}^{n} \sum_{k=1}^{K} d_{i,j} x_{i,j,k}, \tag{2}$$

subject to the following constraints:

$$\sum_{k=1}^{K} \sum_{j=1}^{n} x_{i,j,k} = K, \text{ for } i = 0, \tag{3}$$

$$\sum_{j=1}^{n} x_{i,j,k} = \sum_{j=1}^{n} x_{j,i,k} = 1, \text{ for } i = 0 \text{ and } k \in \{1,2,\ldots,K\}, \tag{4}$$

$$\sum_{k=1}^{K} \sum_{j=0, j\neq i}^{n} x_{i,j,k} = \sum_{k=1}^{K} \sum_{i=0, i\neq j}^{n} x_{i,j,k} = 1, \text{ for } i,j \in \{1,2,\ldots,n\}, \tag{5}$$

$$\sum_{i=1}^{n} q_i \sum_{j=0,j\neq i}^{n} x_{i,j,k} \leq Q, \text{ for } k \in \{1,2.\ldots,K\} \tag{6}$$

$$\sum_{k=1}^{K} \sum_{i=0,i\neq j}^{n} x_{i,j,k}(t_i + b_i + h_i + t_{i,j}) \leq t_j, \quad \text{for } j \in \{1,2,\ldots,n\} \tag{7}$$
$$\text{and } t_0 = b_0 = h_0 = 0,$$

$$e_i \leq (t_i + b_i) \leq f_i, \text{ for } i \in \{1,2,\ldots,n\}. \tag{8}$$

Formulas (1) and (2) define the minimized functions. Eq. (3) specifies that there are K routes beginning at the depot. Eq. (4) expresses that every route starts and ends at the depot. Eq. (5) assures that every customer is visited only once by a single vehicle. Eq. (6) defines the capacity constraints. Eqs. (7)–(8) concern the time windows. Altogether, eqs. (3)–(8) define the feasible solutions to the VRPTW.
Lenstra and Rinnooy Kan (24) proved that the VRP and the VRPTW are NP-hard discrete optimization problems.

3. Sequential simulated annealing

The algorithm of simulated annealing which can be regarded as a variant of local search was first introduced by Metropolis et al. (25), and then used to optimization problems by Kirkpatrick, Gellat and Vecchi (23), and Cěrny (10). A comprehensive introduction to the subject can be found in Reeves (27) and Azencott (5).
Let $C\colon S \mapsto \mathbb{R}$ be a cost function which is to be minimized, defined on some finite solution set (search space) S. Let $N(X)$, $N(X) \subset S$, be a set of neighbors of solution X for each $X \in S$. Usually the sets $N(X)$ are small subsets of S. For the VRPTW the members of $N(X)$ are constructed by moving one or more customers among the routes of solution X. The way in which these sets are created influences substantially the accuracy of results obtained by a simulated annealing algorithm. While constructing the sets $N(X)$ we make sure that their members are built through deep modifications of X. Let R be a transition probability matrix, such that $R(X,Y) > 0$ if and only if $Y \in N(X)$. Let (T_i), $i = 0, 1, \ldots$ be a sequence of positive numbers, called the temperatures of annealing, such that $T_i \geq T_{i+1}$ and $\lim_{i\to\infty} T_i = 0$. The sequence (T_i) is called the cooling schedule, and a sequence of annealing steps within which the temperature of annealing stays constant is called the cooling stage. Consider the sequential annealing algorithm for constructing a sequence (or chain) of solutions (X_i), $X_i \in S$, defined as follows. An initial solution X_0 is computed using e.g. some heuristics. Given the current solution X_i, a potential next solution Y_i is chosen from set $N(X_i)$ with probability $R(X_i,Y_i)$. Then in a single annealing step solution X_{i+1} is set as follows (cf. Fig. 2):

$$X_{i+1} = \begin{cases} Y_i & \text{if } C(Y_i) \leq C(X_i), \\ Y_i & \text{with probability } p_i, \text{ if } C(Y_i) > C(X_i), \\ X_i & \text{otherwise,} \end{cases}$$

where

$$p_i = \exp(-(C(Y_i) - C(X_i))/T_i). \tag{9}$$

If X_{i+1} is set to Y_i and $C(Y_i) > C(X_i)$, then we say that an uphill move is carried out. Eq. (9) implies that uphill moves are performed more often when temperature T_i is high. When T_i is close to zero uphill moves occur sporadically. Simulated annealing can be described formally by non-homogeneous Markov chains. In these chains the probability of moving from one state to another depends not only on these states but also on the temperature of annealing.
A solution $X \in S$ is said to be a local minimum of the cost function C, if $C(X) \leq C(Y)$ for all $Y \in N(X)$, and to be a global minimum of C, if $C(X) = \inf_{Y \in S} C(Y)$. Let S_{min} be the set of global minima of C. We say that the process of simulated annealing converges, if $\lim_{i \to \infty} P(X_i \in S_{\text{min}}) = 1$. It was proved (21) that the convergence is guaranteed by the logarithmic cooling schedules of the form: $T_i \geq \frac{R}{\log(i+1)}$ for some constant R which depends on the cost function landscape. It was also shown (5; 9) that for the logarithmic cooling schedules the speed of convergence is given by:

$$P(X_i \notin S_{\text{min}}) \sim \left(\frac{K}{i}\right)^{\alpha} \tag{10}$$

for i large enough, where $K > 0$ and $\alpha > 0$ are suitable constants. Both constants are connected to the cost function landscape, and for large solution spaces constant K is very large and constant α is very small (5; 9). This implies that the process of simulated annealing converges very slowly. According to Eq. (10) a global minimum is attained only if the process of annealing is infinite. For this reason the question of how to accelerate simulated annealing by making use of parallelism is crucial.
In the sequential simulated annealing algorithm to solve the VRPTW, the chain (X_i) is constructed in two phases. The goal of phase 1 is to minimize the number of routes of the VRPTW solution, whereas phase 2 minimizes the total length of the routes. However in phases 1 and 2 it may happen that both the number of routes and the total length of routes are reduced. The cost of solution X_i in phase 1 is computed as: $C_1(X_i) = c_1 N + c_2 D + c_3(r_1 - \bar{r})$, and in phase 2 as: $C_2(X_i) = c_1 N + c_2 D$, where N is the number of routes (vehicles) of solution X_i, D – the total travel distance of the routes, r_1 – the number of customers of a randomly chosen route which is to be shorten and perhaps eliminated from the current solution, $\bar{r}$ – the average number of customers in all routes, c_1, c_2, c_3 – some constants. For simplicity, instead of the logarithmic an exponential cooling schedule is used, i.e. the temperature of annealing is decreased as $T_{k+1} = \beta_f T_k$, for $k = 0, 1, \ldots, a_f$, and some constants β_f ($\beta_f < 1$) and a_f ($f = 1$ and 2 denote phase 1 and 2).

4. Parallel simulated annealing algorithm

4.1 Independent searches

In the parallel algorithm of independent searches (IS), p independent simulated annealing processes $\mathcal{P}_0, \mathcal{P}_1, \ldots, \mathcal{P}_{p-1}$ are executed. Every process performs its computations like in the sequential algorithm. On completion, the processes pass their best solutions found to the master process, which selects the best solution among solutions it received. This solution constitutes the final result of the IS algorithm.
More formally, suppose that i steps of sequential simulated annealing is taken. Then in parallel IS, p annealing chains of $z = i/p$ steps each are executed. As the result p terminal solutions $\{X_{z,0}, X_{z,1}, \ldots, X_{z,p-1}\}$ are computed, from which the final solution Y_i is selected by: $Y_i = X_{z,0} \otimes X_{z,1} \otimes \ldots \otimes X_{z,p-1}$, where $\otimes$ is the operator of choosing the better solution with respect

to the total length of routes[1]. In terms of convergence we have (5):

$$P(Y_i \notin S_{\min}) = \prod_{0 \le j \le p-1} P(X_{z,j} \notin S_{\min}). \tag{11}$$

Assuming that each simulated annealing chain j of z steps converges at speed determined by Eq. 10: $P(X_{z,j} \notin S_{\min}) \sim \left(\frac{K}{z}\right)^{\alpha}$, we get (5):

$$P(Y_i \notin S_{\min}) \sim \left(\frac{Kp}{i}\right)^{\alpha p}. \tag{12}$$

Consider a chain of $i = 10^7$ steps of sequential simulated annealing, and let $K = 100$ and $\alpha = 0.01$. Then according to Eq. 10 the speed of convergence is equal $\left(\frac{K}{i}\right)^{\alpha} \approx 0.89$. If one uses $p = 5, 10, 15$ and 20 processes, then by Eq. (12) the speeds of convergence of IS are: $\left(\frac{Kp}{i}\right)^{\alpha p} \approx 0.61$, 0.40, 0.27 and 0.18, respectively. Thus the parallel independent searches converge much faster than the sequential algorithm.

4.2 Co-operating searches

The parallel algorithm of co-operating searches (CS) executes in the form of p processes $\mathcal{P}_0, \mathcal{P}_1, \ldots, \mathcal{P}_{p-1}$ (Figs. 1-3). A process generates its own annealing chain divided into two phases (lines 6–19 in Fig. 1). A phase consists of a number of cooling stages, and a cooling stage consists of a number of annealing steps. The processes co-operate with each other every ω annealing step passing their best solutions found to date (lines 12–16 in Fig. 1, and Fig. 3). The chain of annealing steps of process $\mathcal{P}_0$ is entirely independent (Fig. 4). The chain of process $\mathcal{P}_1$ is updated at steps $u\omega$, $u = 1, 2, \ldots, u_{\mathrm{m}}$, to the better solution between the best solutions found by processes $\mathcal{P}_0$ and $\mathcal{P}_1$ to date. Similarly, process $\mathcal{P}_2$ chooses as the next point in its chain the better solution between its own best and the one obtained from process $\mathcal{P}_1$. Thus the best solution found by process $\mathcal{P}_l$ is piped down for further enhancement to processes $\mathcal{P}_{l+1} \cdots \mathcal{P}_{p-1}$. Clearly, after step $u_m\omega$ process $\mathcal{P}_{p-1}$ holds the best solution X_b found by all the processes. To our best knowledge the speed of convergence of co-operating searches given e.g. by equations similar to Eq. (10) and (12) are not known.

As mentioned before, the temperature of annealing decreases according to the equation $T_{k+1} = \beta_f T_k$ for $k = 0, 1, 2, \ldots, a_f$, where a_f is the number of cooling stages. In this work we investigate two cases in establishing the points of process co-operation with respect to temperature drops. In the first case, of regular co-operation, processes interact at the end of each cooling stage ($\omega = L$) (lines 12–13 in Fig. 1). The number of annealing steps executed within a cooling stage is set to $L = (5E)/p$, where $E = 10^5$ is a constant established experimentally, and $p = 5$, 10, 15 and 20, is the number of processes (line 3 in Fig. 1). Such an arrangement keeps the parallel cost of the algorithms constant when different numbers of processes are used, provided the co-operation costs are neglected. Therefore in this case as the number of processes becomes larger, the length of cooling stages goes down, what means that the frequency of co-operation increases. In the second case, of rare co-operation, the frequency is constant and the processes exchange their solutions every $\omega = E$ annealing step (lines 14–15 in Fig. 1). For the number of processes $p = 10$, 15 and 20, the co-operation takes place after 2, 3 and 4 temperature drops, respectively.

[1] In this analysis it is assumed that each chain achieves a solution with the minimum (best known) number of routes.

```
parfor P_j, j = 0, 1, ..., p − 1 do
  Set co-operation mode to regular or rare depending on a test set;
  L := (5E)/p; {establish the length of a cooling stage; E = 10^5}
  Create the initial_solution using some heuristics;
  current_solution_j := initial_solution; best_solution_j := initial_solution;
  for f := 1 to 2 do {execute phase 1 and 2}
    {beginning of phase f}
    T := T_{0,f}; {initial temperature of annealing}
    repeat {a cooling stage}
      for i := 1 to L do
        annealing_step_f(current_solution_j, best_solution_j);
      end for;
      if (f = 1) or (co-operation mode is regular) then {ω = L}
        co_operation;
      else {rare co-operation: ω = E}
        Call co_operation procedure every E annealing step
          counting from the beginning of the phase;
      end if;
      T := β_f T; {temperature reduction}
    until a_f cooling stages are executed;
    {end of phase f}
  end for;
end parfor;
Produce best_solution_{p−1} as the solution to the VRPTW;
```

Fig. 1. Parallel simulated annealing algorithm of co-operating searches

```
procedure annealing_step_f(current_solution, best_solution);
  Create new_solution as a neighbor to current_solution
    (the way this step is executed depends on f);
  δ := C_f(new_solution) − C_f(current_solution);
  Generate random x uniformly in the range (0, 1);
  if (δ < 0) or (x < e^{−δ/T}) then
    current_solution := new_solution;
    if C_f(new_solution) < C_f(best_solution) then
      best_solution := new_solution;
    end if;
  end if;
end annealing_step_f;
```

Fig. 2. Annealing step procedure

The exchange of solutions between processes can be considered as exploitation of the search results, whereas exploration takes place when a process penetrates the search space freely. Let us call a sequence of ω annealing steps executed by a process between points of co-operation as a chain of free exploration. Taking into account Eq. (10) the longer these chains the better.

```
procedure co_operation;
  if j = 0 then Send best_solution_0 to process P_1;
  else {j > 0}
    receive best_solution_{j-1} from process P_{j-1};
    if C_f(best_solution_{j-1}) < C_f(best_solution_j) then
      best_solution_j := best_solution_{j-1};
      current_solution_j := best_solution_{j-1};
    end if;
    if j < p - 1 then Send best_solution_j to process P_{j+1}; end if;
  end if;
end co_operation;
```

Fig. 3. Procedure of co-operation of processes

$$
X_0 \rightarrow \left\{
\begin{array}{ccccccccccc}
X_0^{(0)} & \rightarrow & X_0^{(\omega)} & \rightarrow & X_0^{(2\omega)} & \rightarrow & \bullet & \bullet & \rightarrow & X_0^{(u_m\omega)} & \\
 & & \downarrow & & \downarrow & & & & & \downarrow & \\
X_1^{(0)} & \rightarrow & X_1^{(\omega)} & \rightarrow & X_1^{(2\omega)} & \rightarrow & \bullet & \bullet & \rightarrow & X_1^{(u_m\omega)} & \\
 & & \downarrow & & \downarrow & & & & & \downarrow & \\
\bullet & & \bullet & & \bullet & & \bullet & \bullet & & \bullet & \\
\bullet & & \bullet & & \bullet & & \bullet & \bullet & & \bullet & \\
X_{p-2}^{(0)} & \rightarrow & X_{p-2}^{(\omega)} & \rightarrow & X_{p-2}^{(2\omega)} & \rightarrow & \bullet & \bullet & \rightarrow & X_{p-2}^{(u_m\omega)} & \\
 & & \downarrow & & \downarrow & & & & & \downarrow & \\
X_{p-1}^{(0)} & \rightarrow & X_{p-1}^{(\omega)} & \rightarrow & X_{p-1}^{(2\omega)} & \rightarrow & \bullet & \bullet & \rightarrow & X_{p-1}^{(u_m\omega)} & \rightarrow \; X_b
\end{array}
\right.
$$

Fig. 4. Scheme of co-operation of processes (X_0 – initial solution; X_b – best solution among the processes)

Note that due to co-operation, a process after having completed a chain with solution X, may be forced to explore the search space from a—probably more promising—solution different from X. In order to obtain good results during parallel search the proper balance between exploitation and exploration has to be maintained.

A series of experiments was carried out in order to establish how the number of processes, the length of chains of free exploration, and the frequency of processes co-operation influence the accuracy of solutions to the VRPTW (16). For the experiments, 39 out of 56 benchmarking tests[2] elaborated by Solomon (33) were used. The tests are grouped into three major problem sets named R, C and RC. The geographical coordinates for customers in sets R, C and RC are generated randomly, in a clustered manner, and as a mix of random and clustered structures, respectively. Each of these sets is divided into two subsets, R1, R2, C1, C2, RC1, RC2. The subsets R1, C1 and RC1 have short time windows and permit relatively large numbers of routes (between 9 and 19) in the solutions. The time windows for subsets R2, C2 and RC2 are wider allowing less routes (between 2 and 4) in the solutions. Every test involves 100 customers and the distances are measured using Euclidean metric. It is assumed that travel times are equal to the corresponding distances.

[2] The tests in set C are easy to solve, so they were omitted in the experiments.

In the series of the experiments, the IS and CS algorithms[3] were executed at least 1000 times for each test, a given number of processes p, a number of annealing steps L_2 fixed for it, and a period of communication ω. Based on each sample of results[4] the average of total travel distances of routes $\bar{y}$ and the standard deviation s were calculated. The experiments showed that depending on the test instance, the minimum of the mean value $\bar{y}$ appeared for different values of parameters p, L_2 and ω. E.g. the minimum of $\bar{y}$ for test R101 was obtained for $p = 20$ and $L_2 = \omega = E/4$ (Table **??**). Whether these specific values of parameters give

p	L_2	ω	R101	R102	R103	R104	R105	R106
5	E	E	13.9	17.6	11.4	0.8	1.1	10.6
10	$E/2$	$E/2$	6.5	11.6	3.9	0.5	0.1	5.3
15	$E/3$	$E/3$	1.4	3.3	min	0.7	2.3	2.1
20	$E/4$	$E/4$	min*	min*	0.6*	min	0.3	min
10	$E/2$	E	10.3	13.6	5.5	0.7	1.4	6.7
15	$E/3$	E	15.3	19.9	9.7	1.1	1.0	3.0
20	$E/4$	E	13.8	20.1	8.8	0.6*	min*	0.9*
p	L_2	ω	R107	R108	R109	R110	R111	R112
5	E	E	0.8	1.0	min*	min*	0.3	1.2
10	$E/2$	$E/2$	min	0.1	6.5	3.2	min	1.1
15	$E/3$	$E/3$	1.1	min	6.7	3.7	1.4	min
20	$E/4$	$E/4$	0.7*	1.2*	10.4	5.3	1.9*	0.8
10	$E/2$	E	1.9	1.5	4.1	2.7	1.5	1.6
15	$E/3$	E	3.1	2.7	8.8	3.6	3.0	0.7
20	$E/4$	E	4.6	4.2	10.3	5.5	3.6	1.3*

Table 1. Values of test statistic Z for CS algorithm and set R1;'*' marks the best choice of parameters p, L_2 and ω

statistically superior results can be proved by testing the hypotheses $H_0 : \mu_i \leq \mu_m$ versus an alternative hypothesis $H_a : \mu_i > \mu_m$, where μ denotes the mean value of a population of total travel distances of routes; i – populations whose samples have worse mean values (e.g. cases $p = 5$ and $L_2 = \omega = E$; $p = 10$ and $L_2 = \omega = E/2$; etc. for test R101); m – a population for which the minimum mean value of a sample was observed (i.e. case $p = 20$ and $L_2 = \omega = E/4$ for test R101). In the cases where H_0 are rejected one can claim that their values of parameters p, L_2 and ω give inferior solutions with respect to the values for which $\bar{y} = \bar{y}_{\min}$ occur, or equivalently, the population with $\bar{y} = \bar{y}_{\min}$ comprises superior solutions as compared to other

[3] It was observed (15) that for some Solomon's tests the probability of finding a solution with the minimum number of routes was very low. Therefore phase 1 of the algorithms was executed in the CS fashion with $a_1 = 50$ cooling stages and $L_1 = 10^5$ annealing steps in each stage. In phase 2 the IS and CS modes were used with $a_2 = 100$ and L_2 depending on the number of processes. The following values of parameters were fixed: $c_1 = 40000$, $c_2 = 1$, $c_3 = 50$, $\beta_1 = 0.95$, $\beta_2 = 0.98$.

[4] For some tests the size of the sample was smaller than 1000, since only solutions with the minimum number of routes were considered.

A.	p	L_2	ω	R109	R110	R202	RC102	RC104	RC108	RC202
	5	E	–	2.1*	2.7	5.6	2.4	3.0	min*	3.3
IS	10	$E/2$	–	2.9	4.8	9.4	4.0	6.5	8.5	4.4
	15	$E/3$	–	6.8	6.5	12.0	5.2	11.1	13.6	3.6
	20	$E/4$	–	8.8	9.5	13.1	6.3	11.7	20.3	4.5
	5	E	E	min	min*	min*	min	min*	2.4	min*
CS	10	$E/2$	$E/2$	6.5	3.2	7.2	0.8*	2.7	7.1	4.0
	15	$E/3$	$E/3$	6.7	3.7	10.4	3.4	5.2	12.1	6.7
	20	$E/4$	$E/4$	10.4	5.3	12.8	4.1	8.2	15.2	8.2
	10	$E/2$	E	4.1	2.7	4.7	5.3	3.3	5.1	2.5
CS	15	$E/3$	E	8.8	3.6	7.8	3.5	6.2	10.4	3.4
	20	$E/4$	E	10.3	5.5	9.7	4.3	6.8	13.6	3.9

Table 2. Values of test statistic Z for IS and CS algorithms

populations. For the test statistic:

$$Z = \frac{\bar{y}_i - \bar{y}_m}{\sqrt{\frac{s_i^2}{n_i} + \frac{s_m^2}{n_m}}}$$

the hypotheses H_0 are rejected at the $\alpha = 0.01$ significance level, if $Z > Z_{0.01} = 2.33$ (n_i and n_m are numbers of experiments over which s_i and s_m values are calculated). Table **??** shows the values of Z for set R1 (results for sets R2, RC1 and RC2 are reported in (16)), where min indicates values of p, L_2 and ω which give the minimum of $\bar{y}$. The framed values denote rejections of hypotheses H_0, what means that for the corresponding values of parameters p, L_2 and ω, the results of statistically worse total travel distances of routes are achieved. It can be seen that the values of Z for test R101 and parameters $p = 15$, $L_2 = \omega = E/3$, and $p = 20$, $L_2 = \omega = E/4$, are less than 2.33. So it is justified to claim that these values of parameters give statistically the best solutions to the VRPTW. In other words, using $p = 20$ or 15 processes co-operating after every cooling stage enable us to obtain quickly solutions of the best accuracy. It follows from the experiments (16) that for most Solomon's tests the results of high accuracy can be achieved by making use of $p = 20$ processes. The exceptions are tests R109, R110, R202, RC102, RC104, RC108 and RC202. For these tests the minimum of $\bar{y}$ occurs when $p = 5$ and most of other numbers of processes yield statistically worse results. As already indicated, to keep the cost of parallel computations constant, the number of annealing steps taken by processes between points of co-operation was decreased along with an increase of the number of processes. The results of the experiments prove that for the tests listed above the execution of shorter annealing chains of free exploration of length from $L_2 = E/4$ to $L_2 = E/2$ are not compensated—in terms of accuracy—by the co-operation between processes.

The annealing chains of free exploration are substantially longer in the algorithm of independent searches (IS), in which the processes do not co-operate and execute chains as long as $L_2 = Ea_2$, where a_2 is the fixed number of cooling stages[5]. Table 2 compares the results obtained by the IS and CS algorithms for the specific tests mentioned above. It can be seen that an increase of the length of chains and lack of co-operation in the IS algorithm, make

[5] Note that altogether each process of the IS and CS algorithms executes $a_1 + a_2$ cooling stages.

the results worse for tests R110, R202, RC104 and RC202. Applying the IS algorithm—of low communication cost—can be justified only for tests R109 and RC108.
Considering the results of the experiments and the objective of computing good quality solutions to the VRPTW in a short time, Solomon's tests can be divided into 3 groups:

I – tests which can be solved quickly (e.g. using $p = 20$ processes) to good accuracy with rare co-operation ($\omega = E$). To this group belong 24 tests, out of 39, not listed in groups II and III specified below.

II – tests which can be solved quickly (e.g. with $p = 20$) but the co-operation should take place after every cooling stage (we call this co-operation regular) (e.g. $\omega = E/4$ for $p = 20$) to achieve good accuracy of solutions. This group comprises 8 tests: R101, R102, R103, R107, R108, R111, R207 and RC105.

III – tests whose solving cannot be accelerated as much as for the tests in groups I and II. The solutions of best accuracy are obtained for less than $p = 20$ processes[6]. To this group belong 7 tests: R109, R110, R202, RC102, RC104, RC108 and RC202.

5. Fitness landscape

5.1 Basic definitions

Let C, S and $N(X)$ be a cost function, a search space and a set of neighbors of solution X, respectively, as defined in section 3. A solution $X^o \in S$ is said to be a local minimum of function C, if $C(X^o) \leq C(Y)$ for all $Y \in N(X^o)$, and to be a global minimum X^* of C, if $C(X^*) = \inf_{Y \in S} C(Y)$. In evolutionary optimization function C is often called the fitness and the associated landscape a fitness landscape. More formally (29), a landscape $\mathcal{L}$ for the function C is a triple $\mathcal{L} = (S, C, d)$ where d denotes a distance measure $d\colon S \times S \mapsto \mathbb{R}^+ \cup \{\infty\}$ which for any solutions $P, Q, R \in S$ satisfies the conditions: $d(P,Q) \geq 0$, $d(P,Q) = 0 \Leftrightarrow P = Q$ and $d(P,R) \leq d(P,Q) + d(Q,R)$. If d is symmetric, i.e. $d(P,Q) = d(Q,P)$ for all $P, Q \in S$ then d is a metric on space S.
Discrete optimization can be performed by neighborhood search where the process of searching starts at some initial solution and converges to a local optimum, or an attractor. The searching process is described by a function $\mu\colon S \mapsto S^o$, where $X \in S$ is an initial solution and $\mu(X)$ is the optimum that it reaches (29). A basin of attraction of solution X^o is the set $B(X^o) = \{X\colon \mu(X) = X^o\}$. The set contains the initial solutions from which the search leads to a specified attractor. The basins of attraction for a given function are not unique. They depend on a method adopted for landscape exploration and can be established only if the method is deterministic. Therefore the notion of the basin is of limited use for methods with a good deal of randomization, like simulated annealing.

5.2 Statistical measures of fitness landscape

The nature of a fitness landscape can be unveiled either by mathematical analysis or by gathering some statistical data during the process of searching it. In this work we follow the latter approach. Several statistical measures have been proposed in the literature. Weinberger (36) observed that some characteristics could be obtained from a random walk. Let C_t be the fitness of the solution visited at time t. Then the autocorrelation function of the landscape during

[6] There are two open questions here: whether less than $p = 5$ processes could give solutions of better accuracy for some tests in group III, and whether finding solutions for tests in groups I-II can be speeded up even further by making use of more than $p = 20$ processes with no loss of solutions accuracy.

a random walk of length T is:

$$a_j = \frac{\sum_{t=1}^{T-j}(C_t - \bar{C})(C_{t+j} - \bar{C})}{\sum_{t=1}^{T}(C_t - \bar{C})^2}$$

where $\bar{C}$ is the mean fitness of the T solutions visited, and j is the lag. For smooth landscapes, with neighbor solutions of similar fitness, and small lags, the values of a_j are close to 1. As the lag increases the values of autocorrelation are likely to diminish. The values of a_j are close to zero at all lags for rugged landscapes, where close solutions have unrelated fitness.
A useful indicator of the difficulty of an optimization problem is the number of optima appearing in a corresponding landscape. Indeed, the more optima in the landscape, the harder is to find the global optimum. Suppose that for a given optimization problem the search is restarted r times with random initial solutions. Most likely these solutions lay in different basins of attraction, so as the result of the search a number of different local solutions k, $k \leq r$, will be found. Based on the values of r and k one may estimate the number of optima ν present in a given landscape. Assuming that the probability of encountering each solution is the same, it is easy to show that the random variable K which takes the number of distinct solutions in a series of r independent searches has the Arfwedson distribution (28):

$$P[K = k] = \frac{\nu!}{(\nu - k)!\,\nu^r} rk \qquad (13)$$

where $1 \leq k \leq \min(r, \nu)$, with the mean:

$$\mathrm{E}K = \nu[1 - (1 - 1/\nu)^r]. \qquad (14)$$

After having measured $\mathrm{E}K$ one can solve numerically Eq. (14) and find an estimate for $\hat{\nu}$. Reeves (28) gives an approximation of it as: $\hat{\nu} \approx (\bar{K}^2 - r)/(2(r - \bar{K}))$, where $\bar{K}$ is a measured estimation of $\mathrm{E}K$. When the value of ν is small one may ask how many searches W should be done to be sure with some certainty that all optima have been found. The waiting time W_k for the $(k+1)$th solution provided that k of them have been already found has a geometric distribution, and the mean of the waiting time for ν solutions is (28):

$$\mathrm{E}W \approx \nu(\ln \nu + \gamma) \qquad (15)$$

where $\gamma \approx 0.577$ is Euler's constant. The formulas (13)–(15) are derived under the assumption that the probability of encountering each solution is the same, or in other words that solutions are isotropically distributed in the landscape. Unfortunately in many optimization problems, also in the VRPTW, this assumption is not valid.

5.3 Experimental study

The objective of the study was to gather statistical data concerning the fitness landscapes for 39 (out of 56) VRPTW tests by Solomon.

Fitness landscape characteristics

In the course of experiments the parallel simulated annealing algorithm was executed at least 4200 times (see column Exp. in Table 4) for each test in sets R and RC. The VRPTW is a two-objective optimization problem in which both, the number of routes and the total travel distance, should be minimized. For the landscape studies only solutions with the minimum

number of routes were taken into account. Most of Solomon's tests are relatively easy to solve with respect to the first objective function (the exceptions are tests R104, R112, RC101, RC105, and RC106, see paragraph "Difficulty of test instances"). The minimum number of routes for each test is generally known. Since the VRPTW problem is NP-hard, there is some probability that these numbers are not global minima. However for simplicity, we shall name them as 'minima' instead of 'known minima'.
Table 3 contains the histograms of numbers of solutions[7] produced by the algorithm with the total travel distance y worse by 0-1%, 1-2% etc. than the distance $y_{\min}$ of the best-known solution. The columns denoted by $\bar{\tau}$ and $\tau_{\max}$ show the values of $(\bar{y} - y_{\min})/y_{\min}$ and $(y_{\max} - y_{\min})/y_{\min}$, where $\bar{y}$ and $y_{\max}$ are the average and maximum total travel distances obtained for a given test, respectively. All values in Table 3 are expressed in per cents, and the tests are ordered according to 0-1% column. It can be seen e.g. for test R112 that there is 30% chance of getting a solution with distance y worse by 2-3% than $y_{\min}$. This is because the number of distinct solutions in terms of y for this test, discovered in ranges from 0-1% to >4% were 102, 149, 179, 89 and 81, respectively. Clearly, the distribution of solutions in the fitness landscape is not isotropic, i.e. they are not uniformly scattered across every direction in the search space. There exists a relatively large number of solutions with $y \in [1.02y_{\min}, 1.03y_{\min})$, what increases the probability that the algorithm will finish its computations at a local optimum with y in this range. Fig. 5 plots the distances d of a sample of solutions from the best solution found $X_{\min}$, against the total travel distances of solution routes[8]. As a metric for measuring the distance d between solutions we use the minimum number of customer movements among the routes necessary to convert one solution into another (see subsection 5.1). It was observed that the solutions of all VRPTW tests were not sampled with equal probability. For instance, the majority of solutions of test R112[9] were hit only a few times, but 5 solutions were reached at least 10 times (marked by white circles in Fig. 5). Most likely the sizes of basins of attraction of more popular solutions are larger, although the notion of such a basin is vague in the context of simulated annealing where random uphill moves may take place. The characteristics of the fitness landscape depend also on the search algorithm. Note that the solutions of test R112 reached most often (at least 10 times) are located in range 0-2%, i.e. range of good accuracy (Fig. 5), partly due to good convergence, as we believe, of the parallel algorithm which favors solutions of higher quality. In general, the shape of the landscape which is discovered is as good as thorough is an exploration of the landscape conducted by the algorithm. On the other hand, an excellent search algorithm can give a biased picture of the landscape, since the worse local optima are then found less frequently—if at all—than the better ones. Similar results to that of test R112 were obtained for other Solomon's tests characterized by "long histograms" (see columns 0-1% ...>4% of Table 3). For instance, the numbers of distinct solutions discovered for tests R211 and RC202 in ranges from 0-1% to >4% were 335, 1047, 926, 723, 1351 and 7349, 3105, 14281, 19246, 9027, respectively. The attractors (marked by white circles) were observed in ranges 0-3% (test R211) and 0-5% (test RC202) (Figs. 6–7).

[7] Note that each of these solutions is a local minimum to the VRPTW problem with respect to the total travel distance.

[8] Note that two separate series of experiments were conducted. In the first series the data contained in Tables 3-4 were gathered. The goal of the second series of experiments was to find, up to 700 best solutions to the selected VRPTW tests. The results of these experiments are depicted in Figs. 5-12.

[9] Overall 9200 executions of the algorithm were carried out for this test, 600 executions produced solutions with the number of routes equal 9, which is likely to be minimum, and 399 of these solutions were distinct.

Test	0-1 %	1-2 %	2-3 %	3-4 %	>4 %	$\bar{\tau}$	τ_{max}
R112	17	25	30	15	13	2.4	6.5
R110	45	21	18	7	9	1.6	11.4
R108	47	37	13	2	1	1.2	5.9
R107	61	37	2	0	0	0.8	7.7
R109	70	16	7	3	4	0.8	10.6
R111	72	6	13	5	4	0.9	10.3
R104	82	17	1	0	0	0.5	2.4
R106	91	9	0	0	0	0.6	1.8
R103	96	4	0	0	0	0.6	3.8
R102	100	0	0	0	0	0.4	1.0
R105	100	0	0	0	0	0.2	1.6
R101	100	0	0	0	0	0.1	0.5
R211	8	24	21	16	31	3.4	12.4
R207	25	26	11	20	18	2.4	11.4
R210	41	44	15	0	0	1.2	3.2
R203	56	43	1	0	0	0.9	3.4
R204	75	3	14	8	0	0.9	4.9
R208	77	23	0	0	0	0.6	2.9
R202	88	1	5	5	1	0.5	6.3
R209	97	3	0	0	0	0.2	2.5
R206	99	1	0	0	0	0.4	2.6
R201	100	0	0	0	0	0.1	1.3
R205	100	0	0	0	0	0.0	3.4
RC108	63	25	9	2	1	0.9	11.6
RC104	69	7	24	0	0	0.8	3.1
RC106	72	10	14	4	0	0.7	4.9
RC101	89	11	0	0	0	0.2	2.1
RC102	96	0	1	3	0	0.3	7.6
RC105	99	1	0	0	0	0.3	1.4
RC103	100	0	0	0	0	0.1	3.4
RC107	100	0	0	0	0	0.0	0.4
RC202	14	6	27	36	17	3.2	13.5
RC203	64	23	11	2	0	0.8	4.0
RC206	89	8	3	0	0	0.5	3.3
RC205	91	9	0	0	0	0.5	2.5
RC207	94	4	1	1	0	0.3	4.9
RC201	96	4	0	0	0	0.3	2.8
RC208	97	3	0	0	0	0.2	2.3
RC204	100	0	0	0	0	0.1	3.7

Table 3. Histograms of numbers of solutions in specified ranges 0-1%, 1-2%, ..., >4%, $\bar{\tau} = (\bar{y} - y_{min})/y_{min}$, $\tau_{max} = (y_{max} - y_{min})/y_{min}$ (all values in per cent; tests are ordered according to 0-1% column)

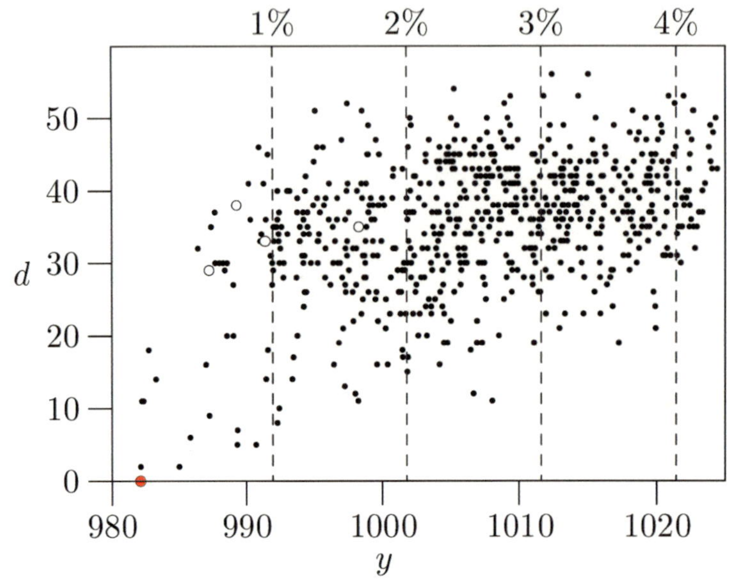

Fig. 5. Distance d from the best solution marked by a shaded circle vs. total travel distance y for test R112 (700 solutions, $X_{\min} = (N_{\min}, y_{\min}) = (9, 982.14)$, $N_{\min}$ is the minimum number of routes)

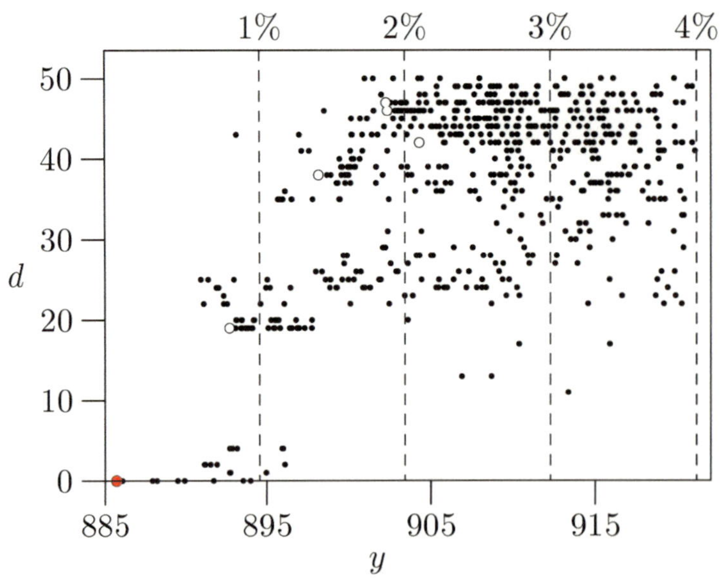

Fig. 6. Distance d from the best solution vs. total travel distance y for test R211 (700 solutions, $X_{\min} = (2, 885.71)$)

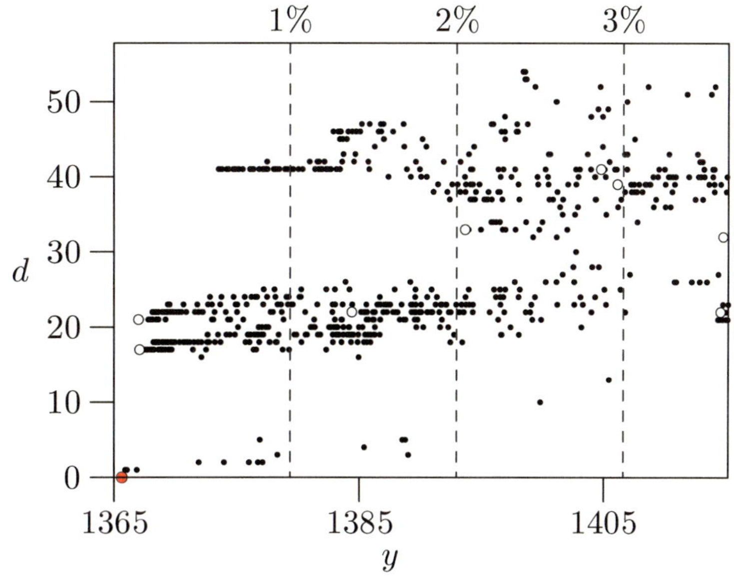

Fig. 7. Distance d from the best solution vs. total travel distance y for test RC202 (700 solutions, $X_{\min} = (3, 1365.64)$)

"Big valley" structure

Several experimental studies in discrete optimization revealed correlations among locations of local optima which suggest existence of a globally convex or "big valley" structures in the fitness landscapes (7). The experiments indicated that local optima are closer (in terms of distance d) to the global optimum than are random points in a search space. The local optima are also closer to each other and form a "big valley" structure with the best local (or global) optimum appearing in a center of the valley. The phenomenon can be illustrated by plotting a graph of fitness against average distance from all other optima. The graph in Fig. 8 shows that the best solution (marked by a shaded circle) has almost minimum distance $\bar{d}$ what implies it is located near the center of the valley. However this is not the case for the graphs in Figs. 9 and 10 where many local optima are much closer to the center than the best solution.

Approximate and exact solutions

Suppose that a hard optimization problem is to be solved. Then getting an approximate solution worse no more than by 0-1% with respect to the optimum can be considered as adequate. In such circumstances a good indicator of the problem difficulty is the value of $\bar{\tau} = (\bar{y} - y_{\min})/y_{\min}$ which exhibits the shift of the average cost $\bar{y}$ of solutions from $y_{\min}$ attained by solving the problem repeatedly. The value of $\tau_{\max} = (y_{\max} - y_{\min})/y_{\min}$ provides some insight into the depth of local optima. If $\bar{\tau} \leq 1\%$ is observed then a problem can be thought of as easy to solve. Assuming that 1% accuracy of solution approximation is acceptable, all VRPTW tests, except R112, R110, R108, R211, R207, R210 and RC202, can be classified as easy[10] (Table 3). Fig. 11 drawn for test R102 shows that all its 700 best solutions found, have their y values within 0.28% margin from $y_{\min}$, what indicates that the fitness landscape

[10] Remembering of course that they are instances of the NP-hard problem being solved by the advanced parallel algorithm.

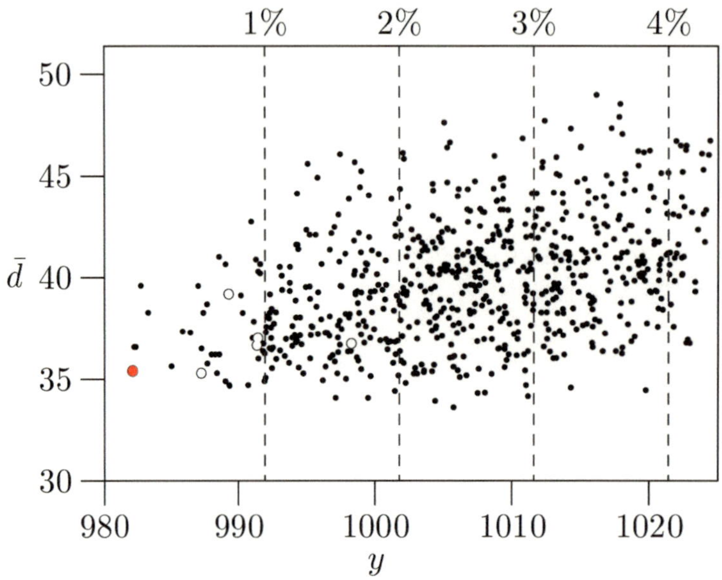

Fig. 8. Average solution distance $\bar{d}$ from the remaining 699 solutions vs. total travel distance y for test R112 (700 solutions)

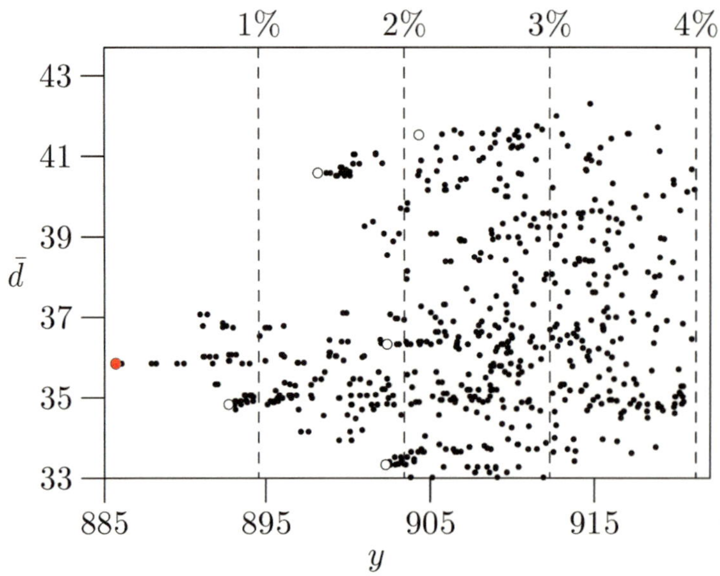

Fig. 9. Average solution distance $\bar{d}$ from the remaining 699 solutions vs. total travel distance y for test R211 (700 solutions)

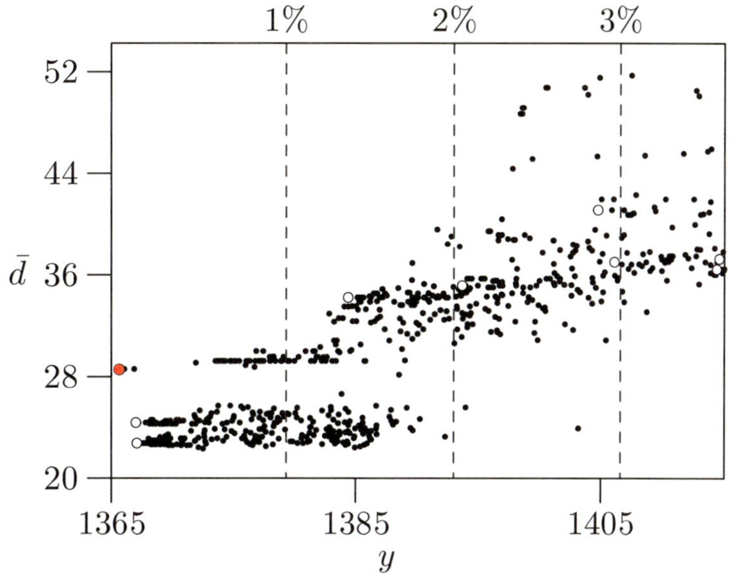

Fig. 10. Average solution distance $\bar{d}$ from the remaining 699 solutions vs. total travel distance y for test RC202 (700 solutions)

of this test is quite smooth. Thus test R102 can be ranked as easy to solve if an approximate solution is sought. However it turns out to be the hardest one in Solomon's set if the optimum is searched for. The smoothness of the landscape is an advantage if one wants to solve a problem with some limited accuracy. In the case when the absolute optimum is desired, the key role plays the number of local optima ν appearing in the landscape. For test R102 the number of these optima was as large as 44773. Table 4 contains the numbers of local optima unveiled for Solomon's tests in the first series of our experiments. Fig. 15 shows the plot of average $\bar{K}$ as a function of the number of unveiled optima ν (see subsection 5.1).

Difficulty of test instances

Since the VRPTW is a two-objective optimization problem, the difficulty of its instances can be estimated by probabilities P_1, P_2 and P_3 that after execution of a searching algorithm i) a solution with the minimum number of routes is found, ii) a solution with the minimum number of routes and minimum distance allowing 1% accuracy is found, and iii) the best-known solution is found, respectively (see Table 4, where $\bar{K}$ – average number of distinct solutions observed in a sample of series of $r = 100$ experiments, ν – number of local optima unveiled; Exp. – number of experiments conducted; $\bar{K}$ and ν are calculated over solutions with minimum number of routes; tests are ordered according to P_2 column). Note that probability P_2 is a product of P_1 and the value of the 1st column of Table 3 scaled to range $[0,1]$. The probability P_3 is counted as a ratio of the number of times the best-known solution is found to ν. If the best-known solution is not found, then probability P_3 is determined by considering the best solution obtained for a given test by the parallel algorithm, see http://sun.aei.polsl.pl/˜zjc/best-solutions.html. The hardest test to solve with 1% accuracy is R104 ($P_2 = 0.002$) and there are many easy tests in this respect, R101, R102, etc. As mentioned before, it is very difficult to solve test R102 to its optimality ($P_3 = 2 \cdot 10^{-5}$). The easy tests in this regard are R205 ($P_3 = 0.997$) and R105

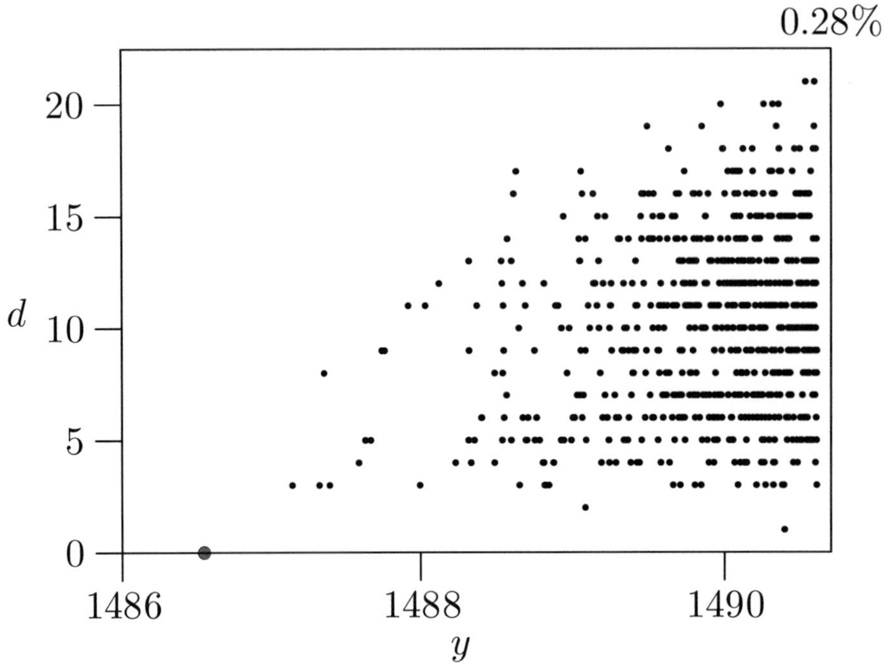

Fig. 11. Distance d from the best solution vs. total travel distance y for test R102 (700 solutions, $X_{\min} = (17, 1486.55)$)

($P_3 = 0.559$). As can be seen in Fig. 12 there are many solutions of test R105 located at small distances d from the minimum. Clearly, such a dense distribution of good quality solutions surrounding the optimum one, facilitates the gradual improvements of the configuration of a current solution during the process of simulated annealing. In contrast, there are not many neighbor solutions close to the minima for tests R112, R211, RC202 and R102 (see Figs. 5-7 and Fig. 11). Each of these minima belongs to a "small valley" of solutions which occurs away from the "big valley" structure. As the result, reaching those minima from an arbitrary initial solution by a process of small enhancements is not easy, and sometimes not possible at all.
The plots in Fig. 13 and 14 show the difficulty of 39 tests by Solomon. For the tests: R104, R112, RC101, RC105, RC106, both probabilities (P_1, P_2 in Fig. 13, and P_1, P_3 in Fig. 14) are less than 0.5. Thus these tests can be classified as the most difficult to solve in Solomon's set.

Taking advantage of landscape properties

In this paragraph we ponder how the features of the fitness landscape can be exploited to improve the performance of the parallel simulated annealing algorithm solving the VRPTW problem. Boese et al. (7) proposed an adaptive multi-start algorithm for the traveling salesman problem. It consists of two phases. In the first, initial phase, a set of R random local minima is computed. In the second phase, which is executed a specified number of times, based on the k ($k \leq R$) best local minima found so far, an adaptive starting solution is constructed. This solution is then improved A times using the greedy descent algorithm, what results in a set of $k + A$ local minima. From this set, the k best minima are selected, a new adaptive starting solution is formed, and the second phase is repeated. An adaptive starting solution is created

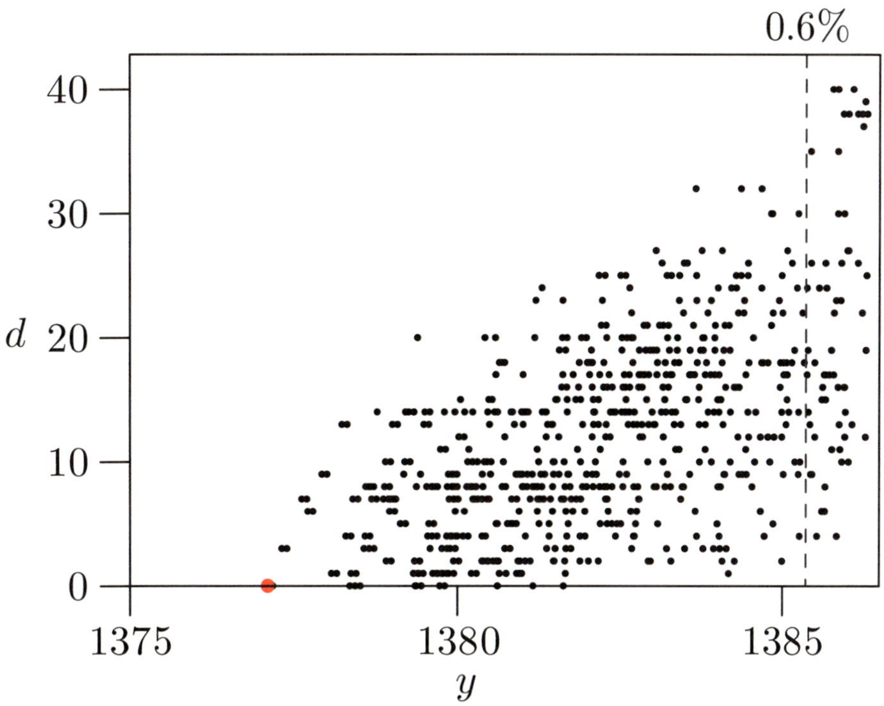

Fig. 12. Distance d from the best solution vs. total travel distance y for test R105 (700 solutions, $X_{\min} = (14, 1377.11)$)

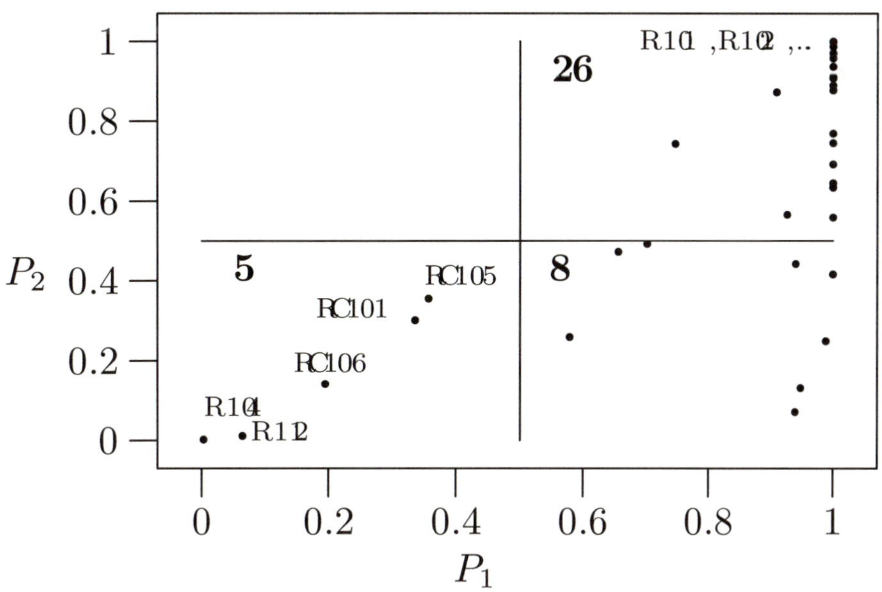

Fig. 13. Difficulty of tests measured by probabilities P_1 and P_2 (1% approximate solution is desired)

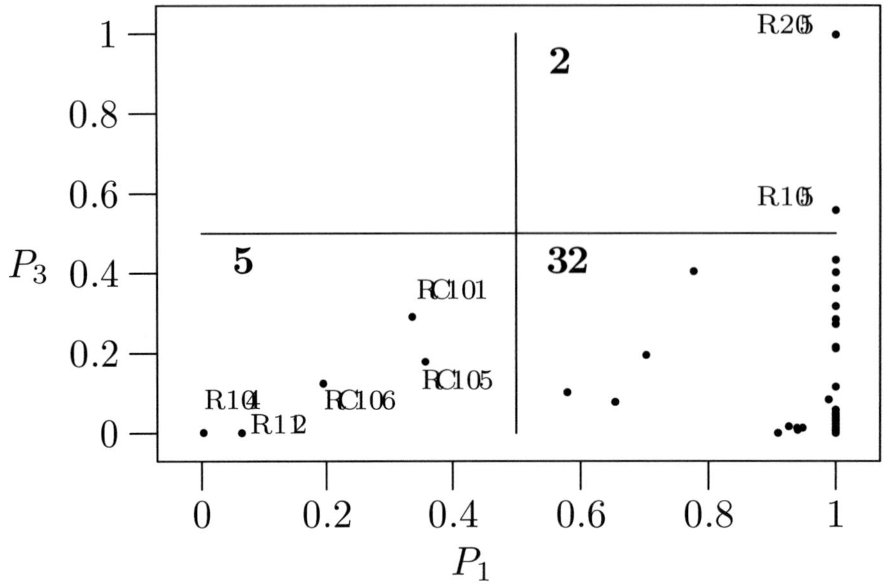

Fig. 14. Difficulty of tests measured by probabilities P_1 and P_3 (best solution is desired)

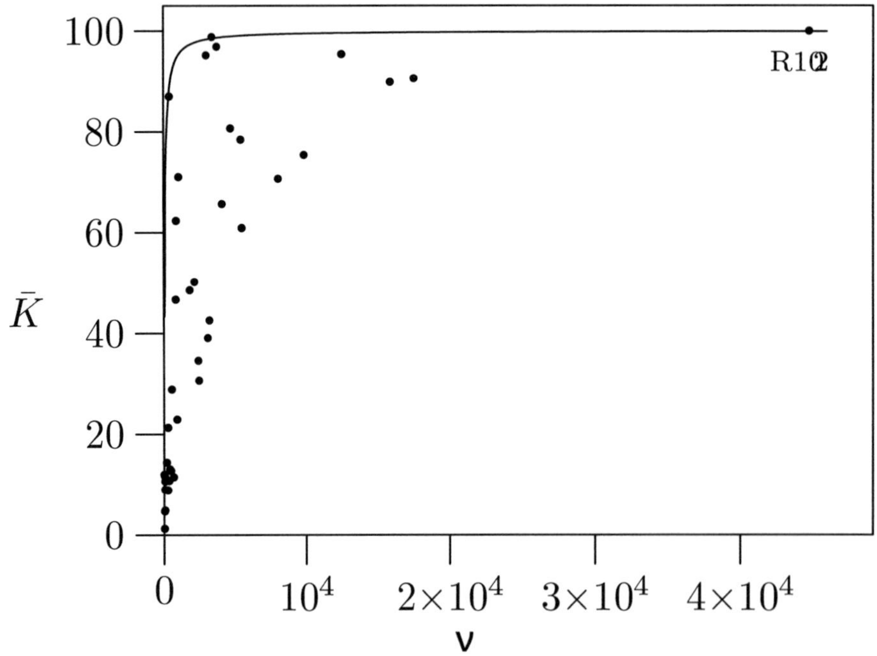

Fig. 15. Average number of distinct solutions $\bar{K}$ observed in a sample of series of $r = 100$ experiments vs. number of unveiled local optima ν for 39 Solomon's tests (for reference, solid line plots Eq. 14)

Test	P_1	P_2	P_3	$\bar{K}$	ν	Exp.
R104	0.003	0.002	0.001	12.00	15	41600
R112	0.065	0.011	$7 \cdot 10^{-4}$	87.00	399	9200
R110	0.579	0.259	0.102	60.91	5486	60600
R108	0.940	0.442	0.008	95.20	2971	4900
R111	0.654	0.472	0.078	65.73	4106	38700
R109	0.703	0.492	0.195	30.61	2435	61400
R107	0.926	0.566	0.017	80.67	4705	19400
R103	0.909	0.873	$2 \cdot 10^{-4}$	98.83	3384	4500
R106	1.000	0.908	0.008	90.57	17523	72200
R105	1.000	0.999	0.559	14.40	185	9100
R101	1.000	1.000	0.006	95.41	12488	56000
R102	1.000	1.000	$2 \cdot 10^{-5}$	99.98	44773	48600
R211	0.939	0.071	0.013	71.07	1028	4700
R207	0.989	0.249	0.084	78.44	5420	23300
R210	1.000	0.416	0.058	70.71	8031	68400
R203	1.000	0.559	0.006	96.91	3734	5300
R204	1.000	0.745	0.216	48.60	1789	10400
R208	1.000	0.769	0.008	75.41	9850	71100
R202	1.000	0.878	0.402	39.11	3070	37200
R209	1.000	0.970	0.433	21.31	279	4200
R206	1.000	0.987	0.049	62.34	854	4400
R205	1.000	0.998	0.997	1.28	36	36500
R201	1.000	1.000	0.317	10.69	72	4500
RC106	0.195	0.141	0.124	11.68	45	22700
RC101	0.336	0.300	0.291	4.91	70	33300
RC105	0.357	0.355	0.178	9.00	69	8900
RC108	1.000	0.634	0.285	42.60	3192	46800
RC104	1.000	0.692	0.031	89.85	15842	40100
RC102	0.777	0.743	0.404	11.51	664	76800
RC103	1.000	1.000	0.022	46.73	823	17700
RC107	1.000	1.000	0.036	4.72	46	15600
RC202	0.948	0.131	0.013	34.55	2387	56000
RC203	1.000	0.645	0.043	50.23	2121	25600
RC206	1.000	0.890	0.273	10.79	351	27800
RC205	1.000	0.911	0.115	22.92	904	42100
RC207	1.000	0.937	0.212	8.89	270	22000
RC201	1.000	0.958	0.362	12.77	472	50100
RC208	1.000	0.971	0.014	13.06	401	18700
RC204	1.000	0.999	0.022	28.86	538	68300

Table 4. Selected statistical measures of fitness landscapes P_1 – probability that solution has minimum number of routes, P_2 – probability that solution has minimum number of routes and minimum distance allowing 1% accuracy, P_3 – probability that solution is the best-known or best-achieved, $\bar{K}$ – average number of distinct solutions observed in a sample of series of $r = 100$ experiments, ν – number of local optima unveiled ($\bar{K}$ and ν are calculated over solutions with minimum number of routes; tests are ordered according to P_2 column)

out of as many frequently occurring edges within the best local minima (salesman's tours) as possible, because it is believed that if the "big valley" structure holds, then very good solutions are located near other good solutions.
Boese et al.'s approach cannot be directly used for the VRPTW problem, since its instances may not have the "big valley" structure (see Fig. 9 and 10). Moreover, an initial solution is not enhanced in simulated annealing into a better local minimum, like in greedy descent. It is rather a starting point for a random walk which ends up at some local optimum. The correlation between the quality of this optimum and the quality of the initial solution where the search began is quite weak.
However a shape of the fitness landscape provides some insight into the procedure which finds the set of neighbors $N(X)$ of a current solution X (see section 3). Figs. 6 and 7 indicate that the optimum solution can be a member of a "small valley" of solutions whose distances from all other solutions—measured by d—are large. Therefore in order to reach any solution in such an isolated "valley", the procedure finding the neighbors should create them through deep modifications of a current solution. This gives some guarantee that both close and distant neighbors will be constructed with equal probability.
The information concerning the ruggedness of the fitness landscape is used to establish the initial temperature of annealing in our parallel algorithm, what is a standard practice. Since the algorithm consists of two phases, the temperature $T_{0,f}$ is computed at the beginning of each phase ($f = 1,2$). The procedure finding a neighbor solution is executed a specified number of times and the average increase of solution cost Δ is computed. The initial temperature $T_{0,f}$ is fixed in such a way that the probability of worsening the solution cost by Δ in the first annealing step: $e^{-\Delta/T_{0,f}}$, is not larger than a predefined constant—in our case 0.01 (15). If this probability is too large then the convergence of simulated annealing is slow.

6. Concluding remarks

The fitness landscape is a useful notion in discrete optimization. It increases the understanding of processes which happen during optimization and helps to improve the performance of optimization algorithms. The experiments conducted for the VRPTW benchmarking tests by Solomon showed that the optimum solution can be located inside a "small valley" placed far away from the "big valley" containing the predominant number of solutions. In order to be able to find such an optimum one should assure that among the neighbors of a current solution built during an optimization process, there are not only the close neighbor solutions but also the distant ones. At the beginning of the process of simulated annealing the initial value of the temperature has to be fixed. It is usually done by taking into account the degree of ruggedness of the fitness landscape of a problem instance being solved. Statistical measures of the fitness landscape can be helpful in establishing the difficulty of instances of the problem. The analysis of this difficulty has several facets. One may ask how hard is to find the exact solution to the problem. In this case the key role plays the number of local optima occurring in the landscape. This number can be estimated by detecting distinct solutions in a series of experiments. The larger is the numer of these solutions, the more local optima are present in the landscape, and the problem instance is harder to solve. If one wants to solve the problem with some accuracy, then the smoothness of the landscape is crucial. An indicator here can be the value of $\bar{\tau} = (\bar{y} - y_{\min})/y_{\min}$ which exhibits the shift of the average cost $\bar{y}$ of solutions from $y_{\min}$ attained by solving the problem repeatedly. For two-objective minimization problems, like the VRPTW, one can ask what are the probabilities that in a final solution produced by an optimization algorithm both objective functions are minimized, or stay within some accuracy limits. For example, we found that among the VRPTW tests these probabilities are the smallest for test R104, and the largest for test R205. Last but not least, the amenability of the problem and its instances for parallelization can be investigated. If the simulated annealing paradigm is used, then shortening the parallel execution time in order to get speedup, decreases the chains of steps of free exploration of the solution space carried out by processes. However short chains cause deterioration of quality of search results, because the convergence of simulated annealing is relatively slow. This difficulty can be alleviated by making processes co-operate. For this goal a suitable scheme of co-operation and its frequency are to be devised. It follows from our experiments that solving most of the VRPTW tests can be accelerated by using up to 20 processes. However for some tests (group III, see subsection 4.2) solutions of best accuracy are obtained for less than 20 processes. We believe that this issue requires further investigation.

7. Acknowledgments

We thank the following computing centers where the computations of our project were carried out: Academic Computer Centre in Gdansk TASK, Academic Computer Centre CYFRONET AGH, Kraków (computing grants 027/2004 and 069/2004), Poznań Supercomputing and Networking Center, Interdisciplinary Centre for Mathematical and Computational Modelling, Warsaw University (computing grant G27-9), Wrocław Centre for Networking and Supercomputing (computing grant 04/97). The research of this project was supported by the Minister of Science and Higher Education grant No 3177/B/T02/2008/35.

8. References

[1] Aarts, E.H.L., and Korst, J.H.M., Simulated annealing and Boltzmann machines, Wiley, Chichester, 1989.

[2] Aarts, E.H.L., and van Laarhoven, P.J.M., Simulated annealing: Theory and applications, Wiley, New York, 1987.

[3] Abramson, D., Constructing school timetables using simulated annealing: sequential and parallel algorithms, Man. Sci. 37, (1991), 98–113.

[4] Arbelaitz, O., Rodriguez, C., and Zamakola, I., Low cost parallel solutions for the VRPTW optimization problem, Proceedings of the International Conference on Parallel Processing Workshops, (2001).

[5] Azencott, R., Parallel simulated annealing: An overview of basic techniques, in Azencott, R. (Ed.), Simulated annealing. Parallelization techniques, J. Wiley, NY, (1992), 37–46.

[6] Azencott, R., and Graffigne, C., Parallel annealing by periodically interacting multiple searches: Acceleration rates, In: Azencott, R. (Ed.), Simulated annealing. Parallelization techniques, J. Wiley, NY, (1992), 81–90.

[7] K. D. Boese, A. B. Kahng, and S. Muddu, A new multi-start technique for combinatorial global optimization, Operations Research Letters 16, (1994), 101–113.

[8] Boissin, N., and Lutton, J.-L., A parallel simulated annealing algorithm, Parallel Computing 19, (1993), 859–872.

[9] Catoni, O., Grandes déviations et décroissance de la température dans les algorithmes de recuit simulé, C. R. Ac. Sci. Paris, Ser. I, 307 (1988), 535-538.

[10] Cĕrny, V., A thermodynamical approach to the travelling salesman problem: an efficient simulation algorithm, J. of Optimization Theory and Applic. 45, (1985), 41-55.

[11] Czech, Z.J., and Czarnas, P., A parallel simulated annealing for the vehicle routing problem with time windows, Proc. 10th Euromicro Workshop on Parallel, Distributed and Network-based Processing, Canary Islands, Spain, (January, 2002), 376–383.

[12] Czarnas, P., Czech, Z.J.,and Gocyla, P., Parallel simulated annealing for bicriterion optimization problems, Proc. of the 5th International Conference on Parallel Processing and Applied Mathematics (PPAM 2003), (September 7–10, 2003), Czestochowa, Poland, Springer LNCS 3019/2004, 233–240.

[13] Czech, Z.J., and Wieczorek, B., Solving bicriterion optimization problems by parallel simulated annealing, Proc. of the 14th Euromicro Conference on Parallel, Distributed and Network-based Processing, (February 15–17, 2006), Montbéliard-Sochaux, France, 7–14 (IEEE Conference Publishing Services).

[14] Czech, Z.J., and Wieczorek, B., Frequency of co-operation of parallel simulated annealing processes, Proc. of the 6th Intern. Conf. on Parallel Processing and Applied Mathematics (PPAM 2005), (September 11–14, 2005), Poznań, Poland, Springer LNCS 3911/2006, 43–50.

[15] Czech, Z.J., Speeding up sequential annealing by parallelization, Proc. of the International Conference on Parallel Computing in Electrical Engineering, PARELEC 2006, (September 13–17, 2006), Bialystok, Poland, 349–354 (IEEE Conference Publishing Services).

[16] Czech, Z.J., Co-operation of processes in parallel simulated annealing, Proc. of the 18th IASTED International Conference on Parallel and Distributed Computing and Systems (PDCS 2007), (November 13-15, 2006), Dallas, Texas, USA, 401–406.

[17] Debudaj-Grabysz, A., and Czech, Z.J., Theoretical and practical issues of parallel simulated annealing, Proc. of the 7th Intern. Conf. on Parallel Processing and Applied Mathematics (PPAM 2007), (September 9–12, 2007), Gdansk, Poland, Springer LNCS 4967/2008, 189–198.

[18] Czech, Z.J., Statistical measures of a fitness landscape for the vehicle routing problem, Proc. of the 22nd IEEE International Parallel and Distributed Symposium (IPDPS 2008), 11th Intern. Workshop on Nature Inspired Distributed Computing (NIDISC 2008), (April 14–18, 2008), Miami, Florida, USA, 1–8.

[19] Czech, Z. J., Mikanik, W., and Skinderowicz, R., Implementing a parallel simulated annealing algorithm, (2009), 1–11 (submitted).

[20] Greening, D.R., Parallel simulated annealing techniques, Physica D 42, (1990), 293–306.

[21] Hajek, B., Cooling schedules for optimal annealing, Mathematics of Operations Research 13, 2, (1988), 311–329.

[22] W. Hordijk and P. F. Stadler, Amplitude spectra of fitness landscapes, J. Complex Systems 1, (1998), 39–66.

[23] Kirkpatrick, S., Gellat, C.D., and Vecchi, M.P., Optimization by simulated annealing, Science 220, (1983), 671-680.

[24] Lenstra, J., and Rinnooy Kan, A., Complexity of vehicle routing and scheduling problems, Networks 11, (1981), 221–227.

[25] Metropolis, N., Rosenbluth, A.W., Rosenbluth, M.N., Teller, A.H., and Teller, E., Equation of state calculation by fast computing machines, Journ. of Chem. Phys. 21, (1953), 1087-1091.

[26] Onbaşoğlu, E.,and Özdamar, L., Parallel simulated annealing algorithms in global optimization, Journal of Global Optimization 19: 27–50, 2001.

[27] Reeves, C.R., (Ed.) Modern Heuristic Techniques for Combinatorial Problems, McGraw-Hill, London, 1995.
[28] Reeves, C. R., Direct statistical estimation of GA landscape properties, in: Foundations of Genetic Algorithms 6, FOGA 2000, Martin, W. N., Spears, W. M. (Eds.), Morgan Kaufmann Publishers, (2000), 91–107.
[29] Reeves, C. R. and Rowe, J. E., Genetic algorithms: Principles and Perspective. A Guide to GA Theory, Kluwer Academic Publishers, (2003), 231–263.
[30] C. R. Reeves, Fitness landscapes, In: Search methodologies. Introductory Tutorials in Optimization and Decision Support Techniques, Burke, E. K. and Kendall, G. (Eds.), 587–610, Springer-Verlag, Berlin, (2005).
[31] C. M. Reidys and P. F. Stadler, Combinatorial landscapes, SIAM Rev. 44, (2002), 3–54.
[32] P. F. Stadler, Towards a theory of landscapes, In: Complex Systems and Binary Networks, Lopéz-Peña, R., Capovilla, R., García-Pelayo, R., Waelbroeck, H., and Zurteche, F. (Eds.), 77–163, Springer-Verlag, Berlin, (1995).
[33] Solomon, M.M., Algorithms for the vehicle routing and scheduling problems with time window constraints, Operations Research 35, (1987), 254–265, see also http://w.cba.neu.edu/~msolomon/problems.htm.
[34] Toth, P., and Vigo, D., (Eds.), The vehicle routing problem, SIAM Monographs on Discrete Mathematics and Applications, Philadelphia, PA, 2002.
[35] Verhoeven, M.G.A., and Aarts, E.H.L., Parallel local search techniques, Journal of Heuristics 1, (1996), 43–65.
[36] Weinberger, E. D., Correlated and uncorrelated landscapes and how to tell the difference, Biol. Cybernet. 63, (1990), 325–336.
[37] S. Wright, The role of mutation, inbreeding, crossbreeding and selection in evolution, In: 6th Int. Congress on Genetics 1, Jones, D. (Ed.), (1932), 356–366.

14

Fine-Grained Parallel Genomic Sequence Comparison

Dominique Lavenier
ENS Cachan / IRISA Rennes
France

1. Introduction

Comparing DNA, RNA or protein sequences is a fundamental process in computational biology. The information deduced by processing genomic sequences remain the base of a large panel of bioinformatics activities such as genome assembly, gene annotation, phylogeny, prediction of 3D protein structures, meta-genomic analysis, etc.

For almost two decades, the amounts of data have steadily increased, nearly doubling every 16-18 months. Hence, from gene level analyses, bioinformatics researches have moved to full genome analysis, leading to extremely large quantities of data to process. Furthermore, recent progresses in biotechnology, such as the next generation sequencing technology able to generate billions of genomic sequences in a single day, still strengthen the needs for fast and efficient solutions.

Basically, genomic data, which are considered here, are DNA or protein sequences. A DNA sequence may be as simple as a single gene (a few thousands of nucleotides) or as complex as a full genome (three billions of nucleotides for the human genome). A protein sequence is shorter. It reflects the DNA to amino acids transcription of genes through the universal genetic code. Their lengths range from a few hundreds of amino acids to a few thousands of amino acids. The alphabet of a nucleotide sequence is composed of only 4 characters: A, C, G and T. The protein alphabet is larger and includes 20 amino acids. From a computational point of view, these data are seen as simple strings of characters.

These sequences are stored in genomic databases. SWISS-PROT and TrEMBL (Apweiler et al., 2004), for example, are two well-known protein sequence databases containing respectively 466739 and 7695149 entries (May 2009). From the DNA size, GenBank (release 171, Apr. 2009) contain more than 100 millions of sequences, representing more than 100 billions of nucleotides (Benson et al., 2008). New releases are made every two months to include new data coming from worldwide research institutes. With the exponential growth of these databases, performing computation on this mass of data is every day a more and more challenging task.

A lot of bioinformatics applications need to compare genomic sequences in their early processing steps. To illustrate our point, we briefly describe some of them in the next paragraphs. The goal is not to provide an exhaustive list, but to give, through some examples, an idea of the volume of data which are routinely processed.

Genome Assembly. Before getting the text of a genome, an initial phase is to *sequence* the long DNA molecule contained in each cell of every living organism. This is achieved by randomly breaking the DNA molecule into billions of short fragments which are re-assembled to compose the final text. Many algorithms have been proposed for reconstructing a genome from these short elements (Pop et al., 2002). However, the pre-processing is always the same: finding overlapping regions between them. This requires making intensive pair-wise comparisons to detect similarity between the beginning and the end of all fragments. In other words, assembling N fragments leads to $N^2/2$ pair-wise independent comparisons. Typically, for eukaryote organisms, N range from 10^7 to 10^8.

Database Scanning. A common task of the molecular biology is to assign a function to an unknown gene. To be functional, a protein must adopt a specific 3D shape related to its sequence of amino acids. The shape is important because it determines the function of the protein, and how it interacts with other molecules. It is assumed that two proteins with identical functions may have similar 3D structures, yielding to a similar sequence of amino acids. Even if this hypothesis is not always verified, a large number of algorithms were proposed to rapidly extract sequences (or portion of sequences) having a high similarity with a query sequence. But the scan of genomic databases is faced to the exponential growth of the data. To be able to query databases of billions of nucleotides within reasonable time (from seconds to minutes), the use of parallel systems is now the only solution.

Full Genome Comparison. Mid 2009, about 1000 genomes have been completely sequenced, and more than 4000 other genome sequencing projects are under progression (Liolios et al., 2008). By comparison, only 300 projects were referenced ten years ago. Actually, no decline in this activity is expected in the next few years. More and more genomes will come from many organisms: virus, bacterium, plants, fishes, vertebrates, etc. This avalanche of data opens the door to new ways of investigating the various genome structures. From a computational point of view, algorithms do not fundamentally differ from standard string comparison algorithms, except that the length of the sequences may seriously limit their use. Strings of hundreds of millions of characters need to be intensively processed to detect any kind of similarities. Compared to gene analysis, which can be satisfactory performed (in time) on a standard computer, genome analysis increases the complexity by several orders of magnitude.

Molecular Phylogeny. On Earth, there are millions of different living organisms. Morphological criteria and gene structure suggest that they are genetically related. Their genealogical relationships can be represented by a vast evolutionary tree. This assumption implies that different species arise from previous forms via descent, and that all organisms are connected by the passage of genes along the branches of the phylogenic tree. To build such a tree, identical (or near identical) genes present in all organisms are systematically compared. This aims to calculate a *distance* between all genes (larger the distance, older the relationship between genes). Based on these distances, trees can be constructed through different phylogenic methods. Again, the pre-processing step involves comparing precisely a large set of genomic sequences.

Next Generation Sequencing (NGS). For the last three years, the very fast improvements of sequencing machines have revolutionized the genomic research field (Shenure & Hanlee, 2008). The equivalent (in raw data) of the human genome can now be generated in a single day. Billions of nucleotides spread in millions of very short fragments (35 to 70 nucleotides) are thus available allowing a large spectrum of new large scale applications to be set up:

genome re-sequencing, meta-genomic analysis, molecular bar-coding, etc. Once again, the preliminary step often deals with intensive genomic sequence comparison.
Since the early 80's, many efforts were made to optimize the genomic sequence comparison problem, both on the software side with powerful heuristics, and on the hardware side with dedicated hardwired systems. Another important effort has also been done on the parallel side, ranging from pure parallel software implementations to highly specific parallel machines.
The goal of this chapter is to present the various strategies which are used to parallelize this essential bioinformatics task, and more specifically strategies using fine-grained parallelism. Section 2 formally introduces the problem and section 3 presents the main algorithms. The three next sections are devoted to three different technologies: VLSI and FPGA accelerators, SIMD instructions, and graphical processing units (GPU). The last section concludes the chapter.

2. The genomic sequence comparison problem

Basically, comparing two genomic sequences is equivalent to find similarities between these two elements. Similarities are symbolized by *alignments* which are the objects that biologists are able to interpret. An alignment is composed of two strings where most characters of both strings match together. For instance, consider the following alignment:

```
A G T G G T C T T A - A C G T T A C A T G T T
| | | : | | | : | |   | | | |     | | : | | |
A G T T G T C A T A T A C G T - - C A A G T T
```

The symbol **|** represents a match between two characters. The symbol **:** represents a mismatch. No symbol indicates a deletion or an insertion. In that case, this operation is referred as a gap. Given two sequences, the game is to find regions which maximize the number of consecutive matches and which represent significant biological similarities. To decide if an alignment is significant or not, a score is associated. If the score exceeds a statistically predefined threshold value, it is then considered as valid.
The score is computed as the sum of three elementary costs:

- Cost of a match
- Cost of a mismatch
- Cost of a gap

If we assign +1 for a match, -1 for a mismatch and -3 for a gap, the score of the above alignment is equal to: 17 x matches + 3 x mismatches + 3 gaps = (17×1) +(3×-1)+(3×-3) = 5. This simple scoring scheme is used for DNA sequences. The values of the match, mismatch and gap costs are given by the user and depend of the applications. To better match the biological reality, the gap cost is often calculated using an affine function giving a highest cost for the first gap and a lower cost for the following ones. Taking again the example, and setting the open gap cost to -3 and the extension gap cost to -1, the value of the score will increase to 7: the cost of the first gap stay the same, but the cost of the second gap rise to -4. For protein comparison, the match and mismatch cost is included in a single operation called substitution given by a *substitution matrix* reflecting the mutation rate between the 20 amino acids.

Depending of the applications, different types of alignment may be considered. Figure 1 depicts the three main variations commonly used in molecular biology: global alignment, local alignment and semi-global alignment. Historically, global alignments were first studied. Global alignments try to find the best match between all characters of two sequences of similar size. They are typically used for phylogeny studies: the score of the alignment between two genes indicates their degrees of proximity.

On the other hand, local alignments aim to detect similarities of any length. Given two sequences, the comparison process aims only to detect part of the sequences having significant similarity. The difficulty is that the position and the length of the alignments are unknown, leading to explore a vast search space. Finding local similarities represents the major needs in bioinformatics. The scan of large databases is the best example. Biologists don't only want to know if there are similar items in the database, they also want to detect if their queries shares some common functionalities with other elements. As proteins (or genes) are often assemblies of different functional domains, extracting only local similarities bring pertinent biological information.

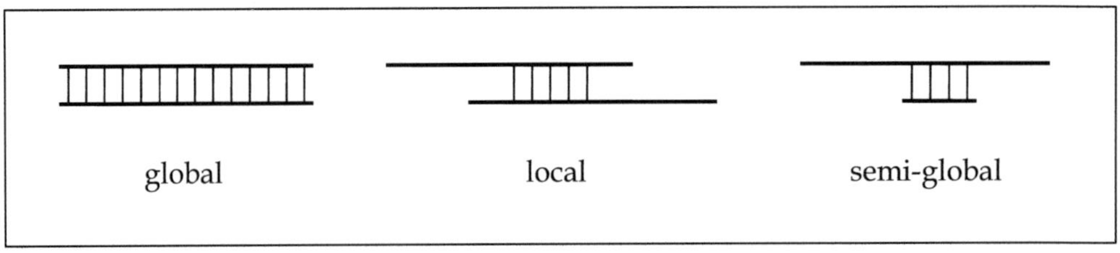

Fig. 1. Schematic representation of the three types of alignments commonly used in molecular biology

The semi-global alignments match all the characters of a small sequence over a large one. The Next Generation Sequencing (NGS) approach which generates a very large number of very short fragments is one of the main activities requiring this treatment. The goal is to map small DNA sequences on full genomes allowing only a restricted number of errors.

Having defined the comparison sequence problem as the search of alignments between two sequences, and having described the main features of an alignment, the next section focuses on the algorithmic side of the problem.

3. The main algorithms

For the last 25 years, due to the tremendous increase of the genomic field, and the growing demand for processing larger and larger amounts of data, many algorithms were proposed to search alignments. The goal, here, is not to review in detail all of them. We will only focus on the two main families which have been widely adopted by the scientific genomic community and which have been implemented on a large panel of parallel structures. The first algorithm introduced in 1970 by Needleman & Wunsch (Needleman & Wunsch, 1970) and revisited in 1981 and 1982 respectively by Smith and Waterman (Smith & Waterman, 1981) and Gotoh (Gotoh, 1982) are based on dynamic programming. They are optimal in the way that they find the best alignments (local or global) between two sequences. But their quadratic complexity - $O(n^2)$ - make them unsuitable for processing large quantity of data. However, for some applications, such as phylogeny or search of weak similarities, there are essential, thereby justifying all the efforts among the last three decades to provide efficient parallel solutions.

By the end of the 80's, however, an important algorithmic breakthrough has emerged, based on a powerful heuristic providing extremely good results. This heuristic drastically reduces the search space by focusing on interesting points, called hits, between two sequences. Using this technique, the execution time could be decreased by nearly two orders of magnitude. Two programs have been immediately proposed to the scientific community, FASTA in 1988 (Pearson & Lipman, 1988) and BLAST in 1990 (Altschul et al., 1990). The later, through many improvements, is now the reference in the bioinformatics community (Altschul et al., 1997). It is maintained by the NCBI (National Center for Biotechnology Information) as an open-source software including parallel implementations.

3.1 Dynamic programming algorithm

The dynamic programming algorithm compares two strings of characters by computing a distance which represents the minimal cost to transform one segment into another one. As stated earlier, two elementary operations are used: the substitution and the gap operations. By using a list of such operations any segment may be transformed into any other segment. It is then possible to take the smallest number of operations required to change one segment to another as the measure of distance between them.

More formally, let $X = (x_1, x_2, \ldots x_n)$ and $Y = (y_1, y_2, \ldots y_m)$ two sequences to be compared. Let $d(x,y)$ the substitution cost to change x into y and g the gap cost. The Needleman & Wunsch algorithm is given by the following recursion:

$$D(i,j) = max \begin{cases} D(i-1,j-1) + d(x_i, y_j) \\ D(i-1,j) - g \\ D(i,j-1) - g \end{cases} \quad (1)$$

with the following initialization:

- $D(0,0) = 0$;
- $D(i,0) = H(i\text{-}1,0) - i \times g$ for $i>0$
- $D(0,i) = H(0,i\text{-}10) - i \times g$ for $i>0$

$D(i,j)$ represents the maximum similarity of the two segments ending at x_i and y_j. Thus, $D(n,m)$ gives the score representing the similarity between the strings X and Y. Higher the score, better the similarity. From the $D(n,m)$ point, a trace-back procedure can be applied to recover the alignment, as shown figure 2. In that case, all the values $D(i,j)$ must be stored in a 2D table. The trace-back procedure consists in reconstructing the optimal path from the last two characters (bottom right) to the first two characters (up left).

		A	T	T	T	G	A	C	G	T	A	T	C
	0	-2	-4	-6	-8	-10	-12	-14	-16	-18	-20	-22	-24
A	-2	1	-1	-3	-5	-7	-9	-11	-13	-15	-17	-19	-21
T	-4	-1	2	0	-2	-4	-6	-8	-10	-12	-14	-16	-18
T	-6	-3	0	3	1	-1	-3	-5	-7	-9	-11	-13	-15
G	-8	-5	-2	1	2	2	0	-2	-4	-6	-8	-10	-12
A	-10	-7	-4	-1	0	1	3	1	-1	-3	-5	-7	-9
C	-12	-9	-6	-3	-2	-1	1	4	2	0	-2	-4	-6
T	-14	-11	-8	-5	-2	-3	-1	2	3	3	1	-1	-3
G	-16	-13	-10	-7	-4	-1	-3	0	3	2	2	0	-2
T	-18	-15	-12	-9	-6	-3	-2	-2	1	4	2	3	1
A	-20	-17	-14	-11	-8	-5	-2	-3	-1	2	5	3	2
T	-22	-19	-16	-13	-10	-7	-4	-3	-3	0	3	6	4
C	-24	-21	-18	-15	-12	-9	-6	-3	-4	-2	1	4	7

Fig. 2. Execution of the Needleman & Wunsch algorithm between two DNA sequences. The cost of a match is set to +1, the cost of a mismatch to -1 and the cost of a gap to -2. Once the similarity score is computed, a trace-back procedure permits to recover the global alignment by reconstructing the optimal path.

Remember that the Needleman & Wunsch algorithm computes a global alignment between two sequences. To find shorter similarities, or local alignments, the Smith & Waterman algorithm introduces a slight modification to the former recursion:

$$D(i,j) = max \begin{cases} D(i-1,j-1) + d(x_i, y_j) \\ D(i-1,j) - g \\ D(i,j-1) - g \\ 0 \end{cases} \tag{2}$$

with the following initialization: $D(0,0) = D(i,0) = D(0,i) = 0$

A threshold value, sets to 0, prevents the score to become negative. The effect is that if, somewhere on the 2D table, a local maximum occurs, it can reflect some local similarity. Figure 3 illustrates this situation. The word ATTGA is present in both sequences and is detected by the highest score inside the 2D table.

		C	G	T	T	G	A	A	T	T	G	A	A
	0	0	0	0	0	0	0	0	0	0	0	0	0
A	0	0	0	0	0	0	1	1	0	0	0	1	1
T	0	0	0	1	1	0	0	0	2	1	0	0	0
T	0	0	0	1	2	0	0	0	1	3	1	0	0
G	0	0	1	0	0	3	1	0	0	1	4	2	0
A	0	0	0	0	0	1	4	2	0	0	2	5	3
C	0	1	0	0	0	0	2	3	1	0	0	3	4
T	0	0	0	1	1	0	0	1	4	2	0	1	2
G	0	0	1	0	0	2	0	0	2	3	3	1	0
T	0	0	0	2	1	0	1	0	1	3	2	2	0
A	0	0	0	0	1	0	1	2	0	1	2	3	3
T	0	0	0	1	1	0	0	0	3	1	0	1	2
C	0	1	0	0	0	0	0	0	1	2	0	0	0

Fig. 3. Execution of the Smith & Waterman algorithm between two DNA sequences. A match is set to +1, a mismatch to -1 and a gap to -2. A trace-back procedure, starting from the highest score, permits to recover the best local alignment.

To better reflect the biological reality, Gotoh improved both algorithms by modifying the cost of N consecutive gaps. The fist gap has an open value g_{open} while the following ones have an extended gap cost g_{ext}. The recursion is modified as follows:

$$D(i,j) = max\begin{cases} D(i-1,j-1) + d(x_i, y_j) \\ V(i,j) \\ H(i,j) \\ 0 \end{cases} \tag{3}$$

$$V(i,j) = \max\begin{cases} D(i-1,j) + g_{open} \\ V(i-1,j) + g_{ext} \end{cases}$$

$$H(i,j) = \max\begin{cases} D(i,j-1) + g_{open} \\ H(i,j-1) + g_{ext} \end{cases}$$

These new equations can be applied both for searching local or global alignments. The complexity for comparing two sequences is the same and is in O(nm), where n and m

represent the length of the two genomic sequences. Note that to get only the similarity score between two sequences, it is not necessary to keep the complete 2D table in memory.

3.2 Heuristic optimization

The dynamic programming algorithm systematically explores a search space equals to $n \times m$. For genomic data mining applications which process billions of sequences, this approach cannot practically be used due to its very high computational complexity. To bypass this constraint, many heuristic algorithms have been developed having in mind to target only regions of interest. These zones can be seen as short regions (sub-sequences) in both sequences with good probabilities of match. The quality and the speed of the algorithms highly depend of the ability to detect these regions.

In the FASTA and the BLAST packages, the idea is the following: Generally, the two strings of an alignment share, at least, one identical word of W characters. These words, called seeds, generate hits between the sequences. From these hits an alignment can thus be reconstructed by extending the search on the left and right hand sides. The size of the seeds has a great influence on the search sensitivity: small seeds have a high probability to belong to all the alignments detected by programming dynamic methods. On the other hand, large seeds often miss weak similarity alignments because such alignments do not include at least one similar word of W consecutive characters. Similarly, small seeds will increase the computation time while large seeds will tend to limit it, just because of the direct relationship between the size of the seed and the number of generated hits: larger the seeds, smaller the number of hits, and smaller the time spent in computing extensions. Users are then faced to a difficult tradeoff: fast and approximate results or slow and sensitive results.

Using this technique, the search of alignments is generally split into a few distinct steps. For example, the BLAST program works as follows:

- Step 1: find hits of W character words
- Step 2: perform ungap extension
- Step 3: perform gap extension

Figure 4 illustrates the process. The first step marks the regions in the 2D space where similar words of W characters are found. These regions are called hits. The second step starts a restricted search on the hit neighborhoods. The complexity of the search is intentionally limited by considering only substitution operations. At this stage, gaps are not allowed. This step aims to investigate if a significant similarity exists near the hit before launching a full alignment computation. An intermediate score is thus calculated. If it exceeds a predefined threshold value, then the third step is run. The last step, only triggered by step 2, performs a dynamic programming on both side of the hit (see Figure 4). Again, a score is calculated. If this new score becomes greater than a statistically significant threshold value, an alignment is generated.

Algorithms based on seed heuristics have been widely adopted by biologists because of their great speed improvements compared to programming dynamic approaches. Furthermore, their sensitivity can be efficiently tuned to match the requirements of many bioinformatics applications just by setting a simple parameter: the size of the seed. Today, these families of algorithms are daily used by thousands of researchers. They represent a large part of the processing time of many bioinformatics centers. Their parallelization on clusters, super-computers or grids has been one of the responses to increase the interactivity with end-users for rapidly processing huge masses of genomic data.

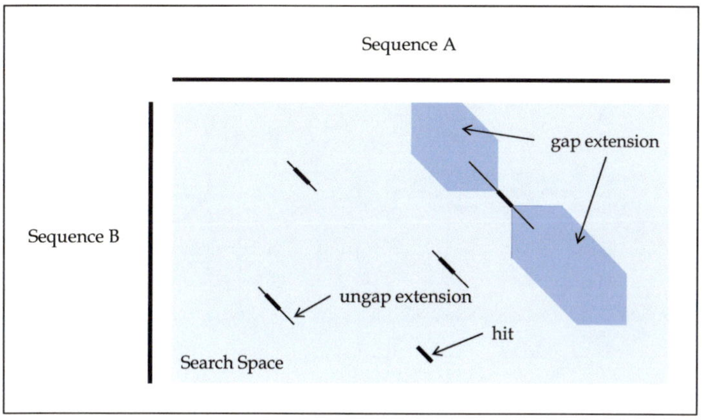

Fig. 4. 3-step BLAST strategy to detect similarity: (1) hit location; (2) ungap extension; (3) gap extension.

However, this type of parallelization is not the only issue. A lot of research works have been done to parallelize the genomic sequence algorithms on other hardware platforms. The next three sections present three different alternatives which exploit the fine-grained potential parallelism of the algorithms

4. VLSI and FPGA accelerators

Historically, the hardware acceleration of the string comparison problem is related to the parallelization of the dynamic programming algorithm on systolic arrays. The immediate implementation consists in hardwiring the recursion of equation (1) on a 2D systolic array as depicted Figure 5. According to the data dependencies, a cell D(i,j) receives data from its three top left neighbouring cells D(i-1,j-1), D(i,j-1), D(i-1,j), computes a similarity score and propagates it to its three bottom right cells D(i+1,j+1), D(i+1,j), D(i,j+1).
If the size of both sequences is n, then, due to the data dependencies, a similarity score is computed in $2n-1$ cycles, providing a speedup of $n^2/2n-1 \approx n/2$. The efficiency of this implementation is far from the optimum, since n^2 cells provide only a speedup of $n/2$. It can be noted that during the computation, only one anti diagonal of cells is active at each cycle. It is thus possible to emulate one column (or one line) on a single cell. The resulting architecture is a linear systolic array of n cells. Details of this kind of architectures can be found in (Lavenier & Giraud, 2005). In that configuration, the number of cycles to compute a similarity score between two sequences of size n stays the same, but the efficiency is much better: a speedup of $n/2$ is obtained with n cells.
To compare one sequence of size n with P sequences of size m with an n-cell array, $n+P\times m-1$ cycles are required. The speedup is thus given by:

$$\frac{n \times P \times m}{n + P \times m - 1} \approx n \qquad with\ P \times m \gg n$$

In that case, a speedup of n is obtained with a systolic array of n cells. This optimal situation occurs, for example, in phylogeny studies where thousands of sequences must be compared together. The systolic array is initialized with one sequence and all the other sequences pass sequentially through the array. This operation is iterated for all sequences.

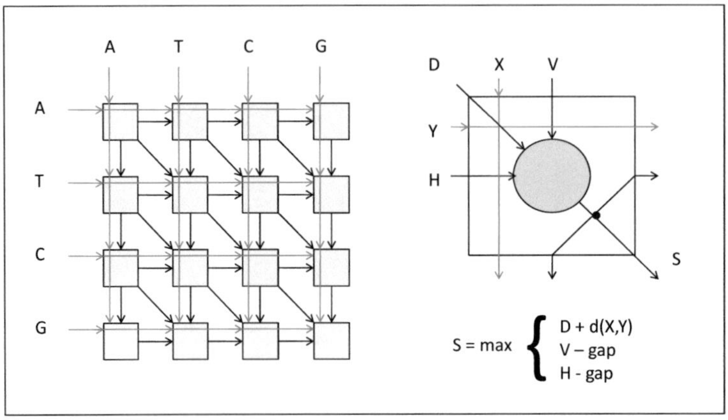

Fig. 5. Implementation of the programming dynamic algorithm on a 2D systolic array. Each cell performs a maximum of three terms. The similarity score is obtained on the bottom right cell in *2n-1* cycles (n is the length of the sequences).

Many systolic implementations have been studied and prototypes have demonstrated the efficiency of the systolic approach. Historically, dynamic programming algorithms were first accelerated with ASIC solutions, such as P-NAC (Lopresti, 1987), BioSCAN (White et al., 1991), Kestrel (Dashe et al., 1997), Samba (Guerdoux & Lavenier, 1997) or Swasad (Han & Parameswaran, 2002) accelerators. The performances of these parallel machines were impressive due to the high number of small processing units running in parallel. However, they suffered from:

- The high cost induced by the design of specific chips and the relatively small market niche where these accelerators were intended.
- The competition with software enhancements, such as seed heuristics, making them not so interested in terms of speed for a wide range of bioinformatics applications.

With the fast evolution of the FPGA technology, the successors of these machines naturally moved to reconfigurable hardware. Basically, their parallel structures didn't change but they could adapt their configuration according to the nature of the data to process (DNA, protein), or according to the type of alignments required by the applications (global alignment, local alignment, with gap, without gap, etc). Pioneer works were realized on the Splash and Splash-2 FPGA systolic machines in the beginning of the 90's (Hoang, 1993). Since this date, a lot of variants have been published in the literature, making this specific domain extremely active to product efficient reconfigurable accelerators (Yamaguchi et al., 2002) (Puttegowda et al., 2003) (Yu et al., 2003) (Dydel et al., 2004) (Pfeiffer et al., 2005) (Li et al., 2007).

It is also interesting to note that commercial products based on these parallel architectures are now available. For example, the DeCypher engine from TimeLogic[1] or the Cube from CLCbio[2] are two FPGA accelerators dedicated to bioinformatics applications, and especially tailored for genomic sequence comparisons. Other generic systems, like the SGI RASC-100 reconfigurable platform, for example, are not specifically devoted to this domain, but permit to implement extremely fast systolic operators (Nguyen et al., 2009).

5. SIMD instructions

The use of SIMD instructions available in each microprocessor for video and image processing purpose is also a very interesting way to parallelize genomic sequence comparison, and especially the dynamic programming algorithm. It can be efficiently speedup by considering groups of cells which can be computed concurrently on the 2D matrix. As stated earlier, the propagation of the computation follows the anti diagonal of the matrix. Cells belonging to a same anti diagonal can thus be processed independently. This can be done with SIMD instructions able to perform K instructions in parallel, as shown figure 6.

A first implementation of the Smith & Waterman algorithm was proposed by Woznia in 1997 (Wozniac, 1997) with the Visual Instruction Set (VIS) available on the SUN ULTRA SPARC processor. It follows the parallel scheme of figure 6. VIS instructions are executed in a specially enhanced floating point unit (FPU) and use its 64-bit registers. Instructions operate on two 32-bit, or four 16-bit integer data packed in a 64-bit double word. In this pioneer implementation, four cells of the matrix are executed in parallel by VIS instructions, storing the running score on 16-bit integers. A speedup of two was obtained.

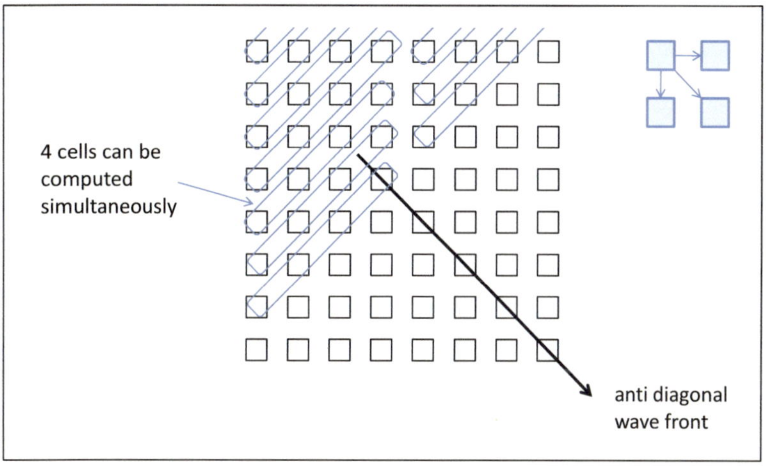

Fig. 6. Diagonal parallelization. Due to the data dependencies of the dynamic programming algorithm, only cells belonging to the same anti diagonal can be simultaneously processed. SIMD instructions can process K cells in parallel.

---

[1] www.timelogic.com

[2] www.clcbio.com

In (Rognes & Seeberg, 2000). the SSEARCH program (a quasi standard implementation of Smith-Waterman for comparing one query with many sequences from a database) was parallelized using the Intel SSE instructions (Streaming SIMD Extension). Eight cells are processed in parallel, each of them manipulating only 8-bit integer values. To increase the precision, unsigned integers are used and a bias mechanism is added to avoid negative values coming from the matrix substitution costs. Speedup of 6 is measured compared to the purely sequential version of SSEARCH.

The speedup improvement, compared to the Wozniac implementation, is due to (1) the superior number of cells computed in parallel, (2) to a clever preprocessing of the query consisting in building a structure called a *profile* and (3) to a programming optimization allowing the cells to be processed in a vertical way as shown figure 7.

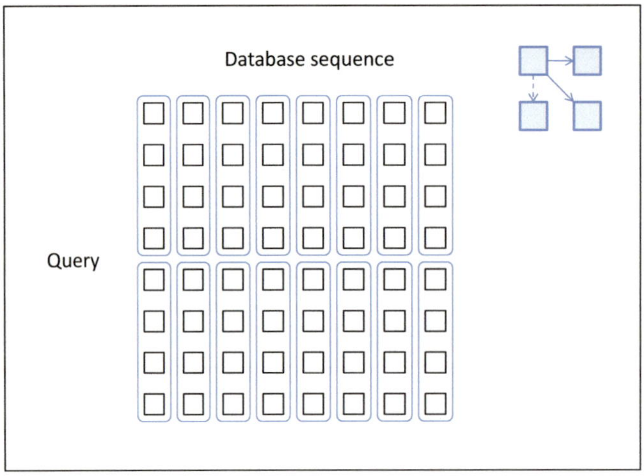

Fig. 7. Vertical parallelization. Under certain assumptions, the horizontal or vertical dependencies can be temporary omitted, leading to the possibility to compute several horizontal or vertical cells in parallel. Here, the vertical dependency is suppressed.

The optimization of the Smith & Waterman algorithm implemented in the Rognes & Seeberg version is based on the observation that in equation (3) V and H are often close to zero and, hence, most of the time, do not participate to the calculation of D. If for K consecutive vertical cells, the V values do not exceed a threshold value, then the vertical dependency can be suppressed, saving many computations. It is possible to check simultaneously if any of the K cells are above a threshold value. If so, the computation of the D values can be very fast. If not, the K scores are computed sequentially.
Farrar (Farrar, 2007) goes one step further by striping the query sequence into T fragments where $T = n/K$ (n is the length of the query and K the size of the SIMD vector). As in the previous implementation, the V values are also neglected to reduce data dependencies. The combination of these two techniques provides better data accesses to the SSE registers and greatly optimizes the SIMD parallelization. After the full computation of the 2D matrix, a lazy evaluation of V is done. Depending of the D scores in some points of the matrix, V values are updated and D scores are recalculated accordingly. This method is very efficient

for sequences with a low level of similarity. The D scores remain low and a very small fraction of the matrix needs to be updated. This situation typically happens in the case of database scanning where only a few sequences have significant similarity among millions of others. Speedup between 2 to 8 is reported compared to the previous SIMD implementations. Performance variations come from the fact that the Rognes & Seeberg implementation is very sensitive to the gap and substitution costs while the Farrar's implementation remains stable.
The Farrar implementation has still been improved in the SWSP3 package (Szalkowski, 2008). Modifications of the code are minors but they significantly reduce the cache footprint especially when long sequences are processed. Furthermore, the lazy V evaluation loop was restructured by transforming it into two nested loops with specific index ranges to hint the compiler at execution counts.
Finally, successive software improvements of the Smith & Waterman algorithm and their clever implementations using SIMD instructions have drastically reduced the performance gap with the seed heuristic algorithms which cannot directly benefit from these SIMD optimizations due to their irregular nature. However, in PLAST, a parallel BLAST-like version for comparing two large databases, SIMD instructions are efficiently used to speedup the computation of the ungap step which represents an important fraction of the execution time (Nguyen and Lavenier, 2008). Identical hits of both databases are grouped together to construct two lists of short sequences. Each sequence of one list is then compared with all sequences of the other list. At this step, gaps are not allowed, easing the computation of the scores to bit fit onto SSE instructions manipulating 16 × 8-bit integers. The parallelization of this part of the algorithm with SSE instructions makes PLAST three to ten times faster than BLAST.
The next generation of microprocessors will increase the SIMD instructions capabilities. New instructions will be provided with larger SIMD registers. For instance, the new Intel set of SSE instructions, called AVX (Firasta et al., 2008), will extend the SIMD integer registers to 256 and/or 512 bits. The genomic sequence comparison will directly benefit from these future improvements.

6. Graphical Processing Units (GPU)

GPGPU stands for General-Purpose computation on Graphics Processing Units. Graphics Processing Units (GPUs) are high-performance many-core processors that can be used to accelerate a wide range of applications[3]. Bioinformatics applications and especially the genomic sequence comparison problem did not escape from deep investigations to evaluate the potential gain these low-cost hardware accelerators can offer.
The last generation of GPU houses hundred of small processing units than can be easily programmed with high-level language, such as CUDA proposed by NVIDIA[4] or OpenCL (Open Computing Language) which is the future standard proposed by the Khronos Group[5]. In such a language, the GPU is viewed as a compute device suitable for massive parallel data application. It can randomly access its own data memory and can run a very

[3] www.gpu.org
[4] www.nvidia.com
[5] www.khronos.org/opencl/

high numbers of tasks in parallel. These tasks, called threads, are grouped in blocks and perform the same algorithms in a SIMD mode. Threads of the same block share data through a complex memory hierarchy and can be synchronized through specific synchronization points.

Again, the dynamic programming algorithm is a good candidate to for GPU because of its high regularity. Different parallelization techniques have been tested. The first relies on the independence of the computation which can be performed on the anti diagonal of the matrix (cf. previous sections). In that case, a thread is assigned to the computation of one anti diagonal. If *n* is the length of the sequences to be compared, then there is the possibility to run simultaneously up to *n* threads performing the recursion of equation (3). This approach has been implemented in (Liu et al., 2007). Speedup from 3 to 10 have been measured compared to the SSEARCH program, depending of the length of the sequences. Long sequences favor the use of GPU accelerators.

The implementation of (Manavski & Valle, 2008) is quite different and targets the scan of databases. The genomic bank is first sorted by the length of the sequences. Then each thread is assigned with a complete comparison between the query and one sequence of the database. As the threads are executed in a SIMD mode, it is important to have the same volume of computation per thread. This is why the sequences are sorted: blocks of sequences of identical size are processed together. Blocks of 64 threads are executed simultaneously, leading to a speedup of 30 compared to SSEARCH (not optimized with SSE instructions). The same style of implementation is done in (Ligowski & Rudnicki, 2009), but with a more efficient use of the global memory bandwidth, providing still better performance.

Another GPU implementation, called CUDASW++, and based on the same parallelization scheme as described above, compares its own performance with one of best multithreaded heuristic implementation (BLAST). A standard Linux workstation (3 GHz dual core processor) equipped with the latest NVIDIA board (GTX 295) including two GPU chips provides much better performance: an average speedup of 10 was reported. In that configuration, the adjunction of a low-cost accelerator outperforms the best seed-based heuristic software while increasing the quality of the results.

In the GPU version of PLAST (cf. previous section), the ungap alignment step for detecting local similarity near the hits are deported on GPU. Two lists (List1 and List2) of short sequences are sent to the GPU in order to make an all-by-all comparison. The parallelization is an adaptation of the matrix multiplication algorithm proposed in the CUDA documentation (Cuda, 2007). Matrices of numbers are simply replaced by blocks of strings. More precisely, suppose that block B1[N1, L] and block B2[N2,L] correspond respectively to List1 and List2, with L the length of the sequences and N1 (N2) the number of sequences in List 1 (List2). A third block SC[N1,N2] stores the scores of all the computation between block B1 and block B2.

The global treatment is done by partitioning the computation into block of threads computing only a sub block of SC, called SC_{sub}. Each thread within the block processes one element of SC_{sub} dimensioned as a 16.x16 square matrix. This size has been chosen to optimize the memory accesses, allowing the GPU internal fast memory to store short sequences which can simultaneously be shared by 256 threads. At the end, the host processor gets back an N1xN2 matrix of scores from which significant ones need to be extracted. Figure 8 illustrates the parallelization scheme of a 16 x 16 string comparison, corresponding to a sub bloc SC_{sub}.

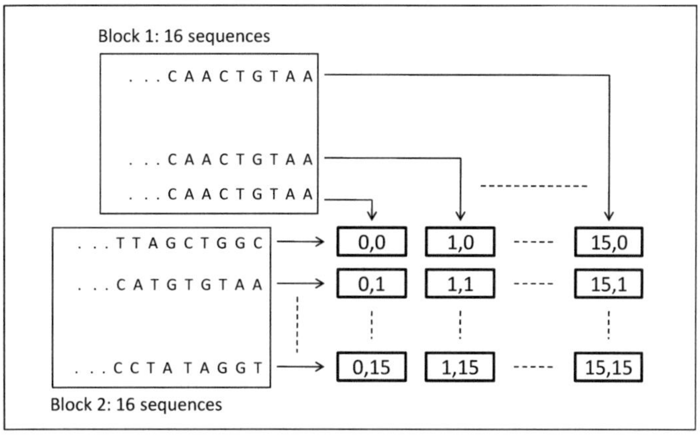

Fig. 8. Principle of the parallelization of an all-by-all string comparison on GPU. A thread (i,j) performs the comparison between the ith and the jth sequences.

Compared to an optimized sequential algorithm an average speedup of 10 is measured for performing this computation on recent NVIDIA graphic boards (GTX 280).

7. Conclusion

This chapter presented three approaches to parallelize the genomic sequence comparison problem: (1) systolic parallelization with VLSI or FPGA accelerators, (2) SIMD parallelization with microprocessor SSE instruction sets, and (3) streaming parallelization with GPU boards. These types of parallelization, referred as fine-grained parallelization, exploit the internal parallelism of the algorithms.

Another possibility is the data-level parallelism. This is actually the approach which is mostly exploited in many bioinformatics applications. A sequence, or a group of sequences, is generally compared with millions of other sequences. There is thus a natural way to split the computation on parallel machines, starting from multicores to clusters or grid platforms. The implementation is immediate: the database is dispatched among the available processing units, and each node works independently on its own subset of data. This approach is very efficient and fit well with the structures of the bioinformatics centres which are mainly composed of clusters of multiprocessors. Besides, MPI versions of the most popular bioinformatics software are now available.

These two alternatives, however, are not antagonist and can be combined to provide higher performance. A few nodes of a general purpose cluster can be equipped with hardware accelerators such as FPGA or GPU boards. When intensive comparisons are required, the system automatically assigns these nodes for this specific process, freeing the rest of the machines for other tasks. As a matter of fact, the scan of genomic databases may represent up to 60%-70% of the execution time of a bioinformatics server. As seen in this chapter, the heart of the algorithms mostly manipulates small integers and, consequently, exploits a relatively small fraction of the microprocessor computational power. Fitting these algorithms into dedicated platforms is much more efficient both in terms of cost and electric power consumption.

With the next generation sequencing technology, the amounts of data to process become a real challenge. Comparing billions of genomic sequences is not the ultimate goal; it is just a necessary step before more complex data analysis in order to filter, organize or classify raw data coming from the fast sequencing machines. In order for this step to not become a serious bottleneck, comparison algorithms must exploit any forms of parallelism available in the next generation of microprocessors. The structures of the genomic sequence comparison algorithms probably need to be revisited to better fit tomorrow architectures such as manycores architectures enhanced with powerful SIMD instruction sets.

8. References

Altschul, S.; Gish, W.; Miller ,W.; Myers, E. & Lipman, D. (1990). Basic local alignment search tool, *J. Mol. Biol.*, vol. 215, no. 3, pp. 403–410

Altschul, S.; Madden, T.; Schäffer, A.; Zhang, J.; Zhang, Z.; Miller, W. & Lipman, D. (1997) Gapped BLAST and PSI-BLAST: a new generation of protein database search programs, *Nucleic Acids Res*, vol. 25, pp. 3389-3402

Apweiler, R. et al. (2004). UniProt: the Universal Protein knowledgebase, *Nucleic Acids Res.*, vol. 32, database issue, pp. 115-119

Benson, D. et al. (2008). GenBank, *Nucleic Acids Res.*, vol. 36, database issue, pp. 25-30

Cuda. (2007). NVIDUA CUDA: Compute Unified Device Architecture, Programming guide, Version 1.0

Dahle, D.; Hirschberg, J.; Karplus, K.; Keller, H.; Rice, E.; Speck, D.; Williams, D. & Hughey, R. (1997). Kestrel: Design of an 8-bit SIMD Parallel Processor, *Proceedings of the 17th Conference on Advanced Research in VLSI (ARVLSI '97)*, September 15 - 16, pp. 145-163, Ann Arbor, Michigan

Dydel, S. & Piotr, B. (2004). Large Scale Protein Sequence Alignment Using FPGA Reprogrammable Logic Devices, *14 th International conference on field-programmable logic and applications*, Antwerp , Belgique, pp. 23-32

Farrar, M. (2007). Striped Smith–Waterman speeds database searches six times over other SIMD implementations, *Bioinformatics*, vol. 23, no. 2, pp. 156-161

Firasta, N.; Buxton, M.; Jimbo, P.; Nasri, K. & Kuo, S. (2008). Intel AVX: New frontiers in performance improvements and Energy Efficiency. *Intel White paper*

Gotoh, O. (1982). An improved algorithm for matching biological sequences. *Journal of Molecular biology*, vol. 162, no. 3, pp. 705-708

Gpu .(2009). http://gpgpu.org

Green, P. (1996). SWAT Optimization, www.phrap.org/phredphrap/swat.html

Guerdoux-Jamet, P. & Lavenier, D. (1997). SAMBA: hardware accelerator for biological sequence comparison, *Bioinformatics*, vol. 13, no. 6, pp. 609-615.

Han, T. & Parameswaran, S. (2002). Swasad: An Asic Design For High Speed Dna Sequence Matching, *Proceedings of the 2002 Conference on Asia South Pacific Design automation/VLSI Design*, January 07–11, Bangalore, India

Hoang, D. (1993). Searching genetic databases on SPLASH2, *IEEE Workshop on FPGAs for Custom Computing Machines*, pp. 185-191, Napa, California

Lavenier, D. & Giraud, M. (2005). Bioinformatcs Applications, in *Reconfigurable Computing: Accelerating Computation with Field-Programmable Gate Arrays,* Gokhale, M. & P.S. Graham P. editor, chapter 9, Springer, ISBN 0-387-26105-2

Liolios, K. et al. (2008). The Genomes On Line Database (GOLD) in 2007: status of genomic and metagenomic projects and their associated metadata, *Nucl. Acids Res.*, vol. 36, database issue, pp. 475-479

Li, IT.; Shum, W. & Truong, K. (2007). 160-fold acceleration of the Smith-Waterman algorithm using a field programmable gate array (FPGA). *BMC Bioinformatics.* vol. 8, no. 185

Ligowski, L. & Rudnicki, W. (2009). An efficient implementation of the Smith-Waterman algorithm on GPU using CUDA for massively parallel scanning of sequence databases, *HiComb 2009: Eighth IEEE International Workshop on High Performance Computational Biology,* Rome, Italy

Liu, Y.; Huang, W.; Johnson, j; & Vaidya, S. (2006). GPU Accelerated Smith-Waterman, *General Purpose Computation on Graphics Hardware (GPGPU): Methods, Algorithms and Applications, LNCS,* vol. 3994, pp. 188-195, ISSN 0302-9743

Liu, W.; Schmidt, B.; Voss, G.; Muller-Wittig, W., (2007). Streaming Algorithms for Biological Sequence Alignment on GPUs, *Parallel and Distributed Systems, IEEE Transactions on Parallel and Distributed Systems* , vol. 18, no. 9, pp. 1270-1281

Liu, Y.; Maskell, D. & Schmidt, B. (2009). CUDASW++: Optimizing Smith-Waterman sequence database searches for CUDA-enabled graphics processing units, *BMC Research Notes,* vol. 2 no. 73

Lopresti, D. (1987). P-NAC: A Systolic Array for Comparing Nucleic Acid Sequences. *Computer,* vol. 20, no. 7, pp. 98-99

Manavski A. & Valle, G. (2008). CUDA compatible GPU cards as efficient hardware accelerators for Smith-Waterman sequence alignment, *BMC Bioinformatics,* vol. 9, no. 10.

Needleman , S. & Wunsch, C. (1970). A general method applicable to the search for similarities in the amino acid sequence of two proteins, *J. Mol Biol.,* vol. 48, no. 3, pp. 443–53

Nguyen, V. ; Cornu, A. & Lavenier, D. (2009). Implementing Protein Seed-Based Comparison Algorithm on the SGI RASC-100 platform, *16th Reconfigurable Architectures Workshop,* May 25-26, Rome, Italy

Nguyen, V. & Lavenier, D. (2008) Fine-grained parallelization of similarity search between protein sequences, *INRIA Report,* (RR-6513)

Pearson, W. & Lipman, D. (1988) Improved tools for biological sequence comparison. *Proc. National Academy of Science,* vol. 85, no. 8, pp. 2444–2448

Pfeiffer G,; Kreft H. & Schimmler, M. (2005) Hardware Enhanced Biosequence Alignment, *International Conference on METMBS'05,* Monte Carlo Resort, Las Vegas, Nevada, USA

Pop,M.; Salzberg, S. & Shumway, M. (2002). Genome Sequence Assembly:Algorithms and Issues, *Computer,* vol. 35, no. 7, pp. 47-54

Puttegowda, K.; Worek, W.; Pappas, N.; Dandapani, A.; Athanas, P. & Dickerman, A. (2003). A Run-Time Reconfigurable System for Gene-Sequence Searching, *Proceedings of the 16th international Conference on VLSI Design,* January 04 - 08, New Delhi, India

Rognes, T., Seeberg, E. (2000). Six-fold speed-up of Smith-Waterman sequence database searches using parallel processing on common microprocessors, *Bioinformatics*, vol. 16, no. 8, pp. 699–706

Shendure, J. & Hanlee, J. (2008). Next-generation DNA sequencing, *Nature Biotechnology*, vol. 26, no. 10, pp.1135-1145

Smith, T. & Waterman, M. (1981). Identification of common molecular subsequences. *Journal of Molecular Biology*, vol. 147, no .1, pp. 195–197

Szalkowski A.; Ledergerber, C.; Krähenbühl, P. & Dessimoz C. (2008). SWP3 - fast multi-threaded vectorized Smith-Waterman for IBM Cell/BE and x86/SSE2, *BMC Research notes*, vol. 1, no. 107

White, C.; Singh, R.; Reintjes, P.; Lampe, J.; Erickson, B.; Dettloff, W.; Chi, V. & Altschul, S. (1991). BioSCAN: A VLSI-Based System for Biosequence Analysis, *IEEE International Conference on Computer Design: VLSI in Computer & Processors*, pp. 504-509, October 14 - 16, Cambridge, Massachusetts, USA

Wozniak, A. (1997). Using video-oriented instructions to speed up sequence comparison, *Comput Appl Biosci.*, vol.13, no. 2, pp. 145–50.

Yamaguchi, Y.; Marumaya, T. & Konagaya, A. (2002). High speed homology search with FPGAs, *Pacific Symposium on Biocomputing*, pp. 271–282, Lihue, Hawaii

Yu C.; Kwon K. ; Lee K. & Leong P. (2003). A Smith-Waterman systolic cell, *13 th International conference on field-programmable logic and applications,* Lisbon , Portugal